T0271938

South–South Globalization

Two prominent features of the current global economy are the worldwide recession brought about by the recent financial crisis, and the emergence of major economic powers from within the developing world such as Brazil, China and India. The former represents the failure of global regulatory policies and macroeconomic imbalances between surplus and deficit countries; the latter is symptomatic of a partial shift in economic power towards developing nations, who are often collectively labelled the global South.

The macroeconomic imbalances are unsustainable in the longer run as they mean greater absorption relative to income in deficit nations; they require corrective action and international policy coordination. Reducing imbalances also requires large developing countries to raise their domestic consumption and also imports from the rest of the world and international financial institutions to operate as a lender of last resort. Furthermore, the engines of global growth, especially for developing countries, may no longer lie solely in the traditional developed country markets in the USA, Europe and Japan, known collectively as the global North. Rather South–South trade is growing rapidly, and that could be an engine of growth for the global economy, including both developed and developing countries. The various chapters in this edited volume address issues surrounding global imbalances and the prospects for growth in developing countries propelled by South–South interaction.

This book should be of interest to students and researchers focusing on political economics, international economics, globalization, global imbalance and the worldwide recession after 2008.

Syed Mansoob Murshed is Professor of the Economics of Conflict and Peace at the Institute of Social Studies, the Netherlands, and is also Professor of International Economics at the University of Birmingham, UK.

Pedro Goulart is a PhD student at the Institute of Social Studies, the Netherlands.

Leandro A. Serino is Researcher and Assistant Professor of Economics at the Institute of Sciences, University of General Sarmiento, Argentina.

Routledge studies in development economics

South–South Globalization

Challenges and opportunities for
development

Edited by Syed Mansoob Murshed,
Pedro Goulart and Leandro A. Serino

Routledge
Taylor & Francis Group

LONDON AND NEW YORK

First published 2011
by Routledge
2 Park Square, Milton Park, Abingdon, Oxon OX14 4RN

Simultaneously published in the USA and Canada
by Routledge
711 Third Avenue, New York, NY 10017

Routledge is an imprint of the Taylor & Francis Group, an informa business

British Library Cataloguing in Publication Data
A catalogue record for this book is available from the British Library

Library of Congress Cataloging in Publication Data
South-south globalization: challenges and opportunities for development/
edited by S. Mansoob Murshed, Pedro Goulart and Leandro Serino.
   p. cm.
   Includes bibliographical references and index.
   1. Economic development–Asia. 2. Economic development–Latin
America. 3. Economic development–Africa. I. Murshed, Syed
Mansoob. II. Goulart, Pedro. III. Serino, Leandro.
   HC412.S59444 2010
   338.9009172'4–dc22

                                                              2010050060

ISBN: 978-0-415-59217-8 (hbk)
ISBN: 978-0-203-81451-2 (ebk)

Typeset in Times
by Wearset Ltd, Boldon, Tyne and Wear

For:
Lenneke Warnars (Syed Mansoob Murshed)
Maria del Piedade (Pedro Goulart)
Beatriz Rearte (Leandro A. Serino)

Contents

Figures

Tables

Contributors

Veronica Bayangos is Acting Deputy Director from the Centre for Monetary and Financial Policy of the Bangko Sentral ng Pilipinas (Central Bank of the Philippines). She holds a Masters and PhD in Development Studies from the ISS-EUR, the Netherlands. Her published works mainly cover the areas of development macroeconomics, monetary and financial policies and macroeconometric modelling and forecasting.

Diadié Diaw is a PhD student affiliated to the Centre for Analysis and Research in Economics at the University of Rouen (France). He has published in journals like the *Third World Review* or the *African Review* and in edited books on issues related to new trade orientations of developing countries (South–South trade).

Pedro Goulart is a PhD student at ISS-EUR. Previously, he has lectured at the undergraduate and master levels. He has published in peer reviewed journals (*Economics of Education Review*; *European Urban and Regional Studies*) and several (edited) books and book chapters in development economics, economic history and labour economics. Website: www.iss.nl/goulart.

Karel Jansen is Associate Professor of Macroeconomics and Development at the ISS. His research interests and publications are in the areas of macroeconomic policy and international finance and geographical focus on Southeast Asia, in particular Thailand, Vietnam and the Philippines.

Mausumi Kar is Assistant Professor of Economics at the Women's Christian College, Kolkata, India. She has been awarded a PhD in Economics from Calcutta University and has worked extensively on international trade in textile and apparel, among other things. She has published in peer-reviewed journals on topics in Public Economics and teaches undergraduate and graduate international economics.

Saibal Kar is a Fellow in Economics (Associate Professor) at the Centre for Studies in Social Sciences, Kolkata, India and Visiting Scholar at Amsterdam School of Economics, University of Amsterdam. He has published in several reputed international journals and edited volumes on Labour Economics and International Trade.

Peter Knorringa is Professor of Private Sector and Development at the ISS, Erasmus University Rotterdam, the Netherlands. His research focuses on the role of private sector actors in development processes, with a particular interest in the developmental relevance of CSR, standards, and alternative economic development initiatives. Website: www.iss.nl/knorringa.

Malte Lübker is a Working Conditions Specialist with the ILO's Conditions of Work and Employment Programme. He obtained an MSc in Development Studies from the School of Oriental and African Studies and taught at the Martin-Luther-University of Halle-Wittenberg. He has worked on financial globalization, employment issues and income distribution and has published in edited volumes and peer reviewed journals (including *International Labour Review* and *Socio-Economic Review*).

Syed Mansoob Murshed is Professor of the Economics of Conflict and Peace at the ISS in the Netherlands and Professor of International Economics at the University of Birmingham, UK. He is the author of six books (including *Explaining Civil War*) and over 100 book chapters and journal articles with interests in conflict, macroeconomics and political economy.

Parthapratim Pal is an Associate Professor at the Indian Institute of Management (IIM), Kolkata. He has a PhD in Economics from Jawaharlal Nehru University, New Delhi. He has also been a fellow at the Cambridge Advanced Programme of Rethinking Development Economics. He works in the areas of macroeconomics, international trade and capital flows.

Kunibert Raffer is Associate Professor at the Department of Economics, University of Vienna, Senior Associate of the New Economics Foundation, and lecturer at UNITAR. He (co)edited seven and wrote five books, two with Sir Hans (HW) Singer, and over 100 articles. He works on sovereign debts, trade and aid. Website: http://homepage.univie.ac.at/kunibert.raffer.

Leandro A. Serino is Assistant Professor of Economics at the University of General Sarmiento, Argentina. Serino obtained his PhD from ISS-EUR in 2009 and between 2008 and 2010 has collaborated with the Ministry of Economy and Public Finances, Argentina. His research interests are on development economics, international finance and applied macroeconomics.

Max Spoor is Professor of Development Studies at ISS, Visiting Professor at IBEI, Barcelona, and Guest Professor at Nanjing Agricultural University, China. He published extensively on macro-economic and rural transformations in Eastern Europe, China and Vietnam, such as: *The Political Economy of Rural Livelihoods in Transition Economies*, London: Routledge, 2009.

Thi Anh-Dao Tran is Associate Professor of Economics at the University of Rouen (France). She coordinates the research area "Globalization, economic interdependence and territorial dynamics" within the Centre for Analysis and Research in Economics (CARE). Her main fields of interest are the macroeconomic issues of international integration and development.

Fiona Tregenna is Associate Professor in the Department of Economics at the University of Johannesburg. She holds a PhD in Economics from the University of Cambridge and an MA in Economics from the University of Massachusetts, Amherst. She has published journal articles and book chapters in the fields of development economics, industrial organization, political economy and labour economics.

Peter A.G. van Bergeijk is Professor of International Economics and Macroeconomics, at the International Institute of Social Studies of Erasmus University, The Hague, and deputy director of the Research School for Resource Studies for Development (CERES), Utrecht.

Rolph van der Hoeven (PhD Free University Amsterdam) is Professor of Employment and Development Economics, ISS-EUR, and has worked for over 30 years for the UN, most recently as Director of ILO's Policy Coherence Group. His work concentrates on employment, inequality, economic reform and globalization. He is board member of (inter)national institutions and journals and has (co-)authored a dozen books, more than 25 articles, four special journal issues and contributed chapters to about 30 books.

Marie-Lise E.H. van Veenstra has an MSc (*cum laude*) in International Economics and Business from Erasmus University Rotterdam and is now studying European Law at Leiden University. Her current research focuses on economic policy coordination within the eurozone.

Rudiger von Arnim is Assistant Professor at the University of Utah in Salt Lake City. He received a PhD in Economics from the New School for Social Research in New York, in 2008. His research focuses on international macroeconomics, trade and development, particularly the application of computer simulated models for policy analysis. Website: www.econ.utah.edu/~rarnim/.

Rob Vos is director of Development Policy Analysis and chief economist of the United Nations Department of Economic and Social Affairs. He is also affiliated Professor of Finance and Development at the International Institute of Social Studies of Erasmus University. His most recent books include *Economic Insecurity and Development* (Oriental Black Swan, 2010) and *Public Policies for Human Development* (Palgrave, 2010).

Mina Yakop (1985) has a BSc (*cum laude*) in International Economics and an MSc in Economics from the University of Amsterdam and is now studying Financial Econometrics at that university.

Preface

Two prominent features of the global economy currently are the worldwide recession induced by the recent financial crisis, and the emergence of major economic powers from within the developing world such as China and India. The former represents the failure of global regulatory policies and macroeconomic imbalances between surplus and deficit countries; the latter is symptomatic of a partial shift in economic power towards developing nations, who are often collectively labeled the global South.[1] The macroeconomic imbalances are unsustainable in the longer run as they mean greater absorption relative to income in deficit nations; they require corrective action and international policy coordination. Furthermore, the engines of global growth, especially for developing countries, may no longer lie solely in the traditional developed country markets in the USA, Europe and Japan, known collectively as the global North. The various chapters in this edited volume address many of the issues surrounding global imbalances and the prospects for growth in developing countries propelled by South–South interaction.

Part I of the volume is concerned with trends in globalization. It begins with the chapter by Syed Mansoob Murshed, Pedro Goulart and Leandro A. Serino who look at the broad analytical patterns of North–South asymmetric economic interaction. The South is postulated to depend on the more industrialized and affluent North to determine its growth rates and terms of trade. The presence of surplus labour in poorer developing countries is key to these types of unequal exchange. However, the rise of certain developing countries like China and India (which may be reverting back to their pre-industrial revolution relative economic positions in the world) is changing patterns of global trade. During the last decade South–South exports increased four times faster than to the North. The chapter further looks at the reserve build-ups by developing countries, and fiscal deficits. Based on the healthier (on average) fiscal positions in developing countries, their substantial foreign exchange reserve build-ups which also promote a competitive exchange rate in favour of their exports, more buoyant growth rates in all regions of the South and burgeoning South–South trade, the prospects for economic interaction between nations in the South seem set fair, and could provide an engine of growth for the South as a whole.

The chapters that follow in Part I focus on macroeconomic imbalances. The chapter by Rob Vos argues that the crisis emerged on the back of an intrinsically unsustainable global growth pattern, characterized by strong consumer demand in the United States, and funded by easy credit and booming house prices. Far-reaching financial deregulation facilitated a massive and unfettered expansion of new financial instruments, such as securitized sub-prime mortgage lending, sold globally. He discusses some key aspects of this process of 'financialization' of worldwide trade and investment. He further attempts to provide some hints at some of the ingredients for global and national policies which could help steer the world towards a fairer and more sustainable pattern of growth.

The chapter by Rudiger von Arnim points to the failure of US-led Bretton Woods institutions to effectively help emerging markets cope with the fallout of bursting asset price bubbles leading them to self-insure. Self-insurance implies accumulation of international reserves and maintenance of a competitive real exchange rate. He then indicates what the three main regions in the saga of global imbalances must do. First, China must rebalance demand towards domestic sources. Proposed government expenditure programmes hint in the right direction, and simulation results indicate that such a programme would help to support growth even in the face of exchange appreciation. Exchange rate realignment does not present a solution by itself, but can help to reduce global imbalances through a broad exchange appreciation and not only against the US dollar. Second, Europe's careful approach to fiscal expansion reflects the political straightjacket of the Maastricht Treaty. Third, the US should institute public expenditure increases sufficient to limit GDP losses. Crucially, these national and regional responses have to be carefully coordinated.

Kunibert Raffer in his chapter argues that neither the oil rich OPEC countries nor China unwound their surpluses, let alone doing so in a way that could trigger shocks as none of these countries issued dubious loans or encouraged unsound practices in the name of the free market. All they did was to accept the necessity of financing (mainly) the US – in terms of real transfers – on credit. Initially highly praised by the international financial institutions (IFIs) for reacting more prudently to price volatility than in the 1970s by investing oil surpluses, these same countries are now accused of not spending them, in stark contrast to the nostrums traditionally meted out to deficit nations to curtail consumption. Petro-dollar Recycling is demanded again: the same policy that led to them being wrongly blamed for the developing country debt crisis in the 1980s. In the same breath, new donors from Asia are accused of granting "rogue aid".

Rolph van der Hoeven and Malte Lübker in their piece on financial liberalization and labour markets in the South argue that external financial liberalization led to a surge in international capital flows since the early 1990s. While the direct growth benefits of financial openness are unclear, many developing countries have experienced greater economic volatility and financial crises since the early 1990s. These crises have had a considerable impact on output and long-term growth prospects; labour has suffered disproportionately as labour market indicators typically lag economic recovery with labour's share in national income typically eroded during a financial crisis. All of this leads to the greater informalization of work.

Part II of the book is concerned with engines of growth in the South. Parthapratim Pal indicates that since the failure of the Seattle Ministerial of the World Trade Organization (WTO) in 1999, developed countries like the USA and the European Union have initiated negotiations on a large number of bilateral and Regional Trade Agreements (RTAs). These agreements tend to push trade liberalization farther than possible under a multilateral trade regime. These RTAs, however, also include rules which are likely to reduce policy space for developing countries as they face stricter trade in intellectual property (TRIPs) regimes, aggressive environment and labour clauses, and extremely restrictive Bilateral Investment Treaties (BITs). The chapter concludes that the net gains from North–South RTAs may be smaller compared to corresponding South–South RTAs and preferential trading agreements (PTAs), which may be more beneficial.

Mausumi and Saibal Kar examine the impact of the end of the multi-fibre agreement (MFA) which governed clothing exports via exporting nation quotas on South and Southeast Asia. They use constant market share analysis from 1995 to 2005 to analyse conditions in clothing and textile industries in these countries. The removal of quotas led to significant changes in countrywise export shares – countries with more efficient production techniques captured larger shares in the post-MFA phase. This supports the proposition that removal of quotas in this case would lead to concentration of textile production in a few larger countries in Asia (because of scale economies) at the expense of many smaller nations that previously enjoyed considerable export shares.

Marie-Lise van Veenstra, Mina Yakop and Peter A.G. van Bergeijk investigate how trade and bilateral economic diplomacy interact. They discuss the economic rationale for public intervention in international activities, investigate whether market failure might provide an explanation and see what instruments are available to solve this problem without bringing about government failure. They use a gravity model to focus on the effectiveness of the two main instruments of commercial and bilateral diplomacy: export promotion agencies and foreign missions, such as embassies. Their findings suggest that diplomatic representation is not a relevant trade enhancing factor for trade within the North, but that it is significant in the bilateral trade relationships of developing countries.

Peter Knorringa's chapter is on responsibility in global value chains and explores where and when responsibility issues in global value chains are more likely to gain a foothold in developing countries. A basic typology identifies a pyramid consisting of four layers with overlapping border zones. The base of this pyramid consists of informal sector firms that do not comply with existing minimum legal requirements in terms of responsible behaviour of firms. The next level consists of formal sector firms that abide by the letter and spirit of the law. A smaller but still sizeable number of firms follow a brand protection strategy, investing in voluntary responsibility initiatives that go beyond legal requirements. Finally, the top layer consists of firms for whom their responsibility profile is a key part of their core value creation strategy. The author describes how this encompassing model can be applied to different contexts.

Fiona Tregenna in her chapter on deindustrialization in some parts of the world argues that it could have a potentially negative impact on growth. A decline in the share of manufacturing in output can be a very different phenomenon from a decline in the share of manufacturing in employment, and these are likely to have different implications for growth. She develops a new method to analyse changes in manufacturing employment levels and shares in 48 developing and developed countries. The analysis separates out changes in the levels and shares of employment manufacturing into components associated with changes in the share of manufacturing in GDP, the growth of manufacturing value added, the labour intensity of manufacturing production and economic growth. The results indicate that in most cases the decline in manufacturing employment is primarily associated with falling labour intensity of manufacturing. Such experiences would not necessarily be expected to have negative effects on growth.

Part III is concerned with case studies in the South. Max Spoor looks at China and India as emerging large economies contributing to new imbalances, such as their appetite for resources (carbon-hydrates, minerals and bio-mass) within these relatively energy-inefficient economies, while at the same time attracting an increasing share of global foreign direct investment (FDI) towards themselves. He also argues that the various imbalances make it more difficult for developing countries (except for those who are resource rich) to get access to necessary development finance.

Leandro A. Serino analyses the recent experience of Argentina. He runs counterfactual simulations using a structuralist CGE model to show that positive external shocks will be expansionary. Further economic integration between Argentina and other developing countries is necessary to preserve export growth and the process of export diversification that Argentina experienced between 2003 and 2008. He also shows the need for expansionary fiscal policies to compensate for the exogenous stimuli that vanished following the crisis. He stresses that a competitive exchange rate regime is fundamental to prevent Dutch disease adjustments associated with positive external shocks, and also to promote an environment favourable to investment.

In their chapter on the macroeconomic impact of remittances in the Philippines, Veronica Bayangos and Karel Jansen point out that remittances are driven by the economic cycle in host countries. They trace the impact of remittances on aggregate demand, money supply, interest rates, exchange rates, labour supply and wages. They demonstrate that the fluctuations in remittance flows over the years are of a magnitude that is significant enough for policy makers to take notice. Their model simulations show that the impact of the US recession on the Philippine economy is more severe once account is taken of the endogeneity and pro-cyclicality of remittances.

Diadié Diaw and Thi Anh-Dao Tran examine the potential for South–South trade expansion by focusing the analysis on Senegal in the context of the West

African Economic and Monetary Union (WAEMU) regional agreement. Does Senegal's participation in the RTA improve its external trade and eventually allow expansion of South–South trade in the sub-region? They calculate three trade indicators: Balassa's Revealed Comparative Advantage (RCA) index, a Contribution to the Trade Balance (CTB) index and a relative trade balance index describing the position (POS) of individual countries on world markets. In order to assess the magnitude of competition among WAEMU members, they look at export similarity indices. Their calculations show that the scope of comparative advantage tends to increase in Senegal, suggesting an improvement in export diversification. Moreover, its export structure is relatively different from WAEMU partners: the low indices of export similarity indicate that these countries are not in competition on global markets, suggesting potential for trade expansion in the sub-region. This points to better prospects for future South–South trade.

The book as a whole examines the nature of global imbalances along with the painfully necessary, therefore difficult to implement, adjustments in consumption patterns, the fragility induced by excessive global financialization, the changing patterns of trade in a world characterized by greater bilateralism making older trade promotion strategies once more salient, and the fact that South–South economic interaction as a locomotive for growth for the developing world *as a whole* is here to stay, notwithstanding the probability of some losers being present within most aggregatively winning situations, as well as the inevitable pitfalls that any new path towards prosperity entails.

The editors

Note

1 We are aware of the somewhat problematic concept of "South" but it contains a useful terminology. For a review of different terminologies and concepts see, for example, Sidaway, J.D. (2011) "Geographies of Development: new maps, new visions?" *Professional Geographer*, in press.

Acknowledgements

The idea of this book evolved as some of the contributors met at Development Dialogue (DD) 2008, a yearly academic event for PhD candidates in development studies organized by young researchers at the International Institute of Social Studies of Erasmus University Rotterdam. Our thanks go to Ariane, Bilisuma, Caizhen, Francisco, Georgina, Henry, Husnul, Mallika, Manohara, Rekopantswe, Roselle, Rose, Shyamika whom with Leandro and Pedro (coordinator) were the organizers of that year. The event also relied on the institutional and financial support of ISS through Louk de la Rive Box (former Rector), Wil Hout (Deputy Rector for Academic Affairs) and Renée de Louw (now Deputy Rector for Executive Affairs), the Research Degree Committee and the Dean's office, and Oxfam-Novib, through Bruno Molijn.

From the panel coordinated by Leandro in the conference to the project of a book was like a great leap forward as the interest in the topics spread rapidly. We thank the various contributors for their earnest commitment. These researchers were drawn from four continents, both in terms of provenance and affiliation, which is a reflection of the changing world order.

We would like to thank Marijn Nieuwenhuis for competent copy editing. Taylor & Francis Ltd graciously permitted the reprinting of material published in Vos, R. (2010) "The Crisis of Globalization as an Opportunity to Create a Fairer World", *Journal of Human Development and Capabilities*, 11(1): 143–160. From Routledge, Thomas Sutton was positive and enthusiastic about our project from the very start, and Louisa Earls provided very helpful guidance and support through the process of publication. We further thank Emily Kindleysides, Phillippa Nichol and Sally Quinn.

A final word must go for Karel Jansen, a contributor for this book. His sudden demise on 28 April 2011, as the book was unfolding, leaves this team weaker. We would like to extend our sincere solidarity to his family.

The editors

Abbreviations

ADB	Asian Development Bank
ANDEAN	Andean Community (Bolivia, Columbia, Ecuador and Peru)
APEC	Asia-Pacific Economic Cooperation
ASEAN	Association of South-East Asian Nations
ATC	Agreement on Textiles and Clothing
BIS	Bank for International Settlement
BITs	Bilateral Investment Treaties
BRIC	Brasil, Russia, India and China
BSP	Bangko Sentral ng Pilipinas
BWIs	Bretton Woods Institutions
CA	current account
CAFTA	Central America Free Trade Agreement
CDSs	Credit Default Swaps
CEE	Central and Eastern European
CEMAC	Economic and Monetary Community of Central Africa
CET	constant elasticity of transformation
CFA	*Colonies françaises d'Afrique* (African Financial Community)
CFIUS	Committee on Foreign Investment in the United States
CGE	Computable General Equilibrium
CIS	Commonwealth of Independent States
CMS	Constant Market Share
COMESA	Common Market of East and South Africa
COMTRADE	Commodity Trade Statistics Database
COS	Cosinus index
CPI	consumer price index
CSR	Corporate Social Responsibility
CTB	Contribution to the Trade Balance
Cusum	Cumulative Sum of Recursive Residuals
CV	coefficient of variation
DAD	Doha Agenda for Development
ECOWAS	Economic Community of West African States
EEC	European Economic Community
EFTA	European Free Trade Association

EMEs	emerging market economies
FDI	foreign direct investment
forex	foreign exchange
FTA	Free Trade Agreements
FTAA	Free Trade Area of Americas
GDP	gross domestic product
GNI	gross national income
GNP	gross national product
GSP	generalized system of preference
HP	Hodrick–Prescott
ICS	Chemical Industries of Senegal
IFIs	international financial institutions
IFS	International Financial System
ILO	International Labour Organisation
IMF	International Monetary Fund
IPCP	index of primary commodity prices
IPR	intellectual property rights
IT	inflation targeting
KILM	ILO Key Indicators of the Labor Market
LAC	Latin America and the Caribbean
LDCs	least developed countries
LES	linear expenditure system
MDGs	Millennium Development Goals
MENA	Middle East and North Africa
MERCOSUR	Mercado Comum del Sur (Argentina, Brazil, Paraguay and Uruguay)
MFA	multi-fibre agreement/arrangement
MFN	most favoured nation
MNCs	multinational companies
NAFTA	North American Free Trade Agreement
NAMA	Non-Agricultural Market Access
NBER	National Bureau of Economic Research
NGO	non-governmental organization
NICs	newly industrialized countries
ODA	Overseas Development Assistance
OECD	Organisation for Economic Co-operation and Development
OF	overseas Filipino
OLS	ordinary least square
OPEC	Organization of the Petroleum Exporting Countries
POS	position
PPP	purchasing power parity
PPP$	purchasing power parity in dollars
PTAs	preferential trade agreements/ arrangements
R/STD	ratio of reserves to short-term external debt
R&D	research and development

RCA	revealed/relative comparative advantage
ROO	Rules of Origin
RTAs	Regional Trade Agreements
SAM	social accounting matrix
SCER	stable and competitive exchange rate
SDRs	Special Drawing Rights
SGP	European Stability and Growth Pact
SITC	Standard International Trade Classification
TRIPs	trade in intellectual property
UIP	uncovered interest parity
UN	United Nations
UNCTAD	United Nations Conference on Trade and Development
VAR	Vector autoaggressive analysis
WAEMU	West African Economic and Monetary Union

Part I
Trends in globalization

1 Globalization and the South at the crossroads of change

Syed Mansoob Murshed, Pedro Goulart and Leandro A. Serino

1.1 Background

We seem condemned to live in interesting times. The rich nations in the global economy (the global North or OECD countries) are mired in recession, while at the same time yet another apparent shift in the global balance of economic power (towards 'emerging' economies) is the subject of considerable chatter amongst economists and within business circles. The current economic crisis is of considerable import, not just because of its size and magnitude, but because it has been accompanied by a change in the macroeconomic policy orthodoxy in the form of a quiet Keynesian counter-revolution which emphasizes counter-cyclical macroeconomic policies instead of inflation control. We employ the expression 'quiet' because there is no return to the earlier post-Second World War commitment of full employment, and fiscal and inflationary profligacy continues to be universally frowned upon. We also speak of another apparent shift in economic power, because present events such as the rise of Brazil, India and the enormous 'surpluses' of China are similar to the rise of the Asian Tigers, and the experience of the surpluses of Japan and West Germany in the global economy a quarter of a century ago. Could it be that the so-called global imbalances, mainly attributed to the USA's current account deficit, which has existed since the 1970s, but accelerated during the 1980s (Edwards 2005) constitute a tribute exacted by the United States, the world hegemon, allowing it to absorb much more than it produces? Be that as it may, the current recession was expected to affect developing countries much less than their developed counterparts, and many developing countries, particularly in Asia are only experiencing a decline in their (positive) growth rates.[1]

Many commentators declare that the engine of growth for the global South is no longer solely in the North (IMF 2008), as has been the case historically ever since the dawn of the Industrial Revolution in England, and the end of the Napoleonic wars that heralded the *Pax Britannica*. So, the processes of development based on globalization (or external trade and finance), as far as the South is concerned, may be at a crossroads. Will the emerging economies of the developing world (China, India, Brazil, South Africa and so on) act as an engine of growth for the rest of the global South, or will global growth be powered by each

Table 1.1 Historical shares of world GDP of present day North and South

	1500	1950	1998
North	27	73	59
South	73	27	41
Of which Developing Asia	62	16	30

Notes
Authors calculations based on Maddison (2001), Table 3–1c.

country growing more on its own steam (domestic demand), or will the United States, Japan and Western Europe continue to play the traditional role of promoting trade and investment-led growth for the rest of the world? For some observers (Frank 1998; Nayyar 2009 among others), global economic history is witnessing yet another 'reversal of fortune' back to the past, with economic power and weight returning to the countries/regions, China and India, who were the most affluent (in both absolute and relative terms) towards the middle of the second millennium of the Christian era and earlier. Table 1.1, based on Maddison (2003), suggests the resurgence of Asia back to its economically ascendant position five centuries ago.

The blame for the present 'great' recession (as it has come to be known) has been squarely laid at the feet of global imbalances between surplus and deficit nations, and the vicissitudes of internationally mobile financial capital, which leaves countries exposed to the contagion of financial crises emanating from outside its frontiers. There are chapters on these two issues to follow, as far as developing countries are concerned. It is not our intention to pursue the pressing issues in the redesigning of the global financial regulatory architecture, but focus instead on the broad swathes of change sweeping across the global economy, and how it affects developing countries (the global South). Since its very inception, shortly after the Second World War, the broad goal of development economics has been to foster growth via industrialization,[2] leading to the elimination of surplus labour. It is important to identify the engines, and the mechanisms, underlying this growth, which for many countries is reliant upon external demand. Thus changing patterns of international trade and investment are important. It is also crucial to focus on the macroeconomic policy backdrop, which is meant to create a stable background for industrialization. We consider both factors in turn.

1.2 Trade as a handmaiden of growth revisited

Before the spurt in mercantile trade, followed by the Industrial Revolution, and the expansion in free trade and economic growth in its wake, most economies could be said to be in a state resembling a Malthusian trap. Their productive sectors, even if not totally agricultural, resembled the limitations of an agrarian economy. Following the exposition in Findlay (2009), we developed a stylized model. In this, the equilibrium real wage is w^*, which equalizes the fertility and mortality rates to maintain a constant population.[3] At any point in time, t, there is a Ricardian total wage fund, $W(t)$, given by saving out of profits in the previous period, which divided by w^*, gives us total employment, $L(t)$. Note that w^* (related to the average product of labour) is the exact counterpart of the latter day exogenously given wage rate due to Lewis (1954). Given a fixed amount of land T, agricultural, $A(t)$, production is:

$$A(t) = f[L(t), T]$$ (1.1)

The rate of profit, r is given by:

$$r = (f_L - w^*)/w^*; = f_L = \text{the marginal product of labour}$$ (1.2)

The point is that given the fixity of land, the marginal product of labour, f_L, will be declining with greater labour input. Countries with greater agricultural productivity, either because the land is more fertile or because of intermediate inputs (irrigation), will be able to sustain larger populations (as in China and India). Otherwise, the economy will be caught in a Malthusian trap, unless there is a nascent manufacturing sector, perhaps subject to increasing returns to scale.

Expanded international trade can release the economy from this Malthusian trap. If there is a phase of mercantilist trade and surplus extraction, where it is the North (England, France, Holland, Portugal) that accumulates surpluses from monopolistic colonial trade and surplus extraction there may be industrialization in some countries of the North (England) following technical progress and institutional change that permit these surpluses to be channelled into industrial capital. Free trade can intensify industrialization where it has occurred in the North and cause de-industrialization in parts of the South (China and India) that had nascent manufacturing.[4] What is less referred to is the use of military power to enforce monopolistic mercantile trade (as with the British and Dutch East India companies) and later on, ironically, even the principle of free trade and the freedom of the high seas. Thus, as Findlay and O'Rourke (2007) put it, prosperity and plenty often emanate from war and even naked aggression.

After the de-industrialization of parts of the South, the economies of these countries will once again be characterized by a Malthusian trap in its subsistence sector, but may have an enclave sector producing commodities demanded by the industrialized North. Many will have surplus labour in the sense of Lewis (1954). Within the sphere of international trade there is an *endogenous* change in endowments which dictates that the South will export commodities (based on the relative abundance of land and labour), and the North manufactures (based upon historically greater capital stocks accumulated via mercantilist trade).

Following Findlay (1980), we can think of the following steady state North–South global equilibrium. Here growth in the South (g_s) is given by:

$$g_s = sPf_k$$ (1.3)

Here f_k is the marginal productivity of capital or land given an exogenously fixed real wage rate, P is the price of the good the South produces and exports and s is the propensity to save out of profit (Pf_k). In the North growth is as in a neo-classical Solow type model; it means equilibrium growth is equal to the growth of the effective labour force, n. In the world steady state n is equal to the growth rate of the South, hence:

$$P = n/sf_k \qquad\qquad (1.4)$$

The South's terms of trade (P) adjust to bring about global growth equilibrium. Technical progress in the South (a rise in f_k) will be immiserizing, as the equilibrium terms of trade for the South (P) declines. Technical progress in the North (a rise in n) benefits the South via higher prices. This is exactly how Raul Prebisch (1950) would have put it. The North is not only the engine of growth for the South but sets its pace based on the North's growth. There is a distinct international division of labour, cemented during the first age of globalization (1870–1914) with the South exporting commodities and the North producing and exporting manufactures. Moreover, this unfavourable system does not change with the simple advent of labour-intensive manufactured goods exports from the South during the 1970s, as long as the South is dependent on the North to determine its rate of growth and the equilibrium terms of trade. An increase in savings rates in the South from (equation 1.3) can raise its growth rate, via capital accumulation. Is this how China and East Asia succeeded by simply accumulating capital and augmenting total factor productivity? That could be partially true, if one considers the writings of Young (1995) and Chang (2007), who argue that the East Asian growth miracle is based on this type of accumulation. Capital mobility between the North and the South driven by the prospect of higher profits in the South will not fully benefit the South except through increased employment at a constant wage rate (in the presence of surplus labour). Its terms of trade will decline with expanded output and a part of profit income has to be repatriated to the North (see Burgstaller and Saavedra-Rivano 1984 for an analytical model of this process).

This bleak picture regarding asymmetric trade and economic interaction can be supplemented by three other strands of thought. The first is to do with economic imperialism, as exemplified in the work of Hobson and Lenin, and elaborated on in a contemporary economic model by Krugman (1981). The developed North may invest in the underdeveloped South, but that does not lead to an increase in living standards (real wage rates) of workers in the South; Northern workers are better off compared to their counterparts in the South. Second, there is the notion of unequal exchange and dependency; see Bacha (1978) for an analytical model encapsulating some of these ideas. Unequal exchange emanates from the fact that North–South trade does not equalize both wages and profits (but only profits), as would be predicted by the Heckscher-Ohlin theory. Factor price equalization would only be applicable to intra-North trade. Finally, we have the experience of the Great Depression of the 1930s, when commodity prices collapsed. This prompted Prebisch (1950) to suggest that because of a low-income elasticity of demand for commodities, specializing in them did not provide dynamic gains in terms of growth. Singer (1950) pointed to a secular tendency for the commodity terms of trade vis-à-vis manufactures to decline. Ergo, industrialize. Somehow, North–South trade was unfair and asymmetric, as it did not provide any more than static gains from trade for developing countries, and was perceived to be inimical to the South's more *dynamic* growth interests. Trade dependence should be minimized, and whenever possible developing countries should rely on their own domestic markets in order to industrialize and grow.[5] But the problem is that a strategy of industrialization is not simple to implement. It requires coordination between sectors, and expectations that the big push towards industrialization will last and not just fizzle out (Murphy *et al.* 1989).

Indeed, the economic history of the world does seem to suggest that there is historical divergence in growth rates (and therefore average living standards) between regions since the Industrial Revolution. Most nations were comparable in per capita income levels at the beginning of the second millennium but after the Industrial Revolution North and South diverged (see Table 1.2). The gap between the average for rich and poor nations as a whole has widened by 350 per cent in 178 years. Until 1950, the Western offshoots (USA, Canada, Australia and New Zealand) grew to take the premier position within the North.[6] The second half of the twentieth century would see Western Europe and Japan catching up and solidifying the world gap. Globalization, which proceeded rapidly between 1870 and 1914, and once again after 1945 (with the biggest surge after 1980), may serve to cement the polarization between rich and poor nations. This polarization has been described by Quah (1996) as the 'persistence and stratification' of the differences between rich and poor. Over time, a bi-modal distribution of world incomes emerges; one for affluent nations, the other for low-income countries. Nations are forced to join one or the other.

Table 1.2 Per capita real GDP levels in 1820 and 2001, and growth rates

	Per capita GDP levels			% annual average*		
	1820	*1950*	*2001*	*1820–1950*	*1950–2001*	*1820–2001*
Western Europe	1204	4579	19,256	1.03	2.86	1.54
Western offshoots	1202	9268	26,943	1.58	2.11	1.73
Japan	669	1921	20,683	0.81	4.77	1.91
Average – rich	*1109*	*6100*	*23,047*	*1.32*	*2.64*	*1.69*
Latin America	692	2506	5811	0.99	1.66	1.18
Asia	577	634	3256	0.07	3.26	0.96
Africa	420	894	1489	0.58	1.01	0.70
Average – poor	*565*	*852*	*3237*	*0.32*	*2.65*	*0.97*

Source: Maddison (2003).

Notes
GDP valued in 1990 international Geary-Khamis dollars.
* Annual average compounded growth rates reported.

In the South, the poorest growth performance in the developing world has been in Africa, with Latin America representing the fastest growing region till the middle of the twentieth century, when Asia seems to take over. At this juncture it is worth noting that there has been a gradual change in the pattern of comparative advantage, from that which emerged from the first great age of globalization before 1914. This was noted by Robertson (1938) as long ago as 1937. The South became more and more capable of manufacturing competitiveness. This introduced a ray of hope for the South, or certain regions within it. Indeed, the product cycle theories developed since the 1960s (see Dollar 1986 for a North–South model) emphasized the innovation of new brands and products along with an accent on increased variety in consumption. As new products were invented, older products would be produced in cheaper (cost competitive) regions of the world.

The presence of large-scale economies of scale and the vertical disintegration of production (see Krugman 1995), meaning that different components could be produced in different locations and countries, only added to this trend that made parts of the South more and more competitive in labour-intensive manufactured goods and components, but also allowed a few countries, such as South Korea and Taiwan, to gradually climb the technological ladder and become inventors of new goods themselves. Consider the following equation which gives the ratio of goods, Q, produced in the North, Q_N, relative to the South, Q_S:

$$Q = Q_N(I)/Q_s(C) \tag{1.5}$$

The number of goods produced in the North depends on innovation (I), and the number of goods imitated by the South is based on diffusion and cost competitiveness, C. Policies can accelerate the pace of diffusion to the South and narrow the North–South wage differential, implying conditional convergence in per capita incomes. Gradually, it is possible to convert oneself from an imitator to an inventor. Will all regions of the South benefit? If we consider agglomeration effects there is a tendency for industries to cluster together. Puga and Venables (1999) present a multi-sector model, which characterizes industrial development in terms of locational agglomeration effects between firms. This encourages the geographical concentration of production. This concentration can spread from one part of the world to the other, but favours some regions of the developing world, such as Asia over Africa. The crucial issues determining success are the presence of infrastructure, and faith in the institutional quality and political stability of a nation. In accordance with the older notion of the fallacy of composition, not all countries can benefit from expanded international trade.

As Table 1.3 indicates growth has been faster in developing East Asia and South Asia since the 1980s, and mirroring that has been the growth in exports from Asia. Growth in Africa picked up after two decades of declining growth rates after the millennium. Despite this unevenness the share of developing countries of world exports has risen to 38 per cent by 2008, compared to 27.4 per cent in 1980 (see Tables 1.4 and 1.6). This has been hastened by the production of

Table 1.3 Annual average GDP per capita growth rates (1995 constant US$)

Area/Country	Annual average GDP growth (%)				
	1960–1970	1970–1980	1980–1990	1990–2000	2000–2006
All developing	3.1	3.3	1.2	1.9	5.7
East Asia and Pacific	2.9	4.5	5.9	6.0	8.6
South Asia	1.8	0.7	3.5	3.2	7.0
Latin America and Caribbean	2.6	3.4	−0.8	1.7	3.1
Sub-Saharan Africa	2.6	0.8	−1.1	−0.4	4.7

Source: World Development Indicators 2002 and 2008, World Bank.

components along globalized value chains at different national locations, which depend on imports that are essentially re-exported after some assembling activity, but also linked to higher prices of primary products. More importantly, there has been a huge spurt (109 per cent) in exports of the South to other countries in that region (Table 1.5). A lot of this has to do with East Asian regional trade.

Despite the decline in multilateralism (mirroring the growth of bilateralism) in international trade and the failure of the Doha rounds, the share of South–South exports as a percentage of world exports grew from 30 per cent in 1980 to

Table 1.4 Relative shares of world exports by region

Export region (%) Import region (%)	1980		1990		2000		2008	
	North	South	North	South	North	South	North	South
North	52.7	19.2	65.9	13.9	57.7	18.7	42.2	23.6
South	19.8	8.2	14.8	5.4	16.6	6.9	19.8	14.4

Source: International Financial Statistics, International Monetary Fund.

Note
North corresponds to IMF's "advanced economies", while South is the rest of the world.

Table 1.5 Destination of the South's exports (as a % of world exports)

Share	1980	1990	2000	2008
South	8	5	7	14
North	19	14	19	24
Variation		*1980–1990*	*1990–2000*	*2000–2008*
South		−34	28	*109*
North		−28	35	*26*

Source: International Financial Statistics, International Monetary Fund.

38 per cent in 2008 (see Table 1.6), along with a 65 per cent increase in South–South exports for developing Asia and a 33 per cent increase in the Western Hemisphere (Latin America and the Caribbean) in the 2000–2008 period. These may have been aided by regional trade agreements and shows that South–South trade is growing faster than North–South trade (see Table 1.5).

The role of Africa in South–South trade deserves special mention. Industrialization did not materialize in that continent as in Asia. Instead, African countries became importers of the South's exports and, by 2008, 46 per cent of its imports had this provenance. Africa's growing integration in a global South's market intensified in the 1990s (see Table 1.6). With the industrialization of some areas in the South and the consequent differentiation of the developing world, Africa seemed to have provided a particularly permeable market for the South's cheaper products. African exports are predicted to increase, but not in the form of manufactures. Other countries in the South have increasingly shown interest in Africa's primary commodities and natural resources. More competition over the demand for these products 'favours' the commercial position of African countries in this regard, but raises other concerns about the environment and human rights. The issue of an undiversified economic structure, however, remains. Additionally, will the countries overcome the old 'resource curse' argument,

Table 1.6 South–South exports, imports and GDP growth (%)

	Share				*Variation*		
	1980	*1990*	*2000*	*2008*	*1980–1990*	*1990–2000*	*2000–2008*
South–South exports							
Africa	32	29	32	34	−10	10	8
Developing Asia	22	19	20	33	−15	6	65
Middle East	30	28	27	38	−7	−4	40
Western Hemisphere	18	32	33	43	77	3	33
All South	30	28	27	38	−6	−4	40
South–South imports							
Africa	15	20	32	46	35	62	42
Developing Asia	23	18	24	37	−22	31	56
Middle East	19	28	33	49	48	18	49
Western Hemisphere	31	22	25	38	−29	15	52
All South	29	27	29	42	−8	9	42
GDP growth (variation)							
Africa					2.7	2.3	5.6
Developing Asia					6.7	7.2	8.2
Middle East					1.2	4.3	5.3
Western Hemisphere					2.1	2.9	3.8
South					3.5	3.3	6.4
North					3.1	2.7	2.4
World					3.2	2.9	4.0

Source: International Financial Statistics, International Monetary Fund.

whereby economic dependence on primary goods delays development? Murshed and Serino (2010) suggest that one way of avoiding the resource curse is to industrially process natural resource based products.

Returning to the global South, it is worth noting that this period also saw more buoyant growth rates for the South *as a whole* (not just Asia) at 6.4 per cent, approximately doubling the average rates for the previous two decades. Does this mean that South–South trade could serve as a new engine for economic growth? Or, is the spurt in South–South trade simply symptomatic of unravelling global value chains? This is particularly relevant, as it is argued that the severity of the recession in the OECD, and specially the need for an export reorientation in the USA makes the importance of new (Southern) engines of growth drawn from countries which did not experience GDP contraction more important.

In 2009, China, India and Brazil's combined share of the world's GDP was 20.5 per cent, according to the IMF (2010), of which China had the biggest share with 12.5 per cent of GDP (India accounted for 5.1 per cent and Brazil for 2.9 per cent). China is the largest and fast growing economy in the South. Its economy is characterized, however, by a high export dependency as a source of growth, along with high savings rates and high investment shares in GDP (Akyüz 2010). The share of wages in national income is lower in China than for many countries. If it reorients towards a smaller export and a higher consumption share in its national income it may exert a smaller beneficial effect on the rest of the South, in terms of final goods demand, compared to the United States. If the USA moves towards less domestic consumption and more exports, imports from the rest of the world will decline by more than they are likely to increase when China's private consumption rises, as the latter's consumption is less import intensive. China's high investment rates may partially result in a domestic property related speculative bubble, which when it bursts, could have negative consequences for the rest of the South. The present pattern is that China has helped keep commodity prices buoyant due its demand for these. These have helped African exporters particularly. It is also an important importer of other intermediate goods, demand for which may decline if its exports decline. If China is to act as a locomotive for the global South's growth it has to keep up its demand for commodities and intermediate inputs, and redirect its consumption towards more final goods imports. Due its vast reserves it may even act as a financier of global trade for deficit nations in the South (ibid.). This will ultimately require greater movement away from reserve currencies, such as the dollar, towards true liquidity in the form of Special Drawing Rights (SDRs).

But there is one area where China may benefit less than advanced regions of the global South. Due to its demographic transition, one child policy, and the effect of growth on wages, surplus labour (in the sense of Lewis) may imminently vanish in China (Cai 2008). In that case its comparative advantage in labour-intensive manufactures will have to shift elsewhere in the South, creating opportunities in low-income countries. We maintain that it is these emerging economic differences within the South that have been driving South–South globalization in the recent past and are likely to continue in the foreseeable future.

1.3 Macroeconomic backdrop

The global picture is that we face rising income inequality and a slowdown in poverty reduction due to the recession. For many of the world's poor, rising food prices in 2007–2008 also contributed to their plight, adding some 100 million people to those who are transitorily food insecure (World Bank 2008). According to WESS (2010), globally the number of people living on less than PPP$1.25 a day declined from 1.8 to 1.4 billion between 1990 and 2005, but this decline was mainly due to a drop in poverty in China and other parts of developing East Asia; poverty is on the rise in South Asia and sub-Saharan Africa. More worryingly, the trend towards greater inequality between skilled and unskilled workers has been on the rise since globalization boosted world trade (see Mamoon and Murshed 2008 and its links with the lack of primary education in many developing countries).

There has been a steady decline in labour's share of national income worldwide (cf. Van der Hoeven 2010). This may have also contributed to the growth in indebtedness of the USA's household sector, as the real earnings compression of the bottom 20 per cent has encouraged borrowing (Blankenburg and Palma 2009). As van der Hoeven (2010) points out, the share of the bottom decile or quintile compared to the top has been steadily declining in most countries, North and South. He argues that every time there is a crisis, a recurrent event since the liberalization of the financial sector, there is a ratchet effect: formal employment recovery after the crisis does not compensate the fall experienced during the downswing. This not only implies declining labour shares (compared to profits), but also the creeping 'informalization' of work.[7]

Three other factors are noteworthy. Since the beginning of financial sector liberalization, the frequency and amplitude of recessions induced by financial crises are rising. Second, the increase in global capital flows is not mirrored in a rise in investment in physical capital (or gross fixed capital formation); see ibid. and WESS (2010). This, of course, is linked to the various housing investment booms globally, and the connection between these bursting house price bubbles and the current great recession. Borrowing with no investment has also increased private and public financial fragility, as debt and interests payments increase in relation to current income and households and firms are more vulnerable to changes in financial markets. This stands as one of the top economic problems in Northern countries today, but has severely affected middle-income countries in the 1990s.

Finally, despite the much vaunted global capital flow surge there are negative transfers between the North and South (between 1997 and 2008, reported in WESS, 2010) because of profit repatriation, debt servicing, and current account surpluses in the South. Similar to the experience of the 1980s, when there were also negative transfers during the debt crisis, the poor South continues to finance the rich North.

There is a great deal made of the global imbalances caused by the US's large current account deficit (see Edwards 2005; Palley 2006 on its unsustainability). This is matched by surpluses in China, Germany and Japan. In addition to China, developing countries have built up huge reserves of foreign currencies. According to figures cited in van der Hoeven (2010), developing countries as a whole had reserves of foreign exchange of up to 27.1 per cent of GNP in 2007 (17.9 per cent of GNP in sub-Saharan Africa), compared to a mere 6.8 per cent in the early 1990s. By contrast, advanced economies hold about 5 per cent of GNP as reserves. Table 1.7 lists reserves build-ups in the developing world. This practice is no doubt driven by the spectre of the 1990s financial crises. International reserves, together with regulation of speculative type of financial flows – in some developing countries, particularly China, India and some South American countries – represent a war chest to combat volatility in financial flows. Although, as Rodrik (2006) indicates that reserves accumulations may have costs in terms of investment and foregone output, after the financial crises in the 1990s developing nations seem to have opted to pay this price to prevent financial crises and the policy conditionalities associated with financial assistance from international financial institutions (IFIs), in particular the IMF.

But reserves build-ups may have another interesting and less obvious rationale. It allows emerging markets to promote competitive real exchange rates. In a context where rigid WTO rules restrict the transfer of technology and commercial and industrial policies, the exchange rate becomes a key policy target to encourage the non-traditional tradable sector in Southern countries (see Frenkel and Taylor 2006) and increase their export market share. Competitive exchange rates promote export growth and import substitution and reserves accumulations prevent exchange rate appreciation in a system of flexible exchange rates, with or without capital mobility. A strategy of export led growth, which as Polterovich and Popov (2003) show, has led to faster growth in developing countries, has to rely on reserve accumulation.

Consider the following equation:

$$R=X(e)-M(e, Y)+K \tag{1.6}$$

Table 1.7 Reserve holdings of leading developing countries in Latin America, Asia, Africa and oil exporters. Millions of US dollars

	1980	1990	1994	1998	2001	2005	2008
Argentina	9297	6222	16,003	22,425	14,556	28,082	46,385
Brazil	6875	9200	38,492	51,706	35,866	53,799	193,783
China	10,091	34,476	57,781	146,448	220,057	831,410	1,966,040
India	12,010	5637	24,221	28,385	49,051	137,825	257,423
Malaysia	5755	10,659	26,339	21,470	29,846	70,458	92,166
Mexico	4175	10,217	6441	28,852	44,805	74,110	95,300
Morocco	814	2338	4622	4197	8669	16,551	22,720
Nigeria	10,640	4129	1649	7781	10,647	28,632	53,599
Russian Fed.	n.a.	n.a.	7206	17,624	36,303	182,272	427,077
Saudi Arabia	26,129	13,437	9139	16,210	18,867	28,888	34,340
South Africa	7888	2583	3295	5957	7627	20,624	34,070

Source: IMF – International Financial Statistics.

Here Y is income, X exports, M imports, R foreign exchange reserves, K other types of financial net inflows and e the nominal exchange rate (a rise in which constitutes depreciation and helps retention of export market share). When there is a balance of payments surplus on the current account, the right hand side of equation (1.6) is positive. This is a feature of most emerging economies. But some variable needs to adjust in the presence of these surpluses. Reserve build-ups ($dR>0$) prevent exchange rate appreciation ($de<0$) in a system of (managed) flexible exchange rates. Thus, a competitive exchange rate is maintained, and sustains global market share. Consequently, a strategy of export led growth has to rely on reserve accumulation to prevent real exchange appreciation.

Export led growth, however, has its pitfalls. It exposes developing countries to a collapse of world trade, which has seen the largest decline in 2009 since the great depression of the 1930s, but is expected to recover in 2010, if vulnerabilities do not materialize; see Table 1.8. Although trade volumes are projected to expand, in part due to the recovery in primary commodity prices, output growth will be promoted by a different component of aggregate demand: government spending and the fiscal stimuli being applied throughout the world. It is worth mentioning, for example, that China applied a fiscal injection of about US$600 billion in 2009, amounting to about 15 per cent of GDP (Akyüz 2010). Thus, the recovery, if any, is based not on private demand but on public sector expenditure. These have also been represented by more 'universal' (or at least categorically targeted) types of programmes rather than 'targeted' types of social safety nets (such as microcredit and means tested benefits so favoured by the Washington based international organizations). Fiscal and monetary stimuli represent the partial Keynesian counter-revolution that we are witnessing worldwide.

Akerlof and Shiller (2009) emphasize the role of a confidence multiplier in engendering recovery in the developed North. Given the depth of the recession, and particularly the negative wealth effects of declining real estate equity on households, as well as the negative impact of toxic assets on banks' balance sheets, the fiscal and monetary stimulus arranged so far may be insufficient and may require an even bigger stimulus. For example, they point out that in Japan where nearly zero interest rates and government expenditure (leading to a debt/GDP ratio of more than 200 per cent) has still been insufficient to revive confidence. Given low confidence, the enforced fiscal prudence demanded by markets

Table 1.8 Global projections in growth and exports (% changes from previous period)

	Output growth (%)		Growth export volume (%)	
	World	*Developing countries*	*World*	*Developing countries*
2003–2007	3.62	6.84	8.08	11.38
2009	−2.60	1.90	−12.60	−8.90
2010 proj.	1.60	5.30	5.50	6.50

Source: UN – DESA.

Table 1.9 Fiscal balance and general government debt

	2007 (pre-crisis)	2009	2010
Overall fiscal balance			
Advanced G20 countries	−1.9	−10.2	−8.7
Emerging market G20 countries	0.2	−4.9	−4.2
G20	−1.1	−8.1	−6.9
General government debt (gross)			
Advanced G20 countries	78.8	100.6	109.7
Emerging market G20 countries	37.5	38.8	40.2
G20	62.4	76.1	82.1

Source: Horton *et al.* (2009), Appendix Table 1.

in the wake of the downgrading of Greek sovereign debt constrains the ability of governments in the North (except perhaps that of the United States, which is in a unique position of being able to issue the international reserve currency that everyone wishes to hold) to aggressively finance a return to macroeconomic confidence. Although, as shown in Table 1.9, advanced nations from the G20 find themselves at present in a much worse fiscal position with a projected deficit of about 8.7 per cent of GDP and total debt stocks rising to nearly 110 per cent of GDP, the way out of the crisis may not be fiscal retrenchment as required by financial markets in Europe, but rather larger counter-cyclical fiscal stimuli. The fragile economic recovery in Europe may otherwise go into reverse.

For the poorest parts of the world, as in Africa, the transmission mechanism of the recession is potentially via declining exports, although commodity prices are buoyant. Weeks (2009) points out that the possibility of fiscal stimuli are constrained by the countries' inability to borrow; the only possibility is money financed fiscal stimuli for many countries; even that is constrained by the history of inflation, aid conditionality and the need for debt servicing. Policies of devaluation or exchange rate depreciation are not feasible for all countries. Some CFA (*Colonies françaises d'Afrique*) zone countries have limited scope in this respect as they are traditionally tied to the French currency, and devaluation may not increase exports in a context of world trade slowdown. A related issue is the possibility of declining aid volumes in real terms. This makes the need to collect greater domestic tax revenues in poorer developing countries all the more pressing. It will require international tax coordination between countries to avoid tax evasion, as garnering more taxes (on the personal and corporate sector) can be a method of domestic resource mobilization in an era where the prospects for increased international development assistance from traditional donors are bleak (WESS 2010).

1.4 Conclusions

During the last decade, countries in the South, particularly China, India and other middle-income countries from Asia and Latin America and to a lesser extent from Africa, have been catching up with the developed world. As described earlier, their rates of economic growth are faster than those of the advanced nations, as reflected in their increased shares of world output and in terms of global financial flows and trade. This is a consequence of not just increased North–South economic interaction, but also increased flows within the South. Regional integration agreements emerged or intensified among developing nations worldwide; new foreign investment flowed from large developing countries, like China, Brazil and South Africa, to other developing nations, particularly in Africa, and most developing countries have been increasing their sales to China and India. As shown in Table 1.5, exports among developing nations doubled since the 1980s and seem to be shaping a new pattern of global commerce. Although some (Dinello and Shaoguang 2009) are sceptical about South–South relationships, others have heralded inter-South exchanges as a potential source of dynamism for the South, and stress that South–South globalization is unlikely to be reversed (cf. Santos-Paulino *et al.* 2010). Only time will tell, whether the divergence between average incomes between North and South will continue to decline, and whether growth in developing countries will be propelled by domestic demand and inter-South trade, rather than the traditional North–South trade channel. Unlike the situation prevailing two decades ago (Murshed 1992), the South as a whole is no longer decoupled from the global economic system.

The growing importance of developing countries, in particular larger ones, is not only economic but also political. IFIs are finally discussing changes in their governance structures to increase the voice and representation of developing countries as a whole and those of underrepresented regions and countries. This has been a long-standing demand from many developing countries denied by rich nations. Several countries in the global South, it is also worth noting, have become international players. These new powers can be observed in the rising power of the Group of 20 (G20) and in the ways economic policies from emerging economies have affected the dynamism of the International Financial System (IFS).

Although the G20 is an informal institution which played no major role between 1999 and 2007, as the US financial crisis became global in 2008, it has become the forum where the largest economies and regions, both from the North and the South, have been discussing and coordinating macroeconomic policies and regulatory changes in the financial system. The G20 explicitly recognizes that many emerging economies, particularly the BRIC countries and other countries such as South Korea, Mexico and Turkey, have a systemic importance for the stability of the IFS, and is the place where, with varying degrees of emphasis and success, developing countries have been pushing for counter-cyclical policies to face the crisis, regulation of financial flows and reforms of IFIs (Abeles and Kiper 2010). Here the important point is that these developments reflect the rise in *part* of the South, but not the whole. In turn, this begs the question as to whether more and more countries from the developing world will become part of this influential club, and whether the G20 will go the way of all flesh and wither away.

The relevance of emerging economies in the IFIs is not only linked to the crises since the 1990s, and their contagion effects, but also to the changes in their attitudes towards international financial markets. Although, until very recently disapproved by the IMF, several emerging economies have (re)introduced measures to regulate their capital accounts – Argentina in 2005 and Brazil in 2010 – while others like China, Chile, Colombia and India have historically always made use of them (Ocampo and Palma 2008). More importantly, emerging economies have been consciously accumulating reserves as *self-insurance* against financial turmoil (Serino and Kiper 2009). This may have fuelled problems associated with current global financial imbalances, yet global imbalances have their roots in the earlier part of the post-war era, when advanced countries like Germany and Japan encouraged the competitiveness of their manufacturing sectors and the USA's role of supplier of the reserve currency prior to 1971.

Reducing imbalances needs more policy coordination among key players such as the US, the UK, Europe, Japan and China, but also increased domestic absorption in the developing world. The latter, however, is unlikely to happen unless the Bretton Woods based IFIs are reformed. If the North needs part of the South to spend more and, in so doing, move from external surpluses to deficits (something countries from the South may be willing to engage in, especially in the context of a crisis), the IMF or other institutions must operate as a lender of last resort and provide financial assistance on terms different from the ones imposed during the Asian crisis. Unfortunately, according to recent estimates and projections for the coming years, imbalances are expected to grow again (cf. WEO 2010).

There are other unaddressed challenges in addition to global imbalances. Growth and trade expansion have had a modest impact towards fairer redistribution. If a growing middle class has enjoyed increased consumption, the bulk of the population continues to be largely left by the wayside by these great transformations. This is reflected in greater inequality in most countries, and the almost universal increase in the skilled–unskilled wage premium. In India, for example, this is reflected in increasingly violent social conflict manifesting itself in Maoist insurgencies. Globalization produces winners and losers, and the losers sometimes violently revolt even in settings where the average level has risen (cf. Murshed 2010: chapter 7). The growing gap within developing countries, adds to the inequality between countries (Milanovic 2005). Targeted safety nets have resulted in modest improvements, but in some cases living conditions actually worsened after the dismantling of previous (formal and informal) general safety nets. Arguably, China avoided social unrest post-2008 by its large, generous and general (untargeted) increase in public expenditure. If growth is to remain buoyant in developing countries, the next challenge is tackling global economic injustice and domestic inequality. If not for humanitarian and ethical reasons, these measures are needed to prevent the potential rise of insecurity.

In spite of still limited mass consumption in many countries, the global South's economic growth raises the issue of the extension of the North's ecological footprint towards the rest of the planet. The increasing utilization of resources under the current 'dirty' technologies in the South has put the environment under further strain. Climate change and carbon emissions further motivate the need for rethinking global governance. Transfers of technology to the South have taken place on a small scale, for example, through the Kyoto's trading of carbon emissions and its clean development mechanism. However, the adoption by the South of cleaner and resource efficient technologies available in the North should be scaled up through cheaper (or free technology). If the aim of development is the elimination of surplus labour (hence mass poverty) in the South via growth, we have to bear in mind that economic progress under the industrial revolutions of the past two centuries, both during the age of steam and electricity, relied on fossil fuel based emissions. The survival of planet Earth necessitates restrictions on these emissions; this ultimately limits global growth in the absence of technological change, and above all the willingness to pay for the global adoption of cleaner technologies by the richer parts of the world.

Notes

1 For example, in 2009 China's growth rate from 9.6 to 8.7 per cent in the previous year; India from 7.3 to 5.6 per cent; with nations like South Korea, Taiwan, Malaysia, Singapore experiencing GDP contractions, but even they are predicted to recover in 2010, see IMF (2010).
2 A convenient shorthand for the growth of the dynamic sector, which can include processed natural resource products.
3 Fertility and mortality rates are a positive and negative function of the real wage rates.
4 The region with the larger capital stock sees its manufacturing sector grow with free trade as happened historically after the Napoleonic wars; it gradually becomes more cost competitive due to economies of scale or increasing returns to scale; the laggard region sees its manufacturing sector vanish after free trade is introduced as it cannot compete in costs; see Krugman (1981) for the analytical model and Bairoch (1982) for the economic history.
5 This includes specialization in processed natural resources, which can also be growth enhancing; see Murshed and Serino (2010).
6 Particularly noteworthy was the growth of population in the Western offshoots relieving Europe of population pressure and perhaps even surplus labour.
7 The share of the informal sector in total employment has been rising since the beginning of financial globalization in the 1980s (which accelerated after the end of the cold war), and the share of the informal sector is greater in low-income countries compared to middle-income countries, where, in turn, it is higher than in advanced industrialized nations (Van der Hoeven 2010).

References

Abeles, M. and E. Kiper (2010) 'El G20: "Hacia una nueva arquitectura financiera internacional" El rol de Argentina, México, Brasil', Paper prepared for the Observatorio de Política Exterior Argentina.
Akerlof, G.A. and J. Shiller (2009) *Animal Spirits: How Human Psychology Drives the Economy and Why it Matters for the Global Economy*, Princeton, NJ: Princeton University Press.
Akyüz, Y. (2010) 'Export Dependence and Sustainability of Growth in China and the East Asian Production Network', 27, Geneva South Centre Research Paper.

Bacha, E.L. (1978) 'An Interpretation of Unequal Exchange from Prebisch-Singer to Emmanuel', *Journal of Development Economics*, 5: 319–30.

Bairoch, P. (1982) 'International Industrialisation Levels from 1750 to 1980', *Journal of European Economic History*, 2: 268–333.

Blankenburg, S. and J.G. Palma (2009) 'Introduction: The Global Financial Crisis', *Cambridge Journal of Economics*, 33: 531–38.

Burgstaller, A. and N. Saavedra-Rivano (1984) 'Capital Mobility and Growth in a North–South Model', *Journal of Development Economics*, 15: 213–37.

Cai, F. (2008) 'Approaching a Triumphal Span: How Far is China Towards its Lewisian Turning Pont?' 2008/9, WIDER Research Paper.

Chang, H.-J. (2007) *Bad Samaritans: Rich Nations, Poor Policies, and the Threat to the Developing World*, London: Random House Books.

Dinello, N. and W. Shaoguang (2009) *China, India and Beyond: Development Drivers and Limitations*, Cheltenham: Edward Elgar.

Dollar, D. (1986) 'Technological Innovation, Capital Mobility, and the Product Cycle in North–South Trade', *American Economic Review*, 76: 177–90.

Edwards, S. (2005) 'Is the U.S. Current Account Deficit Sustainable? And if not How Costly is Adjustment Likely to Be?' NBER Working Paper 11541.

Findlay, R. (1980) 'The Terms of Trade and Equilibrium Growth in the World Economy', *American Economic Review*, 70: 291–9.

Findlay, R. (2009) 'The Trade Development Nexus in Theory and History', 13, WIDER Annual Lecture.

Findlay, R. and K. O'Rourke (2007) *Power and Plenty: Trade, War and the World Economy in the Second Millennium*, Princeton, NJ: Princeton University Press.

Frank, A.G. (1998) *Re-Orient: Global Economy in the Asian Age*, Berkeley, CA: University of California Press.

Frenkel, R. and L. Taylor (2006) 'Real Exchange Rate, Monetary Policy, and Employment', 19, UN DESA Working Paper.

IMF (2008) *World Economic Outlook*, Washington, DC: International Monetary Fund.

IMF (2010) *World Economic Outlook*, Washington, DC: International Monetary Fund.

Krugman, P. (1981) 'Trade, Accumulation and Uneven Development', *Journal of Development Economics*, 8: 149–61.

Krugman, P. (1995) 'Growing World Trade: Causes and Consequences', 25, Brookings Papers on Economic Activity.

Lewis, W.A. (1954) 'Economic Development with Unlimited Supplies of Labour', *Manchester School*, 22: 139–91.

Maddison, A. (2003) *The World Economy: Historical Statistics*, Paris: OECD.

Mamoon, D. and S.M. Murshed (2008) 'Unequal Skill Premiums and Trade Liberalization: Is Education the Missing Link?' *Economics Letters*, 100: 262–6.

Milanovic, B. (2005) *Worlds Apart: Measuring Global and International Inequality*, Princeton, NJ: Princeton University Press.

Murphy, K., A. Shleifer and R. Vishny (1989) 'Industrialization and the Big Push', *Journal of Political Economy*, 97: 1003–26.

Murshed, S.M. (1992) *Economic Aspects of North–South Interaction: Analytical Macroeconomic Issues*, London: Academic Press.

Murshed, S.M. (2010) *Explaining Civil War: A Rational Choice Approach*, Cheltenham: Edward Elgar.

Murshed, S.M. and L.A. Serino (2010) 'An Inquiry into the Competitiveness Explanation for the Resource Curse' (mimeo).

Nayyar, D. (2009) 'Developing Countries in the World Economy: The Future in the Past?' 12, WIDER Annual Lecture.

Ocampo, J.A. and G. Palma (2008) 'The Role of Preventative Capital Accounts Regulations', in J.A. Ocampo and J. Stiglitz (eds) *Capital Market Liberalization and Development*, Oxford: Oxford University Press.

Palley, T. (2006) 'The Fallacy of the Revised Bretton Woods Hypothesis: Why Today's International Financial System is Unsustainable', Levy Economics Institute of Bard College, 85, Public Policy Brief.

Polterovich, V. and V. Popov (2003) 'Accumulation of Foreign Exchange Reserves and Long Term Growth'. Online, available at: http://www.nes.ru (accessed 31 May 2010).

Prebisch, R. (1950) *The Economic Development of Latin America and its Principal Problems*, New York: United Nations.

Puga, D. and A.J. Venables (1999) 'Agglomeration and Economic Development: Import Substitution vs. Trade Liberalisation', *Economic Journal*, 109: 292–311.

Quah, D. (1996) 'Twin Peaks: Growth and Convergence in Models of Distribution Dynamics', *Economic Journal*, 106: 1045–55.

Robertson, D.H. (1938) 'The Future of International Trade', *Economic Journal*, 48: 1–14.

Rodrik, D. (2006) 'The Social Cost of Foreign Exchange Reserves', NBER Working Paper 11952.

Santos-Paulino, W., U. Amelia and G. Wan, Eds. (2010) *Southern Engines of Global Growth*, Oxford: Oxford University Press.

Serino, L. and E. Kiper (2009) 'Acerca de los fundamentos macroeconómicos de la crisis internacional', AEDA's First Annual Conference, August 2009, Buenos Aires.

Singer, H.W. (1950) 'Distribution of Gains Between Borrowing and Investing Countries', *American Economic Review*, 40: 473–85.

Van der Hoeven, R. (2010) *Labour Market Trends, Financial Globalization and the Current Crisis in Developing Countries*, The Hague: ISS.

Weeks, J. (2009) 'The Freetown Declaration: Countercyclical Policy for Africa', SOAS, University of London (mimeo).

WEO (2010) 'World Economic Outlook, Rebalancing Growth', Washington, DC: International Monetary Fund, April.

WESS (2010) 'World Economic and Social Survey', New York: United Nations, Department for Economic and Social Affairs.

World Bank (2008) 'World Development Report Database'.

Young, A. (1995) 'The Tyranny of Numbers: Confronting the Statistical Realities of the East Asian Growth experience', *Quarterly Journal of Economics*, 110: 641–80.

2 New directions for globalization in times of crisis

Rob Vos[1]

2.1 Introduction

In 2008, an unprecedented, though short-lived period of broad-based global economic growth came to an end. During 2002 and 2008, developing countries averaged about 5 per cent of per capita GDP growth per year, outpacing by far welfare increases in developed countries. Also many of the poorest countries witnessed strong per capita income growth (Figure 2.1), leading some observers to make the contradictory claims that globalization was effectively working to enhance living standards worldwide and that some kind of "decoupling" was taking place with strong endogenous growth in developing countries having become less sensitive to downturns in developed economies.[2]

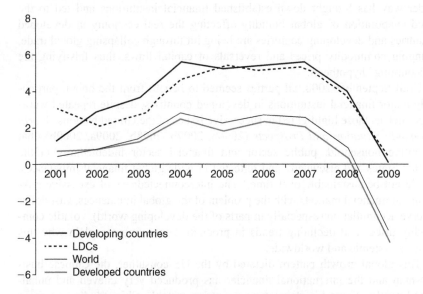

Figure 2.1 Growth of real GDP per capita by major country groups, 2001–2009 (source: UN-DESA, database of World Economic Situation and Prospects. Figures for 2009 are according to baseline forecast of World Economic Situation and Prospects as per mid-2009 (United Nations 2009b)).

As the world economy entered into its worst crisis since the Great Depression of the 1930s, both claims were proven utterly wrong. The present crisis emerged on the back of an intrinsically unsustainable global growth pattern. This pattern was characterized by a strong consumer demand in the United States, funded by easy credit and booming house prices. Far-reaching financial deregulation facilitated a massive and unfettered expansion of new financial instruments, such as securitized sub-prime mortgage lending, sold on financial markets worldwide. This pattern of growth enabled strong export growth and booming commodity prices benefiting many developing countries. Growing United States deficits in this period were financed by increasing trade surpluses in China, Japan and other countries accumulating large foreign-exchange reserves and willing to buy dollar-denominated assets and fuelling mounting global financial imbalances and indebtedness of financial institutions, businesses and households. In some countries, both developed and developing, domestic financial debt has risen four- or fivefold as a share of national income since the early 1980s. This rapid explosion in debt was made possible by the shift from a traditional "buy-and-hold" banking model to a dynamic "originate-to-sell" trading model (or "securitization"). Leverage ratios of some institutions went up to as high as 30, well above the ceiling of ten generally imposed on deposit banks (cf. United Nations 2009a). In the context of a highly integrated global economy without adequate regulation and global governance structures, this risky pattern of financial expansion implied that the breakdown in one part of the system thus would also lead to failure elsewhere. It is this systemic failure we are witnessing today. The deleveraging now under way has brought down established financial institutions and led to the rapid evaporation of global liquidity affecting the real economy in developed countries and developing countries are being hit through collapsing global trade, plunging commodity prices and reversals of capital flows, thus falsifying the "decoupling" hypothesis.

Until September 2008, all parties seemed to benefit from the boom, particularly major financial institutions in developed countries, despite repeated warnings, such as those highlighted in successive issues of the United Nations' *World Economic Situation and Prospects* (2006b, 2007b, 2008b, 2009a, 2009b), that mounting household, public sector and financial sector indebtedness in the United States and elsewhere, and reflected in wide global financial imbalances, would not be sustainable over time.[3] The interconnectedness of excessive risk-taking in financial markets with the problem of the global imbalances, vast dollar reserve accumulation (especially in parts of the developing world), volatile commodity prices and declining trends in productive investment explain why this crisis is systemic and worldwide.

This global growth pattern dictated by the US consumer, the Chinese businessman and the international financier has produced very uneven and unbalanced results. Some big developing countries, notably China, India and some other emerging market economies, have seen strong growth accelerations. Most recently, also low-income countries saw substantial average welfare improvements, epitomizing what might be seen as the "rise of the rest" (Amsden 2001).

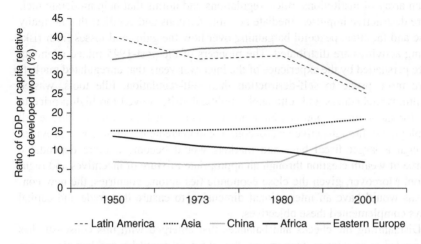

Figure 2.2 Rising global inequality and the rise of (some of) the rest (source: United Nations (2006b)).

Yet, the longer term growth trend has been one of sharply rising levels of income inequality (Figure 2.2).[4] The more recent, more broadly shared global growth took place in a context of increasing macroeconomic disequilibria fuelled by an ever-widening role of finance. The process of "financialization" greased the global growth engine alright, but merely to a point of overheating to reveal the systemic mechanical flaws of the engine itself. Can this engine be fixed or would the objective of a more inclusive and sustainable globalization process be better served by replacing the old engine with a new one? The remainder of this chapter discusses some key aspects of the process of financialization of world-wide trade and investment and gives some hints at some of the ingredients (no blueprint) for global and national policies which could help steer the world towards a fairer and more sustainable pattern of growth.

2.2 The myth of the self-regulating market

The present crisis is also a crisis of the globalization paradigm advocating the virtues of fully liberalized commodity and financial markets. Indeed, the concept of the self-regulating market was the *idée fixe* of the late twentieth century. It was based on the belief that freeing markets would unleash the wealth creating forces of unrestricted competition and risk-taking, resulting in greater prosperity for all while achieving greater stability. A more flexible workforce, greater asset ownership and easier access to financial markets would help households respond better to market signals and smooth incomes as well as consumption over time. Greater economic and social security would naturally follow.

Pushing this idea was always a gamble. At least since Adam Smith, careful observers have understood that markets do not regulate themselves, but depend on an array of institutions, rules, regulations and norms that help moderate their more destructive impulses, mediate possible tensions and conflicts that normally arise and facilitate peaceful bargaining over how the gains and losses from risk-taking activities are distributed. The pioneers of the post-1945 mixed economy were persuaded by the experience of the inter-war years that unregulated markets were more prone to self-destruction than self-regulation. Idle tools, wasted wealth, wretchedness and, ultimately, political strife proved too high a price to pay for stable money and flexible markets. Their stated goal was to achieve full employment through active macroeconomic management, public goods provided through a larger fiscal base and markets would become a more dependable source of wealth creation through an appropriate mixture of incentives and regulation. Moreover, given the close economic ties among countries, the new consensus would have an international dimension to ensure that trade and capital flows complemented these objectives.

Dismantling the checks and balances that emerged with this consensus has proceeded at an uneven pace among the advanced countries and has often been more enthusiastically embraced in the developing world and in transition economies, where "shock therapies" promised rapid and positive effects. As part of a global trend, many of the stresses and burdens of unregulated financial and commodity markets have been unloaded on to individuals and households, and with diminished or only limited offsetting government responses. This has been described, with reference to the United States, as the "great risk shift", but is also characteristic of shifting patterns in global trade and finance.

2.3 Emergence of a debt-dependent trading system

Over the past 20 years, the volume of trade has grown on average by 9 per cent per annum with particularly rapid growth in the period 2002–2007, averaging 14.5 per cent per annum and faster still in developing countries. Four significant forces have helped shape the pattern of international trade in this period: the rise of export-orientated industrializing developing countries; the growth of intra-firm trade in global supply chains (itself made possible by new information and communication technologies and expanded capacity and skill in developing countries); rapid trade liberalization for goods and services, embodied in both multilateral and bilateral agreements; and the explosion of unregulated financial flows. These factors are often treated separately, but in a globalized world they need to be seen as closely interconnected.

At one end of the global supply chains are mostly low-income countries which continue to be highly reliant on more traditional export sectors. Obtaining sustained gains from trade remains a challenge for these countries. In this sense, the contrast between East Asia and other regions is striking. The share of primary products, resource-based and low-technology manufacturing in the total exports of East Asia declined from 76 per cent in 1980 to 35 per cent in 2005. China alone reduced its share from 93 per cent in 1985 to 44 per cent in 2005. Other regions have been less successful in transforming the structure of their

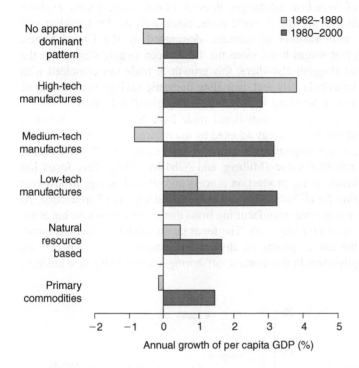

Figure 2.3 Trade specialization and long-term economic growth, 1962–2000 (source: United Nations (2006a)).

production for exports. South American countries still rely on primary products and simple manufactures (around 78 per cent of exports in 2005, down from around 90 per cent in 1983). In Africa, the concentration of exports in low value added products is even greater (83 per cent in 2005). Volatility in commodity prices strongly influences the business cycle in these countries. Strongly booming world market prices of primary products, especially from 2006, and their subsequent collapse from the start of the global financial crisis, have made this fate once again painfully clear. Figure 2.3 shows that long-term growth rates of countries at the lower end of the global value chain are well below those at the higher end, and hence have been a source of perpetuating global inequality.

Creating more dynamic gains from trade also remains a challenge for many developing countries which did manage to diversify into the exporting of seemingly "high-tech" manufactures. In many cases, however, this apparent switch to high-tech exports hides the fact that many countries are rather engaged in mostly low-tech assembly activities than in the exporting of the final good itself. In many cases, production takes place within enclaves, connected though trade and foreign direct investment (FDI) flows to other parts of a corporate supply chain, but with only limited ties to the domestic economy.

The spread of intra-firm exchanges through global value chains explains much of the indicated growth of world trade, albeit with the final product still destined for a small number of markets, dominated by the United States. However, given that wages have, since the 1980s been largely stagnant in the United States and sluggish elsewhere, this growth of trade has coincided with rising levels of household debt and dwindling domestic savings in a number of large industrial economies along with ever-widening global imbalances.[5]

These shifting patterns of international trade have been closely associated with a new global business strategy adopted by many larger firms in the industrialized countries, which emphasizes a focus on "core competence" and a greater attention to shareholder value (Milberg and Schöller 2008). This focus has driven firms to break up the production process and take advantage of low-cost offshore production for all but the highest value added aspects of production. At the extreme this has created manufacturing firms that do no manufacturing at all, such as *The Gap* or *Dell Computers*. The focus on shareholder value has meant an increase in the use of profits for dividend payments, stock buybacks and mergers and acquisitions. In this context, offshoring has served the new business

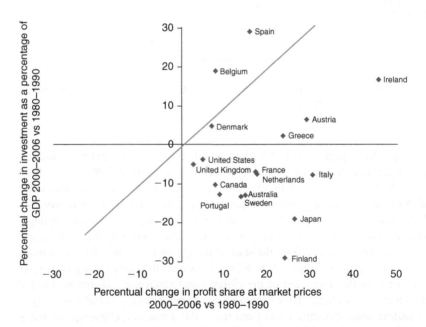

Figure 2.4 Profits and fixed investment in developed economies, 1980s versus 2000s (source: United Nations (2008a: figure II.8). Estimates are UN-DESA's calculations based on AMECO (annual macroeconomic database) of the European Commission's Directorate General for Economic and Financial Affairs).

Note
The profit share is defined as 100% minus the wage share, where the wage share is defined as the compensation per employee as percentage of GDP at market prices. Investment is defined as private sector gross fixed capital formation as divided percentage of GDP at market prices.

model in two ways. First, it has led to cost reductions and thus increased mark-ups over cost, despite the fact that firms face stiff price competition in product markets. Figure 2.4 shows how since the 1970s the share of corporate profits in value added in most developed countries has risen to new highs in the most recent upward swing of the business cycle.

Second, by limiting the scope of the firm and especially its domestic opera-tions, offshoring has reduced investment needs, increasing its ability to return value to shareholders. This has supported a "financialization of non-financial corporations" in many industrialized countries, oftentimes at the expense of pro-ductive investment (as also shown in Figure 2.4), while imports from developing countries were steadily rising. This interplay of financial and corporate dynamics has had far-reaching implications for the real economy, particularly in advanced countries. In many countries, the rise of the financial sector has coincided with the introduction of more flexible hiring practices and less secure employment conditions. Episodes of exceptionally rapid economic expansion driven by spec-ulative financial flows have brought periods of growing prosperity, but have often ended very suddenly in recession or longer periods of slow growth. More-over, losses of investment, employment and income incurred during recessions have not fully recovered when the economy turns up.

All of these factors together spell considerable income and job insecurity, even under conditions of relatively strong expansion. Also, in the majority of developed countries, the increase of wages has not kept pace with labour pro-ductivity, resulting in greater income inequality.

Managing trade pressures are, however, not solely the problem of policy makers in advanced countries. Indeed, the flip side of offshoring jobs by multi-national companies is often low value added and unstable assembly jobs in developing countries. Many of these countries have substantially increased the volume of their international trade over the past two decades, but not necessarily earning more from doing so, thanks to a combination of greater capital mobility, heightened competition in labour-intensive activities and flexible markets. All too often, such production still takes place in enclaves with the shallowest of linkages with the rest of the economy. This can leave them exposed to unex-pected shocks if firms decide to run down or shift the activity. These problems are now exacerbated with the global economic recession, including the acceler-ated decline in world trade and the sharp reversal in FDI that started in the last quarter of 2008.

Policy makers have long sought ways to manage international trade in order to maximize the benefits and limit the costs. Success cases have never relied solely on trade liberalization. Offshoring in the advanced countries and trade shocks in the developing world point to a worrying shift in underlying macro-economic conditions and influence of global financial factors that has made success all the more difficult.

2.4 Unleashing and crashing global finance

In parallel with shift trade patterns, the weight and influence of financial markets, financial actors and financial institutions have increased dramatically. This manifested itself in a massive accumulation of financial assets and by a seemingly "deep diversification" of the financial system through a variety of institutional innovations and introduction of new, then labelled as "exotic", financial institutions, especially through the derivatives markets. These developments fed growing levels of debt in the household, corporate and public sectors. In some countries, domestic financial debt as a share of GDP has risen four- or fivefold since the early 1980s. This process of "financialization", in turn, helped to entrench a singular and narrow macroeconomic policy focus on fighting inflationary threats.

In the decades following 1945, the business cycle was mainly driven by investment and export demand and underpinned by strong wage growth which fed into high levels of consumer spending. This was not always a stable process. Levels of volatility were often quite high, and wages, profits and tax revenues would often outpace productivity growth, leading to inflationary pressures, current account deficits and rising indebtedness. These signalled to policy makers that action needed to be taken, oftentimes ending in cyclical downturn.

This pattern changed fundamentally during the 1990s, as debt, leverage, collateral value and expected asset prices became dominant drivers of the cycle. This exacerbated an already strong pro-cyclical stance of market agents. This could lead to self-inflating bubbles driven by expectations of rising asset prices and by and large detached from improved prospects of real income gains or losses or of the value of the underlying real assets. Intrinsic to financial market behaviour, lenders and investors would tend to underestimate risks in the upswing and overestimate these in the downturn. These attitudes were fortified by the financial innovations through the derivatives markets which promised security against downside risks. This led to ever stronger fluctuations in asset prices: strong asset inflation and extended financial booms in the upswing and steep asset deflation and financial collapses during the downswing. This was already visible during the crises in emerging markets of the 1990s and such factors now turned a broad-based boom into a worldwide bust.

Financial booms give rise to lop-sided investment patterns. These investments often involve little more than rearranging existing assets through leveraged buyouts, stock buybacks and mergers and acquisitions, or are in sectors susceptible to speculative influences, such as property markets. Unlike earlier cycles, these booms have delivered few benefits in terms of rising wages and employment. However, increased access of households to credits has meant that consumer spending can increase, even with stagnant incomes, as (rising) levels of indebtedness substitute for (falling) household savings. But as balance sheets adopt smaller margins of safety, the system becomes more and more fragile.

The shift from an income-constrained to an asset-backed economy has been supported by the liberalization of international capital markets. Indeed, the links between domestic financial markets and capital flows are much stronger in developing countries, many of which opened their capital accounts prematurely in the 1990s.

These flows have been strongly pro-cyclical. Their effects are often transmitted through public-sector accounts, especially through the effects of available financing on government spending and through the effects of interest rates on the public debt service. But the stronger effects typically run through private spending and balance sheets. During booms, private sector deficits and borrowing tend to rise and risky balance sheets accumulate riding on perceived "success", typically seen to be reflected in low risk premia and spreads. Reversals in such perceptions lead to a cut off from external financing and provoke sudden increases in the cost of borrowing, inducing downward adjustment.

The shift towards export-led strategies in the developing world has actually accentuated this pattern in many countries. The growing influence of financial calculation has meant that commodity price volatility operates in an even more exaggerated pro-cyclical manner, which is further amplified by pro-cyclical policies among others, by expanding fiscal expenditures during the boom and reducing spending when prices are down. The latter is reinforced by the conditionality linked to international financial assistance during crises, which involves orthodox, pro-cyclical macroeconomic stabilization policy packages.

These financial dynamics have far reaching implications for the real economy. Episodes of exceptionally rapid economic expansion driven by financial bubbles can bring periods of growing prosperity, but they can end very suddenly leading to deep recessions or even longer periods of stagnation. Vulnerability to a sharp reversal of flows varies but, in many emerging markets, it is often triggered by factors beyond the control of recipient countries, including shifts in monetary policies or the bursting of a housing and financial bubble in a major developed economy.

The suggestion that the growth of cross-border financial flows would trigger a greatly improved investment climate is belied by the global trend of weaker capita formation since the 1990s (Figure 2.5) and the increased volatility of investment relative to that of output. This applies to both developed and developing countries (Figure 2.6).

With the exception of South Asia, and despite a recent worldwide recovery, this heightened volatility has resulted in average rates of capital formation still well below those enjoyed in the 1970s. Infrastructure investment and additional manufacturing capacity appear hardest hit, both critical to improving the resilience of countries against external shocks.

Moreover, losses of investment, employment and income incurred during recessions are not fully recovered when the economy turns up, pulling down the longer-term average (Akyüz 2008). The rise of the financial sector has, in many countries, also gone hand in hand with more flexible hiring practices. All this spells considerable income and job insecurity, even under conditions of relatively strong expansion. A clear sign of this has been the failure in the majority of advanced industrial countries for growth of labour compensation to keep pace

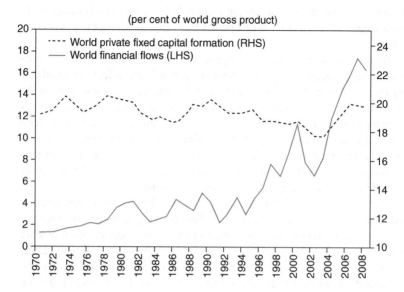

Figure 2.5 A not so healthy global investment climate (source: United Nations (2010; Chapter V)).

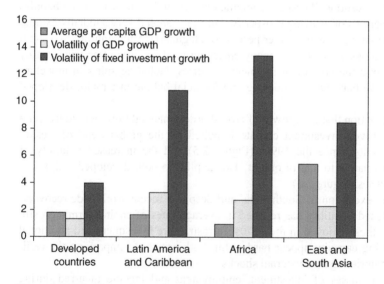

Figure 2.6 Volatility and growth, 1991–2006 (source: United Nations (2008a)).

Note
Volatility is measured through the standard deviation of output and fixed investment growth, respectively.

with labour productivity, but the same trend is apparent in emerging markets as well. Oftentimes, rising levels of income inequality have been the flip side of this development.

2.5 Political economy

No social or economic order is secure if it fails to benefit the majority of those who live under it. This demands nothing less than what European political philosophers in the seventeenth and eighteenth centuries called a "social contract": an implicit understanding among members of a community to cooperate for mutual benefit, along with formal rules and institutional mechanisms to help build trust, balance competing interests, manage disputes and provide a fair distribution of the rewards that are generated.

No single institutional blueprint prescribes what arrangement works best under particular historical and political circumstances. In the modern era, that contract has been forged around the challenges and risks generated by expanding markets and a more complex industrial division of labour. In response to those challenges and risks, new institutions and mechanisms for managing economic risk and extending social protection emerged, including a much more prominent role for the public sector. This period lasted until the early 1970s, when, beginning in the more advanced economies, a combination of internal tensions and external shocks began to threaten the existing consensus. At the end of the decade, an abrupt tightening of macroeconomic policy in these countries signalled a break with past practice, and a willingness to rethink the social contract. Citizenship, cooperation and social protection slipped down the agenda and, in some cases, dropped off altogether; in their place, consumer choice, competition and risk-taking moved to centre stage. The political checks and balances that had previously determined how markets could best serve the objectives of growth and stability were rolled back, leaving strong property rights, the rule of law and low transaction costs – the "good governance" agenda – to guarantee the legitimate functioning of the emerging market order.

The trend has been somewhat restrained in advanced countries by practical and social constraints on policy making. Resistance has proved much weaker in many developing countries, leaving them more vulnerable to downside risks. The present global crisis has made evident to policy makers worldwide that deregulation and the erosion of checks and balances had gone too far, given rise to reconsidering many aspects of existing global arrangements.

Against the growing backdrop of increasing economic and political insecurity in inter-war Europe, John Maynard Keynes (1963 [1925]: 336) called for

new policies and new instruments to adapt and control the workings of economic forces, so that they do not intolerably interfere with contemporary ideas as to what is fit and proper in the interests of social stability and social justice.

Those words resonate just as strongly today. Responsibility for the choice and mix of policies to guarantee prosperity, stability and justice, remains, of course, with national institutions and constituencies, but in an increasingly interdependent world and on a fragile planet, building a more secure home is a truly international endeavour.

2.6 What is to be done?

In today's world of increased economic and political interdependence, achieving a broad-based, rapid and sustained growth in income and employment involves even more complex policy challenges than in the past. The complexities of global interdependence in trade and finance are but one dimension of these challenges. A rapidly ageing world population, the catastrophic threat of climate change, continued widespread poverty and social exclusion, as well as raging civil conflicts and wars in many parts of the world are those putting heavy weight to the challenges ahead. The systemic nature of the present crisis has made overly clear that no benign solutions are likely to be found by relying on market forces. It would be a mistake, however, to let the pendulum swing back to the other extreme and put all our faith in state dirigisme to steer towards optimal solutions. The agenda rather should be one of making economic and social security and cohesion the basis for the unleashing of the creative impulses created by market forces, as much as through public–private partnerships. This will require strategic vision and leadership of governments and international organizations to give substance to a new social contract which strikes a balance between achieving greater (global) horizontal equity for present generation prosperity and peace and intergenerational equity ensuring sustainable development for future (though ageing) world populations and overcoming the threat of climate change. In a world of great uncertainty, it is far from obvious how to strike such a balance, let alone what policies will work best.

The crisis of globalization and the huge global challenges ahead suggest the need for going back to the drawing board. New grand ideas are needed to reshape the global economy and to redefine the regulatory and multilateral frameworks to redraw the rules of the game and allow for a return of checks and balances in the system. Grand ideas may provide a guide, but there is no certainty any of those will work in practice and much experimenting with concrete policies may be needed to find a more sustainable global growth path.

2.6.1 A global new deal

Grand schemes easily can end up in wishful thinking and no workable policy action. Yet the challenges of our time ask for big ideas that are global and address the links between core issues. Ahead of the present crisis, the United Nations' *World Economic and Social Survey 2008: Overcoming Economic Insecurity*, called for a "Global New Deal" (United Nations 2008a). The 2008 food security crisis had led the World Bank to plead for a "new deal" on global food policy. At the time, the Bank suggested that market forces through further agricultural trade liberalization, more compensatory financing and strengthened social safety nets should strike the right balance between the interests of food importers and exporters. However, this proposal underplayed some of the key elements that comprised President Roosevelt's original New Deal in response to the Great Depression, in particular the mechanisms that were created to expand and better manage markets, along with redistributional measures which aimed to better distribute the burden of shocks.

Just how far the redistribution agenda can be pushed to rebalance globalization and prevent a potentially damaging backlash is an open debate.

One possible complementary suggestion is to develop universal systems that would provide a minimum basic income in the form of a cash grant to all households. This picks up and extends the idea of a basic pension proposed by the United Nations (2007a) and Vos *et al.* (2008) in response to the global population ageing challenge. Such measures are, of course, fraught with complications and difficulties. Yet, this idea has been pushed further in response to the crisis by the International Labour Organization (ILO) in its proposal for a "Global Jobs Pact" which sees that a sustainable and equitable recovery requires the pursuance of full-employment and universal social protection objectives (ILO 2009a, 2009b).

Similarly, UN agencies have proposed a Global Green New Deal (UN-DESA 2009a; UNEP 2009) with the objective of pushing the world economy on a green and thus more sustainable growth path. Apart from new market incentives for households and businesses worldwide to allocate much more resources in energy efficiency, renewable energy and green products, this foremost will require massive public investment efforts to facilitate a transition towards carbon-free economic growth. Developing countries would need large-scale transfers of resources and access to relevant technologies to be able both to contribute to the greening of global growth and to sustain sufficiently high growth rates to respond to the poverty challenge.

Until recently, such grand ideas would seem elusive and unrealistic. World leaders have shown willingness to think out of the box and have included resources for addressing climate change, providing additional social protection and overcoming crises in pension schemes in the massive fiscal stimulus packages for economic recovery. World leaders at the G20 Summit held in April of 2009 also recognized the need for large amounts of additional resources needed for developing countries to overcome their immediate liquidity problems caused by the global financial crisis and engage in counter-cyclical responses which could be aligned with their long-term development needs. Likely, even the promised $1.1 trillion in additional resources will be far from sufficient (UN-DESA 2009b), as much as that it is far from clear how the aforementioned "new deals" add up to a workable global strategy for sustainable growth. Yet, with further elaboration in more concrete directions they could provide starting points that could evolve into new national and global social contracts that could live up to the challenges ahead.

2.6.2 Back to the multilateral drawing board

Getting there will also require a return to the multilateral drawing board. The global economic crisis has already triggered a reconsideration of a range of existing multilateral arrangements. As with the case of the crises of the 1930s, which led to the Great Depression, the systemic causes of the present crisis are ultimately based on fundamental weaknesses in global economic governance and overcoming these defects is the only genuine solution. These weaknesses underpin haphazard financial deregulation, the explosion of global imbalances and vulnerabilities, and irresponsible behaviour promoted by the international reserve system. Much more fundamental changes are needed to reform the international financial system in order to provide better safeguards that can prevent it happening again, and to create a framework for global economic governance in line with twenty-first century realities.

This will require a renewed Bretton Woods system for global financial stability. The multilateral arrangements designed at Bretton Woods in 1944 did not include a global regime for capital movements, given that capital mobility was expected to be limited. However, no such regime has emerged even after the breakdown of these arrangements, and despite the surge in private capital flows. In the aftermath of the Asian crisis, various codes and standards were established through international institutions, not just with respect to the financial sector, but also with regard to auditing and accounting, data collection and so on. None of this helped prevent the present crisis. New rules of the game will need to be established.

A major challenge for the new multilateralism is to help both developed and developing countries, though especially the latter, mitigate the damaging effects of volatile capital flows and commodity prices, and provide counter-cyclical financing mechanisms to compensate for the inherently pro-cyclical movement of private capital flows. A number of options are available to dampen the pro-cyclicality of capital flows, provide counter-cyclical finance and thus help create a better environment for sustainable growth. A first set of measures would include improved international financial regulation to stem capital flow volatility and provide advice in designing appropriate capital controls, including on a counter-cyclical basis.[6]

As new systems of regulation are being elaborated, immediate financing constraints should be addressed by enhancing available international liquidity and by reconsidering the terms of access to such resources, especially the access for developing countries to compensatory financing mechanisms to cope with external shocks. It is also important to end the tendency to impose pro-cyclical macroeconomic conditionality at higher access levels. Improved multilateral surveillance will also need to take on board all possible international spillovers of national economic policies.

None of this will work well, however, if the democratic deficit that is undermining the credibility of the Bretton Woods institutions is repaired. The IMF and the World Bank must be comprehensively reformed so that they can more adequately reflect changing economic weights in the world economy and be more responsive to current and future challenges and to strengthen the legitimacy and effectiveness of these institutions. Beyond the rebalancing of voting power in these institutions, it is important to introduce a fundamental revision of their functions and equip them with the necessary resources, such that they can effectively safeguard global financial stability, coordinate macroeconomic policies and provide adequate long-term development financing.

Further, a new global reserve system must be created which no longer relies on the US dollar as the single major reserve currency. The dollar has not proven to be a stable store of value, a requisite for a stable reserve currency. Also global instability and deficiencies the international financial institutions to address this instability have led many developing countries to accumulate vast amounts of reserves on their own. This build-up has contributed to the deflationary pressures to the world economy. A new system needs to be developed which allows for better pooling of reserves at the regional and international levels and which is not based on a single or even multiple national currencies, but which permits the emission of international liquidity (SDRs or an equivalent thereof) so as to create a more stable global financial system.

The interest of developing countries in the stability of the international financial system is underpinned by the wish that it allows greater participation in international trade through a full exploitation of their development potential. Despite the general acceptance of the benefits of freer trade, the international division of labour is still heavily influenced by commercial policies that favour products and markets, in which more advanced countries have a dominant position and a competitive edge. The recent collapse of the Doha trade talks should provide the breathing space for a much needed reassessment of the rules and norms governing international trade. In particular, high tariffs, tariff escalation and subsidies in agriculture and fisheries are applied extensively to products that offer the greatest potential for export diversification in developing countries. The panorama of protectionism is no better for industrial products including footwear, clothing and textiles where many developing countries have competitive advantages. The trading system is also vulnerable to the increasingly volatile working of the international financial system, reversing the original intentions of the post-war multilateral architects and adversely affecting developing country prospects. A major concern is the destabilizing and deflationary feedbacks among trade and financial flows, which can create impediments to development, including through unstable and misaligned exchange rates and boom–bust cycles which lead to excessive expansion of investment, production and trade in particular sectors, which eventually come to an end with the collapse of the bubble, resulting in sharp declines in trade flows and prices.

Reforming the international financial system should be undertaken with the basic objective of easing the integration of developing countries into the international trading system. The interest of developing countries in the stability of the international financial system is that it allows greater participation in international trade to be combined with the full exploitation of their development potential.

It is also to be expected that the internationalization of production will continue, and that the *outsourcing* of jobs will influence employment outcomes as emerging economies tap deeper into global supply chains in attempts to create additional job opportunities for their workers. Indeed, there are reasons to expect this trend to become even more significant. Consequently, as labour markets become more integrated and ever more dependent on large and more footloose multinational enterprises, there may be a need for a "more transparent, coherent and balanced framework" at the global level to address the employment dimensions of globalization.[7] Whether or not that materializes, a strategy of lifting all boats (and avoiding beggar-my-neighbour responses) requires a faster pace of investment in the advanced countries, including, in particular, public investment in infrastructure development and for managing the shift to low-carbon technologies consistent with commitments to mitigating the adverse impact of climate change.

Moreover, a more balanced pattern of domestic demand will only be achieved when rising wages (in line with productivity gains), rather than increased levels of debt, provide a solid basis for expanding domestic market demand. The challenges ahead will also require economies to continuously increase their skill and knowledge base in order to successfully integrate themselves into the global production process, to ensure that the net effect of globalized production is not simply the displacement of workers and to uphold core labour standards in order to ensure decent and productive work for all.

Active labour market policies (including skill development) should be strengthened to better prepare workers for the future job market. When temporary dislocation of workers cannot be avoided, appropriate social protection measures can be introduced to provide worker security. In all cases, the benefits that global production can bring should be properly weighted against the costs, and these costs can only be minimized through active involvement of all the major actors.

The responsibility for the choice and mix of policies required to guarantee prosperity, stability and justice, remains, of course, with national institutions and constituencies, but in an increasingly interdependent world and on a fragile planet, building a more secure home is a truly international undertaking.

Notes

1 This chapter is based on material published in Vos, R. (2010) "The Crisis of Globalization as an Opportunity to Create a Fairer World", *Journal of Human Development and Capabilities*, 11(1): 143–160. Taylor & Francis Ltd, the publisher, graciously permitted the reprinting.
2 Both the IMF and the World Bank, while recognizing trends towards rising global inequality, sustained the decoupling hypothesis till shortly before the present crisis (IMF 2007, 2008; World Bank 2008).
3 See further United Nations (2006b, 2007b, 2008b, 2009a, 2009b).
4 For further discussion of these trends see United Nations (2006a, 2008a), Ocampo *et al.* (2008) and Ocampo and Vos (2008).
5 See United Nations (2006b, 2007b, 2008b).

6 See United Nations (2005: chapter IV, 2008a: chapter II) and Ocampo and Vos (2008) for an elaboration of the principles for a fundamental reform of financial regulatory frameworks and their international coordination.
7 See discussion in World Commission on the Social Dimension of Globalization (2004).

References

Akyüz, Y. (2008) "Financial instability and countercyclical policy", UN-DESA background paper to World Economic and Social Survey 2008. Online, available at: www.un.org/en/development/desa/policy/wess/wess_bg_papers.shtml (accessed 11 February 2011).

Amsden, A. (2001) *The Rise of the Rest: Challenges to the West from Late-Industrializing Economies*, Oxford: Oxford University Press.

ILO (2009a) *The Financial and Economic Crisis: A Decent Work Response*, Geneva: International Labour Organization.

ILO (2009b) "The Global Jobs Pact: Policy Coherence and International Coordination", Working Party on the Social Dimensions of Globalization, Governing Body, GB306/WP/SDG/1 (November), Geneva: International Labour Organization.

IMF (2007) *World Economic Outlook: Spillovers and Cycles in the Global Economy*, Washington, DC: International Monetary Fund.

IMF (2008) *World Economic Outlook: Housing and the Business Cycle*, Washington, DC: International Monetary Fund.

Keynes, John Maynard (1963) "Am I a Liberal" (1925), in *Essays in Persuasion*, London, New York: W.W. Norton (first published in 1932).

Milberg, W. and D. Schöller (2008) "Globalization, offshoring and economic insecurity in advanced countries", UN-DESA background paper to World Economic and Social Survey 2008.

Ocampo, J.A. and R. Vos (2008) *Uneven Economic Development*, London: Zed Books.

Ocampo, J.A., K.S. Jomo and R. Vos (eds) (2008) *Growth Divergences: Explaining Differences in Economic Performance*, London: Zed Books.

UN-DESA (2009a) "The Global Green New Deal and Sustainable Development", New York: United Nations Department of Economic and Social Affairs, Policy Brief No. 12. Online, available at: www.un.org/en/development/desa/policy/publications/un_desa_briefs.shtml (accessed 22 February 2011).

UN-DESA (2009b) "The Trillion Dollar Plan", New York: United Nations Department of Economic and Social Affairs, Policy Brief No. 13. Online, available at: www.un.org/en/development/desa/policy/publications/un_desa_briefs.shtml (accessed 22 February 2011).

UNEP (2009) "Global Green New Deal", Nairobi, United Nations Environmental Programme, Policy Brief (March). Online, available at: www.unep.org/pdf/A_Global_Green_New_Deal_Policy_Brief.pdf (accessed 22 February 2011).

United Nations (2005) *World Economic and Social Survey 2005: Financing for Development*, New York: United Nations.

United Nations (2006a) *World Economic and Social Survey 2006: Diverging Growth and Development*, New York: United Nations.

United Nations (2006b) *World Economic Situation and Prospects 2006*, New York: United Nations.

United Nations (2007a) *World Economic and Social Survey 2007: Development in an Ageing World*, New York: United Nations.

United Nations (2007b) *World Economic Situation and Prospects 2007*, New York: United Nations.

United Nations (2008a) *World Economic and Social Survey 2008: Overcoming Economic Insecurity*, New York: United Nations.

United Nations (2008b) *World Economic Situation and Prospects 2008*, New York: United Nations.

United Nations (2009a) *World Economic Situation and Prospects 2009*, New York: United Nations.

United Nations (2009b) *World Economic Situation and Prospects as per mid-2009*, New York: United Nations. Online, available at: www.un.org/en/development/desa/policy/wesp/archive.shtml (accessed 22 February 2011).

United Nations (2010) *World Economic and Social Survey, 2010: Retooling Global Development*, New York: United Nations.

Vos, R., J.A. Ocampo and A.L. Cortez (2008) *Ageing and Development*, London: Zed Books.

World Bank (2008) *Global Economic Prospects 2008*, Washington, DC: The World Bank.

World Commission on the Social Dimension of Globalization (2004) *A Fair Globalization*, Geneva: International Labour Organization.

3 Global imbalances, financial crisis and globalization

Rudiger von Arnim[1]

3.1 Introduction

The past world-economic decade opened with a strike of lightning, and goes out with thunder that has not yet stopped ringing in our ears. In between, it was characterized by a deepening and acceleration of *Bretton Woods II*, the floating dollar standard that had emerged after the collapse of Bretton Woods. The strike of lightning, of course, is the Asian crisis of 1997/98, and the thunder today only part of the ongoing global financial (and, in consequence, real) disaster. How are these events related?

The failure of US-led Bretton Woods institutions to effectively help emerging markets cope with the fallout of bursting asset price bubbles led them to self-insure. Self-insurance implies accumulation of international reserves and maintenance of a competitive real exchange rate. The export-driven success of this model put developing countries in a position to confidently stand against giving up further policy space in the current WTO trade negotiations, touted as the *Doha Development Round*. Indeed, talk abounded of successful "South–South" globalization and even of decoupling from Northern economies. However, it turns out still to be true that if the US sneezes – admittedly, rather violently, in this case – Europe, Japan, China, and all the rest of the emerging market and developing countries are subjected to a perfect storm of slumping export volumes, falling commodity prices and a crippling dearth of liquidity.

In the next section of this chapter I describe key linkages between global imbalances, the current global financial crisis, and the ongoing process of globalization. This section serves as motivation for a simple global model of imbalances presented in later sections. The model extends the heuristic analysis here, and suggests which policies could speed up global recovery.

3.2 The political economy of the past decade

3.2.1 The export-driven model in the South and the demise of the Bretton Woods institutions

Since the bursting of the bubbles in Asia, East Asian countries have refocused on what got them where they are. Exports of increasingly sophisticated and competitive high value added products hold the largest growth potential by foster-ing economy-wide productivity growth. Stabilization of the rate of exchange at a reasonably competitive level has been an important component of policy for many countries in the area. The "new mercantilist" development strategy centers on the manipulation of the exchange rate to (1) provide broad support for export-oriented activities with increasing returns to scale, and to (2) bolster a national insurance fund against balance of payments crises, capital flight, and exchange volatility. It is often to the detriment of "thy neighbor," and appears to have been perfected by China, whose dollar reserve accumulation has become a matter of national security concern in the US. The entrance of China into global markets, her tremendous success and sheer size have indeed sent ripples all throughout the world.

The triple whammy of reserve accumulation, commodity price rises, and increased South–South lending enabled the global South to forego budgetary support from the Bretton Woods institutions. Most importantly, the cord was cut on IMF and World Bank loans burdened with conditionalities. Indeed, the IMF appears to have been rocked by a series of events that severely undermine its legitimacy and effectiveness. Compared to the debt and balance of payments crises-ridden 1980s and 1990s, lending has virtually ceased. Remaining borrow-ers are African countries, Colombia and Turkey, whose Stand-by agreement expired summer 2008. The resulting lack of revenue from lending operations forced the managing director to offer buy-outs to employees, to announce country office closures, and prepare to sell Gold holdings. Moreover, internal evaluations find remaining lending still tied to "fundamentalist" conditionalities, neither supported by economic theory and evidence, nor part of the IMF's mandate. The IMF (2008b: 1), in reference to (IMF 2008a), notes that

> during the evaluation period, 1995–2004, conditions became more focused on areas within the Fund's core mandate but one third [of structural conditionalities] still remained in areas where the Fund had little or no expertise. Also, conditions remained too numerous and many were not tied to key program goals.

The practice continues unabated in the current crisis. The World Bank's Michael Pomerleano (2009) wrote at VoxEU.org that:

> [s]ince the crisis began, recipient countries have turned a cold shoulder toward the IMF. The fund's $100 billion lending program announced in October 2008 hasn't attracted a single borrower among the countries tar-geted: Mexico, Peru, Chile, Brazil, Singapore, South Korea, Taiwan, and perhaps Poland. Even when the IMF approached Mexico, a country whose finance minister, Agustín Carstens, is a former IMF deputy managing direc-tor, to break the logjam in its lending program, the offer was rejected.

Similarly, recent IMF voting reform, aimed at providing a rejuvenating jolt of legitimacy, utterly failed to distribute power more evenly. Political horse-trading at the IMF's conception determined initial voting power, but strongly favored the US and its allies, and has since been, in its essential bias, fairly untouched. The increase in basic vote shares was only marginal, and the total increase in quotas insufficient. Most importantly, however, the formulas applied would even have decreased developing countries' aggregate number of votes; only introduction of arbitrary and politically driven adjustments to the formula adjustments made a compromise possible.

Across the street, the World Bank's research has been found to lack even minimum quality, and has been too quick with and "pushing too hard" their own, ideologically driven policy recommendations. The evaluation, chaired by Angus Deaton and made available by Banerjee *et al.* (2006), comes to quite damning conclusions, i.e., that on the one hand much of Bank research remains unpublished due to low quality, but that on the other hand these "groups are almost entirely inward looking," so that "the degree of self-reference rises almost to the level of parody" (ibid.: 73).

Hence, throughout our decade of interest, increasingly confident developing countries were unwilling to play within a multilateral financial and commercial system geared towards interests of and dominated by developed countries. Their response to the radical Washington Consensus-type policies of the 1980s and 1990s is to self-insure and wait for the North to realize that the agenda discussed in the "Green Rooms" of the world has to reflect their concerns. Viewed through this lens, Asian mercantilism of the new millennium is not a renunciation from a previously "free" multilateral economic system, but a well-defined national policy response to the biased multilateral system of IMF conditionalities, unbalanced trade agreements, ignored WTO rulings, and politically driven World Bank-funded projects. Confidence culminated in the belief that Asian economies, and indeed much of the South, pulled largely by Chinese demand, were to decouple from the imminent turn of the cycle in Northern countries.

How are emerging markets doing now? It has quickly become obvious that growth in the South depended not only on booming consumption demand in the North, but furthermore on some kooky credit originating practices on Wall Street, and that, true to style, the global recession might hit hardest in the developing world.

3.2.2 The debt-driven model in the US, and the various ways to look at that

Aggressive monetary easing after the bursting *new economy* stock market bubble, recycling of Asian emerging economies, as well as petroleum exporters' trade surpluses into US financial assets, and a wave of financial innovation fueled a liquidity boom that enabled US households to deepen consumption's role as the dominant component of US effective demand, driving an ever larger trade deficit.

The "Greenspan put" supported asset prices, which in turn fueled further asset sales to, initially, private investors seeking a stake in returns to US productivity gains but increasingly and by now almost exclusively monetary authorities in various corners of Asia and oil rich regions. Securitization of mortgages and loans and thus their liquefaction ensured that the recovery was accompanied by buoyant financial conditions, epitomized by strong appreciation in housing prices. Households had been the motor of US growth for the past two decades, and mortgage equity withdrawals, cheap finance, and predatory lending only reinforced the steep and unsustainable trend in private debt to income ratios. Collapsing real estate prices, subsequent events in financial markets, particularly since the bankruptcy of Lehman brothers in the late summer of 2008, and a string of bad news on real activity led to a December 2008 NBER announcement that the US recession began a year earlier, in December 2007.

How could all of this happen? It is not a simple endeavor to develop coherent causal storylines in a world with highly interdependent real and financial markets. What drives floating exchange rates remains a conundrum, as the US dollar appreciated between the mid-1990s and early 2002, evidently confuting both a Humean exchange rate response to trade as well as uncovered interest parity (UIP).[2] The *reverse* of UIP, however, might fit the data better, and is consistent with carry trading and inflation targeting. The difficulties economists have sorting through data generated by an increasingly complex, globalized world economy are bypassed by imposing causal schemes that help to explain correlations, and serve as a basis for a discussion of the question of how the unraveling might come about. The following paragraphs summarize widely discussed views, and motivate the modeling approach taken up below.

First, international financial arrangements matter. The *Deutsche Bank* view (cf. Dooley *et al.* 2005), often dubbed *Bretton Woods II*, claims that Chinese authorities need to maintain an undervalued exchange rate in order to provide employment opportunities in exporting sectors for vast amounts of rural surplus labor. The government accepts possible losses on reserve holdings following a revaluation in the future in order to reap real gains now: industrialization and development. While the story is plausible, it does by no means imply that US growth of (private) debt can continue forever. More generally, *Bretton Woods II* describes the international financial system that has emerged after the collapse of Bretton Woods (one) in the 1970s. The system relies on US dollars as the unit of account. The provision of US dollar denominated "riskless" assets as international reserves requires the center country to run a balance of payments deficit. Crucially, *Bretton Woods II* is as much subject to Triffin's dilemma as the original version; meaning international liquidity needs breed a dollar devaluation, but a dollar devaluation limits international liquidity provision.

US interest rate shocks and systemic financial events – i.e., the Volcker shock, contagion throughout the Asian financial crisis, and the current credit crisis – often have drastic consequences for emerging markets. Calvo and Talvi (2006) suggest that a shock to global imbalances would lead to a soft landing in the US and a hard landing in the global South due to a "flight to quality" for global capital. US privilege appears not to go that far, but there is no doubt that the recession would already be much more severe had the US not enjoyed continued capital inflows. McKinnon (2005) aptly describes this world as being *trapped by the international dollar standard*. Along similar lines, Eatwell and Taylor (2001, 2002) have argued that divergence between an increasingly globalized economy and only nationally regulated currencies and banking systems threatens global financial stability. Structure and closure of the model applied here aim to reflect this general problematic.

Second, domestic imbalances both in the US and Asia matter. A series of papers have suggested that an important driver of global imbalances are US household saving and investment characteristics; see Barbosa-Filho *et al.* (2008), Papadimitriou *et al.* (2006), Godley and Zezza (2006) and Godley *et al.* (2005). Decompositions of net borrowing flows by sectors – public, corporate, household, and foreign – show that the US's external deficit correlates with excess expenditures of households. If consumption drives growth while real wages and incomes are stagnating, *debt levels will rise*. As it turned out, Asian central banks were happy to do the lending. Thus, this chapter focuses on the US's original problem, if not sin, which lies with *private rather than public* borrowing trends. Similarly, Mussa (2007) writes

> it is ... important to emphasize that US fiscal consolidation is not the be-all and end-all of policies to address the US external deficit. In particular, the "twin deficits theory" that asserts that the US external deficit is primarily the consequence of the US fiscal deficit is largely nonsense.

Certainly a strong opinion, but principally reasonable for two reasons. First, the flows of funds constraint always has to be satisfied. Given investment, an increase in external borrowing correlates either with a decrease in private saving or a decrease in public saving, or a combination thereof. As mentioned before, such correlation does not imply causation, but if blame is to be attributed, it is net borrowing of households that increased dramatically in the mid to late-1990s – at a time when the government managed a surplus. To be sure, Bush's tax cuts did not help. As Frankel (2006) reminds us, the reason for their regressivity was to increase saving among the wealthy, increasing loanable funds and subsequently physical investment. However, with firms still earning the returns to computerization, all those loanable funds were not channeled into accumulation, Ramsey-style, but consumption, Minsky-style. Second, the link between government and external deficits supposedly works through the interest channel. The argument, if ever valid, misses the peculiarities of the international environment during the build-up of global imbalances. Asian dollar reserve accumulation and recycling of oil exporter's revenues pushed up bond and equity prices, and depressed interest rates. The inverted yield curve showed the difficulties the Fed had in increasing the relevant rates at the medium to long end of the curve. While the model applied here does not include interest rates, specifying savings and investment functions as well as government policy in all three regions provides some insights.

Lastly, Ben Bernanke (2005) has contended that imbalances are largely driven by global excess saving, saying

> that over the past decade a combination of diverse forces has created a significant increase in the global supply of saving – a global saving glut – which helps to explain both the increase in the US current account deficit and the relatively low level of long-term real interest rates in the world today.

There is no disagreement on the data – where to situate causality is the question. Obviously, priors matter. Principally, the savings-glut hypothesis fits well into modern open-economy macroeconomics, where payments imbalances are an optimal result of given intertemporal preferences. Individuals in Asia want to save more, individuals in the US want to consume more, and the whole exchange is the best possible, because otherwise nobody would do it. Deep financial markets are the efficient means to achieve such consumption smoothing. The perspective adopted here is that agents are not rational. Rather, Tom's, Dick's, and Harry's expectations have always included the next credit card, and that even a major stock market crash will not affect him (or her) negatively. More specifically, governments play an important role in shaping international economic transactions.

3.2.3 Bretton Woods II, *and its central role in the current crisis*

Indeed, the very particular international (and inter-governmental) relations of *Bretton Woods II* should be recognized as the heart of the matter. Both the export-driven model in the South and the debt-driven model in the US are rooted in an international financial system that (1) rests on US dollar hegemony and (2) is supported by the US dominated multilateral Bretton Woods institutions. In fact, outside the (shrinking) camp of market fundamentalists, who tend to believe that history has ended and a "free market" is the flatline that remains, exists a fairly broad consensus about the nature of the problem: the US has to run payments deficits in order to provide liquidity to the world, and those deficits undermine the credibility a liquidity-providing currency requires. The resulting net capital flows in and out of developing countries tend to be strongly pro-cyclical, as the issuer of the key currency recycles funds from surplus countries to deficit countries. Vasudevan (2008: 1055) aptly summarizes this mechanism, writing:

> [t]he stability of the international monetary system hinges on a dominant country acting as an international lender of last resort, injecting liquidity by recycling surpluses to countries facing balance of payments problems. The efficacy of this mechanism does not depend on the dominant country retaining a "creditor" status. Rather it has depended historically, on the dominant country's ability to continue to borrow, in the face of growing external deficits without undermining the status of its currency as international money. A pivotal role is played by the institutional mechanisms that allow

the dominant country to borrow from surplus countries on one hand and lead to increasing fragility in peripheral debtor countries on the other.

The key difference of this crisis is – beside its magnitude – that financial markets have recycled some of the surplus funds to a "developing economy that exists within the United States' own borders" (Reinhart and Rogoff 2008: 11). Hence, as the build-up to the crisis is rooted in international relations, so is recovery. Beyond recovery, true reform of the international payments system, including reform of Bretton Woods institutions, is necessary to avoid recurring crises either in core or periphery.

Now, global imbalances should be readjusted through international policy coordination. Model and simulation discussed in the following sections hint at a way forward. In anticipation of results, savings and investment balances in US and Asia have to shift for global rebalancing, but the increase in savings in the US should be undertaken by the *private* sector, while a decrease in *public* savings – deficit spending – should be launched to cushion possibly large output losses. (Analog, though for different reasons, the increase in absorption in Asia should come from the public sector.) There is some agreement on the first point; see, for example, Salvatore (2007) and Rogoff (2007). Agreement on fiscal policy has been much more elusive, but a global recession might bring many around. Importantly, the real transfer necessary for adjustment can be made without large exchange rate changes. McKinnon (2007) made this point, and the analysis here principally confirms it, even if his focus is on an increase in public saving. Accounting for unemployment and a deepening recession force an increase in private saving, and make public dissaving necessary. Conversely, real appreciation in Asia by itself is unlikely to *trigger* significant adjustment, and the many calls for such action from Treasury and Think Tanks (e.g., Lardy 2007) might best be left unheeded. Still, the model applied here shows that *some* real and broad appreciation of Asian currencies would support effecting the transfer.

3.3 A model of global imbalances

The structure of the model is simple, so that the exposition here is kept brief, and confined to a one-sector, one-country open economy without a government or domestic intermediates.

Table 3.1 lays out a social accounting matrix (SAM) with the relevant accounting. Along the first column costs of domestic firms are decomposed into factor costs and imports, the former the total of wage bill wL and profits rK and the latter imports fX valued at foreign prices in domestic currency, eP_f. The import–output coefficient, f, is a function of the real exchange rate. Following standard bookkeeping practice, the first column total PX is equal to the first row total, which aggregates production across buying agents. In the second column, households allot real GDP V valued at the GDP deflator Q to consumption PC and private saving S. Nominal GDP QV is equal to the sum of row 2, GDP at factor cost. Investment PI figures in the material balance in row 1 and balances

Table 3.1 Symbolic, simplified SAM for a one-country, one-sector economy without government and domestic intermediates

	Costs	Households	Investment	Exports	Sum
Production		PC	PI	PE	PX
Factor income	$wL+rK$				QV
Flow of funds		S	−PI	S_f	0
Foreign income	$eP_f fX$			$eP_f fX$	
Sum	PX	WV	0	PC	

in the flows of funds with total saving, which are the sum of private saving and foreign saving S_F, the negative of the current account $PE-eP_f fX$. Evidently, macroeconomic equilibrium is attained when saving equals investment. Costs are the sum of factor and import bill,[3] and assuming that in the short run real value added is proportional to real output, $V=(1-f)X$, the cost decomposition gives P as a weighted average of factor and import costs,[4]

$$P=(1-f)Q+fe. \tag{3.1}$$

The import coefficient f itself is a function of the real exchange rate,

$$f = f_c \left(\frac{e}{P}\right)^{-\sigma}, \tag{3.2}$$

where f_c is the base year ratio of imports to sectoral output, and σ the import price elasticity. Consumption is equal to expenditures after saving, so that real consumption becomes a function of relative prices and output,

$$C = \frac{(1-f)(1-s)Q}{(1-f)Q+fe} X, \tag{3.3}$$

which is modeled as a standard Linear Expenditure System (LES) in the multi-sector version. Saving is a function of distribution. $\psi=wL/QV$ is the wage share, and the profit share $\pi=1-\psi$. The macroeconomic savings propensity follows from the accounting identity $s=s_w\psi+s_\pi\pi$ as

$$s = s_\pi - (s_\pi - s_w)\psi. \tag{3.4}$$

Investment increases with capacity utilization and the current rate of profit. Using the accounting definition for the profit share $r=\pi u=\pi(V/K)$, the investment function can be written as

$$I = i_0 + (i_1(1-\psi)+i_2)\frac{V}{K} \tag{3.5}$$

and output follows from aggregate demand as

$$X = C + I + E = F[Q,e](I+E),$$ (3.6)

where

$$F[Q,e] = \frac{f_e + (1-f)Q}{f_e + (1-f)sQ} > 1$$

is the multiplier, decreasing in s and f, the "propensities to leak," and furthermore in e, but increasing in Q.

The price of value added Q is modeled as a CES-unit cost function for value added. Dual to it is a CES-production function that smoothly combines labor and capital with the elasticity of substitution θ. The derivative of the cost function with respect to factor prices gives conditional factor demand functions,

$$Q = (\alpha w^{1-\theta} + \beta r^{1-\theta})^{\frac{1}{1-\theta}},$$ (3.7)

$$\frac{L}{V} = \alpha \left(\frac{w^*}{Q}\right)^{-\theta},$$ (3.8)

and analog for capital, which implies a trade-off between employment and real wages.[5] Expanding equation (3.8) by w/Q gives the wage share as $\psi = \alpha(w/Q)^{1-\theta}$. The propensity to spend out of wage income is higher than that out of capital income, meaning total saving responds negatively to wage increases,

$$\frac{\Delta s[w,r]}{\Delta w} < 0$$

as long as $\theta < 1$.

3.3.1 Macroeconomic adjustment: non-clearing goods and labor markets

Let us now discuss model closure. Goods markets do not clear.[6] With demand-driven macro adjustment, investment is not driven by savings, but follows from an investment function (equation (3.5) above) with a standard accelerator and a Neo-Kaleckian response to redistribution. *Ceteris paribus*, an increase (decrease) in the profit share (wage share) provides incentives for investment; as long as investment responds more strongly to increases in profits than saving, effective demand is characterized as profit-led; see the contributions in Setterfield (2002). Barbosa-Filho and Taylor (2007) estimate such a model and find that the US is indeed profit led. In a model without asset markets or at least an interest rate, this Kaleckian formulation connects investment to profitability. Prices of goods are driven by costs, see equation (3.1). The factor cost index is a geometric average of wage and profit rate, and output prices a simple average of factor costs and import prices.

Second, labor markets do not clear. Employment varies with activity, but inversely with the real wage. Analog, capital is subject to diminishing returns. In contrast to labor markets, however, it is the factor return – profit rate *r* from *K*'s Shephard's Lemma – that varies with activity. The money wage is set institutionally, leaving *Q* pro-cyclical. Resulting counter-cyclical real wages allow for job growth in an expansion. Furthermore, with two sectors the degree of factor mobility becomes relevant. Capital is assumed perfectly immobile in the short run, but labor perfectly mobile. (A real depreciation shifts production towards tradables and consumption towards non-tradables. Hence, the more flexible labor markets, the smoother is transition, and the smaller is the real depreciation necessary for adjustment.) The baseline *domestic* causal configuration can be summarized as

$$r_{ci} = r[X_{ci}; \bar{K}_{ci}] \tag{3.9}$$

and

$$L_{ci} = L_{ci}[X_{ci}; \bar{w}_c] \tag{3.10}$$

where *c* = *US, EU, AS* is the index of countries and *i* = *T, NT* the index of sectors. A bar defines a variable as exogenous.

Internationally, balance of payments adjustment requires reduction *and* shift of expenditures. Real depreciation increases traded goods prices ($\Delta P_T > \Delta P_{NT}$), so that consumption shifts toward non-traded goods, whereas production shifts toward traded goods. However, international goods arbitrage does not lead to price equalization across borders, because domestic output prices are anchored by domestic factor costs. Given base year data determines the degree to which import price changes can pass through to output prices. Partial pass-through, in turn, is the driving force behind inflation differentials across countries, and thus determines real exchange rate changes.

The complete model features intermediates and a government. The latter is conceived to borrow just as much as necessary in order to finance its expenditures, a quite realistic assumption at least in the short run all too often forgotten by CGE-modelers.

3.3.2 *International adjustment: standard BOP approaches and less standard* Bretton Woods II

Let's consider a few more details on the international closure applied between the three regions. First, a note about data, accounting, and calibration appears in order. The SAM is fed by GTAP v6.0 database with a base year of 2000. The base year aggregation presents composite regions with the USA, UK, Spain, and Portugal as the dominant deficit countries, Japan, China and other emerging Asian economies with competitive exchange rates the most important surplus countries, and the EU and remaining developing countries the more passive middle. Oil exporters are separately accounted for, but without their small domestic economies.[7] The base year data is calibrated to fit the headline figures of the first quarter of 2006, representing the last quarter of positive growth in US residential investment, and as such arguably the peak of the (real-side) expansion. The figures are necessarily ballpark, but should give a fair representation of the relative sizes of the involved domestic production and international trade flows. See Table 3.2 for the SAMs, and von Arnim (2007) for more detail on data and calibration. Low-income countries are not taken account of separately. Necessarily, the discussion of the impact of the crisis on the poorest countries cannot be based directly on model results. However, the Asian region includes many emerging markets, and some conclusions can be drawn from their performance.

The accounting broadly follows Godley's scheme to arrange SAMs in a multi-country model side by side and "flip" cross-border transactions across SAMs, currency-converted and summing to zero. See Godley and Lavoie (2007) and Taylor (2004) for examples. Note the accounting of payments flows financing trade deficits and the oil-exporting row. First, the US as the issuer of the single reserve asset is the epicenter of excess saving. Whatever happens globally, it happens through the accounts of Wall Street and Treasury bankers. The *exorbitant privilege* to borrow in own currency belongs to the single hegemon, despite recent and still small shifts in reserve allocation toward the euro. The oil region appears essentially as a balance of payments row, the international head of an economy without a rump. As petroleum transactions are commonly conducted in US dollars, the oil-row's trade flows are quoted in dollars.

In a model with one or two countries with one bilateral nominal exchange rate and one current account, either the former or the latter can be endogenized. Following the *income (or absorption) approach to the balance of payments*, the nominal exchange rate can be taken as exogenous, leaving trade to follow incomes and relative prices. Suppose the exchange rate is exogenous and trade flows respond freely to relative price changes. The current account then is a function of the real exchange rate,

$$CA = PE\left[\frac{e}{P}\right] - ef\left[\frac{e}{P}\right]X, \tag{3.11}$$

and the question typically asked is whether a depreciation leads to an improvement in the balance of payments. Marshall–Lerner conditions can be derived, and effects of a devaluation on output and income distribution can be analyzed. Alternatively, along the lines of the *elasticities approach to the balance of payments*, trade is assumed balanced or fixed, or is forced to balance, providing an estimate of exchange rate changes necessary to bring that about. The nominal exchange rate e then becomes the variable that equilibrates demand-driven trade flows against a set trade balance,

$$e = e[fX, PE, \overline{CA}] \tag{3.12}$$

where a typical question is by how much e would have to change in order to achieve $\overline{CA} = 0$.

Table 3.2 Three region SAMs

	US						
	Cost	*Priv.*	*Gov.*	*Exp.*	*Inv.*	*For.*	*Sum*
Prod.	11,932	10,383	2,765	2,006	3,298		30,384
Labor	9,492						9,492
Capital	6,113						6,113
Gov.		2,075					2,075
S-I		3,148	−690		−3,298	840	0
Capital flows						−200	
						−350	
OIL	165			−98		−290	
Trade flows	1,584						
	759						
	339			−339			
				−1,241			
Sum	30,384	15,606	2,075	0	0	0	

Table 3.2 continued

	EU						
	Cost	*Priv.*	*Gov.*	*Exp.*	*Inv.*	*Inv.*	*Sum*
Prod.	9,750	6,373	2,142	4,459	2,979		25,704
Labor	6,054						6,054
Capital	5,640						5,640
Gov.		1,930					1,930
S-I		3,391	−212				0
Capital flows					−2,979	−200	
						−200	
OIL	255			−195			
Trade flows				−1,584			
	1,241			−2,199			
	2,199						
	565			−481			
Sum	25,704	11,694	1,930	0	0		

Adding a third region grants a second degree of freedom. Without asset markets in the model, some assumptions have to be made about capital accounts in order to balance international payments. Table 3.3 lays out three asset markets, read along the rows and all reported in US dollars. Each region's two principle agents, the private and public sector, add along their respective

Table 3.2 continued

Asia

Cost	Priv.	Gov.	Exp.	Inv.	For.	Sum
8,189	4,238	1,135	2,167	2,717		18,445
4,801						4,801
3,639						3,639
	1,006					1,006
	3,196	−128		−2,717	−350	0
						0
					350	0
255			−91			0
						0
			−759			0
						0
						0
					0	
			−565			0
751			−751			0
329						0
481						0
18,445	8,440	1,006	0	0	0	0

Notes
Prod. = production; Gov. = government; S-I = savings-investment; Priv. = private; Exp. = exports; Inv. = investment; For. = foreign.

Table 3.3 Balance of payments-accounting

	Priv.	Gov.	Priv.	Gov.	Priv.	Gov.	Sum
US	$\Delta R_{P1}^{\$}$	$\Delta R^{\$}$	$\Delta R_{P2}^{\$}$	0	0	$\Delta R_{G3}^{\$}$	0
Europe	$e_{12}\Delta R_{P1}^{E}$		$e_{12}\Delta R_{P2}^{E}$	$e_{12}\Delta R^{E}$			0
Asia					$e_{13}\Delta R_{P3}^{¥}$	$e_{13}\Delta R^{¥}$	0
Sum	CA_1		$e_{12}CA_2$		$e_{13}CA_3$		

columns to net lending balances, which in turn sum to current accounts. Each government issues a reserve asset, $\Delta R^{¥}$ in Asia,[8] which is held exclusively domestically, $\Delta R_{P3}^{¥}$. Europe, on the other hand, issues an asset, ΔR^{E} that is bought by private agents domestically and abroad in the US. US treasuries are demanded by the same private agents in the West and by government in Asia, $\Delta R_{P1}^{\$} + \Delta R_{P2}^{\$} + \Delta R_{G3}^{\$}$. Two assumptions are implicit. First, EU governments do not pursue active reserve policies, and due to capital controls private agents in Asia are limited to invest in domestic debt instruments. Asia's balance of payments follows directly,

$$e_{13}CA_3 = \Delta R_{G3}^{\$} \tag{3.13}$$

substituting row 2 in the European column sum gives

$$e_{12}CA_2 = \Delta R_{P2}^\$ - e_{12}\Delta R_{P1} \qquad (3.14)$$

and the US's balance of payments follows as

$$CA_1 = -(e_{12}CA_2 + e_{13}CA_3) \qquad (3.15)$$

Equations (3.13) and (3.14) grant two degrees of freedom, and (3.15) constrains accounts to add up. *Six* variables are candidates for endogeneity – three bilateral exchange rates and three trade balances – for two degrees of freedom. Let's look at the three relationships from an *income approach*. All exchange rates are policy variables, and all three current accounts are determined by trade flows following income and relative prices. (Strictly speaking, two *CA*s are endogenous, and the third closes accounts.) Alternatively, looked at from an *elasticities approach*, two current accounts can be set exogenously. Two endogenous bilateral rates imply the third; and the "closing" current account ensures that things add up. Both approaches are used for simulations below, and complement analysis with what I call the *Bretton Woods II* closure.

The *Bretton Woods II* closure reflects realities of recent international financial arrangements. Put simply, neither Europe nor the US are claiming a degree of freedom between the three major blocs, leaving Asia to use both. Thus, Asia's current account surplus CA_3 is driven by reserve accumulation, $\Delta R_{G3}^\$$. One could say that *finance rules trade*, which in this context means that the fixed capital account binds aggregate net exports. Second, Europe's current account surplus determines the flows of finance between the EU and the US, in the sense that *trade rules finance*. Third, the US's current account deficit CA_1 follows residually as the borrower of last resort. As mentioned above, the modeler imposes causal storylines in order to make sense of a complex world. Given the nominal peg of China and crawling pegs of other Asian currencies vis-à-vis the US dollar it seems natural to fix e_{13}. Neither Europe nor the US conducts exchange or capital market policies, leaving the second degree of freedom up for grabs.

Essentially, as will be seen in the discussion of simulations below, controlling net exports through reserve accumulation and undervaluation of the exchange rate limits the variation of real value added in Asia, and transfers the burden of international adjustment in absorption to Europe.

3.4 Simulation results

3.4.1 US consumption crunch and Asian deficit spending

The Case–Shiller house price index, published by Standard & Poor's, has seen phenomenal increases from a trough in the mid-1990s. The ratio of Case–Shiller house prices to an index of housing costs suggests a return to fundamentals could imply house price falls in excess of 30 percent.[9] Indeed, by September 2008 the index had fallen more than 17 percent over a year, and has dropped 23 percent from its peak in May of 2006. How does this wealth effect impact private consumption demand? Menegatti and Roubini (2007) discuss evidence on passthrough of changes in wealth to consumption, and find the wealth effect to range between 3 percent and 10 percent. Fed Governor Mishkin (2007) argues that evidence on *housing* wealth effects particularly for the US is inconclusive, but suggests that they could be larger than equity wealth effects – simply because a lot more people own houses than stocks, and their consumption behavior might vary more strongly with income and wealth changes.

Assuming the value of outstanding (household) real estate falls by 30 percent, roughly US$6.3 trillion of wealth will be lost; based on 2007:Q2 Federal Reserve balance sheets. Stipulating that households pass 5 percent thereof through to consumption, demand decreases by US$315 billion, which represents roughly a 5 percent adverse consumption shock;[10] see Table 3.4 for results. With the rise in the savings propensity, value added in the US falls. Due to the *Bretton Woods II* closure, the negative impact of the demand shock on Asia is contained. Indeed, all hinges on Asian external lending. Continued Asian reserve accumulation in combination with slowing US demand requires Europe to act as the "consumer of last resort." The Asian real exchange rate is barely affected, given the peg to the dollar, whereas Europe's real exchange rate appreciates noticeably, turning a current account surplus of 1.7 percent relative to GDP to a (very small) deficit. Importantly, EU GDP contracts more sharply than US GDP. How to interpret this simulation? First, Europe is less willing than the US to take on the burden of consuming for the world. Second, it is less suited to do so, because it does not (yet) offer a reserve asset for the surplus region to hold. Third, a transfer of the debt bubble from US to EU financial markets is very unlikely in current circumstances. Hence, this simulation does not point toward adjustment, but suggests that continued Asian export targeting policies are likely to increase structural imbalances in the world economy.

If Asia were to loosen her grip on external demand, and instead increase domestic demand, some rebalancing can be achieved. Simulation (2) shows results from a combination of shocks; (a) consumer recession in the US and (b) an increase in government spending in Asia. International closure here follows the traditional income approach to the balance of payments, with three bilateral exchange rates as policy variables and three endogenous current accounts.

(Note that an increase in US savings due to recession and decrease in Asian savings due to government deficit spending represent a transfer of real resources.) The domestic demand increase in Asia is slightly inflationary. In combination with a fixed exchange rate inflation leads to some real appreciation, particularly because government spends only in the non-traded sector. Despite the loss in export revenue – CA_3 decreases by 40 percent – GDP expands. The US and the EU contract; the US quite sharply. Fiscal expansion in these two regions should provide a buffer against the negative impact of rebalancing, and simulations (5) and (6) in Table 3.4 return to the issue. Let's first have a look at the potential for rebalancing from exchange rate appreciation in Asia.

3.4.2 Exchange rate revaluation in Asia

Chinese and other Asian monetary authorities or state-controlled institutions are actively accumulating US debt instruments, many at truly astonishing rates. Mid 2008, Chinese dollar reserves stood well above US$1 trillion, and could be as high as US$1.5 trillion. The many interventions target exchange rates. The Chinese yuan, for example, is allowed to fluctuate within a narrow band on a daily basis. That trading band has been widened, first to 0.3 percent and more recently to a whopping 0.5 percent. The resulting nominal appreciation of the Chinese yuan from the hard peg of 8.28 CNY per US dollar, at which the currency was held between 1995:Q2 and 2005:Q2, to 6.84 CNY per US dollar in 2008:Q3 appears as a step toward rebalancing. In real effective terms, however, the Chinese currency is virtually unchanged relative to its low 2002:Q1, and has only since early 2005 appreciated by about 5 percent annually. How would further guided appreciation affect global imbalances?

Simulation (3) shows results of under the *income approach*. Here, e_{12} is set to follow from the ratio of the other two bilateral rates. Both are assumed to depreciate by 10 percent against Asian currencies. Thus, Asia does loosen her policy grip, and the external surplus decreases to 3.6 percent of GDP, versus 4.2 percent initially. However, the loss of export markets triggers as well a contraction, making this an unattractive policy option in Asia. Moreover, overall external imbalances do not improve significantly. The next simulation (4) is based on the *elasticities approach*, where I set the level of two current accounts exogenously, and two bilateral rates adjust to attain these. By how much would e_{13} and e_{23} have to depreciate in order to accommodate a 50 percent reduction in the level of CA_3 and CA_1? Thus, the third exchange rate (e_{12}) and third current account (CA_2) follow residually. Results in Table 3.4 indicate that adjustment induced by large relative price changes is very volatile. Adjustment does not come with changes in domestic savings and investment balances – as in simulation (2) – but from income changes following very large trade flow changes. The necessary increase in US savings stems from a substantial gain in real income, and the necessary decrease in surplus countries' savings stems from a substantial contraction. It seems unlikely that this scenario is feasible. Yes, the US economy is famously flexible, but there does not seem to be a burning desire on the part of Germans, Koreans and Japanese to drive Suburban XL Hybrids. Indeed, both size of income changes and structural reality of world markets suggest that such a turnaround would require many, many years. (It would as well require some other country to provide liquidity to the world.)

Comparing these simulations clarifies a couple of things. Shifts in domestic S and I place the burden of adjustment on the US – the transferor – whereas shifts in relative prices place the burden on Asia – the transferee. The former appears much more likely, or even feasible, because "reasonable" relative price changes (and the concomitant income changes) are insufficient to trigger the transfer necessary for rebalancing. With this in mind, the crucial question is what governments can do, and how that could aid global rebalancing and limit GDP losses.

Table 3.4 Simulation results

	Sim #	Closure	Region	CA/GDP (%)	S[G]/GDP (%)	Real GDP (%)	eP*/P (%)	Real wages (%)	Inflation (P) (%)
US consumer recession	(1)	BWII	US	-4.2	-5.4	-5.0	5.6	3.6	-2.0
			EU	0.0	-2.9	-6.3	-4.5	6.8	-8.6
			AS	4.1	-1.5	0.4	-0.8	-0.3	0.8
US consumer recession and Asian deficit spending	(2)	Income	US	-4.6	-5.7	-6.8	2.0	5.1	-4.3
			EU	1.1	-2.1	-1.5	0.0	1.6	-1.6
			AS	2.4	-4.0	3.5	-1.5	-2.6	1.9
Revaluation of CNY against US and EU	(3)	Income	US	-5.3	-4.3	0.7	1.1	-0.5	0.8
			EU	1.9	-1.7	0.8	0.5	-0.8	1.0
			AS	3.6	-1.8	-2.1	-1.6	1.9	-2.7
Halving current accounts in US and Asia	(4)	Elasticities	US	-1.9	-1.5	21.2	31.6	-13.4	23.2
			EU	-0.3	-3.4	-11.0	-14.0	12.4	-17.7
			AS	2.5	-2.6	-8.8	-17.2	8.3	-13.0
Recession, appreciation, and fiscal expansion, 1	(5)	BWII	US	-3.9	-6.7	4.2	8.9	-3.0	5.3
			EU	0.3	-3.8	-3.6	-6.0	3.7	-6.6
			AS	3.2	-5.0	9.0	-4.1	-6.9	6.7
Recession, appreciation, and fiscal expansion, 2	(6)	Income	US	-1.6	-7.4	0.3	2.6	-0.2	0.9
			EU	1.7	-2.8	2.7	0.4	-2.7	2.9
			AS	2.2	-5.6	5.5	-3.4	-4.1	2.4

3.4.3 Recession, Asian appreciation and fiscal expansion

The endogenous investment decrease in simulation (1) due to the accelerator is a bit more than 2 percent, which is "not enough." Over the post-World War II period in the US, investment contracted on average 6 percent from (own) peak to trough. Third quarter 2008 data suggest that large parts of Europe are already in recession, and that Asia is as well contracting. Hence, in the following two simulations I assume a global adverse shock of 5 percent to (autonomous) investment in combination with the US consumer recession. Furthermore, let's take the guided appreciation of the Asian currency vis-à-vis the US dollar as given, and consider whether (global) fiscal expansion can put a floor under GDP losses. The public expenditure packages on the table at the time of this writing are about US\$500 billion in the US, US\$250 billion in the EU, and US\$500 billion in China, representing roughly 3 percent, 1.5 percent, and about 5 percent of GDP. In the following two simulations, I assume that the model's three Gs are increased by these percentages relative to GDP.

Thus, the set of shocks in simulation (5) is a 5 percent consumption decrease in the US, a global shock to autonomous investment of 5 percent, nominal appreciation of Asian currency against US dollar of 10 percent and global fiscal expansion as outlined. Additionally, it is assumed that Asia "allows" a reduction of the external surplus, implemented by a 10 percent decrease in CA_3. Simulation results show that despite a relatively large domestic stimulus in Asia, continued export targeting, even though at a reduced rate, transfers the burden of adjustment to Europe. Recall that in the *Bretton Woods II* closure US/EU rate e_{12} adjusts endogenously to satisfy the international accounting constraint, so that the "passive middle" experiences real exchange appreciation. External demand contracts and GDP declines with it. A stimulus of 1.5 percent of European GDP is not enough to balance the drop in export demand, given the unfavorable Asian exchange policy. Nevertheless, a switch in demand from traded to non-traded goods and from external to domestic sources leads to some global rebalancing (see CA/GDP ratios).

The set of shocks in simulation (6) is the same as in (5), except for Asia's current account CA_3. Here I apply the *income approach*. The key difference is that Asia does not any longer target exports – and it shows. CA_3/GDP_3 falls from 4.2 percent to 2.2 percent, all the while the strong domestic stimulus buffers the region from a serious GDP contraction. The US's external imbalance improves as well, as deficit relative to GDP decreases from 5.4 percent to 4.6 percent. The nominal exchange rate shock in simulation (6) to e_{13} of 10 percent implies a 10 percent rise of e_{23}, because the EU/Asia rate follows residually. The US/EU rate does not change; therefore EU's CA_2 – exports largely to the US – is unaffected.

An increase in US private savings is unavoidable in order to improve hard hit balance sheets, *and* is necessary for rebalancing. Public deficit spending can cushion the negative impact on GDP. Higher government expenditures in the non-traded sector lead to some real appreciation, which is why further nominal appreciation in Asia is necessary for the transfer to pan out. In summary, the unfortunate reality of the financial crisis and recession present an opportunity for global rebalancing that should not be passed on.

3.5 Summing up

What can the three main regions do to unwind imbalances, and to speed up recovery? First, China must rebalance demand toward domestic sources. Proposed government expenditure programs hint in the right direction, and simulation results indicate that such a program would help to support growth even in the face of exchange appreciation. Some further exchange rate realignment should help to reduce global imbalances, but does not present a solution by itself. Crucially, exchange appreciation should occur broadly and not only against the US dollar. Second, Europe's careful approach to fiscal expansion reflects the political straightjacket of the Maastricht Treaty. Simulations show that a continuation of *Bretton Woods II* spells doom for German exports, making reflationary policies all the more important. However, the increasingly tense transatlantic dialogue does not bode well for coordinated policy responses. Third, the US should institute public expenditure increases sufficient to limit GDP losses. The need for infrastructure investment presents an opportunity to weather collapse in the construction sector, and to improve the situation in the labor market. Simulations show that government *dissaving* is essential to avoid a protracted recession, given the expected – and indeed necessary – change in household savings behavior. Crucially, these national and regional responses have to be carefully coordinated. It is not clear where lack of cooperation could lead, but it is unlikely to be a smooth reduction of external imbalances in the near future.

What does the current situation imply for developing countries? Certainly, some developing countries have more resilient economies today than ten, twenty, or thirty years ago. Some developing economies have diversified their production structure away from primary export dependence. Some of those developing countries are finding their voice in multilateral committees, and are speaking with much greater, and greatly deserved confidence about their economic performance and strategies. However, many developing countries have not generated sufficient domestic demand to withstand external demand contractions. Many developing countries still boom and bust with commodity price cycles, and are hard hit by sharp drops in remittances, and all the most recent indicators confirm this pattern of dependency. The pattern is perpetuated by the current international financial architecture, where the key currency country exports macroeconomic volatility through pro-cyclical capital flows. Hence, the 800 lb gorilla in the room wants to know – from rich and poor countries, from North, South, and East and West, for that matter – what will replace *Bretton Woods II*, when it ends? It certainly cannot continue indefinitely.

Notes

1 Assistant Professor of Economics at the University of Utah. I am particularly grateful to Lance Taylor, Duncan K. Foley, and Alex Izurieta for comments. The standard disclaimer applies.
2 Following UIP, we would have expected that lower interest rates lead to a depreciated exchange rate.
3 Domestic production X is a composite of home value added V and imports and is therefore higher than in national income accounts. The assumption is that all imports pass through domestic firms.
4 The foreign output price is here normalized to unity, $P_f = 1$.
5 This trade-off is contradicted by the data. A Phillips-curve or some other construct that produces a positive co-movement between real wages and activity fits data better. Nevertheless, deriving conditional demand functions from CES aggregations is probably the single most important exercise in standard CGE models, and even though output and import demands do not rest on optimizing "first principles" it grants a degree of comparability to the relevant models. However, in simulations below, the focus *cannot* be on real wages, productivity, and distribution, but only on GDP, and external and public balances.
6 See Taylor and Lysy (1979) for the original discussion on macro-closures; as well as Taylor (2004: chapter 5).
7 The US profile – industrialized country with a sizeable current account deficit – is augmented by UK, Portugal, Spain, Austria, Luxembourg, and Australia. The characteristics of the Asia region are (1) a current account surplus, (2) an undervalued exchange rate either due to a fixed or managed peg or other reasons, and (3), a massive reserve build-up. The EU closes the accounts as the *rest of the world*. Oil exporters match three characteristics: (1) large export share of petroleum and related products, (2) a current account surplus, driven by those exports, and (3) an economy heavily reliant on commodity exports with relatively little domestically created value added. The list comprises twenty-eight countries, most importantly Russia alongside OPEC members.
8 Currency symbols are chosen merely for convenience. The Asian currency reflects a composite, including Chinese yuan, Korean won, and others; and analog for dollar and euro. All entries are in US dollars. The US/EU rate is e_{12}, e_{13} the US/Asia rate; the EU/Asia rate follows directly as the ratio e_{13}/e_{12}.
9 "Owner's equivalent rent" is an index (component of the CPI and calculated by the BLS) of housing costs that includes a survey of owner occupied homes and the prices they think could be captured if the property were rented.
10 The shock is implemented by calibrating savings parameters with a 5 percent lower base year consumption level, essentially increasing the aggregate savings rate. The procedure should sit well with a "traditional" wealth effect, according to which households will save more, if falling asset prices or inflation devalue their wealth. Here, however, households give up to finance consumption directly out of wealth, *and on top of that might change their savings behavior* – leaving these estimates arguably on the optimistic side.

References

Banerjee, A., A. Deaton, N. Lustig, and K. Rogoff (2006) *An Evaluation of World Bank Research, 1998–2005*, Washington, DC: World Bank.
Barbosa-Filho, N.H. and L. Taylor (2007) "Distributive and Demand Cycles in the US-Economy: A Structuralist Goodwin Model," *Metroeconomica*, 57: 389–411.

Barbosa-Filho, N.H., C. Rada, L. Taylor, and L. Zamparelli (2008) "Cycles and Trends in US Net Borrowing Flows," *Journal of Post-Keynesian Economics*, 30: 623–648.

Bernanke, B.S. (2005) "The Global Saving Glut and the US Current Account Deficit." Online, available at: www.federalreserve.gov/boarddocs/speeches/2005/20050414/default.htm (accessed February 25, 2010).

Calvo, G. and E. Talvi (2006) "The Resolution of Global Imbalances: Soft Landing in the North, Sudden Stop in Emerging Markets?" *Journal of Policy Modeling*, 28: 605–613.

Dooley, M., D. Folkerts-Landau, and P. Garber (2005) *International Financial Stability: Asia, Interest Rates, and the Dollar*, London: Deutsche Bank.

Eatwell, J. and L. Taylor (eds.) (2001) *Global Finance at Risk: The Case for International Regulation*, New York: New Press.

Eatwell, J. and L. Taylor (eds) (2002) *International Capital Markets: Systems In Transition*, Oxford: Oxford University Press.

Frankel, J. (2006) "Could the Twin Deficits jeopardize US Hegemony?" *Journal of Policy Modeling*, 28: 653–663.

Godley, W. and M. Lavoie (2007) "A Simple Model of Three Economies with Two Currencies: The Eurozone and the USA," *Cambridge Journal of Economics*, 31: 1–23.

Godley, W., D.B. Papadimitriou, C.H.D. Santos, and G. Zezza (2005) "The United States and Her Creditors: Can the Symbiosis last?" Levy Economics Institute of Bard College Strategic Analysis: September.

Godley, W. and G. Zezza (2006) "Debt and Lending: A Cri de Coeur," Levy Economics Institute of Bard College Policy Note: April.

IMF (2008a) *An IEO Evaluation of Structural Conditionality in IMF-Supported Programs*, Washington, DC: IMF.

IMF (2008b) *Progress Report on the Activities of the Internal Evaluation Office*, Washington, DC: IMF.

Lardy, N.R. (2007) "China: Rebalancing Economic Growth." In C.F. Bergsten, B. Gill, N.R. Lardy, and D.J. Mitchell (eds.) *The China Balance Sheet in 2007 and Beyond*, Washington, DC: Peterson Institute and CSIS.

McKinnon, R.I. (2005) "Trapped by the International Dollar Standard", *Journal of Policy Modeling*, 27: 477–485.

McKinnon, R.I. (2007) "The Transfer Problem in Reducing the U.S. Current Account Deficit," *Journal of Policy Modeling*, 29: 669–675.

Menegatti, C. and N. Roubini (2007) "The Direct Link between Housing and Consumption: Wealth Effect and Home Equity Withdrawal", RGE Monitor Brief.

Mishkin, F.S. (2007) "Housing and the Monetary Transmission Mechanism," *Finance and Economics Discussion Series* 2007-40.

Mussa, M. (2007) "The Dollar and the Current Account Deficit: How Much Should we Worry?" *Journal of Policy Modeling*, 29: 691–698.

Papadimitriou, D.B., E. Chilcote, and G. Zezza (2006) "Can the Growth in the U.S. Current Account Deficit Be Sustained?" Levy Economics Institute of Bard College Strategic Analysis: May.

Pomerleano, M. (2009) "The IMF's Global Fumble: As the IMF Tries to Please Everyone, it Serves No One." Online, available at: www.voxeu.org/index.php?q=node/3347 (accessed March 26, 2009).

Reinhart, C.M. and K. Rogoff (2008) "Is the 2007 U.S. Sub-Prime Financial Crisis So Different? An International Historical Comparison," NBER Working Paper: 13761.

Rogoff, K. (2007) "Global Imbalances and Exchange Rate Adjustment", *Journal of Policy Modeling*, 29: 705–709.

Salvatore, D. (2007) "US Trade Deficits, Structural Imbalances, and Global Monetary Stability", *Journal of Policy Modeling*, 29: 697–704.

Setterfield, M. (2002) *The Economics of Demand-Led Growth*, London: Edward Elgar Publishing.

Taylor, L. (2004) *Reconstructing Macroeconomics: Structuralist Proposals and Critiques of the Mainstream*, Cambridge, MA: Harvard University Press.

Taylor, L. and F.J. Lysy (1979) "Vanishing Income Redistributions: Keynesian Clues about Model Surprises in the Short Run," *Journal of Development Economics*, 6: 11–29.

Vasudevan, R. (2008) "The Borrower of Last Resort: International Adjustment and Liquidity in a Historical Perspective," *Journal of Economic Issues*, 4: 1055–1081.

von Arnim, R. (2007) "Short-run Adjustment in a Global Model of Current Account Imbalances", SCEPA Working Paper: 2007-7.

4 Global imbalances and the US crisis

Is a bad excuse really better than none?

Kunibert Raffer

4.1 Introduction

Global imbalances seem to have become a catchword for putting at least part
– if not all – of the blame for the present US crisis on the South, more precisely on some OPEC members, some Asian countries, and China in particular. Already around and presented as a concern by the IMF before the US
crash, "global imbalances" were soon singled out as one main reason for the
crisis, in the same way the debt crisis of the 1980s was blamed on OPEC
("recycling of petrodollars") – against facts, truth, and fairness (cf. Raffer and
Singer 1996: 127ff., 2001: 133ff.). In plain English: it is claimed that the
crisis was not caused by highly leveraged instruments, "liar" and "ninja" (No
Income, No Job nor Assets) loans, slack regulation pursuant to the Greenspan
doctrine that markets can do no wrong or CDSs (Credit Default Swaps) sold
by institutes incapable of doing more than cashing the pertinent fees, and
foreseeably going belly-up when these contracts would have to be honoured.
At least in part if not mainly, it is China's fault, as well as the fault of OPEC
countries. Lorenzo Bini Smaghi (2008), member of the Executive Board of
the European Central Bank, titled his speech in Beijing: "The financial crisis
and global imbalances – two sides of the same coin". Predictably, he starts his
speech: "When analysing the current financial crisis the temptation might
arise to attribute all the responsibilities to the excesses of the US financial
system. I think this would be a mistake." Unlike Oscar Wilde, he proved able
to resist temptation.

While accepting that toxic assets originated in the major financial centres (the
plural excludes logically thinking of the US alone), Bini Smaghi deplores "an
insufficient production of alternative assets [alternatives to toxic assets, or alternative toxic assets?] around the world, compared to the large amount of savings
available". By necessity, this leads to a "close intertwining of the current crisis
and global imbalances" and to the conclusion: "In fact, many of the macro roots
of the current crisis were behind the widening of global imbalances in the last
decade" (ibid.). Starting at not putting all the blame on the US, he finally scores
his homerun, discovering that many – if not all – roots are actually in the South.
Finally, the Bush administration is quasi innocent.

A report published by the Council of Foreign Relations is more explicit (Dunaway 2009), quoting Treasury Secretary Paulson, who saw "addressing" global imbalances as more critical than mere "regulatory issues" as these imbalances would otherwise simply find "another outlet". However "Secretary Paulson did not go far enough" as "Global imbalances ... did indeed play a major role in creating the current crisis". The "savings glut helped to reduce world interest rates" (ibid.: 13), driving investors into asset bubbles and subprime mortgages: just as OPEC surpluses in the 1970s drove banks to lend to Southern countries (SCs) without any regard to the most basic principles of sound banking. The real problem was the inflow of money "enforcing" such investor behaviour. This argument strongly recalls the "blame OPEC arguments" for the debt crisis of the 1980s. The "Fed is a convenient scapegoat" (ibid.: p. 18) for loose monetary policies. The historically low level of interest rates over years and frequent rate cuts by the Fed go unmentioned, as does deregulation allowing if not encouraging ninja and liar loans.

Once mentioned, global imbalances quite correctly found their way into the list of causes of the financial crises prepared by the Congressional Research Service (Jickling 2009). What seems strange is that this "explanation" made it into the report of the President of the UN General Assembly, obviously so because his Commission of Experts (2009: 11) also sees global imbalances as playing "an important role in this crisis". According to Miguel D'Escoto Brockmann (2009: 12) "The *global imbalances which played an important role in this crisis* can only be addressed if there is a better way of dealing with international economic risks facing countries than the current system of accumulating international reserves." There is – exercising one's membership rights to control capital (Raffer 2010), but it goes unmentioned. While the President at least indirectly refers to the IMF's inappropriate policies of capital account liberalisation, this perfectly wrong "explanation" is nevertheless gaining ground. The IMF (2009) – much to its credit – seems the only global player stating that global imbalances were neither the reason nor the trigger of the present mess.

McKinley (2009: 1) spotted a "bandwagon" on which "[M]any commentators in the West have jumped ... lately to blame China for playing a leading role in causing the current global crisis, as well as for preventing a sustainable recovery". He traces this back to "Martin Wolf, the well-known columnist of the *Financial Times*", who laid out a case for pinning the principal blame for global imbalances on China.

Economically as well as logically, this is a patently wrong explanation. Neither China nor OPEC countries have unwound their surpluses. They could not have done so without losing a substantial amount of money, let alone did so in a way that triggered shocks. Thus their disorderly unwinding able to aggravate the crisis may remain a not unjustified fear of the Commission of Experts, but it has never turned into reality. None of these Southern surplus countries issued liar or ninja loans or encouraged unsound practices in the name of the free market and pursuant to the Robichek/Greenspan doctrine. After the putsch by Chile's fascist junta, which provided ideal preconditions to implement neoliberal ideas, the IMF's Director of the Western Hemisphere, E. Walter Robichek, had assured Latin Americans that exchange and other risks would presumably be taken into account as private firms can be expected to be careful. Private borrowers (as opposed to governments) were very unlikely to overborrow, even with official guarantees. Briefly, private, voluntary transactions were the private sector's own business, and unquestionably optimal. This view is sometimes called the Robichek doctrine. It might as well be called the Greenspan doctrine. Exactly as nowadays, the private sector was finally bailed out at great cost in Chile by the military junta. The Chilean catastrophe was one early test-run for the US crisis.

In the interest of fairness, this contribution must therefore pierce the wool the North is busy pulling over the eyes of the world. It discusses the nature and reasons of surpluses, putting things right. It shows that the basic line is very similar to the blame put at OPEC surplus countries' door after 1982. An English proverb rightly says: "Throw dirt enough and some will stick." The purpose of this contribution is to clean away whatever dirt willingly thrown might be about to stick. It discusses the specific and different situations of country groups with large forex reserves:

- OPEC countries with a lot of crude and relatively few inhabitants that cannot but accumulate surpluses unless they decided to export just enough to cover their current forex, especially their import, needs, which no one really wants them to;
- poor SCs, forced by the IMF not to use resources productively because the Fund still forces them not to use capital controls if and as necessary;
- Asian countries that have learned the lesson of the Asian crisis and obviously prefer to "self-insure" at considerable costs rather than using their IMF membership right of controlling capital flows – a political rather than an economic decision;
- China, the one outstanding case, whose surpluses are explained by her political decision to follow an export-led development path.

4.2 OPEC surplus countries

The case of the OPEC is particular since its countries supply a product considered crucial for the global economy: crude oil. If oil producers followed microeconomic optimisation, such as Hotelling's profit optimising firms, or if large producers restricted production to their own absorption capacity, a perceptible reduction in supply would ensue. Some of the biggest surplus countries are characterised by large crude reserves and small populations. Limiting sales to needs would have quite unpleasant consequences on the global economy, especially so at a time when demand is said to grow substantially due to newly increased consumption in India and China. If oil producers were not prepared to export more than they can absorb – even though crude in the ground might well be a better and safer asset given the evolution of global demand – they would be blamed for throttling the global economy. Now, they stand accused of "causing" the US crisis because they did not throttle economic activity and behaved in a way commended shortly before. Apparently for SCs the saying seems to hold: "damned if you do, damned if you don't".

Quite recently, the IBRD (2005: 27), for example, saw "evidence ... of the adoption of a more prudent spending stance compared to previous boom periods". The "robust revenue increases ... have largely been saved, leading to a marked improvement in both fiscal and external balances" (ibid.: 32). Briefly: "Thus, in many ways, MENA oil exporters are reacting to the current windfall revenues with a fair degree of prudence in comparison to previous booms" (ibid.: 35). The IMF judged in an equally positive light (cf. Raffer 2007: 36f.) before it started to worry about global imbalances. With the US in dire straits because of the irresponsible policies of its own government and financial sector, these same countries are now accused of not spending these surplus resources – critics as honest as Iago.

Technically, oil deposits in the ground and receipts from oil exports deposited in financial markets are merely an asset swap (Raffer 2007). The US crisis may suggest that exporters might have fared better to leave crude where nature had put it instead. It must be recalled that initially the Bretton Woods Institutions (BWIs) highly praised OPEC countries for avoiding the wrong decisions of the 1970s of spending too much, reacting more prudently to price volatility by investing surpluses caused by high prices.

Sterilising inflows during booms secures many advantages. Obviously, resources can be used to smooth out downswings and external shocks. Past experience definitely proves that such countervailing policies may be necessary. But it also eliminates appreciation pressures on domestic currencies and inflationary pressures, thus eliminating important Dutch disease effects. Investment income from such resources diversifies revenues.

This prudent use of large current account surpluses has increasingly come under attack. The IMF's *World Economic Outlook* (IMF 2005b: 111) already strikes a critical tone. Identifying the "recent increase in oil prices" as "adding to global imbalances", the IMF concludes: "This clearly has important implications for how existing imbalances can be resolved." A "5 per cent of GDP permanently higher investment rate" (ibid.: 113) of oil producers could reduce the US current account deficit visibly. The IMF (2005a: 10) suggested that oil exporters might "contribute to the adjustment of global imbalances". To do so "these countries may need to increase spending on imported goods, which could be facilitated by further liberalizing international trade in some countries" (ibid.). Speaking again of an "oil shock", Nsouli (2006: 1), an IMF director, sees necessary adjustment of global current account balances as "the bottom line" (ibid.: 11), demanding higher government spending by oil exporters in order to contribute to reducing global imbalances via increased imports. The fact that oil exporters import relatively little from the US, having "turned into large buyers of goods from Asia, a region where they also sell the bulk of their oil" (ibid.) is of particular concern to the author, even though that could simply be a clear sign of Asia's revealed comparative advantage, in other words, the proof that the global market functions well. Consumer sovereignty, a cornerstone of free market economies loses its value when it comes to help the US. Countries with low absorption capacity should "recycle their petrodollars through capital out-flows to the rest of the world, contributing to dampening interest rates in the oil-importing world" (ibid.). OPEC countries are openly requested to recycle their petrodollars through capital outflows to the rest of the world, in other words, to engage in the same policy, which has been used so far wrongly to blame the debt crisis of the 1980s on OPEC. Following this advice would automatically provide a scapegoat for the next debt crisis.

Unfortunately, it is hardly assured that these resources would be used to import from the US – they might as well be used to import from Asia or Europe without "appropriate" conditionality.

Such demands on surplus countries differ markedly from the usual IMF advice when it comes to dealing with countries having balance of payments defi-cits. One may, however, doubt whether they are the first signs of a fundamental reorientation of the IMF's policies towards deficit countries. Recent experience of how the IMF acts in SCs justifies doubts whether these concerns regarding "global imbalances" are the first signs of such a fundamental reorientation towards what had initially been wanted by Keynes, unless they happen to be the US: Keynesianism for one country, or for more equal countries after the US crisis, as one might say looking at the IMF's advice to Western Europe. The double standard in fighting the crisis (large government spending in the North, old austerity policies in the South) clearly reflects E.A. Blair's *Animal Farm*, where one species is "more equal". At the same time, though, new donors from Asia are condemned as granting "rogue aid", and investment by surplus SCs in the North is fought or prevented.

Now that oil exporters have successfully engaged in handling their surpluses in the best interest of their own economies as well as of the global economy, pressure is building up to fall back to the ways of the past mercilessly criticised just shortly before. Arab countries would be well advised to analyse quite thoroughly where their economic interest lies, and whether increasing spending is the optimal policy.

High volatility of crude markets in 2009 has again proved the advantages of oil surpluses available to cushion export shocks. UN/DESA (2009: 7f.) expected substantial trade shocks from

> a 35 percent drop in the average price of crude oil in 2009 (compared with the 2008 average).... In line with the regional trend, oil exporters such as Saudi Arabia are forecast to experience a pronounced contraction in their trade surpluses due to lower oil prices and, albeit to a smaller extent, lower oil export volumes.

As could be expected, oil exporters are among the countries hardest hit by trade shocks. Self-insurance is more than just advised.

4.3 IMF policies increasing imbalances

4.3.1 Asia

Under the trauma of the crash of 1997–1998, Asian countries have meanwhile amassed huge reserves to shield their economies against future crises. Arguably, this is the most important and visible policy change. It also may be interpreted as falling into another BWI trap, believing the IMF's new mantra about open capital accounts cum huge reserves as preferable to appropriate reserves plus using the right to capital controls enshrined in the IMF's very statutes. Much smaller reserves would suffice if countries decided to use the membership right of any IMF member if and when necessary: controlling capital flows.

The Asian crisis is thus also a tale of two standards: international financial institutions (IFIs) have routinely infringed on the membership rights of SCs. The IMF gravely breached its statutes to the detriment of Asian members. This would be unthinkable when and if big shareholders wanted to exercise the same statutory rights, as the present double standard of encouraging deficits in the North and old-style austerity policies in SCs documents. Talked again into not using their membership rights to control capital flows, Asian countries have attempted to shield themselves against a recurrence of the crisis by following once again IMF advice, accumulating large foreign exchange reserves. Now they are the villains of the piece.

According to the BIS (2007: 89), East Asia and India (ten countries) held over 44 per cent of the world's official foreign exchange reserves in December 2006, of which China held nearly half. Korea ($238.4 billion) and Taiwan ($266.1 billion) held more reserves than the whole Euro area, 1.3 and 1.45 times as much respectively. At the end of 2005, Korea's reserves amounted to about 28 per cent of GDP, up from some 9 per cent at the start of the 1990s (Ra 2007: 150). Ra compares this to the US, Germany, and Britain, all with a ratio below 2.5 per cent, citing criticisms that Korea shoulders unnecessarily high costs for these reserves. Pointing out that "some reserves have been accumulated through government bond sales" he states the financial problem succinctly: "reserves earn a current market rate of 2–3%, but the government bonds carry an interest rate of 9%" (ibid.). Ra (ibid: 148) also points out that the yield of US Treasuries (one main form of holding reserves) are much below "the expected return on local investments". According to Akyüz (2008: 27), "about half of the total stock of reserves in Asia now would be 'borrowed' reserves". Assuming a "moderate 500 basis points margin" between costs and returns, Akyüz estimates costs of reserve holding "of $50 billion for the region as a whole" (ibid.). Considering the average spread of emerging markets over the full boom–bust cycles he calls his estimate "quite modest". Substantial opportunity costs are suffered just to keep capital accounts open to please the IMF.

Once, and possibly because, Asians appear to have started thinking about the usefulness and costs of large reserves, coincidence has it that the BIS (2007: 46) warned: "Some similarities to pre-1997 crisis conditions are apparent" in emerging market economies (EMEs). Fortunately, the BIS identifies "also important differences compared with the earlier period", mainly "foreign exchange reserves" at "record levels, exceeding conventional thresholds of reserve adequacy in most EMEs" (ibid.). The BIS speaks of those global imbalances that are meanwhile the root of all evil.

The IMF (2000: 6) supports and advises the choice of accumulating surpluses, defining the ratio of reserves to short-term external debt (R/STD) as the "Single most important indicator of reserve adequacy in countries with significant but uncertain access to capital markets." Positing that "conditions to ensure private sector access to international capital markets reduces the need" (ibid.) for reserves, the IMF continues to pursue its liberalisation agenda, though. Especially with regard to Asia this assertion sounds courageous (in a Sir-Humphreyesque sense) and definitely not in tune with historical facts. The IMF (2000: 16) goes on: "A smaller reserves to short-term debt ratio [= logically, less global imbalances] is associated with a greater incidence and depth of crises", which is only valid if and as long as capital accounts are kept open. Under such conditions, the suggestion "that the weaker a country's liquidity position prior to the onset of the crisis, the stronger the exchange market pressure and thus potential for a crisis during the crisis period" (ibid.: 16) is to be expected. Capital controls are a better alternative *and* a membership right of any IMF member. The IMF does not like this option, though, fighting it as hard as it can in violation of its own Articles of Agreement. It is all the more important to point out that such reserves are not necessary, especially so as the IMF meanwhile started to see "global imbalances" as the new problem. Again, dammed if you do and dammed if you don't – both small and large reserves cause crises and they are always the SC's fault.

4.3.2 Poor SCs under BWI control

BWI pressure to liberalise capital accounts has made increased stocks of international reserves necessary. The IMF has forced many countries to use inflows of Overseas Development Assistance (ODA) to build up reserves. These reserves have been anointed one of the widely used targets of poverty reduction strategies in Africa, although any IMF member has the right to capital controls pursuant to the IMF's Articles of Agreement. To some extent, the IMF's statutes even encourage capital controls. Only current transactions are to continue. Using these rights, which the BWIs force their clients not to do – the IMF in open breach of its own constitution – would not cost anything, unlike large reserves squirreling resources away from poverty alleviation, financing MDGs or development at large. A Eurodad study (Molina-Gallart 2009: 11) showed that "a constant in almost all IMF programmes reviewed is the requirement to *increase the country's international reserves position*, up to three or four months of imports".

Evaluating the IMF and aid to Africa, the IMF's (2007: viii, 40) own Independent Evaluation Office (IEO) found:

PRGF-supported macroeconomic policies have generally accommodated the use of incremental aid in countries whose recent policies have led to high stocks of reserves and low inflation; in other countries additional aid was programmed to be saved to increase reserves or to retire domestic debt.

Increased disbursements are literally sterilised, while many poor countries fall back behind schedule to meet the MDGs. The IEO found this practice so common that "outside observers perceive the Fund as 'blocking' the use of aid" (ibid.). Countries with reserve levels below 2.5 months of imports were programmed to use almost all of the anticipated aid increases (95 per cent on average) to raise reserve levels. But the amount of reserves is not the only indicator. Inflation plays an important role too: "The estimated inflation threshold for determining whether the country got to spend or save additional aid lies within the 5–7 percent range" (ibid.). Economists call this a trade off. Fighting inflation is privileged: tough luck for underweight children under five years of age or infants dying if the country's inflation is above this critical range, maybe only by a few basis points. Even though the money is there, it must not be used to help them. Tough luck also for global imbalances.

One cannot but understand the shock suffered by the General Director of Médecins Sans Frontières in Belgium, G. Ooms, when reading this IEO Report:

> It really was an eye-opener. It reveals, almost casually, that the IMF did not block the reception of additional aid at all; it simply blocked the use of additional aid. ... On the one hand you have hundreds if not thousands of organizations and individuals pleading their government to provide more aid to provide better health care or education, to realize the MDGs, to keep children from starving and to keep people with AIDS from dying perfectly avoidable deaths; and on the other hand you have the IMF making sure that 80% of all that aid is not being used. This picture is too grotesque for my imagination, and yet it is what has happened since 1999, and as far as I know it simply continues to happen.
>
> (Rowden and Thapliyal 2007: 1f.)

Some SCs have at least a fair chance to be allowed to use these reserves to iron out aid volatility, which means going on financing their fight against poverty and infectious diseases: "Countries with very high initial levels of reserves are, on average, allowed to finance the aid reductions to avoid fiscal adjustments, mainly through the depletion of reserves" (IMF IEO 2007: 56). This is, however, asymmetrical: countries

> with very low initial levels of reserves, by contrast, have to fully bear anticipated reductions in aid, in the form of full fiscal and current account adjustments. The programmed fiscal response to aid reductions does not depend on inflation levels.
>
> (ibid.)

Who could any longer doubt official IFI claims that countries actually "own" their programmes – and are therefore also fully responsible for creating global imbalances?

This IEO evaluation documents one further interesting point: "Case study analysis indicates that debt sustainability concerns may be an additional factor reducing the programmed level of absorption – and increasing the programmed build up of reserves – in response to an increase in aid" (ibid.: 6). Thus, at least the IMF assumes that debt relief has not been sufficient in quite a few cases and that reserves therefore also have to serve as a cushion. Similar to the case of outright debt cancellation such funds are in a way double-counted: "aid" technically substitutes proper reductions.

Seen with this IMF strategy in mind, the attacks on new creditors and donors, culminating in the hypocritical phrase "rogue aid" gain a wholly new perspective. These flows do not only increase poor countries' policy space, but they may also allow continuous financing of the MDGs not guaranteed by "old" donors, and put at risk by the IMF. They might save the lives of a few infants, but this does not seem to be a concern in the North. Although sums are small in the case of each of these poor countries, they add up, accumulating to those global imbalances the IMF is fond of decrying on other occasions.

4.3.3 Other SCs

Arguing that "the US forced the rest of the world to convert to policies of export-led growth", Kregel (2009: 3) identifies "four basic forces driving global trade. Virtually all ... linked to the US." While his first two are arguably more relevant to China, the so-called shadow banking system creating "large increases in international capital flows, many to developing countries, joining current account surpluses to support exchange rates and further increase foreign reserves" is more relevant for other countries. Kregel's "final factor", commodity investment funds accelerating the rise in commodity prices, which in turn increased forex reserves, is particularly important for the poorest and primary commodity exports focused countries. It also makes cushions against volatility mandatory. Doubtlessly though, the security motivation (guarding against speculative attacks) discussed for Asia was present in other regions too.

All in all surplus and relatively high reserves countries in the South are rather victims than perpetrators of the US crisis. This fact, as well as the IMF's open violation of its own statutes and the Fund's harmful role in increasing "global imbalances" – helpful as it might have been for some time to finance US deficits – must be recalled.

4.3.4 China

China's case differs. Clearly, it is impossible to provide a full in-depth analysis on a few pages. Nevertheless, some problems can be signalled, hoping that they might be picked up by later research and that a more balanced and fairer picture might eventually emerge. Considering present power structures this might be seen as a pious wish, though. Following an export-led development trajectory, as several other countries had done successfully before her, China has focused on the US market. Given China's domestic average income, this had to produce surpluses. Her high savings rate, an autonomous consumer decision, aggravates them.

In a textbook world with homothetic preferences (i.e. a Chinese consumes precisely the same basket as a US-American, just proportionally less of each product due to lower income), China could make up low incomes by numbers. The Chinese would, of course, have to change their saving habits and their way of life. This would diminish trade surpluses. In reality very different consumption patterns (with or without government encouragement to import) exist, and export opportunities for US consumption goods are limited. Surpluses must accumulate automatically.

Not all surpluses have been generated by trade. Between 1999 and 2007 continuous inflows of net direct investment amounting to 2–4 per cent of GDP contributed to China's surplus (McKinley 2009: 4), inflows that by definition cannot stem from export surpluses. This is often conveniently forgotten. When bashing China, attempts to separate trade effects from other balance of payment effects are usually and conveniently not made. Chen (2009: 48) points out that "American and other foreign banks and firms are invited to be strategic partners with China's state-owned firms for improving China's competitiveness." To the extent retained profits have been reinvested rather than repatriated – e.g. because an appreciation of the renminbi is expected – surpluses were not reduced. Kregel (2009: 3) sees an impact of private equity firms demanding increased rates of return, driving producers to outsource production to take advantage of lower foreign labour costs linked to US technological dominance. Lum and Nanto (2004: 10f.) already pointed out in a CRS Report:

> In addition, the bulk of China's exports are manufactured under foreign brand names, and over half of China's exports are produced by foreign-owned companies. According to PRC official estimates, 70% of PRC exports to the United States contain foreign components, particularly from Taiwan, South Korea, and Singapore.

Interestingly, they also point at the substantial inaccuracies in balance of payments statistics: while Chinese figures showed a US deficit of "only $58.6 billion in 2003, the United States report it to be $123 billion" (ibid.: 12). They reveal that China ran a trade surplus with the US since 1993, according to Chinese data, while US data show trade deficits with China since 1983. Some analysts argued that the US Department of Commerce overstated the trade deficit with China by as much as 21 per cent, because of the way that it calculates entrepôt trade through Hong Kong (ibid.: 6, 8). According to the same source, some trade specialists suggested that the surge of US imports from China does not pose an additional threat to US industries and workers because it merely represented a shift of investment and production from other Pacific Rim countries. If so, China's surplus would be counter-balanced by lower surpluses or higher deficits elsewhere.

Speculative inflows betting on the appreciation of the renminbi, flowing into the country legally or otherwise are said to be one engine of the exchange rate too. Foreign investors tried to profit from the booming housing market in China, where house prices skyrocketed recently. This speculation was no doubt encouraged by US pressure on China to appreciate its currency. Given dimensions it should not be attempted to counter such non-trade effects via the trade policy.

US consumers, on the other hand, were quite willing to import. Kregel (2009: 3) speaks of households using "their home equity as an ATM and providing for rising demand for the exports of developing countries, often produced by US companies operating abroad". This specific lending practice of Anglo-Saxon countries fuelled imports. It is unknown in continental Europe where banks routinely insist on a certain percentage of self-financed down-payments. Thus the US crisis could only spread via US junk papers avidly bought by European expertise. Unlike China, neither US consumers nor outsourcing US companies are blamed. Like China, they ought not to be blamed.

McKinley (2009: 2) points out that the US's propensity to "live beyond its means" had been well entrenched long before China became a significant exporter of capital: "The US's tendency to run sizeable current-account deficits dates from the early 1990s, when China's current-account surpluses were still negligible."

However, returning to presently existing reserves whatever their origin, it seems plausible to assume that China's long-term development strategy might already have factored in losses as the price of her chosen development strategy – an export drive such as China's is impossible without high surpluses, simply because domestic consumption falls necessarily behind export capacity. It remains to be seen how high losses of dollar held surpluses will eventually be, but it seems rational to assume that China would be inclined to keep losses low. Thus, she has no incentive to rock the boat. Be that as it may, it is very interesting, even unique, that the seller (given the high share of transnational exporters in China not even the seller but the host country) not buyers are accused of causing imbalances – in sharp contrast both to the traditional view blaming deficit countries (profligate spenders) and to the differences in IMF advice now given to Northern countries (finance expansionary policies) and SCs, where austerity policies have to bring import capacity in line with export proceeds.

Chen (2009: 48f.) concludes:

> More than half of China's exports are by foreign firms – and most export channels are controlled by multi-national firms such as Wal-Mart. Chinese companies and the Chinese Government has no pricing power in the international market. For any Chinese product sold in the United States, Chinese companies receive 2–5 per cent of the sale value. As a result, China's domestic market is more open and more competitive than those of the United States, Japan or any other country in Asia and Europe.

Reducing surpluses will be difficult as Chinese foreign direct investment (FDI) is not welcome and Chinese aid gets criticised. Thus the same countries decrying imbalances are actively hindering reductions. Quite routine acquisitions, such as the attempt by the Dubai Ports World to buy US harbours even triggered considerations to pass special laws prohibiting this. The fact that these harbours had been managed by a foreign (British) company before was obviously no problem. Australia is presently fighting Chinese investments. Routinely, the Committee on Foreign Investment in the United States (CFIUS) vets FDI whether it poses concerns, such as making the US dependent on foreign-controlled suppliers of crucial goods or services. This closely mirrors the concern *dependentistas* expressed when dependency theory discussed the power of transnational corporations, but which was ridiculed by the North. Foreign investment seems to be wonderful unless investors are from those surplus countries encouraged to reduce their accumulated surpluses. The alleged benefits of FDI seem only to accrue if Northern companies invest in the South, not the other way round. Simultaneously, sovereign wealth funds attract fire, unless they happen to be Norway's *Statens pensjonsfond – Utland.* These impediments to reducing surpluses in turn increase global imbalances. Of course, lending this money unconditionally to the IMF would be welcome, at least but not only by the Fund. Apparently due to criticism of her surpluses, China signalled her intention to invest up to US$50 billion in notes issued by the Fund in June 2009. Is doling out their wealth to the North or the IMF – but not (directly) to SCs – the only accepted alternative? Do these dollars now miraculously reduce the US deficit since they are no longer held by China?

Chen (2009: 48) argues: "If world trade were free and based on rules of symmetry, China would be buying much more US technology than it really does." But the US does not allow high tech exports to China, in contrast to Japan and other East Asian countries that have enjoyed persistent trade surpluses with China, "quite comparable with China's trade surplus with the United States".

McKinley (2009: 3) sees a political background in China bashing. Although "the combined current-account surpluses of Germany and Japan (in 2007: $464 billion) exceed those of China", ($372 billion), "few economists or politicians in the West are heaping blame on them for global imbalances". The former "have been running large current-account surpluses for a long time without having triggered" negative reactions, which McKinley explains by the "main difference" that "China is realigning the global balance of economic and political power while Germany and Japan are not" (ibid.). One might add: Japan and Germany are Northern countries. Their surpluses are thus as acceptable as a counterfactual US surplus would no doubt be. Then, the IMF would fervently pressure deficit countries – reckless spenders – to correct their deficits.

4.4 Surpluses – really a concern?

Demonstrably, the crisis was not triggered by erratic movements or large sales of surplus dollars. Surplus holders continued to behave as they had done before.

Consequently, no one of those blaming surplus countries goes into details, arguing how and why precisely they are culpable.

Much to its credit (as already mentioned above) the IMF (2009: 34) is one of the very few putting things into perspective:

> [A]lthough global imbalances may have been a factor behind the buildup of macroeconomic and financial excesses that led to the crisis, the crisis was largely caused by weak risk management in large institutions at the core of the global financial system combined with failures in financial regulation and supervision. Despite earlier concerns, a disorderly exit from the dollar has not yet been part of the crisis narrative.

It states that "a reversal of capital inflows to the United States and the deprecia- tion of the dollar clearly were not the trigger for the current global crisis" (ibid.: 35), singling out a "reversal of the overoptimistic assessment of risk on U.S. subprime and other mortgage-backed assets, which prompted a massive increase in risk aversion, a loss of financial capital, and deleveraging". While agreeing that global imbalances were an integral part of low interests and capital inflows to the US, which fostered leverage and "a search for yield, and the creation of riskier assets and house price bubbles in the United States and some other advanced economies" (ibid.: 36), the IMF concludes: "But a central role in the current crisis has been played by the failure of risk management in financial institutions and weakness in financial supervision and regulation." Or, Green- span not China is to blame. Even if venom were abundant, proper regulation would still prevent people from drinking it.

Although no reason for the US crisis, are China's surpluses a reason for future concern? A large chunk has been invested in Treasuries. China has financed, so to say, her own export drive. Technically, dollars earned from US imports were handed over to the Treasury in exchange for mere paper and the hope that it would be honoured as stipulated – trust in God (written on the greenback) was exchanged for trust in God's own country, switching from God to his ground staff. The money stayed in the US, as did exported goods; "the large amount of savings available" Bini Smaghi (2008: 1) decried is to a large extent money put at the US government's disposal and spent by it, e.g. in Iraq, Afghanistan, or for Wall Street. As long as owners do not start big financial manoeuvres nothing happens. They have no economic incentive to do so, and a lot to lose by disturbing the delicate (im)balance. Normally, this situation is called a stable equilibrium in economics. But textbooks do normally pretend not to take low politicking into account.

On the other hand, the realistic danger exists that the dollar might strongly lose in value due to US policies, i.e. surplus countries forced to invest in the dollar are going to lose. Thinkers at the Peterson Institute meanwhile stress the necessity to increase US exports strongly in order to reduce US dependency on foreign creditors, quoting papers written by known experts and speeches by top politicians. All agree that a strong devaluation of the dollar would be the precondition. This necessity "is not just economic. It is also strategic" (Bergsten and Subramanian 2009). In plain English: surplus countries are bound to lose part of their wealth due to US policies. If quick unwinding is likely at all, it is more likely to be done by the US than by SCs. Quite a few people might be inclined to agree with Chen (2009: 48) when he argues that "US Treasuries turned out to be a trap.... When the dollar goes down, Japanese or Europeans can buy US assets, but Chinese cannot – blocked as they are by the United States' national security policy".

As the share of China's exports to the US "declined from about 20% in 2000 to about 16% in 2007" McKinley (2009: 2) argues that neither pegging the renminbi to the dollar, nor "pumping reserves into US securities in order to abate depreciation of the dollar" does make a great deal of sense. The latter is technically equivalent to revaluing the renminbi vis-à-vis the dollar accordingly. His conclusion that China must abandon this ineffective and risky strategy is correct, but China is also caught in a dollar trap. Moving out too quickly would trigger substantial losses, of which her government is obviously aware. Thus fears about a disorderly unwinding are wholly unjustified as long as one credits the Chinese with some rationality and assumes no global war to be about to start where destruction of whatever dimension is just a collateral.

There is no other currency able to perform the dollar's role as the global currency, thus no alternative. Although rooted in an equally potent economy, the euro cannot do so because the quantity of xenoeuro necessary for performing this role would mean much larger balance of payments deficits than the euro area has had and seems willing to run. Such deficits are the only way that enough euros could get into the global economy outside the zone. All surplus countries are thus prisoners to the dollar and US policy decisions. While they might wish to unwind, they know that this can only be done slowly, if at all.

Another question mercifully allowed to sink into oblivion is whether the exchange rate of the dollar that is likely to have trade effects is mainly or uniquely determined by China's (or other) trade surpluses. This is clearly not the case, as the fluctuations of the dollar show, e.g. it appreciating during the US crisis when money flowed back into the US. Thus the US dollar's exchange rate to the euro fluctuated between 0.8252 (26 October 2000) and 1.5990 (15 July 2008) according to the European Central Bank. Against which dollar value should China have depreciated her currency, of 2000 or of 2008? Should it have followed the changes of the dollar just to keep the US happy? According to the Asian Development Bank the renminbi appreciated by roughly one-fifth against the dollar between 2000 and 2008.

This raises the question why China's trade policy alone should correct all changes of the dollar's exchange rate vis-à-vis the renminbi and other currencies. Since the dollar's exchange rate is to a considerable amount determined by global speculative flows, capital believing the US to be a safe haven, or – more recently – simply by US corporations selling off their foreign assets to fill the holes the crisis they had caused had torn into their balance sheets at home, it remains unclear why China alone should be held responsible for all changes, in stark contrast to US authorities aiding and abetting destructive speculation. As the exchange rate between the dollar and the renminbi is definitely not caused by China's trade policy alone, why should China even out the impacts of all other US policies?

4.5 Conclusion

The purpose of this chapter was to show that the blame for the US crisis brought about by inefficient regulation, neoliberal liberalisation, greed, and sometimes fraud cannot simply be put on surplus countries. In essence this crisis is not different from other neoliberal crises. It is only larger, which, however, had to be expected considering the build-up of neoliberal crises since the 1980s. Just as the debt crisis caused by unregulated xenomarkets in the early 1980s was blamed on OPEC, SCs (including OPEC countries) are once again targeted as scapegoats. Very much as in the Bible, the goat is perfectly innocent. SCs under the IMF's thumb had no choice. Asian countries fell into an IMF trap. At most they may be blamed for not defending their membership rights. OPEC countries chose the best policy for themselves as well as responsibly for the global economy. Reducing their output to their needs would have caused pure catastrophe, especially in the case of countries with relatively large oil reserves and a relatively small population. To attack them now for not causing catastrophe by accommodating global demand is somewhat disingenuous. To some extent they acted selflessly, because maximising self-interests would doubtlessly have suggested different policies. Having learned the lessons of the past they avoided the failures of the 1980s for which they have been scolded until very recently.

Regarding China, this chapter has not tried more than to show that present criticism is politically motivated and biased, arguing for a more nuanced analysis. It is to be hoped that this chapter may trigger more research on the issues discussed and that such elaborations prove to be more truthful (academic) than politically biased. Expecting so much seems preposterous, but don't let's lose hope in truth eventually prevailing.

The "arguments" brought forward against surplus countries nowadays are a deplorably poor copy of those "arguments" trying to pin down the Southern debt crisis and global recession on OPEC after 1974. Apparently, the success of the latter encouraged this encore. In a way, it is always the fault of the South. This disingenuous "excuse" is worse than none.

References

Akyüz, Y. (2008) "The Current Global Financial Turmoil and Asian Developing Countries". Bangkok Paper presented at the ministerial segment of ESCAP's 64th commission session, 29 April (mimeo).

Bergsten, C.F. and A. Subramanian (2009) "Cannot Resolve Global Imbalances on Its Own." Online, available at: www.iie.com/publications/opeds/oped.cfm?ResearchID=1283 (accessed 6 September 2009).

Bini Smaghi, L. (2008) "The Financial Crisis and Global Imbalances: Two Sides of the Same Coin". Asia Europe Economic Forum Conference: The Global Financial Crisis: Policy Choices in Asia and Europe, Beijing.

BIS (2007) "77th Annual Report". Basel: Bank for International Settlement.

Chen, P. (2009) "From an efficient market to a viable international financial market". In R. Garnaut, L. Song, and W.T. Woo (eds) *China's New Place in a World in Crisis: Economic, Geopolitical and Environmental Dimensions*, Canberra: ANU E-Press.

Commission of Experts (2009) "Recommendations by the Commission of Experts of the President of the General Assembly on reforms of the international monetary and financial system". Sixty-third session, Agenda item 48, Follow-up to and implementation of the outcome of the 2002 International Conference on Financing for Development and the preparation of the 2008 Review Conference (Chair: Professor J. Stiglitz) A/63/XXX (Draft), New York.

D'Escoto Brockmann, M. (2009) "United Nations Conference World Financial and Economic Crisis and its Impact on Development, Draft Outcome Document Presented by the H.E. Miguel D'Escoto Brockmann, President of the General Assembly", New York.

Dunaway, S. (2009) "Global Imbalances and the Financial Crisis", No. 44, March, Council on Foreign Relations, Special Report.

IBRD (2005) *Oil Booms and Revenue Management, 2005 Economic Developments and Prospects, Middle East and North African Region*. Washington, DC: Bank for Reconstruction and Development.

IMF (2000) "Debt- and Reserve-related Indicators of External Vulnerability". Online, available at: www.imf.org/external/np/pdr/debtres/index.htm (accessed 11 September 2009).

IMF (2005a) "Regional Economic Outlook (September)", Middle East and Central Asia Department, Washington, DC: International Monetary Fund.

IMF (2005b) "World Economic Outlook 2005 (September)", Washington, DC: International Monetary Fund.

IMF (2009) "World Economic Outlook, Crisis and Recovery (April)", Washington, DC: International Monetary Fund.

IMF, Independent Evaluation Office (2007) "An Evaluation of the IMF and Aid to Sub-Saharan Africa (12 March)". Online, available at: www.imf.org/external/np/ieo/2007/ssa/eng/index.htm (accessed 6 September 2009).

Jickling, M. (2009) "Causes of the Financial Crisis", CRS Report for Congress, Washington, DC, 29 January.

Kregel, J. (2009) "The Global Crisis and the Implications for Developing Countries and the BRICs: Is the 'B' really Justified?" Revised draft of a paper prepared for the XXI Forum Nacional, Opening Session: The New Role of the BRIMCs and the Global Crisis, Rio de Janeiro, 18 May.

Lum, T. and D.K. Nanto (2004) "China's Trade with the United States and the World". CRS Report for Congress, Washington, DC, updated 19 November.

McKinley, T. (2009) "Will Pinning the Blame on China Help Correct Global Imbalances?" Policy Brief 2, Centre for Development Policy and Research, SOAS, London.

Molina-Gallart, N. (2009) "Bail-out or Blow-out? IMF Policy Advice and Conditions for Low-income Countries at a Time of Crisis". Online, available at: www.eurodad.org/uploadedFiles/Whats_New/Reports/Bail-out%20or%20blow-out.pdf?n=8936 (accessed 6 September 2009).

Nsouli, S.M. (2006) "Petrodollar Recycling and Global Imbalances". Paper presented at the CESifo's International Spring Conference, Berlin, 23–24 March.

Ra, H.-R. (2007) "Demand for International Reserves: A Case Study for Korea". *Journal of the Korean Economy* 8, n.1: 147–76.

Raffer, K. (2007) "Macro-economic Evolutions of Arab Economies: A Foundation for Structural Reforms". *OFID Pamphlet Series* 36.

Raffer, K. (2010) *Debt Management for Development: Protection of the Poor and the Millennium Development Goals*, Cheltenham, Elgar.

Raffer, K. and H.W. Singer (1996) *The Foreign Aid Business: Economic Assistance and Development Co-operation*, Cheltenham: Elgar.

Raffer, K. and H.W. Singer (2001) *The Economic North–South Divide: Six Decades of Unequal Development*, Cheltenham: Elgar.

Rowden, R. and N. Thapliyal (2007) "IMF Still Blocking Progress on HIV/AIDS, Health, and Education: New Report Outrages Aid Advocates". *Policies and Priorities* 2(1), Actionaid.

United Nations/DESA (2009) "Monthly Briefing, World Economic Situation and Prospects and Monitoring of Global Vulnerability", 11 (12 August), United Nations.

5 Employment in the South[1]

Rolph van der Hoeven and Malte Lübker[2]

The consequences of mistakes in financial markets, where capital is volatile and mobile globally, far exceeds the consequences of mistakes in the labor markets, where labor is largely immobile across national lines.

Richard Freeman (2003)

5.1 Introduction: some characteristics of financial globalization

The current wave of globalization is characterized by widespread adoption of policies for financial openness.[3] Over the past two decades, many countries have liberalized their capital accounts and almost all policy measures related to foreign direct investment (FDI) favored a more open regime (UNCTAD 2009). These measures have been adopted autonomously by some countries, and also as conditions of adjustment loans. The major expected result from financial openness was that it would allow developing countries to better utilize resources and to increase capital formation by stimulating FDI and other international capital flows such as private portfolios investment. A more open national financial system was seen as a necessary complement to the lifting of impediments to international capital flows.

Capital has become more globally mobile as a result of these policy changes, especially since the mid-1990s. Worldwide gross private capital flows (the sum of the absolute values of foreign direct, portfolio, and other investment in- and outflows) have exceeded 20 percent of world GDP every year since 1998 and reached a new record of 32.3 percent of GDP in 2005 – compared to less than 10 percent of world GDP before 1990 (World Bank 2009c). Worldwide FDI flows, a sub-category of private capital flows, also rose substantially during the 1990s. They peaked at 4.9 percent of world GDP in 2000 and declined with the downturn of the early 2000s, but strongly rebound before the current global financial and economic crisis. On average, global FDI flows doubled between the 1980s and the 1990s, and again in the years from 2000 to 2007. The increase in capital flows contrasts with that of labor, whose movement is still highly restricted. The world's approximately 86.3 million migrant workers accounted for only 3.1 percent of the economically active population in 2000.[4]

In spite of this substantial increase in capital flows, the expected benefits have not materialized for many countries. During the surge in foreign capital flows since the mid-1990s, actual investment into new infrastructure and productive capacity stagnated. This can in part be attributed to the fact that much FDI was spent on mergers and acquisitions, rather than on investment into new factories or equipment that would have added productive capacity.[5] Gross fixed capital formation (the most commonly used measure for physical investment) averaged 21.6 percent of GDP in the 1990s and 21.0 percent in the years from 2000 to 2006 (the last year for which global estimates are available) (ibid.). Hence, it fell well short of the level reached in the 1970s and 1980s. In fact, Figure 5.1 shows an overall declining trend in capital formation since the early 1970s. It is thus not surprising that world GDP growth, too, was slower in the 1990s and the 2000s than in previous decades (see also Figure 5.2).

Moreover, despite much excitement about the promise of 'emerging markets', cross-border capital flows are still largely a phenomenon of developed countries. In 2005, gross private capital flows equaled 37.2 percent of GDP in high-income countries, but only 12.7 percent of GDP in low- and middle-income countries (ibid.). While there was a positive balance between in- and outflows for developing countries as a group, these flows by-and-large bypassed the poorest countries since the early 1990s as middle-income countries accounted for more than 90 percent of the total (World Bank 2009a). FDI, as well, is highly concentrated among industrialized countries and a small group of middle-income countries (UNCTAD 2009). Low-income countries, to a large extent, still draw their foreign resources from official development assistance which decreased over the 1990s and only rebound in the past few years.[6]

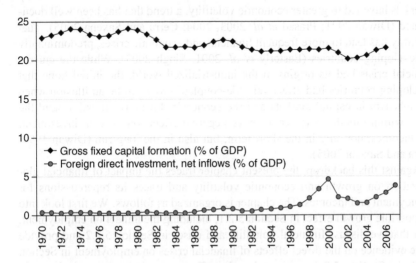

Figure 5.1 FDI and investment as share of GDP, world, 1970–2007 (source: World Bank (2009c), online database (May 2009)).

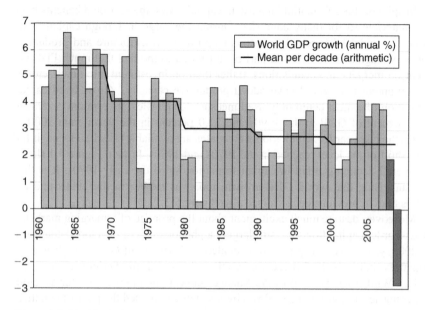

Figure 5.2 World GDP growth, 1961–2009 (annual change in percent) (source: World Bank (2009c), online database (as of April 2009) and World Bank (2009a) (June 22, 2009)).

Note
Figures for 2008 and 2009 (shaded bars) are a World Bank estimate/forecast.

Meanwhile, international capital movements and their sometimes sharp reversals have led to greater economic volatility, a trend that has been well documented (Diwan 2001; Prasad *et al.* 2003, 2004; Cerra and Saxena 2005). That volatility has lead to more frequent financial and economic crises, predominantly in developing countries (Easterly *et al.* 2001; Singh 2003). While the current financial crisis had its origins in the industrialized world, the initial hope that developing countries had effectively 'de-coupled' proved to be an illusion when the upheaval in capital markets and the economic downturn spread around the globe within months. Such crises have negative effects on growth, investment, and incomes, not only in the short term, but also in the long run (Diwan 1999; Cerra and Saxena 2005).

Against this backdrop, the present chapter traces the impact of financial globalization on growth and economic volatility and traces its repercussions for employment and incomes. The chapter is organized as follows. We first look into the possible growth effect in Section 5.2.1, including the impact on employment, after that we discuss financial volatility and crises in Section 5.2.2 and provide some evidence on the direct effects of financial crises on employment in Section 5.2.3. In Section 5.2.4 we examine the effects of crises on wage shares in national income. A short summary of the main findings follows in Section 5.2.5.

Section 5.3 discusses policy responses that could make the international financial system more conducive to the goal of adequate employment generation and better returns to labor. Policies in industrialized countries, new rules for the international system, and policies in developing countries are addressed, followed by a discussion of the role of institutions in designing and implementing coherent policies. We end with a short postscript to situate our discussion in the context of the current financial crisis that hit the world economy after the first version of this chapter was written, and whose devastating effects on labor far exceed what we would have thought possible when first starting work on the topic.

Since we focus on private capital flows (i.e. those private international transactions that are recorded under the balance of payments' financial account), we make only reference in passing to other important sources of foreign finance, such as official and private development assistance, income generated from exports, and workers' remittances. Although the latter are a form of private financial flows, they do not establish an investment position and are, therefore, recorded under the current account.[7] Using a broad definition, the World Bank estimates that remittances to developing countries amounted to US$166.9 billion in 2005, compared to US$85.6 billion in 2000 and US$31.2 billion in 1990 (World Bank 2005b: 88). Remittances are not only a rapidly growing source of external finance, but they are generally continuous over the years and not prone to sudden reversals of direction (Ratha 2005). They tend to be countercyclical for crises in developing countries (i.e. migrants send more money home to support their families) and hence help to smoothen consumption volatility. However, the current financial and economic crisis engendered by the sub-prime mortgage crisis in the United States is leading to greater job losses than ever, in particular in industries such as construction that have a disproportionate share of migrant workers, and will have a negative impact on remittances. Although very large remittance flows can cause 'Dutch disease' problems, their overall economic impact is generally thought to be positive (Giuliano and Ruiz-Arranz 2005; World Bank 2005b: chapters 4 and 5). In particular, remittances can make a significant contribution to poverty reduction since they often directly benefit poorer households (Adams and Page 2005).

5.2 Financial globalization and labor

How does financial openness affect labor? There are several potential channels of influence. First is the potential effect of openness on growth. In addition to the potential direct positive effect of capital flows on growth (as countries gain additional resources that can be invested), there can also be an indirect negative effect on growth when financial liberalization forces countries to hold larger foreign reserves, which reduces consumption and/or investment and hence growth potential. If financial flows have, on balance, a positive impact on growth, this would be generally beneficial for labor, while slow growth is usually disadvantageous for labor. However, even in the case of fast or steady growth, the distributional impact of financial openness on different categories of labor needs to be taken into account. Labor might benefit less than necessary for long term institutional and human capital development and for growth of domestic consumption.

We then look into the effects of international financial flows on economic volatility, and their role in provoking financial crises. If financial crises become more frequent or more severe, their negative consequences for growth (both in the short and long run) could cancel out earlier benefits of financial openness or even lead to a net negative effect on growth. Moreover, financial crises can have impacts on labor that go over and above their general economic impact. Since, as indicted above, volatility and the frequency of financial crises have increased, we review their direct impact on employment. This is followed by a discussion of wage shares, and how they have evolved during crises, and a summary of the main findings.

5.2.1 Financial globalization, growth, and employment

Direct effects on growth

It has proven difficult to establish a robust causal relationship between financial openness and growth. A study by IMF researchers (Prasad *et al.* 2004) has confirmed the main findings of earlier studies, such as those undertaken in UNCTAD (2001), that find that growth depends more on the quality of domestic institutions and careful macro-economic management than on financial liberalization. Edison and others (2004) argue in the same direction and demonstrate that the findings of previous research (that found a positive association between capital account openness and growth) crucially depended on the country coverage, the choice of time periods, and the indicator for capital account openness. They also find evidence for a suggestion that was first made by Rodrik (1998),[8] namely that conventional indicators for capital account openness closely proxy the reputation of a country's government. If governance is controlled for, capital account openness has no significant effect on economic performance (Edison 2004: 243ff.). By contrast, Tornell *et al.* (2003) study a sub-set of countries with functioning financial markets (thus excluding the majority of developing countries) and argue that switching to a regime of de facto financial openness will ease credit constraints, which leads to higher growth but also increased risk of financial crises. By their account, the growth effect outweighs the cost of crises. This result runs counter to the findings presented by Lee and Jayadev (2005) who use a *de jure* measure of capital account liberalization (rather than a de facto measure that reflects the success in attracting inflows). For the period from 1973 to 1995 (i.e., even when excluding the negative impact of the East Asian crisis), they find no positive effect on growth rates and – contrary to mainstream economic theory – some indication that openness reduces the investment share in GDP.

The conflicting results could in part be caused by differences in country coverage, but also by differences between the indicators employed in the literature.

Prasad and others (2004) and Collins (2005) highlight the crucial difference between '*de jure*' or 'de facto' measures of financial openness. '*De jure*' openness includes abolishment or changes in rules and regulations concerning foreign capital, as it is often required as part of the conditionality for financial support by the international financial institutions. Many countries in Latin America fall under this category. By contrast, 'de facto' openness relates to increases in a financial openness indicator, irrespective of whether rules have changed or not (India, China, and some other Asian countries fall into this category). In the latter case, the causal relationship between financial openness and growth is more difficult to establish. Did openness lead to higher growth, or did higher growth induce financial flows and integration? Rodrik (2003) and Singh (2003) argue that the latter is the case especially for India and China where growth induced greater financial integration.

Another factor to explain the difference in results could be the different impact of financial openness across countries. Levine (1997) has argued that financial deepening, which often is undertaken in tandem with financial openness, may ease foreign exchange constraints and growth, but this conclusion depends strongly on the assumption of an efficient economy and of a two gap model, which is not always valid for developing countries. Edison *et al*. (2004) argue that capital account liberalization can be beneficial to middle-income countries under certain conditions, while low-income countries with a poor regulatory framework and weak institutions have little to gain. The importance of institutions and the policy framework as a precondition for capital account liberalizations is also pointed out by Gilbert *et al*. (2001). They conclude that '[b]y itself, capital account liberalisation will deliver relatively little' (ibid.: 121) while leaving poor countries more vulnerable to crisis. An even more pessimistic view emerges from the study by Lee and Jayadev (2005), who find that even when the most commonly mentioned preconditions are met, capital account liberalization has, overall, no positive effect on growth.

While the argument that the impact of financial flows depends on country characteristics is most frequently applied to portfolio equity and short-term debt flows, it has also been made for FDI. Ghose (2004) found that the effects of FDI on the host country crucially depended on country specific circumstances, in particular whether they met an unmet demand for investment finance (e.g. to build up export-oriented manufacturing industry). However, FDI does not always add to the productive capacity of the recipient country, but can also crowd out domestic investment when foreign entrepreneurs seize upon investment opportunities that would have otherwise been taken up by domestic enterprises (ibid.). A similar point is made by Hanson (2001), who argues that there 'is weak evidence that FDI generates positive spillovers for host economies'. Global financial liberalization encourages cross-border mergers and acquisitions, which implies often a greater informalization of the total labor force. Furthermore Tokman (2003) argues that the slow growth that has accompanied financial liberalization in Latin America has led to a greater informalization of the work force, persistent poverty, and greater inequality.

Indirect growth effects through increased reserve holdings

The repeated financial crises of recent years have led many developing countries to build up foreign reserves. For some countries these reserves were created by surplus on the current account, while others built up reserves through capital inflows which were not spent on foreign goods. As Feldstein (1999) argues, increasing international liquidity is an effective 'self-help' strategy in the absence of an international lender of last resort. However, while giving countries some protection against financial crises, holding large international reserves is also a costly strategy as foreign reserves are held in low interest bearing instruments such as US treasury bills, rather than earning much higher returns on the capital market or through investment into human or physical capital. Baker and Walentin (2001) estimate that the increased reserve level of the late 1990s compared to that common in the 1960s implies an annual cost of around 1 percent of GDP in most regions, and of between 1.2 and 2.5 percent in East Asia and the Pacific. This lower level of growth also led to lower levels of employment growth. They argue that the gains of trade liberalization in terms of higher GDP growth were actually 'eaten up' for most countries in the 1990s by the earnings forgone on higher reserve holdings (ibid.). In a more recent study, Rodrik (2006) estimates the cost of increased reserve holdings to be 1 percent of GDP on average for developing countries. While imposing costs on developing countries, increased reserve holdings are an indirect subsidy to the countries in whose currencies the reserves are held (see Stiglitz 2000).

The trend has accelerated in recent years to a somewhat alarming level (see Figure 5.3). Overall, reserves held by low- and middle-income countries were equal to 27.1 percent of their GNI in 2007, compared to 6.8 percent in the first half of the 1990s – a fourfold increase.[9] The increase took place in low- and middle-income developing countries alike, and across regions. Even a poor region like sub-Saharan Africa now holds foreign reserves equal to 17.9 percent of its GNI, more than three times the ratio in the early 1990s. The trend is particularly strong in South Asia, East Asia, and the Pacific. Even when China (the developing country with the largest foreign reserves) is excluded, there remains a substantial increase from an already high 15.0 percent of GNI (1990–94) to 27.6 percent in 2007 for the rest of the region (World Bank 2009b).

Part of the explanation for the accelerated build-up of international reserves is that developing countries, particularly those from Asia, accumulated reserves after the financial crises of the late 1990s to avoid dependence on the international financial institutions in times of future crises (see Bird and Mandilaras 2005). In a recent cross-country study, Aizenman and Lee (2006) find that changed risk perception after the Mexican and the East Asian crises (as proxied by dummy variables) and the degree of capital account openness are indeed the main factors behind the surge in reserve levels. By contrast, variables linked to export promotion regimes, such as a depreciated real exchange rate and high lagged export growth rates, had a small impact on reserve levels. The results also confirm that China is not an outlier with respect to the level of its international

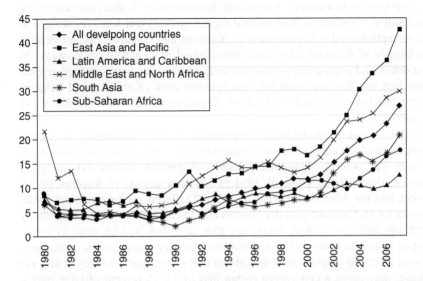

Figure 5.3 Reserve holdings by developing countries, 1970–2007 (in % of GNI) (source: World Bank (2009a) (May 2009); based on series 'International Reserves (US$)' and 'Gross National Income (US$)'.

reserves (ibid.: 3). This refutes arguments that attribute China's reserve levels to the country's exchange rate policies (see, e.g., Dooley *et al.* 2003; Goldstein 2004). As Prasad and Wei (2005) demonstrate, the recent steep rise in China's foreign reserves is mostly due to large non-FDI capital inflows.

5.2.2 Financial globalization, volatility, and crises

Financial liberalization in developing countries is associated with increased GDP volatility and higher consumption volatility (Kose *et al.* 2003; Prasad *et al.* 2004; Levchenko 2005). Kaminsky (2004) pointed out that the absence of sound financial regulation, both at the national and international levels, makes developing countries much more vulnerable to negative impacts of capital flows. When institutions with the ability to manage greater volatility are absent or not fully effective, the generally procyclical nature of international capital flows ('when it rains it pours' syndrome) adds to the effects of fiscal policies, and, to a certain extent, also macroeconomic policies, that tend to be procyclical in most developing countries. Such behavior deepens and prolongs a crisis.

Other research confirms that developing countries have indeed become more prone to both currency and banking crises after financial liberalization (see, e.g., Weller 2001; Tornell *et al.* 2003). Countries across East Asia and Latin America have suffered from such crises, with the Argentinean crisis of 2000/01 being a particularly sharp example. Russia and Turkey have also been severely affected.[10] When crises break out, they often cannot be sufficiently explained by any deterioration in a country's so-called 'fundamentals'. Rather, they can occur as a result of volatility in international capital markets that leads to changes in risk perceptions and risk averseness of investors and creditors. Second generation models of financial crises have investigated this channel of contagion in great detail, and argued that a crisis can spread from one country to another even when there are few economic linkages between them (Kaminsky and Reinhart 2000; van Rijckeghem and Weder 2001; Caramazza *et al.* 2004; Goldstein and Pauzner 2004).

Financial crises typically have a large impact on the real economy. In the five countries most affected by the East Asian crisis of 1997/98, GDP per capita fell between 2.6 percent (Philippines) and 14.8 percent (Indonesia). In Latin America, the Mexican crisis of 1994/95 led to a decline in incomes of 7.9 percent, and the Argentinean crisis of 2001/02 reduced the country's per capita incomes by 16.5 percent (van der Hoeven and Luebker 2006). A recent study by Hutchison and Noy (2006) documents that so-called 'sudden stop' crises (a reversal in capital flows and a simultaneous currency crisis) have a particularly harmful effect on output – over and above that of 'normal' currency crises. On average, they cause a cumulative output loss of 13–15 percent of GDP over a three-year period. One important factor behind this trajectory is the disarray financial crises often cause in the banking sector. Burdened with non-performing

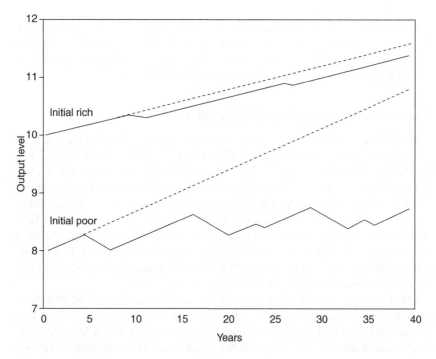

Figure 5.4 Typical growth path after a financial crisis in rich and poor countries (source: Cerra and Saxena (2005: 24)).

loans, the domestic banks fail to perform their function of providing credit at a time when it is most needed. An extreme case of a prolonged credit crunch is Mexico, where real credit continued falling until 2002 – eight years after the crisis of 1994 (see Tornell *et al.* 2003: 54ff.).

Financial crises can therefore have long-term implications, although there is some controversy about how big and permanent the costs of financial crises are. Tornell *et al.* (2003: 23) argue that crises 'are the price that has to be paid in order to attain faster growth', and that that it is possible for GDP growth to recover rapidly from a crisis (although this did not happen in Mexico, the case they study in detail). The view that crises pose only a temporary setback is challenged by Cerra and Saxena (2005), who deconstruct what they call the 'myth of recovery' by using panel data for broad datasets of countries. They document that recessions are typically not followed by high-growth recovery phases, either immediately following the trough, over several years of the subsequent expansion, or even over the complete subsequent expansion that follows a recession (Figure 5.4). When output drops, it tends to remain well below its previous trend. Cerra and Saxena also find that frequent crises and instabilities interfere with convergence between rich and poor countries:

> Countries that experience many negative shocks to output tend to get left behind and their long-term growth suffers. Thus, while standard growth theory may work well in explaining expansion, a fruitful direction for future research would be to explain the proclivity to wars, crises, and other negative shocks.
>
> (2005: 24)

This is related to the point Rodrik (2003) makes, namely that policies for stimulating growth are different from policies to sustain growth and that frequent crises require frequent policy regime switches.

5.2.3 Financial openness, crises, and employment

Financial crises are generally not only associated with an economic decline, but also with severe social costs. These are most prominently felt in terms of rising open unemployment, falling employment-to-population ratios, falling real wages, or a combination of the above (see, e.g., Lee 1998). Moreover, the social costs can usually be felt longer than the economic impact: even when GDP per capita has recovered to pre-crisis level, the other indicators usually lack behind. This pattern can be observed in a majority of countries that were most affected by the financial crises of the past decade. Mapping the observed trends against a counterfactual with limited financial openness and no financial crises would, from an analytical perspective, of course be the empirical strategy of choice. However, such a counterfactual is excessively difficult to construct.

Figure 5.5 demonstrates clearly the consequences of financial crises on employment. In all but one case (Argentina) the unemployment rate, even three

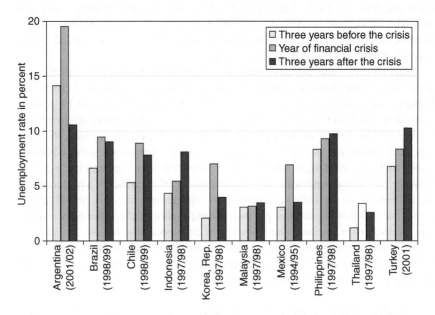

Figure 5.5 Unemployment rates before, during, and after financial crises (source: ILO (2007)).

Notes
* If a financial crisis extended into a second calendar year, the unemployment figure refers to the later year where the economic impact of the crises usually peaked.
The unemployment figures for Argentina refer to urban areas only; the pre-crisis unemployment rate for Indonesia refers to 1996.

years after the crisis, had not returned to its pre-crisis level. A higher post-crisis unemployment rate could be the consequence of sluggish growth after the crisis, but van der Hoeven and Lübker (2006), reviewing several crises in Latin America, East Asia, and in Turkey, demonstrate that in almost all cases GDP growth has picked up much faster than employment growth after the crisis. A return to pre-crisis GDP levels was not accompanied by a return to pre-crisis levels of unemployment, and unemployment often continued to rise even when growth had resumed. The worrying conclusion is that financial crises affect employment more than temporarily and may lead to unwarranted structural changes in the long-term creation of employment.

5.2.4 The impact on labor shares of financial globalization and financial crises

Contrary to the conventional wisdom that sees the labor share in GDP as relatively constant, research by Diwan (2001) and Harrison (2002) shows that the proportion of GDP that goes into wages and other labor income is variable over time. Using a data set from 1960 to 1997, Harrison (2002) splits her sample of over 100 countries into two even groups (based on GDP per capita in 1985). Her data show that, in the group of poorer countries, labor's share in national income fell on average by 0.1 percentage points per year from 1960 to 1993. The decline in the labor share accelerated after 1993, to an average decline of 0.3 percentage points per year. In the richer sub-group, the labor share grew by 0.2 percentage points prior to 1993, but then fell by 0.4 percentage points per year. These means indicate a trend reversal for the richer countries post-1993, and an acceleration of an already downward trend for the poorer sub-group.

Harrison (ibid.) tested for factors that could explain changes in labor shares, combining detailed national accounts data from the United Nations with measures of trade openness, capital account restrictions, and capital flows. Overall, the results suggest that changes in factor shares are primarily linked to changes in capital/labor ratios. However, measures of globalization (such as capital controls or direct investment flows) also play a role. Harrison found that exchange rate crises lead to declining labor shares, suggesting that labor pays a disproportionately high price when there are large swings in exchange rates (i.e., wages are more severely affected than GDP). Capital controls are associated with an increase in the labor share, an effect that Harrison attributes to the weaker bargaining position of capital vis-à-vis labor if the cost of relocating production increases with capital controls. Foreign investment inflows are also associated with a fall in the labor share. The weak bargaining position of labor under open capital accounts, where jobs can be exported, is also a causal mechanism explored by Lee and Jayadev (2005). They find that financial openness exerts a downward pressure on the labor share both in developed and developing countries for the period from 1973–95. The effect is independent of the negative impact of financial crises. Harrison also finds that increasing trade is associated with a fall in the labor share. This result is robust across specifications. These results point to a systematic negative relationship between various measures of globalization and the labor share.

Diwan (2001) reports, based on a large sample of countries, an average drop in the labor share of GDP per crisis of 5.0 percentage points, and a modest catch-up thereafter. In the three years after the crisis, labor shares were still 2.6 percentage points below their pre-crisis average. Given the fact that most countries have undergone more than one crisis, the cumulative drop in the wage share over the last 30 years is estimated at 4.1 percent of GDP, and is especially large for Latin America, where the figure reached 6.7 percent of GDP over the period from the 1970s to the 1990s.

The overall decline in the labor share is partly explained by what some call the ratchet effect: after an economic shock or a financial crisis the labor share in gross national income decreases (van der Hoeven and Saget 2004). In the 1980s, some authors argued that the decline in labor share after economic shocks was, in effect, the consequence of a too high labor share before the crisis, partly blaming labor for the build-up of the crisis. However, only in a minority of cases have financial crises been caused by bidding up wages and labor shares. In most cases, the crisis was caused by external events or rent-seeking behavior of capital owners. In a study of the manufacturing sector in a large sample of developing countries, Amsden and van der Hoeven (1996) argue that a decline in real wages and fall in wage share of value added in most non-Asian developing countries in the 1980s reflect a redistribution of income from labor to capital, as low wages were made to bear the burden of uncompetitive manufacturers.

5.2.5 The effects of financial globalization on labor: summary of main findings

On balance, the capital account liberalization that many developing countries embarked upon in the 1990s has delivered disappointing results.[11] The preceding discussion has shown that capital account liberalization fell not only far short of expectations, but did serious harm to some countries and had a disproportionately negative effect on labor. Six main conclusions emerge:

1   In the absence of adequate institutions, capital account liberalization has little direct benefit for growth. This is especially true for poor countries where the institutional gap is greatest, but also for middle-income countries where capital inflows were not used to fill unmet investment needs.
2   Even if capital account liberalization is managed prudently, it has cost to developing countries. In order to cushion the effects of sudden outflows, developing countries have sterilized inflows and built up large reserves. Since these are mainly held in low-yield treasury bonds issued by industrialized countries, the opportunity cost is large.
3   Capital account liberalization has left developing countries vulnerable to crisis. These are often not triggered by a deterioration of a country's fundamental economic status, but by forces in the international financial system. The output losses associated with such crises are large, and even a subsequent recovery is usually insufficient to bring a country back on to its old growth path.
4   The negative effects of financial crisis on the labor market can be detected in a number of indicators. Open formal unemployment typically rises substantially during a crisis, real wages often fall, underemployment rises, and workers shift from the formal sector to the informal economy and agriculture.
5   Labor markets typically lag the economic recovery by several years. Even when GDP per capita has reached its pre-crisis level, the consequences of the crisis are normally still evident in higher unemployment compared to pre-crisis levels. This lag means that labor pays a disproportionate cost.
6   Tracking the evolution of the labor share in national income also shows that financial openness and financial crises diminish labor's share. Financial openness is associated with stronger bargaining power for capital vis-à-vis labor. Financial crises have a negative and persistent effect on the share of labor compensation in GDP.

5.3 Financial globalization and employment: the need for greater policy coherence

The experience of recent decades makes clear that growth, employment, and income should be more explicitly taken into account in policies governing the financial system if economic and social goals are to be achieved. Adelman (2000) argues that it might be advisable to restore a global financial environment which carries some of the characteristics of the so-called Golden Age – steady development for developing countries, combined with high stable growth for industrialized countries – while maintaining some of the virtues of a more liberalized trading and investment climate (ibid.: 1058). In order for such a system to function more efficiently in terms of growth and employment, it must have three properties:

- *First, it should provide liquidity in the international system.* Liquidity is needed to respond to demands for foreign exchange and for foreign investment. In effect the downfall of the original Bretton Woods system was in part due to illiquidity of the system as a whole and the reliance on only one currency to provide liquidity.
- *Second, an international system should provide stability for global markets.* As indicated above the absence of stability during the last decade has caused severe damage to the growth potential of a number of developing countries.
- *Third, an international financial system should provide a large degree of policy autonomy for participating countries.* This is extremely important as countries not only have different factor endowments (capital, labor, and technology) but also different socio-economic systems. In order to find equilibrium between different policies to satisfy both economic and social demands, each country must be able to use the policy instruments and institutions best fitted to the country.

These three properties are not necessarily compatible with each other.[12] Policy coherence is therefore required at three different levels in order to achieve an international financial system that is more benign for labor markets in developing countries. These are policies in industrialized countries, the set of multilateral rules that has been developed since World War II, and policies in developing countries themselves.

5.3.1 Policies in industrialized countries

Policies in industrialized countries and their outcomes circumscribe the economic and social policies of developing countries. A useful list of relevant policy changes was compiled by the World Commission on the Social Dimensions of Globalization (WCSDG 2004). It called for more coherent economic policies between Europe, Japan, and the United States, whose uncoordinated fiscal, monetary, and foreign exchange policies have created a highly volatile and instable system which is not geared toward growth. A greater concern for growth and employment creation in general is called for from all industrialized countries. Japan and Europe should give greater importance to growth and employment in their fiscal and monetary policies. This would enable the United States to reduce its double deficit without serious repercussions for global growth. The effect of the deficit rules of the European Stability and Growth Pact (SGP) should be opened to public debate. As Annett and Jaeger (2004) argue, an ideal fiscal rule would combine medium-term fiscal discipline with short-term fiscal flexibility. Beetsma and Debrun (2005) present an argument in favor of increasing the pact's procedural flexibility to improve welfare. The developed countries also have a responsibility to provide development assistance and to stimulate other sources of finance to enhance growth of less developed countries and contribute to a more balanced international financial system.

5.3.2 Rules of the international system

Changes in policy goals and priorities should be embedded in multilateral rules and the international financial agencies. Specifically, capital account liberalization should depend on a country's circumstances, with national flexibility to achieve investment, growth, and employment goals while avoiding volatility. The international system should have a greater resort to emergency financing to reduce volatility and contagion, given the damaging and persistent effects of crises on growth and employment. Developing countries should be accorded a greater role in the international financial institutions (IFIs) and the system of debt reduction should be improved.

An important point in considering the rules of the international system and the policies applied by the IFIs is that the international financial landscape has changed considerably since the 1980s. One of the most salient points is that the continuous opening of trade and the application of fairly drastic adjustment and stabilization policies in the 1980s and 1990s have dampened worldwide inflationary tendencies (see Akyüz 2006). In some respect, inflation rates resemble those which were current during the decades of high growth and development in the 1950s through mid-1970s. A decade ago, many countries had inflation rates of 10 percent or higher, however today very few do.[13] The expansion of trade and downward pressure on prices makes it unlikely that inflation will return in the near future. Meanwhile, the heavy emphasis in monetary policy on price stability has not resulted in financial and macro-economic stability, because financial liberalization has led to increasingly sharp cycles and fluctuations in economic activity.

The focus of the international system should shift from concerns on price stability to concerns for asset stability. This would require first a greater surveillance by the IMF on asset instability and second a review of its approach to capital account liberalization, leading to an internationally accepted system of managed capital account liberalization. There are signs that the international policy agenda is shifting in this direction.[14]

5.3.3 Policies in developing countries

Changes in rules and policies at the international level and the current low level of inflation would allow developing countries to undertake more coherent policies in order to stimulate development, employment, and growth. A potentially effective set of policies would combine a flexible system of capital controls with a managed real effective exchange rate (Diwan 2001; Charlton and Stiglitz 2004; World Bank 2005a). The flexible system of capital controls would allow for more coherent national policies to be undertaken and reduce volatility which has serious consequences not only in terms of short-term welfare losses but also in terms of reduced growth potential.

The aim of a system of a managed real effective exchange rate is to keep the economy at high levels of capacity utilization and so aim for full employment.

Is a coherent approach of social and economic policies possible? There is a so-called 'policy trilemma' of international economic policies[15] which states that national policy cannot pursue the following three policies simultaneously: open capital account, fixed exchange rates, and independent monetary policy. The trilemma posits that only two out of these three policies can be combined. For example, under a system of an open capital account and fixed exchange rates, countries cannot pursue an independent monetary policy since interest rates are determined by world interest levels. Conversely, if countries need to undertake an independent monetary policy, they have either to revert to flexible exchange rates or opt for a closed capital account. However, some more recent research argues that the policy trilemma can be relaxed by avoiding corner solutions. This means to go beyond the traditional alternatives of fixed versus flexible exchange rates, or open versus closed capital accounts, to adopt intermediate options in these three policy domains – like a capital account management through the selective application of capital controls, or a managed real exchange rate (see Bradford 2004).[16]

Although capital controls have, much like any other policy instrument, not always been fully effective in reaching their stated objectives (see Ariyoshi *et al.* 2000), they have contributed to regaining greater policy autonomy in several cases. For example, controls imposed on inflows have helped to reduce their level and to change the composition of inflows toward longer maturities in Chile, hence increasing the autonomy of monetary policy (Gallego *et al.* 1999): an important side-effect is that the level of international reserves can be reduced when the amount of short-term liabilities falls, lowering the opportunity cost of reserve holdings. An important lesson is that controls need to have comprehensive coverage and be forcefully implemented to be effective (Ariyoshi *et al.* 2000: 17). The more controversial issue is controls on outflows, but Edison and Reinhart (2001) argue that such controls have enabled Malaysia to stabilize exchange rates and interest rates during the East Asian crisis and to gain more policy autonomy. Kaplan and Rodrik (2001) conclude that the Malaysian approach has led to a faster economic recovery and smaller declines in real wages and employment than if the country had adopted orthodox policies as advocated by the IMF at the time.[17]

How could a system of a managed real exchange rate, the second element mentioned earlier, affect employment? Rodrik (2003) and Frenkel (2004) provide three channels.

- It would allow for higher capacity utilization in times of unemployment, if applied in combination with the appropriate mix of macroeconomic and fiscal policies.
- It would also stimulate output growth and hence employment, if combined with appropriate industrial policies, as the experience in various Asian countries has shown (Amsden 2001).
- It could shift the sectoral composition of exports toward more labor intensive goods, and hence increase the employment elasticity of the economy as a whole.[18]

Employing a policy mix with intermediate options such as a managed capital account and a managed real exchange rate requires more fine-tuning and coherence in policies rather than relying on rule-of-thumb policy interventions. While this can help to avoid corner solutions, it necessitates national institutions with explicit mandates and capabilities to achieve this and an international setting with consultations and considerations of the global financial structure so as to avoid beggar thy neighbor policies.

Another possible, supplementary element to relax the policy trilemma would be to include one or two additional policy instruments to complement the fiscal and monetary tools (see also Tinbergen 1970 [1952]: 40f.). Bradford (2004) suggests, for example, social pacts or coordinated wage bargaining to hold down inflation and so to 'free up' fiscal, monetary, and exchange rate policies to aim at growth and employment creation. Also, a greater concern for inequity and a reduction of national inequalities could contribute to reducing inflationary pressure and could be added either as part of a social pact or as a stand-alone policy instrument (see van der Hoeven and Saget 2004). Hence by giving more prominence to social policies thereby reducing potential conflicts over resources, and thus reducing inflationary pressures, national policies can focus more on growth and employment creation.

5.4 The challenges of the 2008 financial crisis

To what extent is the analysis on financial openness during the period 1995–2007 relevant in the current context? We would argue not only that both the analysis and the policy recommendations are still relevant, but will even go further in arguing that the observations and suggestions regarding a three-pronged approach (changes in the North's policies for ample liquidity, changes in the international rules and regulations, as well as greater policy autonomy in developing countries to pursue growth and employment) have in fact gained in relevance over the last year. The initial optimistic view which prevailed in 2007 and early 2008 and which predicted that the strengths of many developing countries, especially India and China, would lead to a greater decoupling between the South and the North,[19] has been proven wrong. In fact, globalization has made economies in the North and the South more dependent on each other. The decline of demand in industrialized countries, as well as the decline in investment flows and migrant remittances, places a heavy adjustment burden on developing countries, with corresponding consequences for their growth prospects.

Reinhardt and Rogoff (2009) expect deceleration or decline in growth both in the North and the South to lead to rising unemployment with a longer duration than the deceleration or decline in GDP. Based on a sample of crises in the past they observe that, on average, a slump in employment lasts 4.8 years while the deceleration or decline in output growth lasts only 1.9 years. These observations by Reinhart and Rogoff are congruent with the observations we presented in Section 5.2.3. Their data also confirm the argument made in Section 5.2.2 (as depicted in Figure 5.4) that the decline in GDP during a crisis is larger for developing countries than for developed countries, as has been the case since World War II. At the time of writing, no data are available to verify whether the current crisis is similar to previous crises in that respect or whether this crisis is characterized by a larger percentage decline in output in industrialized than in developing countries, as was the case with the crisis in 1929. But even if this were the case, the effects on developing countries would still be severe and could have a more lasting impact.

Reports prepared for meetings of the G-20 in early 2009 emphasize that, with the expectation of falling revenues and a scarcity of affordably priced capital, protecting core social infrastructure spending will become more difficult (World Bank 2009b). This in itself is cause for concern, but what is even more worrying is that indicators for social advancements exhibit a similar ratchet effect as we observed in Section 5.3 for unemployment. For example, Arbache and Page (2007) argue that in Africa child mortality increases during growth decelerations, but hardly falls during growth accelerations. Further, primary school completion rates and life expectancy are substantially lower in countries experiencing growth decelerations.

Reports end 2009 point indeed to a deterioration in employment conditions both in developed countries and in developing countries. ILO (2009b) estimates that, even under rather optimistic assumptions, levels of employment in industrialized countries will not return to pre-crisis level before six years and that of developing countries before three years. But even worrying macro figures mask deterioration in labor conditions for those who work.

In industrialized countries many have remained in employment by working fewer hours, receiving lower wages. Also employment figures are flattered because many workers are discouraged and leave the labor force putting a greater strain on the social welfare and security system. Such options are often not available in developing countries, where workers join or remain active in informal activities. The ILO (ibid.) predicts that many will face increased informality for even over five years after the crisis.

The challenge for international and national policy makers to prioritize both economic and social policies while bearing in mind the distributional effect of the current crisis has, therefore, only become more pressing, as has the need for policy coherence. Fiscal stimuli and other measures to regulate growth patterns should therefore be aimed specifically at the key priorities of maintaining employment and investment in social infrastructure. If these are not protected, large parts of the developing world will find themselves even more disadvantaged after the crisis than they were before.

Notes

1 This chapter relies on 'Financial Openness and Employment: The Need for Coherent International and National Policies' Chapter 2 in Ocampo J.A. and Jomo K.S., 2007, *Towards Full and Decent Employment*, London, Zed Books. This current chapter however is based on a newer data set, which contains a more detailed country analysis and has a section on the financial and economic crises which hit the world in 2008.
2 Rolph van der Hoeven is from the ISS, The Hague, and Malte Lübker is with the Conditions of Work and Employment Programme, International Labour Office, Geneva. The views expressed in this chapter are those of the authors and do not necessarily reflect those of the ISS or the International Labour Office.
3 Financial openness is used here as an umbrella term that includes both financial integration and financial liberalization. Financial liberalization in turn incorporates the liberalization of the capital and financial account. Congruent with the literature, we henceforth use 'capital account liberalization' as shorthand for the liberalization of the capital and financial account (while acknowledging that, strictly speaking, the relaxation of rules that refer to direct investment and portfolio flows should be called 'financial account liberalization'); for the standard presentation of the Balance of Payments see IMF (2005). We also include other elements such as less or different supervision and regulation of the banking sector and often a liberalization of the foreign exchange rate regime.
4 International Labour Office, Geneva, ILO (2004: 7), and the ILO database, Laborsta (ILO, 2009a), EAPEP, Version 5.
5 UNCTAD data show that the FDI boom was in part driven by mergers and acquisitions (M&A). In 2007, the value of worldwide M&As was US$1,637 billion – some 21 percent higher than during its previous peak in 2000. This compares to global FDI inflows of US$1,833 billion in the same year. See UNCTAD, *World Investment Report 2008* (UNCTAD various years).
6 Official development assistance and official aid (ODA/OA) to all low- and middle-income countries actually declined through most of the 1990s, falling from current US$63.7 billion in 1991 to a low of US$51.7 billion in 1997. The recovery thereafter brought it back to US$64.7 billion in 2002 and to US$105.1 billion in 2007. However, the increase is far smaller when adjusted for inflation. While it amounted to 1.7 percent of GNI in recipient countries in 1991, the ratio fell to 0.7 percent in 2007. See World Bank (2009c); based on series 'Official development assistance and official aid (current US$)' and 'Aid (% of GNI)'.
7 See the classification in IMF (1993) and the technical discussion in World Bank (2005b: 105ff.).
8 The authors note that much of their analysis focuses on de facto rather than on *de jure* globalization as capital controls come in so many flavors and enforcement varies widely among countries.
9 By contrast, foreign reserves have remained at under 5 percent of GDP in industrialized countries (Rodrik 2006: 15).
10 For a comprehensive overview see Capario and Klingebiel (2003).

11 This disappointment is well summarized in a World Bank report that reviews the growth performance of the 1990s:

> Contrary to expectations, financial liberalization did not add much to growth, and it appears to have augmented the number of crises. As expected, deposits and capital inflows rose sharply as a result of liberalization. But, other than in a few East Asian and South Asian countries, capital markets did not provide resources for new firms. Numbers of stock market listings declined, even in the newly created markets in the transition countries that were sometimes used for privatizations. Also, although relevant time-series data on access are weak, and contrary to expectations, it appears that access to financial services did not improve substantially after liberalization.
>
> (2005a: 21)

12 Tinbergen's rule that the number of policy instruments must at least be equal to the number of policy targets remains relevant (see Tinbergen 1970 [1952]).

13 In 2001 and 2002, roughly 80 percent of the *c*.180 countries with available data had inflation rates below 10 percent, compared to less than 50 percent of all countries during most of the mid to late 1970s and early 1980s. Current conditions are not too dissimilar from the 1960s. Back then, 85 to 90 percent of the *c*.160 100 to 120 countries with available data had inflation rates below 10 percent (see World Bank 2009c).

14 See for example World Bank (2005a) and a report from the IMF's Independent Evaluation Unit (2005). Also the deliberations after the G-20 Summit in London, March 2009, are expected to lead to substantial review of IMF monitoring role.

15 For further discussions see Mundell (1963); Cohen (1993); Obstfeld *et al.* (2004).

16 For example, in the case of China, research from the IMF argues that making the quasi-fixed exchange rate more flexible would allow the country to pursue a more independent monetary policy. The same paper also argues for a cautious approach to capital account liberalization, given institutional weaknesses of China's financial system (see Prasad *et al.* 2005).

17 For a detailed review of the Malaysian experience see Jomo (2005). For a comprehensive discussion of the management of capital flows in developing countries and policy conclusions see UNCTAD (2003).

18 This is a comparative static argument comparing two equilibria under different policy regimes. This is independent of a secular decline of employment elasticity, which various observers have been discussing.

19 See for example the discussion in IMF (2008: 1).

References

Adams, R. and J. Page (2005) 'Do international migration and remittances reduce poverty in developing countries?' *World Development* 33: 1645–69.

Adelman, I. (2000) 'Editor's introduction (Special section: Redrafting the architecture of the global financial system', *World Development* 28: 1053–60.

Aizenman, J. and J. Lee (2006) 'International reserves: Precautionary versus mercantilist views, theory and evidence', Washington, DC: National Bureau of Economic Research (mimeo).

Akyüz, Y. (2006) 'Issues in macro-economic and financial policies, stability and growth', Policy Integration Department Working Paper 73, Geneva: International Labour Office.

Amsden, A. (2001) *The Rise of the Rest: Challenges to the West from the Late-Industrializing Economies*, Oxford: Oxford University Press.

Amsden, A. and R. van den Hoeven (1996) 'Manufacturing output, employment and real wages in the 1980s: Labour's loss until century's end', *Journal of Development Studies* 32: 506–30.

Annett, A. and A. Jaeger (2004) 'Europe's quest for fiscal discipline', *Finance and Development* June: 22–5.

Arbache, J. and J. Page (2007) 'More growth and fewer collapses? A new look at long run growth in Africa', World Bank Policy Research Paper 4384, Washington, DC: World Bank.

Ariyoshi, A., K. Habermeier, B. Laurens, I. Ötker, J.I.C. Kriljenko, and A. Kirilenko (2000) 'Capital controls: Country experiences with their use and liberalization', IMF occasional paper 190, Washington, DC: International Monetary Fund.

Baker, D. and K. Walentin (2001) 'Money for nothing: The increasing cost of foreign reserve holdings to developing nations', CEPR policy paper, Washington, DC: Center for Economic and Policy Research.

Beetsma, R. and X. Debrun (2005) 'Implementing the stability and growth pact: Enforcement and procedural flexibility', IMF Working Paper 05/59, Washington, DC: International Monetary Fund.

Bird, G. and A. Mandilaras (2005) 'Reserve accumulation in Asia: Lessons for holistic reform of the international monetary system', *World Economics* 6: 85–99.

Bradford, C., Jr (2004) 'Prioritizing economic growth: Enhancing macroeconomic policy choice', Paper presented at the XIX G24 Technical Group Meeting, September 27–28, Washington, DC, Intergovernmental Group of Twenty-Four.

Capario, G. and D. Klingebiel (2003) 'Episodes of systemic and borderline financial crises', Washington, DC: World Bank (mimeo).

Caramazza, F., L. Ricci, and R. Salgado (2004) 'International financial contagion in currency crises', *Journal of International Money and Finance* 23: 51–70.

Cerra, V. and S. Saxena (2005) 'Growth dynamics: The myth of economic recovery', IMF working paper 05/147, Washington, DC: International Monetary Fund.

Charlton, A. and J. Stiglitz (2004) 'A development round of trade negotiations?' in F. Bourguignon and B. Pleskovic (eds) *Proceedings from the Annual Bank Conference on Development Economics*, Washington, DC: World Bank.

Cohen, B. (1993) 'The triad and the unholy trinity: Lessons for the Pacific region', in I. Higgott, R. Leaver, and J. Ravenhill (eds) *Pacific Economic Relations in the 1990s*, London: Allen and Unwin.

Collins, S. (2005) 'Comments on financial globalization, growth and volatility in developing countries by Eswar Prasad, Kenneth Rogoff, Shang-Jin Wei, and M. Ayhan Kose', Cambridge, MA: National Bureau of Economic Research (mimeo).

Diwan, I. (1999) 'Labor shares and financial crises', Washington, DC: World Bank (mimeo).

Diwan, I. (2001) 'Debt as sweat: Labour, financial crisis, and the globalization of capital. Draft as of July 2001', Washington, DC: World Bank (mimeo).

Dooley, M.P., D. Folkerts-Landau, and P. Gaber (2003) 'An essay on the revived Bretton Woods System', NBER Working Paper 9971, Cambridge, MA: National Bureau of Economic Research.

Easterly, W., R. Islam, and J. Stiglitz (2001) 'Shaken and stirred: Volatility and macroeconomic paradigms for rich and poor countries', in B. Preskovic and N. Stern (eds) *Annual Bank Conference on Development Economics 2000*, Washington, DC: World Bank.

Edison, H., M. Klein, L. Ricci, and T. Sløk (2004) 'Capital account liberalization and economic performance: Survey and synthesis', *IMF Staff Papers* 51: 220–56.

Edison, H. and C. Reinhart (2001) 'Stopping hot money', *Journal of Development Economics*, 66: 533–53.

Feldstein, M. (1999) 'A self help guide for emerging markets', *Foreign Affairs* 6: 93–101.

Freeman, R. (2003) 'Responding to economic crisis in a post-Washington Consensus world: The role of labor', Paper presented at the ILO Meeting on Cooperation for Argentina, January 13–17, revised May 2003, Buenos Aires: International Labour Office (mimeo).

Frenkel, R. (2004) 'Real exchange rate and employment in Argentina, Brazil, Chile and Mexico', Paper presented at the XIX G24 Technical Group Meeting, September 27–28, Washington, DC: Intergovernmental Group of Twenty-Four.

Gallego, F., L. Hernández, and K. Schmidt-Hebbel (1999) 'Capital controls in Chile: Effective? Efficient?' Central Bank of Chile Working Paper, 59, Santiago de Chile: Central Bank of Chile.

Ghose, A. (2004) 'Capital flows and investment in developing countries', Employment Strategy Paper 2004/11, Geneva: International Labour Office.

Gilbert, C., G. Irwin, and D. Vines (2001) 'Capital account convertibility, poor developing countries, and international financial architecture', *Development Policy Review* 19: 121–41.

Giuliano, P. and M. Ruiz-Arranz (2005) 'Remittances, financial development, and growth', IMF Working Paper 05/234, Washington, DC: International Monetary Fund.

Goldstein, I. and A. Pauzner (2004) 'Contagion of self-fulfilling financial crises due to diversification of investment portfolios', *Journal of Economic Theory* 119: 151–83.

Goldstein, M. (2004) 'Adjusting China's exchange rate policy', Paper presented at the IMF seminar on China's Foreign Exchange System, May 26–27, Dalian.

Hanson, G. (2001) 'Should countries promote foreign direct investment?' G-24 discussion paper no. 9, New York and Geneva: United Nations Conference on Trade and Development.

Harrison, A. (2002) 'Has globalization eroded labor's share? Some cross country evidence', Cambridge, MA: National Bureau of Economic Research (mimeo).

Hutchison, M. and I. Noy (2006) 'Sudden stops and the Mexican wave: Currency crises, capital flow reversals and output loss in emerging markets', *Journal of Development Economics* 79: 225–48.

ILO (2004) 'Towards a fair deal for migrant workers', International Labour Conference, 92nd Session 2004, Report VI, Geneva: International Labour Office.

ILO (2007) 'Key Indicators of the Labour Market', 5th edn, Geneva: International Labour Office.

ILO (2009a) 'ILO database Laborsta, EAPEP (Version 5)', Geneva: International Labour Office.

ILO (2009b) 'World of Work report 2009: The Global Jobs Crisis and Beyond', International Institute of Labour Studies, Geneva: International Labour Office.

IMF (1993) 'Balance of payments manual, 5th edition'. Washington, DC: International Monetary Fund.

IMF (2008) 'World economic outlook 2008', Washington, DC: International Monetary Fund.

IMF Independent Evaluation Office (2005) 'The IMF's approach to capital account liberalization', Washington, DC: International Monetary Fund.

Jomo, K. (2005) 'Malaysia's September 1998 controls: Background, context, impacts, comparisons, implications, lessons', G-24 Discussion Paper Series 36, Geneva and New York: United Nations.

Kaminsky, G., C. Reinhart, and C. Végh (2004) 'When it rains, it pours: Procyclical capital flows and macro economic policies', NBER Working Paper 10780, Cambridge, MA: National Bureau of Economic Research.

Kaminsky, G.L. and C.M. Reinhart (2000) 'On crises, contagion, and confusion', *Journal of International Economics* 51: 145–68.

Kaplan, E. and D. Rodrik (2001) 'Did the Malaysian capital controls work?' NBER Working Paper 8142, Cambridge, MA: National Bureau of Economic Research.

Kose, A., E. Prasad, and M. Terrones (2003) 'Financial integration and macroeconomic volatility', *IMF Staff Papers* 50: 119–42.

Lee, E. (1998) 'The Asian financial crisis: The challenge for social policy', Geneva: International Labour Office.

Lee, K. and A. Jayadev (2005) 'Capital account liberalization, growth and the labor share of income: Reviewing and extending the cross-country evidence', in G. Epstein (ed.) *Capital Flight and Capital Controls in Developing Countries*, Cheltenham: Edward Elgar.

Levchenko, A. (2005) 'Financial liberalization and consumption volatility in developing countries', *IMF Staff Papers* 52: 237–59.

Levine, R. (1997) 'Financial development and economic growth: Views and agenda', *Journal of Economic Literature* 53: 688–726.

Mundell, R.A. (1963) 'Capital mobility and stabilization policy under fixed and flexible exchange rates', *Canadian Journal of Economics and Political Science* 29: 475–85.

Obstfeld, M., J. Shambaugh, and A. Taylor (2004) 'The trilemma in history: Tradeoffs among exchange rates, monetary policies, and capital mobility', NBER Working Paper 10396, Cambridge, MA: National Bureau of Economic Research.

Prasad, E. and S.-J. Wei (2005) 'The Chinese approach to capital inflows: Patterns and possible explanations', IMF Working Paper, Washington, DC: International Monetary Fund.

Prasad, E., T. Rumbaugh, and W. Qing (2005) 'Putting the cart before the horse? Capital account liberalization and exchange rate flexibility in China', IMF Policy Discussion Paper 05/1, Washington, DC: International Monetary Fund.

Prasad, E., K. Rogoff, W. Shang-Jin, and A. Kose (2003) 'Effects of financial globalization on developing countries: Some empirical evidence', Washington, DC, International Monetary Fund (mimeo).

Prasad, E., K. Rogoff, W. Shang-Jin, and A. Kose (2004) 'Financial globalization, growth and volatility in developing countries', NBER Working Paper 10942, Cambridge, MA: National Bureau of Economic Research.

Ratha, D. (2005) 'Workers' remittances: An important and stable source of external development finance', in S.M. Maimbo and D. Ratha (eds) *Remittances: Development Impact and Future Prospects*, Washington, DC: World Bank.

Reinhart, C. and K. Rogoff (2009) 'The aftermath of financial crises', NBER Working Paper 14656, Cambridge, MA: National Bureau of Economic Research.

Rodrik, D. (1998) 'Who needs capital-account convertibility?' *Princeton Essays in International Finance* 207: 55–65.

Rodrik, D. (2003) 'Growth strategies', NBER Working Paper 10050, Cambridge, MA: National Bureau of Economic Research.

Rodrik, D. (2006) 'The social cost of foreign exchange reserves', NBER Working Paper 11952, Cambridge, MA: National Bureau of Economic Research.

Singh, A. (2003) 'Capital account liberalization, free long-term capital flows, financial crisis and development', *Eastern Economic Journal* 29: 191–216.

Stiglitz, J. (2000) 'Capital market liberalization, economic growth, and instability', *World Development* 28: 1075–86.

Tinbergen, J. (1970 [1952]) *On the Theory of Economic Policy*, Amsterdam: North-Holland.

Tokman, V. (2003) 'Towards an integrated vision for dealing with instability and risk', *CEPAL Review* 81: 79–98.

Tornell, A., F. Westermann, and L. Martínez (2003) 'Liberalization, growth, and financial crises: Lessons from Mexico and the developing world', *Brookings Papers on Economic Activity* 2: 1–88.

UNCTAD (2001) 'Trade and development report 2001', Geneva and New York: United Nations Conference on Trade and Development.

UNCTAD (2003) 'Management of capital flows: Comparative experiences and implications for Africa', Geneva and New York: United Nations Conference on Trade and Development.

UNCTAD (2009) 'Handbook of statistics 2008' (online version), Geneva and New York: United Nations Conference on Trade and Development.

UNCTAD (various years) 'World investment report', Geneva and New York: United Nations Conference on Trade and Development.

van der Hoeven, R. and C. Saget (2004) 'Labour market institutions and income inequality: What are the new insights after the Washington Consensus?' in G.A. Cornia (ed.) *Inequality, Growth, and Poverty in an Era of Liberalization and Globalization (WIDER Studies in Development Economics)*, Oxford: Oxford University Press.

van der Hoeven, R. and M. Lübker (2006) 'Financial openness and employment: The need for coherent international and national policies', Working Paper No. 75, Policy Integration Department, Geneva: ILO.

van Rijckeghem, C. and B. Weder (2001) 'Sources of contagion: Is it finance or trade?' *Journal of International Economics* 54: 293–308.

WCSDG (2004) 'A fair globalization: Creating opportunities for all', World Commission on the Social Dimension of Globalization, Geneva: International Labour Office.

Weller, C. (2001) 'Financial crises after financial liberalisation: Exceptional circumstances or structural weakness?' *Journal of Development Studies* 38: 98–127.

World Bank (2005a) *Economic Growth in the 1990s: Learning from a Decade of Economic Reform*, Washington, DC: World Bank.

World Bank (2005b) *Global Economic Prospects 2006: Economic Implications of Remittances and Migration*, Washington, DC: World Bank.

World Bank (2009a) 'Global development finance, online database', Washington, DC: World Bank.

World Bank (2009b) *Swimming against the Tide: How Developing Countries are Coping with the Global Crisis*, Washington, DC: World Bank.

World Bank (2009c) 'World development indicators, online database' (CD-Rom), Washington, DC: World Bank.

Part II

Engines of growth in the South

6 The asymmetry of North–South Regional Trade Agreements

Parthapratim Pal[1]

6.1 Introduction

One of the most striking developments in the world trading system since the mid 1990s is a surge in Regional Trade Agreements (RTAs).[2] The number of RTAs notified to the World Trade Organization (WTO) increased from about 50 in 1990 to cross 250 in 2003. According to the latest data (till 1 July 2010) of the WTO, more than 450 RTAs have been notified to WTO. Among these RTAs, more than 250 are currently active. The World Bank (2005) estimated that about 40 percent of total global trade is done among regional trading partners. Given the rise in the number of active RTAs, this number is likely to have increased in the last few years.

Initially the WTO encouraged the growth of RTAs because it believed that regional integration initiatives can complement the multilateral trade regime. The idea was that RTAs can promote further trade liberalization and act as 'building blocks' to the multilateral trade system. However, as the number and spread of RTAs surged, the WTO increasingly became more concerned about the possible negative effects of the RTAs on the multilateral trade regime. There are two possible reasons why the proliferation of RTAs can create problems for the WTO. First, RTAs represent an important exception to WTO's principle of non-discrimination (i.e., the 'Most Favoured Nation' clause). According to the WTO rules, countries within an RTA (or, in other words, members of an RTA) can trade among themselves using preferential tariffs and easier market access conditions than what is applicable to other WTO member countries. As a result, WTO member countries that are not members of the RTA lose out in these markets. Second, trading within the regional trade blocs does not come under the purview of the WTO. As an increasing amount of global trade is being diverted through this route, there is a growing apprehension that RTAs might undermine the role of the WTO in the global trading system. In a speech, the Director General of the WTO has mentioned that the continued proliferation of regional trade agreements is indeed 'breeding concern' for the WTO.[3]

It is notable that this surge in RTAs is largely driven by developed countries. Since the failure of the Seattle Ministerial of WTO in 1999, the European Union and some developed countries, notably the USA, have initiated negotiations on a large number of bilateral and regional Trade Agreements. Traditionally developed countries have always been big markets for exports from developing countries and the prospect of preferential access to such markets have induced many developing countries to seek Preferential or Free Trade Agreements (PTA/ FTA) with developed countries. The motivation to go for a PTA with a developed country becomes particularly strong for a developing country if other countries, with which it is competing to supply goods to the developed market, are preferential trade partners of the developed country. In such cases the motivation comes from a defensive necessity against a possible exclusion from these markets. But preferential market access comes at a cost. As a quid pro quo, developing countries are expected to accept certain commitments to make the trade agreement attractive to the developed country partner. There are apprehensions that these commitments may reduce the policy space available to developing countries.

Therefore, from the point of view of a developing country, the tradeoff is essentially between possible better market access in developed countries vis-à-vis accepting stricter rules imposed by the developed country partner. As there is such a huge increase in the number of North–South RTAs[4] it tends to indicate that developing countries feel that overall North–South RTAs will be beneficial, as costs arising from new commitments will be more than offset by increased trade and market access in the developed country markets. As market access plays such an important role in the formation of RTAs, it is important to investigate whether North–South RTAs have indeed given developing countries increased market share in the developed country markets. Using data from a number of North–South RTAs, this chapter seeks to find out whether there is any clear pattern between the signing of RTAs and an increase in market share in developed countries. This chapter also analyzes the possible factors which can prevent a developing country from gaining market access in a developed country even when they are part of a PTA.

6.2 Why this sudden proliferation of RTAs?

The traditional theory of gains from trade suggests that removal of trade barriers allows consumers and producers to purchase from the cheapest and most competitive source of supply. This enhances efficiency and increases welfare. Following this logic, it was traditionally believed that regional trade blocs should generate gains from trade as member countries reduce trade barriers among themselves.

This view was first challenged by Viner in his book entitled *The Customs Union Issue* (1950). Viner, in his seminal contribution, introduced the concepts of 'trade creation' and 'trade diversion' and showed that the net effect of trade liberalization on a regional basis is not unambiguously positive. Viner pointed out that RTAs can lead to trade creation if, due to the formation of the regional agreement, RTA members switch from inefficient domestic producers and import more from efficient producers from other members of the RTA. In this case, efficiency gains arise from both production efficiency and consumption efficiency. On the other hand, trade diversion takes place if, because of the RTA, members switch imports from low-cost production in the rest of the world and import more from higher-cost producers in the partner countries. Trade diversion lowers welfare of not only the partner countries but the rest of the world also.[5]

Viner's analysis shows that trade creation and trade diversion have opposite welfare implications and the net effect will depend upon which of these two effects dominate. However, he did not unequivocally establish the net welfare effect of RTAs. In the last 50 years, in spite of various enhancements to the basic concepts of trade creation and trade diversion, economists cannot tell, on an a priori basis, which of the two effects will dominate.

Since the late 1960s, recognition of market imperfection in international trade has added a new dimension to this literature. The introduction of imperfect competition in trade models altered the perception of gains from trade and hence about the motivation behind regionalism. The traditional trade theory has always assumed perfect competition and full employment while discussing various aspects of trade theories. However, the traditional theories were finding it difficult to explain the trade patterns of the post World War period, which were characterized by intra-industry trade and trade among countries with similar factor endowments. To explain this phenomenon, a new class of trade models emerged. These models challenged the concept of perfect competition inherent in the classical trade models and introduced imperfect market structures like monopoly, monopolistic competition or oligopoly in trade models. Pioneering work in this field has been done by Brander (1981), Brander and Spencer (1984), Dixit (1984) and Krugman (1980).[6] Introduction of imperfect competition in trade theory changed the predictions of traditional trade theories completely. Some results that came out of these models have profound implications for the present topic. Using monopolistic competition and oligopoly models, this new generation trade models were able to explain why and how countries with very similar economies can gain from mutual trade of similar products (intra-industry trade). Taking a cue from these models, it is easy to establish that if economies of scale exist in the industries of the preferential trading partners, then these countries can benefit from trading with each other. This happens because the industries of member countries can take advantage of their scale economies by exploiting the larger union-wide markets. However, once imperfect competition and scale economies are simultaneously introduced in these multi-country preferential trade models, they get very complex and the welfare impact of PTAs becomes more ambiguous.

But this strand of theoretical analyses of RTAs does not fully explain why there has been a sudden increase in regionalism during the 1990s. There is an emerging consensus among economists that frustration with the multilateral trading system is one of the prime reasons behind the current growth of regionalism. In 1993, answering a question about 'what are the problems of the GATT that lead countries to turn to their neighborhood', Krugman (1993) suggests that countries find regionalism an easier alternative because large numbers of participants in multilateral trade negotiations reduce the cost of non-cooperation and creates rigidity in the system. Also according to him, modern trade barriers are much more complicated to negotiate in a multilateral forum and most countries find it easier to deal with these issues on a bilateral or regional level.

There is another set of studies which suggests that, in a multilateral framework, countries tend to favor preferential agreements against multilateral ones because of some strategic reasons. For example, Limão (2003) suggests that developing countries may resist a multilateral system in fear of erosion of their preferential treatments in regional agreements with developed countries. Similarly, industrial countries can have a strategic incentive in keeping their multilateral tariff level at a higher level than they otherwise would so that they can have more bargaining power when negotiating market access at the bilateral/regional level. On the other hand, Mansfield and Reinhardt (2003) argue that multilateral trade negotiations, in fact, motivate countries to conclude RTAs. This is so because as WTO membership expands, individual countries' ability to influence the content and pace of MFN liberalization reduces and the large membership makes it difficult for countries to have a coordinated strategy. As formation of regional blocs lead to increased negotiating power at the multilateral level, countries want to become a part of a regional grouping to increase their leverage in the multilateral negotiations.

However, it appears that the surge in regionalism during the WTO years has been largely driven by a handful of developed countries. Many economists including Bhagwati (1993), Panagariya (1996) and Bergsten (1996) believe that the USA's transformation from a supporter of multilateralism to a follower of regionalism is the major reason behind this growth of regionalism since the 1990s. According to Bhagwati, 'the main driving force for regionalism today is the conversion of the United States, hitherto an abstaining party to Article XXIV' (Bhagwati 1993: 29).

To support this hypothesis, it is pointed out that as some big developed countries are getting involved in Free Trade Agreements (FTAs) with developing countries on a bilateral or regional level, this has prompted many developing countries to seek participation in FTAs with these countries as a defensive necessity against a possible exclusion from these markets. The motivation to go for an FTA with a developed country will be particularly strong for a developing country if other countries, with which it is competing to supply goods to the developed market, are part of a PTA with the developed country. This leads to a configuration which is known as the 'hubs and spokes' configuration of RTAs. A hub is defined as a country which is a member of two or more distinct RTAs. Spokes arise when a hub country forms a bilateral RTA with another country. Alternatively, a spoke can also be formed when a hub country establishes an RTA with another trading bloc (see Figure 6.1 for an illustration of its working).

From Figure 6.1, it can be seen that the hub enjoys access to all its spokes on a preferential basis. As most hubs are developed countries, most gains of PTAs have gone to them. On the other hand, each spoke enjoys preferential access

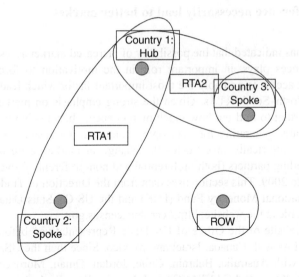

Figure 6.1 Hubs and spokes in international trade.

only to the hub. Therefore, spokes have less market access than the hub. Or, in other words, a hub enjoys preferential access to all its spokes but a spoke has preferential access only to its hub. A spoke country tries to avoid this problem by becoming a hub in its own right by entering into its own set of RTAs. This has led to the acceleration in bilateral agreements at the present time. Moreover, if some countries cannot form an FTA with a developed country, they attempt to create their own market by joining an RTA among excluded members. This creates a bandwagon effect where no countries want to be left out of some major regional groupings. It is also notable that the Rest of the World (ROW) is left out of this set of preferential agreements and loses out in the markets in hubs and spokes.[7]

Along with economic factors, political and strategic factors also motivate countries to join RTAs. Trade linkages between economies can increase the cost of conflict and improve cross-border cooperation. Due to this reason, RTAs are used as a strategic move to consolidate peace and increase regional security among member countries. RTAs are often used by developed countries to forge geopolitical alliances and build up diplomatic ties. By providing increased discriminatory access to a larger market, these countries seek to garner increased support on the political front. It is apparent that most political RTAs are not driven by economics, however, in the political RTA arrangements, particularly where a large developed country is involved, there is always the possibility that the interests of smaller countries would be of secondary concern.

6.3 Does tariff preference necessarily lead to better market access?[8]

The previous section has indicated that the possibility of increased market access through tariff preferences plays an important role in the motivation to form RTAs. In fact, market access is probably the most important factor which leads to the formation of North–South RTAs. Given the strong emphasis on market access, it deems important to find out how much market access benefits North–South RTAs are actually generating for developing countries. To answer this question, this chapter empirically investigates the change in market share of some of the USA's trading partners (both preferential and non-preferential) over the period from 1990 to 2009. This section uses data from the Direction of Trade Statistics of the International Monetary Fund (IMF) and the US CenStats Databases, which are available at the website: http://censtats.census.gov.

According to the website of the Office of US Trade Representative,[9] before 2000, the USA had RTAs with Canada, Israel and Mexico. Since then the USA has negotiated RTAs with Australia, Bahrain, Chile, Jordan, Oman, Morocco, Singapore, Peru, South Korea and CAFTA (Central America Free Trade Agreement). In certain cases like the South Korea–US and the CAFTA–US FTAs, negotiations have been completed. However, legislative ratifications for these agreements are still pending.

The USA is also negotiating FTAs with a number of countries including Malaysia, Panama, Thailand, UAE, Colombia and Ecuador (part of ANDEAN). There are some regional initiatives as well which include the talks on Free Trade Area of Americas (FTAA) and the US–ASEAN proposed FTA.

To investigate whether the signing of an FTA with the USA necessarily leads to increased market access in the USA, we look at the market shares of traditional and the new trading partners. For the sake of comparison we compare their performance with a couple of other countries that are not yet preferential trade partners of the USA.

To see how these countries have fared in the US market, we divide the countries in three groups. The first group (Group 1) consists of the traditional preferential trading partners of USA. They are Mexico, Canada and Israel. In the second group (Group 2) we placed a set of countries that are the new preferential trading partners of USA. These include Australia, Singapore, Chile, Peru, Jordan, Oman, Morocco and Bahrain. In Group 3, there are five countries, Brazil, China, India, Malaysia and Thailand. These countries are not yet a member of a PTA with the USA, although Malaysia and Thailand are negotiating a PTA with the USA.[10]

From the market share data of these three groups of countries, the following observations can be made.

For Group 1 countries, it is notable that their market share in the USA increased during the first half of the 1990s and has stagnated or declined since 2000. For Mexico this increase in market share is pronounced during the 1990s. For Canada, it grew till 1995. It is notable that the NAFTA came into force during this period in which both Canada and Mexico are the preferential trading partners of the USA. However, since 2000/2001 these two countries have not gained market share in the USA. In fact Canada's share in the US market has declined from around 19 percent in 2001 to around 14 percent in 2009. Mexico also has not managed to increase its market share by much; the market share of Mexico has remained stagnant during the last decade (Figure 6.2).

The US–Israel FTA was signed in 1985 and following the same trend as above, Israel gained some market share during the early to mid 1990s, but the growth in market share has stopped and Israel's market share in USA has stabilized around the 1 percent mark since 2000.

In all the three cases, there was an initial increase in market share after the PTA/FTA was signed but the growth in market share was not sustained. In fact, over the years these countries lost some of their share of the US market to others.

For the Group 2 countries, i.e., the countries that signed an FTA with the USA after 2000, the data show a more mixed picture. Two of the most high profile free trade partners of the USA, i.e. Singapore and Australia, face declining market shares in the USA even after signing FTAs with the US in 2003 and 2004 respectively. However, from Figure 6.3, it does not appear that these FTAs have helped these countries to improve the size of their market share in the USA.

The situation looks somewhat better for the new preferential trade partners from South America. Both Chile and Peru seem to be gaining market share in the US market. To understand whether these gains are due to the preference margins, this chapter looked into the export pattern of these countries to the USA. This analysis shows that both Chile and Peru are large exporters of metal

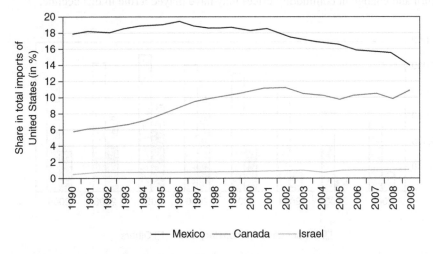

Figure 6.2 Market share of the three traditional preferential trade partners of the USA (source: Direction of Trade Statistics, IMF).

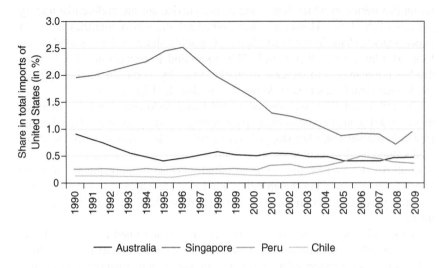

Figure 6.3 USA market share of new preferential trading partners of the USA (source: Direction of Trade Statistics, IMF, accessed July 2010).

products to the USA and that they have significantly benefited from increasing metal and commodity prices. For example, copper and copper products made up a very high proportion of Chile's exports to the USA, and there has been a significant growth in exports of this commodity to the USA (Figure 6.4). For example, in 2002, Chile's exports of these products to the USA were about US$723 million. In 2006, the figure has swollen to more than US$4000 million. After that year, exports of copper products have come down. The global downturn and change in commodity prices may have played a role in this decline.

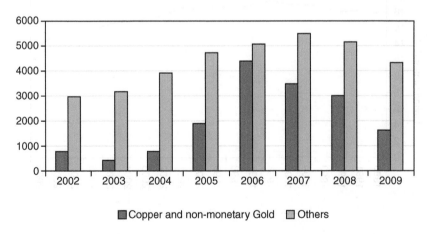

Figure 6.4 Exports of Chile to the USA: high growth of exports of metals and related products till 2006 (source: US Censtat database, accessed July 2010).

But it is important to be noted that tariff preferences do not seem to play a major role in this massive expansion of Chilean exports of copper to the USA. The preference margins (or the gap between MFN rates and preferential tariff rates) are very low for copper products. For HS chapter 74 (HS code for 'Copper and articles thereof'), maximum MFN tariff rate charged by the USA is 3 percent, and the average MFN rate for this chapter is less than 2 percent. Therefore, the preference margins have been quite low for these products and it is unlikely that preferential trading has played a major role in the surge in Chile's exports of copper to the USA. Similarly, for Peru, gold and copper are the major export items and the export growth in these two sub-sectors has been higher than others. And as in the case of Chile, preference margins of these products are not very high.

It is also worth pointing out that the four biggest suppliers of copper (SITC-682) to the USA are Chile, Canada, Peru and Mexico with 31.5 percent, 24 percent, 8.2 percent and 7.2 percent market share respectively in 2006. As all four countries are members of an FTA with the USA, the effective preference margin enjoyed by each of them is almost zero.

In this group, there is another set of countries that is from the Middle East and North Africa (MENA) region. They are Morocco, Bahrain, Jordan and Oman. These countries have a very low market share in the USA. But data show that over the last few years, there has been some increase in their market share in the USA. However, the total market share of Morocco, Bahrain, Jordan and Oman remains less than 0.2 percent in the USA. Among these countries only Jordan has managed to increase its market share significantly. However, even in Jordan's case we see that the market share has stagnated after an initial rise (Figure 6.5).

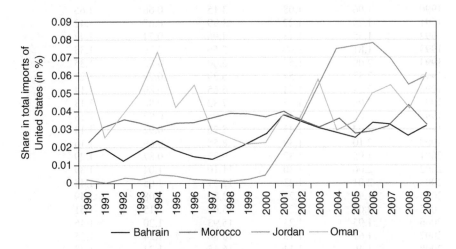

Figure 6.5 Market share of some new preferential trade partners of the USA (source: Direction of Trade Statistics, IMF, accessed July 2010).

The Group 3 countries are a sample of countries that are not yet a member of any FTA with the USA, although some of them are currently negotiating PTAs/FTAs with the USA. We have included five countries in this group: Brazil, China, India, Malaysia and Thailand. Table 6.1 shows how their market share in the USA has changed over the years.

From Table 6.1, it is quite clear that China has managed to increase its market share phenomenally over the concerned period. It shows that China's market share increased by about sixfold over 1990 and 2009. India has also increased its share in the US market steadily, albeit at a much slower rate. For the other three countries, there is no definite trend observable. It is notable here that Malaysia, Thailand and Brazil are in the process of negotiating FTAs with the USA, while China and India are not yet involved in such negotiations.

To summarize the results:

1   Some FTA members have lost market share in the US, this list includes traditional FTA partners like Mexico and Canada and new partners like Australia and Singapore.
2   A few FTA members have managed to maintain/improve their market share (Peru, Chile).
3   A few non-members have done very well/well and increased their market share (China, India).
4   Most ASEAN countries did not manage to increase their market share.

Table 6.1 Market share of some MFN trading partners of the USA (market share in USA, percent)

	Malaysia	Thailand	China	India	Brazil
1990	1.06	1.08	3.15	0.66	1.66
1991	1.25	1.27	3.99	0.67	1.42
1992	1.55	1.43	4.96	0.74	1.47
1993	1.81	1.49	5.56	0.79	1.33
1994	2.09	1.57	6.00	0.82	1.35
1995	2.33	1.54	6.29	0.79	1.22
1996	2.24	1.44	6.65	0.80	1.14
1997	2.06	1.45	7.32	0.86	1.13
1998	2.07	1.48	7.95	0.92	1.13
1999	2.07	1.43	8.25	0.92	1.13
2000	2.10	1.39	8.58	0.89	1.16
2001	1.95	1.32	9.27	0.87	1.29
2002	2.06	1.30	11.10	1.04	1.39
2003	2.01	1.23	12.51	1.05	1.45
2004	1.90	1.22	13.80	1.08	1.49
2005	2.00	1.21	15.00	1.15	1.51
2006	1.95	1.23	15.93	1.20	1.46
2007	1.67	1.18	16.86	1.24	1.35
2008	1.46	1.14	16.45	1.24	1.48
2009	1.49	1.24	19.30	1.37	1.31

The results of this exercise do not give us a clear picture of market access gains by PTA/FTA partners in the USA. For most traditional preferential trade partners of the USA, their market share is stagnating or declining. While the new trade partners exhibit a mixed pattern, some of them have actually lost market share in the USA after having signed an FTA, while some others have managed to gain an additional share in the US market.

If one divides the trading partners of the USA into two broad groups, i.e. preferential trading partners and others, then one can observe that the FTA/PTA partners have lost some market share to the rest of the world in the period between 2000 to 2009 (Figure 6.6). Here it might be argued that China's explosive export growth to the USA is responsible. However, it is interesting to note that China's export boom to the USA has indeed played its part in the reduction of market share of the preferential trading partners but even excluding China's share, the PTA/FTA partners as a whole have not gained any market share from the rest of the world.[11] This is shown in Figure 6.6.

It can also be argued that PTAs/FTAs may have allowed the preferential trading partners to perform better than they would have done in the absence of such agreements. It is of course not easy to prove or disprove such counterfactual arguments. The task is even more difficult here because the techniques of time-series econometrics could not be used due to a lack of data points. As most new US FTAs have been signed after 2002, there are not enough time-series data and with such limited number of observations, it may not possible to carry out meaningful time-series econometric tests.

Overall, using the US data, this section does not find unequivocal support for the hypothesis that there is a positive relationship between the signing of FTAs and the gaining of market share in a developed country. From this set of evidence, it is not possible to give a verdict on whether or not FTAs are either necessary or sufficient for guaranteeing increased market access in developed countries.

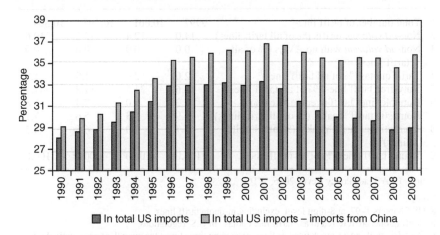

Figure 6.6 Total market share of all preferential trade partners of the USA (source: Direction of Trade Statistics, IMF).

6.4 Possible explanations

The previous section indicates that the signing of RTAs may not guarantee increased market access in developed countries. This is an interesting observation, because most of the North–South FTA/PTAs are signed to ensure increased market access for the country from the South. But these results are not very surprising. In fact, there are a number of reasons why signing up for a PTA/FTA may not necessarily lead to increased market access in a developed country. These are discussed below in more detail.

6.4.1 The tariff preferences received in North–South RTAs are generally not very high

A major advantage of a PTA stems from the difference between the MFN rate and the preferential tariff rate of that agreement. This difference in tariff rates allows certain market access advantages to the preferential trade partner. It should be obvious that a greater difference between the MFN and the preferential rates results in more market access advantages from a PTA.

If one looks at the tariff structure of the USA, it shows that the average level of an MFN tariff is not very high in that country. According to the latest WTO Trade Policy Review of the USA, in 2004, the average MFN applied tariff was 4.9 percent. Table 6.2 shows the tariff structure of the USA.

Table 6.2 shows that close to 19 and 38 percent of all tariff lines of the United States were duty free in 1998 and 2004 respectively. This implies that for 38

Table 6.2 Structure of the tariff schedule of the United States, 1998–2004

		1998	2000	2002	2004
1	Total number of tariff lines[a]	9997	10,001	10,297	10,304
2	Non-*ad valorem* tariffs (% of all tariff lines)	14.0	12.4	12.2	10.6
3	Non-*ad valorem* with no AVEs (% of all tariff lines)	0.0	0.0	0.0	0.0
4	Tariff quotas (% of all tariff lines)[b]	2.0	2.0	1.9	1.9
5	Duty-free tariff lines (% of all tariff lines)	18.6	31.5	31.2	37.7
6	Dutiable lines tariff average rate (%)	7.2	8.0	7.4	7.8
7	Domestic tariff 'peaks' (% of all tariff lines)[c]	4.9	5.3	5.6	7.1
8	International tariff 'peaks' (% of all tariff lines)[d]	7.7	7.0	6.6	5.5
9	Bound tariff lines (% of all tariff lines)	100.0[e]	100.0[e]	100.0[e]	100.0[e]

Source: USA Trade Policy Revue 2006, WTO.

Notes
a HS Chapters 1–97, at 8-digit level, excluding in-quota tariff lines.
b Tariff quotas are referred to as "tariff rate quotas" in U.S. regulations.
c Domestic tariff peaks are defined as those exceeding three times the overall average applied rate.
d International tariff peaks are defined as those exceeding 15%.
e Two lines applying to crude petroleum are not bound.

percent of the total tariff lines, there is no possible market access gain from having preferential or zero duty access to the US domestic market. Moreover, the US data indicate that the coverage of duty-free tariff lines is increasing over the years. If this trend continues then gradually the effectiveness of tariff preferences will come down.

Moreover, if one of the major export items attracts a low MFN tariff rate in a developed country market, then the advantage of having a PTA becomes much less for that sector. For example, as it could be seen in the previous section, Chile's biggest export productto the USA is copper and articles made of copper. In this sub-sector, the preference margin is almost inconsequential as the average MFN rate itself is less than 1 percent. Similarly, for the top export products of Singapore, which comes in the HS sectors 16, 17 and 18, the preference margin given to Singapore is quite modest (Table 6.3). This pattern of trade preference explains why RTAs or PTAs have not helped countries to significantly improve their market share in the USA.

Table 6.3 Summary analysis of U.S. tariffs under selected preferential agreements, 2004

		Average tariff rate for the HS sub-sector		
		MFN	Chile	Singapore	GSP
1	Live animals and products	11.4	9.1	8.5	8.6
2	Vegetable products	4.0	2.1	2.6	0.9
3	Fats and oils	3.5	1.5	1.8	0.2
4	Prepared food, etc.	13.3	9.9	10.3	8.9
5	Minerals	0.6	0.1	0.2	0.0
6	Chemicals and products	3.5	0.0	2.4	0.0
7	Plastics and rubber	3.7	0.0	1.5	0.1
8	Hides and skins	4.3	0.9	1.4	2.1
9	Wood and articles	2.2	0.1	1.2	0.2
10	Pulp, paper, etc.	0.0	0.0	0.0	0.0
11	Textile and articles	9.0	0.1	0.1	8.8
12	Footwear, headgear	13.3	3.5	11.2	12.3
13	Articles of stone	5.0	2.0	3.3	0.4
14	Precious stones, etc.	3.0	0.0	1.5	0.0
15	Base metals and products	1.9	0.2	0.7	0.1
16	Machinery	1.6	0.0	0.3	0.0
17	Transport equipment	2.6	0.2	1.4	0.0
18	Precision equipment	3.0	0.9	1.5	0.7
19	Arms and ammunition	1.5	0.0	0.8	0.0
20	Miscellaneous manufacturing	3.2	0.3	1.7	0.1
21	Works of art, etc.	0.0	0.0	0.0	0.0
By ISIC sector					
Agriculture and fisheries		5.7	4.2	4.4	3.6
Mining		0.4	0.0	0.1	0.0
Manufacturing		4.9	1.2	2.1	2.6

Source: US Trade Policy Review, WTO.

To further illustrate this point, Table 6.3 shows the actual tariff preference received by the two recently concluded US FTAs with developing countries, namely, Chile and Singapore. It is evident from Table 6.3 that on average the preference margins are quite low. Apart from two sectors for Chile (textile and articles; footwear, headgear) and one sector for Singapore (textile and articles), the preference margins on average are less than 4 percent (Figure 6.7). Interestingly, these countries are marginal players in the US markets in sectors where they have received maximum tariff advantage. For example, for the sub-sector SITC-65 ('Textile yarn, fabrics, made-up articles, n.e.s. and related products') in the USA, Chile had a market share of 0.016 percent in 2000 and 0.04 percent in 2006. Singapore is an even smaller player in that sector with 0.01 percent market share in 2006 and 0.03 percent market share in 2000. Incidentally, China and India's market share in this segment in 2006 was 29.6 percent and 9.7 percent respectively. The other sector where Chile has got a relatively high preference margin is footwear and headgear. To understand Chile's position in that sector, exports of Chile to USA for the sub-sector SITC-61 is checked. It shows that Chile had a market share of 0.05 percent in 2000 and 0.036 percent in 2006. From Chile's point of view also these two sectors are not important export sectors. SITC-61 and SITC-65 together account for less than 0.1 percent of Chile's exports to the USA.

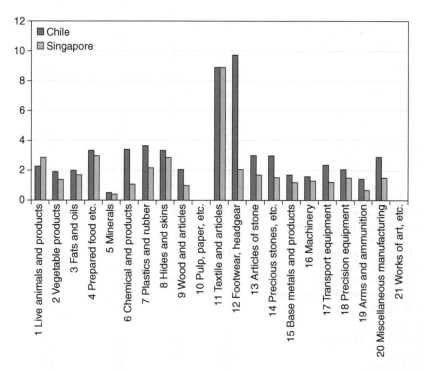

Figure 6.7 Preference margin of Singapore and Chile in the USA (MFN preferential tariff) (hs sector wise), 2004 (source: US Trade Policy Review, WTO, 2006).

On the other hand, the sectors where Chile (and Peru) has strong a competitive advantage, namely, items of copper and gold, the preference margins are not very high. This is because the MFN rates are themselves low in such sectors. The maximum and average MFN tariff rates for copper and items manufactured by copper are only 3 percent and 2 percent respectively.

It is also worth mentioning here that apart from PTAs and FTAs, developed countries also have unilateral tariff preferences given to developing and least developed countries (LDCs). One of them is called the GSP (generalized system of preference). As can be seen from the Table 6.3, the margin between the preferential tariff rates and the GSP rates are not only very low but also in some cases, the GSP tariff rates are even lower than that of preferential tariff rates.

Second, some LDCs have been given duty-free–quota free access to developed country markets and they tend to enjoy better market access conditions than provided under the PTAs/FTAs.

6.4.2 Even this narrow preference margin is expected to be eroded over time

Another problem with tariff preferences given in the North–South RTAs is that these preferences are likely to erode over time. This will happen because the Doha Round of trade talks has very ambitious tariff reduction proposals. For example, for non-agricultural goods, it has been decided that a Swiss Formula will be used for tariff reduction.[12] According to the latest official document on the negotiations on Non-Agricultural Market Access (NAMA),[13] for developed countries, a Swiss Formula with a coefficient of 8 or 9 will be used. One of the mathematical properties of the Swiss Formula is that the coefficient acts as the post cut ceiling. This means that, irrespective of what the initial level of tariff is, the post cut tariff rate will always be less than the coefficient value. Therefore, if the WTO members agree to the coefficient of 8 and assuming that the current round of negotiations concludes in two years' time, in another seven years' time (by the end of the implementation period of the Doha Round), the maximum non-agricultural tariff rate of developed countries will be less than 8 percent. This will further reduce the tariff margins enjoyed by the developing country partners in a North–South RTA.

For agriculture, it has been decided that the tariff cuts will be implemented by a tiered formula that cuts higher initial tariff by a higher margin. The latest draft indicates that the developed countries will have to cut their existing tariff rates at least by 48 percent. For the tariff lines where the initial tariff rate is more than 75 percent, the tariff rates need to be cut by around 70 percent. These facts indicate that the Doha Round has ambitious plans for tariff reduction and once the commitments of the new WTO round are implemented, the preference margins enjoyed by the trading partners of developed countries in RTAs will come down. It is indeed not certain yet when the Doha Round of trade talks will be concluded. But if the Doha Round proposals are implemented, it will lead to deep tariff cuts both in developed and developing countries.

Another source of erosion of preference margins may come from the RTAs themselves. As developed countries are engaging with more and more RTAs, they are increasingly becoming hubs of a large number of preferential agreements. This reduces the advantage of a preferential partner in that market. For example, if almost all the major suppliers of a certain commodity become preferential trade partners of a developed country then the preference margin for each of the suppliers gets diluted. This may lead to a situation where the formation of RTAs will be important to merely maintain a status quo rather than to gain additional market access. In fact, in such cases, the MFN trading partner becomes the least favored supplier. However, if the MFN rates come down significantly, this source of discrimination will gradually matter less for developing countries.

6.4.3 Treatment of non-tariff measures

As it has been discussed above, in developed countries tariffs are not generally very high. Though there exist spikes in tariff rates (or tariff peaks), on average, tariffs are on the lower side in most developed countries. In such countries, the level of protection is being maintained by various non-tariff measures (NTMs),[14] such as standards, technical barriers, trade restrictive anti-dumping rules etc. In fact, a recently released set of data from the World Bank on 'Trade and Import Barriers' indicates that the use of non-tariff barriers is highest among the high-income OECD countries (Table 6.4). It is not surprising that in WTO negotiations, negotiators from developing countries complain more about NTMs than about tariff rates in developed countries. According to them, the NTMs tend to be high on products which are of export interest to the developing countries (Table 6.5) and these measures provide much higher levels of protection, because they are much more restrictive, opaque and difficult to measure.

Therefore, to gain any meaningful increase in market access, along with obtaining tariff preference, it is important to also lower the level of protection through NTMs. However, in an RTA with a developed country, the lowering of NTMs depends very much on the negotiating abilities of the partner country. In a multilateral forum, smaller countries can free ride using the negotiating power of the bigger countries. But the asymmetry of bargaining power is much more pronounced in bilateral negotiations and, therefore, it is unlikely that in a North–South RTA, a developing country will be able to significantly lower the NTMs of a developed country. But on the other hand, because a developed country manages to push through 'WTO Plus' clauses which deal with issues like labor and environment, it can actually happen that in a North–South RTA, the level of NTMs may be higher than in the multilateral route. This can happen because the RTA-specific labor and environmental clauses can be used by the developed country as protectionist devices for sectors, which they want to protect.

The RTAs also contain very complicated Rules of Origin (ROO) and value addition norms. This reduces transparency and creates the 'spaghetti bowl' problem highlighted by Bhagwati and Bhagwati and Panagariya in their works

Table 6.4 Frequency coverage ratio of non-tariff barriers (NTBs) by country

Country/group	Year	Simple average (%)	Import-weighted average (%)
Australia	1999	20.6	29.1
Canada	2000	28.4	19.7
European Union	1999	34.4	24.8
Japan	2001	36.8	36.2
Korea Republic	1998	36.9	25.6
New Zealand	1999	36.5	43.8
Norway	1996	14.9	12.2
Switzerland	1996	22.0	27.0
United States	1999	30.3	47.1
Memo: average			
Developing countries (65)	1992–2001	15.7	18.9
Low-income countries (20)	1993–2001	6.2	10.0
Middle-income countries (45)	1992–2001	20.0	22.9
High-income non-OECDs (7)	1994–2001	17.69	18.24
High-income OECDs (9)	1996–2001	28.98	29.51

Source: http://go.worldbank.org/LGOXFTV550.

(see Bhagwati 1992, 1994, 1995, and Bahgwati and Panagariya 1996). Given the large number of RTAs with possible overlapping of agreements with different preferential tariff rates and a plethora of ROOs and value addition norms, it can be a logistical nightmare for the customs offices in developing countries. Such complex trade rules have the potential to create major trade facilitation problems for developing countries. It is particularly true for developing countries because, the World Bank (2005) has shown that the ROOs tend to be more restrictive in North–South RTAs than other types of RTAs.

6.4.4 Exclusions of certain sectors

Many North–South RTAs tend to exclude certain sectors from preferential tariff coverage. The most common example of such exclusions is agriculture. Almost all trade agreements between EU and developing countries have kept agriculture out of any preferential market access. The same is true for RTAs with Japan. Exclusion of this critical sector can limit market access gains for developing countries. It is notable here that most LDCs get duty-free–quota-free access for their products (including agricultural products) in developed country markets. But most of these concessions are given on a unilateral basis and these are not part of PTAs.

Another notable exception in North–South RTAs focuses on the free movement of labor. Almost all North–South FTAs have restrictions on free movement of labor. Even when issues regarding the temporary movement of workers are included in these RTAs, they are largely confined to professional and skilled

Table 6.5 Non-tariff barrier (NTB) frequency coverage ratio by product in selected developed countries

Product category (SITC)	Australia	Canada	European Union	Japan	United States
Primary products (0–4, 68)	0.54	3.23	1.98	7.49	4.69
Agriculture (0–2, 4)	0.63	3.52	2.30	7.69	4.56
Mining (3, 68)	0.00	1.51	0.47	6.31	5.44
Manufactures (5–8, less 68)	0.31	20.89	10.77	5.08	5.23
Iron and Steel (67)	0.24	83.33	51.94	0.48	42.44
Chemicals (5)	0.89	0.16	4.18	1.15	3.35
Other semi-manufactures (61–4, 66, 69)	0.49	1.47	0.86	0.64	4.59
Machinery and transport equipment (7)	0.07	0.11	2.41	0.05	5.18
Textiles and clothing (65, 84)	0.06	81.26	87.21	23.06	1.13
Other consumer goods (81–3, 85, 87–9)	0.00	0.35	4.82	0.68	0.92
Other products (9)	0.00	0.00	0.00	0.00	0.00
All products (0–9)	0.36	16.88	5.79	5.61	5.08

Source: Same as the previous Table (Table 6.4).

workers, mostly dealing with intra-corporate transfers. It can generally be observed that in North–South RTAs, developed countries are willing to go much beyond the rules of the WTO in areas like TRIPS, investment, services sector liberalization and labor and environmental conditionalities. However, in issues like agricultural market access and the free movement of labor, they are clearly reluctant to take any step toward greater liberalization. In fact, some of the North–South RTAs try to impose additional restrictions in these areas. Exclusion of these key sectors is a major reason why the formation of RTAs often does not help developing countries expand their market access significantly in developed countries.

6.5 The costs of North–South RTAs

The previous section has indicated that there are a number of reasons why developing countries that are joining North–South RTAs may not secure better market access in developed countries. However, there are some potential drawbacks of such RTAs, which can have a significant impact on the growth and development process of a developing country.

Most new RTAs, especially the North–South RTAs, tend to cover much more than liberalization of tariffs and quotas. Most of these RTAs have provisions on enforcement of labor laws, environmental laws, services, intellectual property rights issues, competition policy, government procurement and investment. It is notable that many of these provisions, especially issues like labor and environment, investment and competition policy are no longer on the mandate of the WTO negotiations. These issues have been dropped from the Doha Development Agenda mostly because of strong opposition from developing countries. During the current round of negotiations, it was felt that these issues are 'extraneous issues', which should not be discussed as part of multilateral trade negotiations or in the context of a 'single-undertaking' framework. Because of the structure of WTO negotiations (the so-called 'consensus' based approach) coupled with increased assertiveness of developing countries in the multilateral negotiations, these issues were dropped from the Doha Round. However, most North–South FTAs contain these issues and because of the asymmetry in negotiating power in bilateral negotiations, developed countries not only manage to include these new issues but also impose stricter rules on issues like TRIPS and the opening up of services in developing countries. In fact, RTAs are also being used by some developed countries to remove controls on capital flows. Williamson (2006) points out that in the post Asian crisis period, trade agreements are used by the US treasury to impose free movement of capital on developing countries.[15]

Inclusion of these clauses in the trade agreement leads to a number of problems for developing countries. *First*, these rules further reduce the policy space available to developing countries. Some researchers like Akyüz (2005) and Chang (2002) have argued that WTO commitments restrict policy space available to the developing countries and prevent them from adopting domestic and industrial policies used by currently developed countries during their phase of development. An illustrative example of such policies and the corresponding WTO restrictions is given in Table 6.6.

It is important to note that the provisions of most North–South RTAs go well beyond the WTO rules and are likely to impose higher levels of restrictions on the developing countries. It will also force countries to adopt more 'market friendly' measures in areas such as investment and IPR issues. As the 2007 UNCTAD *Trade and Development Report* (2007) points out, these new RTAs have increasingly included provisions for deeper integration among countries and include policies which require a much higher degree of harmonizing national policies with 'a reform agenda that favors greater freedom for market forces' (ibid.: 54). For a developing country, where the level of industrialization is not high, such measures can have serious negative impact on the industrialization and growth of its economy. It will also constrain the policy space available to these countries.

Second, one can argue that by pushing aggressive trade treaties on a bilateral basis, developed countries are weakening the power of developing countries in multilateral trade negotiations. As discussed above, in an RTA between a developed and a developing country, the developed country often manages to include aggressive trade liberalization clauses, investment protection clauses and extraneous issues in the treaty. Having abandoned objections about these issues on a bilateral level, the developing country cannot oppose these issues on a multilateral platform. This not only helps developed countries push these issues into the WTO, but it also breaks the alliance of developing countries in the multilateral negotiations. Given the diversity among developing countries and the kind of coalition we are seeing in the WTO negotiations, maintaining a unified stance will be of critical importance for the developing countries. However, there is a possibility that this position may be weakened because of the involvement of many developing countries in North–South RTAs.

Third, in North–South RTAs, developing countries are accepting long-term commitments in exchange of uncertain and often transient market access promises. As mentioned before, in such RTAs, developed countries manage to push through a number of conditions like stricter TRIPS regulations, highly unfavorable bilateral investment treaties (BITs), a wide range of market access openings and extraneous clauses like labor and environmental rules. These can result in serious, long-term repercussions for a developing country. Whereas stricter TRIPS laws can lead to serious issues like availability of life saving drugs and medicines at an affordable price, BITs can restrain the options of developing countries to use FDI as a policy instrument to improve the sectoral/regional balance of their economy. BITs are particularly troublesome because not only are they used to introduce harsh labor and environmental requirements in developing countries, but the BITs clauses also try to align a developing country's financial and legal systems to a market-oriented system which favors such enterprises. This can have serious implications for developing countries.

Table 6.6 Policies followed by now-industrialized countries during their phase of development and current WTO rules which prohibit them

Country	Policy	Economic rationale	WTO restriction
USA	High tariff and non-tariff barriers	Infant industry protection	Tariff liberalization, removal of non-tariff measures
UK	High tariff and non tariff barriers Colonial exploitation	Infant Industry protection Extraction of resources	Tariff liberalization, removal of non-tariff measures
Japan	1 State supported investment in R&D 2 Adaptation of designs of products developed by other countries 3 Learning curve pricing	1, 2 Improve competitiveness 3 Taking advantage of economies of scale	1 Countervailing duties 2 Trade related intellectual property rights 3 Anti-dumping laws
South Korea	1 State supported export growth 2 Directed credit 3 Export subsidies 4 Learning curve pricing 5 Interventionist industrial policy	Strategic and innovationist trade policy Economies of scale	Countervailing duties Outright ban of export subsidies Anti-dumping duties Privatization as pushed by the World Bank

Source: Collated from Chang (2002) and Akyuz (2005).

6.6 Conclusions and the importance of South–South trade

The results of this chapter prompt us to question the prevalent tendency of developing countries to treat North–South RTAs as the best way to expand their market. In North–South RTAs, developing countries get supposedly better market access and the perceived gains for developing countries come from the 'preference margin' derived from the gap between the MFN rate and the preferential tariff of the RTA. But as discussed in this chapter, due to a plethora of reasons, this preference margin may not translate into better market access or higher market share. Moreover, this preferential access is temporary and it is not going to provide developing countries with long-term market access benefits. As the Doha Round of trade negotiations aims to reduce the MFN rates significantly, the present tariff preference margins will be eroded by a significant extent as and when these new commitments are implemented.

Also, with more and more RTAs being signed by developed countries, the preference margin enjoyed by an existing developing country partner in North–South RTAs will get diluted. If almost all the major suppliers of a certain commodity become preferential trade partners of a developed country, then the preference margin for each of the suppliers gets further reduced. This, coupled with the fact that MFN rates are themselves low in developed countries, indicates that with the proliferation of RTAs, most developing countries will end up with little or no tariff preferences in a developed country market. Also, in a North–South RTA, the developing country partner loses the privilege of non-reciprocity and Special and Differential Treatment, which are available to them under the multilateral system.

But, on the other hand, in North–South RTAs developing countries are undertaking long-term commitments in areas like labor, environment, investment and competition policy. So, what is essentially happening is that developing countries are binding themselves in long-term commitments on a number of inconvenient issues against temporary and small tariff preferences granted by developed countries. As Ghosh (2004) pointed out developed countries, particularly the USA and the EU members, are pushing RTAs, under the influence of large capital, to force developing countries make deeper trade and investment commitments than is now possible multilaterally given the divisions in the WTO. Developing countries, in their pursuit for export led growth, are accepting all sorts of very damaging conditions in terms of foreign investment protection, IPR and the opening up of markets, simply to avail of what may be transient or minor gains in terms of market access.

In this context, South–South trade blocs may emerge as a viable alternative to developing countries for expanding their market. With growing income in many parts of the developing world, this may provide significant market access for many countries from the South. There might be some concerns about the lack of trade complementarities among the developing world, but it could be pointed out here that developing countries are currently a diverse group and have enough variety in their export basket to generate sufficient trade among themselves. Also, with increased industrialization, it will be possible for some developing countries to engage in intra-industry trade and allow their firms to exploit the economies of scale. As a late UNCTAD Trade and Development Report (2007) points out, all regional blocs involving developing and transition economies, regionally produced manufactures, including the more skill- and technology-intensive product categories, find markets more easily in countries in the same region than in international markets farther away. The report then concludes that there is considerable scope for developing and transition economies to benefit from advantages of geographical and cultural proximity when seeking to develop their industries and upgrade their production.

To sum up, theoretically trade liberalization through regionalism may not offer the best solution but in the current state of distorted multilateralism RTAs are used by many developing countries to improve market access. But the North–South RTAs have their own share of problems. The problems associated with unequal power structures and the exploitation of smaller members by bigger economic powers is more acute in such regional trade blocs. In this context, South–South RTAs can become a useful solution for many developing countries for expanding their market. This is particularly true for small developing countries that do not have a domestic market which is big enough to allow the advantages of economies of scale to their domestic industries.[16] These RTAs are likely to be beneficial for developing countries because not only it will allow these countries to expand market access without compromising on national policy autonomy but also it will help them forge and foster stronger South–South alliances at the multilateral trade negotiations. However, there are also some obvious arguments against regionalism. Apart from the problems of trade diversion, the complex web of regional agreements can also introduce even more uncertainties and opacity in the present global trade system, which already has a myriad of market access barriers and other forms of standards and regulations. Widespread adoption of RTAs, along with the RTA specific barriers and concessions, may make the system even more complex. It is also possible that if the world would be divided into a number of mega trade blocs, weaker countries could become marginalized.

Notes

1 Address for correspondence: Parthapratim Pal, A204, Faculty Block, Indian Institute of Management Calcutta Joka, Kolkata.
2 There are subtle differences among the concepts of Regional Trade Agreements (RTAs), Preferential Trade Agreements (PTAs) and Free Trade Agreements (FTAs). But in this chapter, these terms will be used interchangeably.
3 Proliferation of regional trade agreements 'breeding concern': Pascal Lamy, dated September 10, 2007, online, available at: www.wto.org/english/news_e/sppl_e/sppl67_e. htm (accessed July 2010).
4 Here North–South refers economic North and South. That is, North–South RTAs refer to trade agreements between developed and developing countries.
5 In Viner's own words:

> where the trade-diverting effect is predominant, one at least of the member countries is bound to be injured, the two combined will suffer a net injury, and there will be injury to the outside world and to the world at large.
>
> (1950: 44)

6 However, it must be mentioned here that Ohlin (1924) and Graham (1923) have recognized the possibility of increasing returns to scale and its impact on international manufacturing trade long before this modern strand of literature.
7 Incidentally, almost all WTO members are currently involved in one or more RTAs.
8 Unless otherwise mentioned, data for this section are taken from the website http://censtats.census.gov (accessed July 2010).
9 Online, available at: www.ustr.gov/Trade_Agreements/Section_Index.html (accessed July 2010).
10 Together, these three groups of countries account for about 60 percent of the total US market in 2006. Other notable trading partners of the USA are the EU countries, Japan, Taiwan and Saudi Arabia.
11 The formula used here is =100X(total imports by USA from all its PTA/FTA partners/(total US imports–imports from China).
12 The Functional Form of the Swiss Formula is like this: $t_1=Ct_0/(C+t_0)$, where t_0=initial tariff rate, t_1=final tariff rate and C=agreed coefficient. This formula has some interesting mathematical properties. It cuts higher tariffs by a larger proportion, lower the value of coefficient, higher the cut lower the coefficient lower the post cut dispersion and the coefficient becomes the effective ceiling for the post cut tariff rates.
13 Revised draft negotiating text for market access for goods, dated February 8, 2008, online, available at: www.wto.org/english/tratop_e/markacc_e/namachairtxt_feb08_e.doc (accessed July 2010).
14 Non-tariff measures (NTMs) and non-tariff barriers are sometimes used synonymously in the literature though, strictly speaking, they are not exactly the same thing. This chapter uses these terms interchangeably.
15 Williamson says

> Since then the main pressure for liberalising capital flows has come from the US treasury. When countries wanted to negotiate bilateral free trade agreements with the US, they found the treasury insisted that US negotiators demand that the partner country should commit itself to never reimposing effective capital controls for any length of time. Several of the partner countries that had made effective use of such controls in the past, like Chile and Singapore, found themselves forced to choose between abandoning their aim of securing a free trade agreement with the US and abandoning their ability to control capital movements with the object of avoiding or at least attenuating crises. Given that governments, like markets, typically take a rather short-term view of costs and benefits, and that the countries could not see the prospect of a crisis on the horizon at the time the negotiations were taking place, the US treasury got its way.

(2006: 1848)

16 For bigger developing countries, where domestic markets can potentially support large industries, there is another option. They can strive to develop and expand the size of their domestic market instead of relying completely on external demand. However, this option is not there for smaller countries.

References

Akyüz, Y. (2005) 'The WTO negotiations on industrial tariffs: what is at stake for developing countries?' RIS Discussion Paper No. 98, New Delhi: Research and Information Service for Developing Countries.
Bergsten, C.F. (1996) 'Competitive liberalization and global free trade: a vision for the early 21st century', Asia Pacific Working Paper Series No. 96–15, Washington: Institute for International Economics.

Bhagwati, J. (1992) 'Regionalism versus Multilateralism', *World Economy*, 15: 535–55.

Bhagwati, J. (1993) 'Regionalism and Multilateralism: An Overview', in J.D. Melo and A. Panagariya (eds) *New Dimensions in Regional Integration*, Cambridge: Cambridge University Press.

Bhagwati, J. (1994) 'Threats to the World Trading System: Income Distribution and the Selfish Hegemon', *Journal of International Affairs*, 48: 279–85.

Bhagwati, J. (1995) 'U.S. Trade Policy: The Infatuation with Free Trade Areas', in J. Bhagwati and A. Krueger (eds) *The Dangerous Drift to Preferential Trade Agreements*, Washington, DC: American Enterprise Institute for Public Policy Research.

Bhagwati, J. and Panagariya, A. (1996) *The Economics of Preferential Trade Agreements*, Washington, DC: AEI Press.

Brander, J. (1981) 'Intra-industry Trade in Identical Commodities', *Journal of International Economics*, 11: 1–14.

Brander, J.A. and Spencer, B.J. (1984) 'Tariff Protection and Imperfect Competition', in Henryk Kierzkowski (ed.) *Monopolistic Competition and Product Differentiation and International Trade*, Oxford: Oxford University Press.

Chang, Ha-Joon (2002) *Kicking Away the Ladder*, London: Anthem Press.

Dixit, A. (1984) 'International Trade Policy for Oligopolist Industries', *Economic Journal*, 94: 1–16.

Ghosh, J. (2004) 'Regionalism, foreign investment and control: the new rules of the game outside the WTO', Paper presented at a seminar on the Economics of New Imperialism, Jawaharlal Nehru University, New Delhi, January, 2004.

Graham, F. (1923) 'Some aspects of protection further considered', *Quarterly Journal of Economics*, 37: 199–227.

Krugman, P. (1980) 'Scale Economies, Product Differentiation, and the Pattern of Trade', *American Economic Review*, 70, 950–9.

Krugman, P. (1993) 'Regionalism versus Multilateralism: Analytical Notes', in J. de Melo and A. Panagariya (eds) *New Dimensions in Regional Integration*, Cambridge: Cambridge University Press.

Limão, N. (2003) 'Preferential Trade Agreements as Stumbling Blocks for Multilateral Trade Liberalization: Evidence for the U.S.', University of Maryland, College Park.

Mansfield, E.D. and Reinhardt, E. (2003) 'Multilateral Determinants of Regionalism: The Effects of GATT/WTO on the Formation of Preferential Trading Arrangements', *International Organization*, 57: 829–62.

Ohlin, Bertil (1924) 'The Theory of Trade', PhD dissertation, republished in 1991, 'The Theory of Trade', in Bertil Ohlin and Eli Heckscher (eds) *Heckscher–Ohlin Trade Theory*, Cambridge: The MIT Press.

Panagariya, A. (1996) 'The Free Trade Area of the Americas: Good for Latin America?' *World Economy*, 19: 485–515.

UNCTAD (2007) *Trade and Development Report 2007: Regional Cooperation for Development*, New York and Geneva: United Nations.

Viner, J. (1950) *The Customs Union Issue*, New York: Carnegie Endowment for International Peace.

Williamson, J. (2006) 'Why Capital Account Convertibility in India is Premature', *Economic and Political Weekly*, 41: 1848–50.

World Bank (2005) *The Global Economic Prospects 2005: Trade, Regionalism and Development*, November 2004, Washington, DC: World Bank.

World Bank (2010) Data on Trade and Import Barriers, online, available at: http://go.worldbank.org/LGOXFTV550 (accessed August 2010).

7 The multi-fibre arrangement and South Asia

Mausumi Kar[1,2] *and Saibal Kar*[3,4]

7.1 Introduction

High degrees of economic transactions within the South vis-à-vis those between North and South countries was long described as the 'flight of the chicken' – one that is always promising, but failing to materialize. The reasons behind this observed trend, naturally eclectic, have been discussed in various ways. Among these however, the lack of intra-industry trade was considered reasonably potent in explaining why the North–South interactions are still overwhelmingly important. Differences in production technologies, according to the Heckscher–Ohlin–Ricardo model of trade (1995 for APEC region and so on) or imperfect competition *à la* Krugman (1980, 1981), provide strong grounds for intra-industry trade, and yet smaller domestic markets and other institutional barriers did not allow these to successfully explain intra-South trade in goods. In more recent times, however, there has been a significant growth in the flow of goods and services within the countries of the South, mainly owing to the benefits of globalization reaching large masses in the South. What we argue in this chapter is that certain changes, ushered in with regime shifts in the WTO policies, have caused to bring the South countries closer through competition than they ever were. With regard to such exogenous policy shifts we shall invoke the well-known Multi-Fibre Arrangement (henceforth, MFA) in clothing and textile and its slow phasing out over a period of ten years. For a large number of Asian countries that traditionally enjoyed high comparative advantages in the production of these commodities, the demise of the MFA brought in varied and significant economic changes. This chapter traces the impact of MFA withdrawal for a handful of Asian countries and reflects on the implications for the global South. Although much has been written on the role of MFA and its implications, a cross-country analysis of the nature, as the one developed here, is not yet available in the current literature.

The focal point of this analysis is the state of competitiveness for India in the manufacturing of textiles and clothing vis-à-vis other Asian exporters. As we have already mentioned, choice of textile and clothing sector is an outcome of the importance it carries for India and competing Asian countries. For India, in particular, it is the largest industry as well as the largest net foreign exchange earner. The contribution of this industry to the gross export earnings of India is over 20 per cent, while it adds only 2–3 per cent to the gross import bill. Between the textile and apparel industries, it is the apparel (clothing) industry, which is of a more recent origin and primarily produces exportable items. Second, in spite of being the largest net foreign exchange earning sector in India the industry's share in world exports of textile and apparel is still quite low when compared to other countries, such as the Asian Giants; South Korea, Singapore and Hong Kong. Not surprisingly then, export promotion policies in India strongly support this sector, which in recent times has become quite sensitive to the changing of the global economic order and newly adopted rules.

In analysing the impacts, we must keep in mind that the Agreement on Textiles and Clothing (henceforth, ATC) ensured the dismantling of only quotas on textile and apparel items, while tariff on these items were not abolished.[5] The MFA provided a framework under which developed countries imposed quotas on exports of textiles and apparel from developing countries. These quotas were typically applied on a bilateral basis and were product-specific as defined by fibre and functionality. This allowed discrimination not only against specific fibres and products but also among exporting countries. The exporting countries' governments administered the MFA export quotas, which were allocated to them based on predetermined criteria.[6] This iniquitous system of quotas thus violated all the fundamental principles of the multilateral trading system, and discriminated against the poorest countries and those seeking to move up from a reliance on primary commodities to manufacturing.

Hence, it is important to note as a starting point that despite removal of the MFA, trade in clothing and textile would still not be entirely free, but merely 'quota free'. In addition, in the presence of political equations in an increasingly complicated world of multilateral negotiations, the extent of compliance with the ATC on the part of importing countries remains unclear. This impending reality brings the issue of competitiveness to the fore for all countries including India. In fact, as we shall observe in the following sections, the changes give rise to a make or break proposition in which some Asian countries will do much better than the rest. This should additionally serve to empirically verify a recent proposition that quotas can function as a competitive device. This stands contradictory to the accepted wisdom that quotas are anti-competitive in nature. Marjit *et al.* (2009) have argued that the entry of China in the WTO and the removal of the MFA shall work against the interest of many smaller countries in the South. The scale of production or sheer efficiency of Chinese manufacturers would negatively affect the erstwhile quota protected market shares of a large number of countries and might lead to a monopoly outcome. However, as long as the monopoly price set by a large exporting country remains below the import competing price in the importing countries, gains from trade via removal of quota at destinations still improve. Note that, between the North and the South the results are likely to be asymmetric. With India at the core of our analysis, we intend to see if a withdrawal of the MFA actually brings forth more competition or drives monopoly concentration within a host of Asian countries.

Section 7.2 examines India's performance in textile and clothing exports to the major world markets in comparison with her seven most important Asian competitors during the decade just before liberalization. As a follow up, we evaluate India's performance vis-à-vis these countries except for Sri Lanka during the transition to the MFA phase-out. In both cases we use the well-known 'Constant Market Share Analysis' that is widely applied in measuring the export growth performance of a country. In Section 7.3 we offer an analysis of the trends and stability patterns for export growth in textile and clothing for each country. Section 7.4 concludes. The Appendix to this chapter has three sections. An outline of the methodology employed in Section 7.2 is discussed in Appendix A.1. Relevant tables containing data and results are available in Appendix A.2. The charts and diagrams in support of our trend analysis are presented in Appendix A.3.

7.2   Effects of MFA on major Asian exporters

It is important to note as a starting point that the present section discusses the impacts of the quota withdrawal on *aggregate* exports of textile and apparel items for a group of Asian countries and the evolving relative international competitiveness for each country. Since understanding changes in the domestic market structure following the MFA dismantling at the country level is of critical importance, we would briefly comment on the extent of such investigations. We have studied the implications of changes in concentration ratios of each category of garment manufacturing firms during 1990–2005 for India in a separate exercise (Kar 2009). The study drew on firm level statistics for a large number of Indian garment manufacturers. The study on the concentration of different sectors is followed by an investigation dealing with the causal relation between economies of scale and the structure of the industry. Besides, we have also tried to evaluate the barriers to entry, faced by different sectors of this industry, by estimating the average cost facing the firms vis-à-vis their respective sizes. Subsequently, we use the degree of cost-effectiveness at the firm level to calculate the critical size of a firm within the industry. In the typical industrial organization framework it is argued that the firm structure is exogenously determined by technical factors, more precisely, by economies of scale. We used a similar framework to measure how scale economies affect the structure of an industry.[7]

We now focus on the present contribution and discuss the pre- and post-ATC situations for a group of Asian exporters of textiles and apparels.

7.2.1   The pre-ATC period

As discussed in the previous section, our analysis pivots on the status of India vis-à-vis other Asian exporters. We shall include the pre-WTO period to compare the trends to that observed in the post-WTO era. An analysis of India's export performance in textile and clothing to the five large regional markets in the world in comparison with seven major Asian countries is what we shall begin with. The period of our analysis is set between 1985 and 1994. The seven Asian competitors include China, Bangladesh, Pakistan, Sri Lanka, Indonesia, Malaysia and Thailand. However, the elite group comprising newly industrialized countries (NICs) of South-East Asia, such as Hong Kong, the Republic of Korea, Taiwan and Singapore, have already established themselves as large players in the field of textile and clothing exports to the world market and are excluded. Also, the markets and the composition of exports for these NICs are largely different from that of India. On the other hand, although China is the world's third largest exporter of textiles and the largest exporter of garments, we have included it for the following reasons. First, China's textile industry is heavily based on domestic cotton like that of India and her competitors. Second, China's major markets for textiles and clothing are Hong Kong, Japan, the EU and the USA offering the ground for direct competition with a number of other Asian countries. Interestingly, however, China's garments exports are understated by its own export figures. According to the World Bank, in 1991 China's clothing exports as reported by importing countries were 46 per cent more than those reported by China's own statistics (Debroy 1996).

The five major destinations for the group of exporters thus selected are the USA, Canada, EEC, EFTA, Japan and the Middle East and are chosen on the basis of high import volumes in any of these years. Note that, since this subsection covers the period 1985–1994 the formation of the European Union was yet to be completed, which is the reason for considering the EEC and the EFTA as distinctly different destinations. This study focuses on three prime categories of textiles and clothing chosen from the Standard International Trade Classification (SITC). The items are (i) textile fibres and wastes (SITC-26), (ii) textile yarn, fabrics etc. (SITC-65) and (iii) clothing and accessories (SITC-84).

As a methodology we use the Constant Market Share (CMS) analysis (Richardson 1971; Hickman *et al.* 1979). A detailed methodological treatment is also available in Leamer and Stern (2006: 171). The basic idea behind this method is the assumption that a country's share in the world market should remain constant over time. If there is a difference between the export growth according to this constant share norm and the observed export performance as per aggregate returns, it is attributed to the competitiveness effect broadly. Furthermore, the actual growth in exports is divided into three components: the *competitiveness effect*, the *market size effect* and the *interaction effect*. In terms of the data for the pre-ATC years we rely on the UN Commodity Trade Statistics, Statistical Papers: Series D (different issues), the *Trade Statistics Yearbook* and the *Statistical Yearbook* (different volumes) for Asia and the Pacific. For the following subsection covering the period 1995–2005, we solely rely on COMTRADE, the database of the UN Commodity Trade Statistics. This database is formed mainly by the reported statistics of different member countries of the UN for different years.[8] The CMS analysis is regularly used in many important studies to ascertain the role of competitiveness in the export growth for several countries (namely, Ichikawa 1996 for APEC region and so on; Lohrmann 2000 for Turkey; Simonis 2000b, 2000a for Eastern Europe and Belgium; James and Movshuk

2004 for Japan, Korea, Taiwan and USA; Danninger and Joutz 2007 for Germany; Piezas-Jerbi and Nee 2009 for a cross-country analysis).[9]

The concept of 'international competitiveness' can be looked at from different angles. It may either be defined as the ability of the country to improve its sales in international markets at the expense of its competitors, or as the success of the country in import substitution in the domestic market in competition with overseas suppliers. Whatever be the approach, the direct consequence of improvement in international competitiveness of a country is real income gain. Moreover, gains from trade do not grow automatically with an increase in the volume of trade, because the terms of trade for the country and the commodity composition of trade are also very crucial in this respect.

The export market share can be used as a crude, but reliable indicator of international competitiveness. The indicator directly shows the ability of a country to sell in international markets. Indirectly, it is supposed that by harnessing a growing share of international demand, the real incomes of the factors employed in a country's international sector increase vis-à-vis real incomes of its trading partners (Bhattacharya and Raychaudhuri 1994). Koopman and Langer (1988) have also empirically shown a fairly close (positive) correlation between the GNP/GDP growth rate and a changing export market share. There, GNP/GDP growth rate serves as a proxy for real income growth whereas market share is considered as the index of competitiveness. Furthermore, Misra (1993) asserts that CMS analyses also serve as a simple method of quantifying the relative impact of different factors in determining the shifts in market shares. In terms of applications for India, Marjit and Raychaudhuri (1997) notably show that export performance can be largely explained by the competitiveness effect and there is an indication of an improvement in India's price competitiveness in terms of a downward movement of the relative Wholesale Price Index for India over time.[10] However, these studies also suggest that price factors do not explain changes in the aggregate competitiveness of exports in a significant way when costs have little or no influence on the competitiveness of the manufacturing sector.

According to the CMS analysis a percentage change in the export share of a country for any item ($\dot{y}$) can be decomposed into three constituent parts, namely: (i) percentage change in export share explained by the *competitiveness effect*, (ii) percentage change in export share explained by the *market size effect* and (iii) percentage change in export share explained by the *interaction effect*.

This *competitiveness effect* isolates the influence of change in the competitiveness of country *i* in specific regional markets. The *market size effect* implies that the total exports of country *i* may increase or decrease without any change in its export competitiveness. The *interaction effect* measures the interaction between changes in market shares and market sizes. For the interested reader, components of $\dot{y}$ are explicitly derived in expression (A.1.f) in Appendix A.1. We present calculations of these three components of $\dot{y}$ in Appendix A.2 for India and its competitors for each of the three textile items during 1985 to 1994. For India, the calculations have been performed on an annual as well as on a quinquennial basis. For computing the quinquennial changes, we have divided the period under survey into three time intervals constituting four years each. These are: (i) 1985 to 1988, (ii) 1988 to 1991 and (iii) 1991 to 1994. The years 1985, 1988 and 1991 have been used as base years with respect to which the changes in export share in the final years of the respective intervals have been computed. The latter exercise has been carried out for all the countries considered, whereas the first one has been carried out only for India, in order to compare India's competitive position with those of other countries without much statistical complexity.

Tables 7.1–7.3 (Appendix A.2) offer country-wise export of the three categories of textile and clothing items selected. Tables 7.4–7.6 (Appendix A.2) show the final results of our CMS analysis for the period 1985 to 1994. It offers the annual changes in India's export share along with its three constituents. Tables 7.7–7.9 offer results based on a quinquennial estimate. Each table has three parts; part A corresponds to textile fibres (SITC-26), part B corresponds to textile fabrics and yarns (SITC-65) and part C to clothing (SITC-84).

It is observable from Tables 7.4, 7.5 and 7.6 that none of the items of India's textile and apparel exports showed consistent trends over this period. However, one aspect quite similar to the world trend was that in the final year export of textile fibres underwent negative percentage change with respect to the preceding year while both textile fabrics and clothing reflected positive percentage changes. Although, the results are just reversed if we consider the percentage changes in 1993 with respect to 1992, yet it can be argued that textile fibres gradually lost their importance in India's export basket of textile and clothing items and clothing expanded its portfolio. This can directly be observed from Tables 7.1–7.3, where export values of textile fibres for most countries including India, declined considerably since 1990, whereas that of clothing increased significantly over time. Another remarkable feature is that in almost all the cases the competitiveness effect is the dominant component for percentage change in export performance of India. Although for 1985–1986 and 1989–1990 (for textile fabrics and yarns) and for 1985–1986 (clothing) the market size effect dominates the competitiveness effect, differences are not statistically significant, unlike in the textile fibres case, in which the competitiveness effect dominates significantly all through. The *interaction effect* has little or no contribution to change in export shares.

It can be inferred from the above results that the internal production strength for India, as reflected in the competitiveness effect, were more important than external factors. Hence, a removal of export quota should imply greater competition among suppliers and countries with strong domestic production base would be able to extract maximum benefits from a withdrawal of the quota. Moreover, for all of these three items the *market size* effect for India shows a declining trend over the time span, especially in the final intervals. Since about three-quarters of India's exports were destined for those countries, which imposed MFA restrictions, the share of quota exports within total exports was fairly high. It is expected that the removal of quotas should stimulate India's textile and clothing exports.

7.2.2 Are these effects similar for other Asian countries?

Tables 7.7–7.9 presents the quinquennial changes in export shares along with their constituent parts for eight exporting countries. These tables give a rough idea of the relative gainers (and/or the losers) over each interval and over the entire time span and also indicate the specific factors (namely, relative market shares or market sizes), which contribute significantly to the country's gains (or losses). With the help of this empirical exercise we can make a broad comparative study of India's export performances in textile fibres (Table 7.7), textile fabrics and yarns (Table 7.8) and clothing (Table 7.9) vis-à-vis seven major competitors in the same markets following the CMS norm.

First consider Table 7.7, which provides us with the outcomes for textile fibres. During the first interval, i.e. 1985–1988, only four countries (India, Indonesia, Malaysia and China) showed improvement in export shares to major regional markets of the world. In the second interval (1988–1991) Pakistan and China were the only losing countries. Pakistan was the country that suffered most, while Indonesia was the largest gainer in this interval followed by Thailand. India's percentage change in export share for textile fibres was highest in this interval among all quinquennial intervals. However, Sri Lanka and Bangladesh also showed remarkable increases in their shares, while Malaysia's performance drastically fell. The final interval (1991–1994) showed a reduction in shares of exports for all the countries (except China) when compared to the previous interval, implying a gradual decline in importance of textile fibres in the export basket. The effects essentially show a roller coaster change for most countries. The export performance of both Pakistan and Indonesia, for example, took nosedives in the final quarter.

Table 7.8 offers results for textile fabrics and yarns. Here, during the first interval (1985–1988) the only losing countries were Bangladesh and Malaysia. The best performer was Indonesia, followed by Sri Lanka. In the second interval (1988–1991) Bangladesh remained the net loser with China. India, Pakistan, Indonesia and Malaysia were able to improve their performances in comparison to the previous interval.

The last interval (1991–1994) reveals a dramatic increase in the share of exports for Bangladesh by about 126 per cent. More surprisingly, such an improvement in the performance of Bangladesh was accompanied by a reduction in percentage shares for India, Pakistan, Indonesia, Malaysia and Thailand. Over the entire period the competitiveness effect, unambiguously, remained the most crucial determining factor in explaining changes in export shares of all the countries except China.

Finally, we consider Table 7.9, which shows quinquennial percentage changes in export shares of India and its seven competitors for clothing. The table records Sri Lanka as the market that suffered most during the first interval (1985–1988) with large negative percentage changes for the market size effect. India and China were also net losers in this period and the highest gain was accrued to Thailand (a growth of more than 39 per cent). In the second interval (1988–1991)

India, Malaysia, Thailand and China were the net losers, though India and China saw improvements in their relative positions compared to the previous interval. Indonesia was again the largest gainer followed by Sri Lanka. The last interval (1991–1994) shares some common features with the previous one. India remained a net loser in clothing exports recording the worst performance. However, China and Bangladesh registered considerable gains. The market size effect was the major explanatory factor for the unsatisfactory performances of India and Pakistan but for other countries the competitiveness effect remained the strongest one.

A salient feature of Table 7.9 is that while Pakistan, Malaysia and Thailand show a monotonically declining trend over the entire period, China has been successful in gradually increasing its percentage share of exports of clothing and has become the largest gainer in the final period. India's experience was fairly unique for clothing exports; percentage change in India's export share explained by the competitiveness effect was negative but gradually declining in magnitude. On the other hand, the market size effect revealed a gradual loss for India's export of clothing. Previously, the market size effect had been dominated by the competitiveness effect but in the final interval the former dominated the latter and thereby confirmed that the loss of market size was so high that it largely influenced India's performance. Therefore, it appears that the market size effect, as determined by quotas and other protectionist measures of the MFA, may function as the major constraint for growth in clothing exports from India.

7.2.3 The post-ATC period

The enactment of the regulation to put an end to textiles quotas worldwide was a huge step for the industry and for a large number of activities directly or indirectly linked to it. It is best to admit that it would require a mammoth effort to capture all these effects in one attempt. Presently, therefore, we shall restrict ourselves to the output effects and subsequently its implications for the state of competitiveness among the Asian exporters. Importantly, this is also the period when the EU took shape and is now treated as a composite importing country. Here, we chose six Asian competitors of India, namely, China, Bangladesh, Pakistan, Indonesia, Malaysia and Thailand, and three regional markets namely, North America, the European Union and Japan. North America consists of the United States of America, Canada and Mexico. The European Union is the association of 27 European countries. Lastly, Japan is the single largest importer of textiles and clothing in Asia. However, unlike in the previous sub-section, we have to exclude Sri Lanka due to the non-availability of matching data of the country after 1995. Since textile fibres and yarn steadily lost ground for India during the pre-ATC period, we concentrate on the implications of MFA phase-out for clothing sector alone (SITC-84) during the post-ATC regime. The period of this study starts from 1995 (the beginning year of quota liberalization) and ends in 2005 (the year of the full integration of textile and apparel trade into the ATC).

Once again, the approach is to calculate the three components of expression (*vide* expression A.1.f in Appendix A.1) for India and her six competitors for SITC-84 during 1995–2005. The calculations are done on an annual basis, where changes in the relative export shares and their components are calculated by considering the preceding year as the base year. The calculations are based on the original values of total exports of clothing of each exporting country to all the importing regions, clubbed together and depicted in Table 7.10 in Appendix A.2.

We offer detailed numerical results of the CMS analysis along with its constituent parts in seven consecutive tables (Table 7.11 to Table 7.17). Each table exhibits annual percentage change in the export shares of each country, as well as its constituent parts in a time series with the preceding year held as the base year. The most remarkable feature of all these tables is that in almost all the cases the competitiveness effect is the most dominant component of change in export performances of India as well as for all of her competitors. For example, during 1995–1996 the share of Indian export of clothing in all markets taken together has declined by more than 16 per cent out of which about 14 per cent decline was caused by the internal factors. This is due to the competitiveness effect as against only 1.5 per cent decline resulting from other market restraints. This pattern replicates for the following years where roughly 10 per cent of the decline is caused by the declining competitive edge. The trend saw a turnaround by 2003–2004, when India's export share started rising substantially and still the competitiveness effect accounted for much of it. China (Table 7.12) exhibits almost a consistent pattern of the dominance of the competitiveness effect over the entire period with the exception of 1997–1998 and 1998–1999 when the market size effect dominates over the competitiveness effect by a small margin. The role of competitiveness effect is even more prominent in the second interval. Pakistan also is not an exception in this regard (Table 7.14). However, with few exceptions the magnitude of the market size effect is smaller than the competitiveness effect although this difference is not significant enough to bestow the entire change to the second factor up to 2001–2002. The last three intervals again show that the competitiveness effect is dominant.

Tables 7.15, 7.16 and 7.17 describe a similar kind of situation for Indonesia, Malaysia and Thailand respectively. For all these countries, the competitiveness effect very significantly dominates over the market size effect. Interestingly, for all these countries the export shares are on a steady but unmistakable decline, except for one or two years of positive changes. Bangladesh (Table 7.13) on the other hand, is one of the countries that reaped the maximum benefit from the MFA withdrawal. The huge percentage change in its export share during 1995–1996 is largely owed to improvements in its internal conditions captured by the competitiveness effect. More precisely, Bangladesh is among the first beneficiaries of the ATC, as indicated by the magnitude of the percentage change in export share for the first phase of integration, i.e. up to 1997–1998. In the following years, competition aggravated and her export share also faced fluctuations over time with respect to previous intervals. In general, Bangladesh has been able to improve its export share vis-à-vis close competitors from a miniscule 3 per cent to a respectable 9 per cent by 2004–2005 and has caught up with India (at approximately 10 per cent). Clearly, the growth performance of Bangladesh is better than all of her competitors except China. Although the plan we have set for ourselves in this study precludes us from venturing into finer details on what might have caused this, it is certainly worth exploring.

In fact, according to the proposition by Marjit *et al.* (2009) it is a distinct possibility that the country with the most efficient production technique would move towards monopoly market share when quotas are lifted. Our numerical results display that while China, Bangladesh, India and Pakistan benefited from the abolition of the quota, the textile sector went into steady contraction for a number of other countries. The existence of quota in other words should then be deemed as purveyor of greater competition at the country level. Stated simply, the existence of quotas actually provided a protected market for a large number of countries, which had a positive demand for their exports without being exposed to threats from low cost, relatively efficient and better quality product suppliers. In brief, the net global gains from the withdrawal of the MFA needs to be evaluated by incorporating all these changes and preferably in a dynamic setup in the future.

In addition, much in contradiction to the conventional belief, the regime of bilaterally negotiated quotas did not actually restrain exports of clothing from the developing nations. The insignificant percentage changes explained by the market size effects for most of the years bear direct testimony to this fact. The net gains accruing to China and Bangladesh in particular have come at the cost of countries like Malaysia whose export share went down to an all time low.

7.3 Trends and stability

In the previous section we discussed the patterns of changes in export performance for India and a number of other countries classified over pre-ATC and post-ATC periods. This section analyses certain characteristic features in the growth patterns over the entire span of 20 years. Among these, we are interested in simple observations such as the existence of structural breaks, stability and time dependence (projections) of industry level growth paths for all of these countries. Note that, since the data we acquired is up to the year 2005 these projections can now be retested against actual data. But, it would still be interesting to see in retrospect what the estimates suggested. Following Brown *et al.* (1975) we test for structural change over time, which is an important application of the recursive residuals. Recursive residuals are a set of residuals, which, if the disturbances are independently and identically distributed, will be independently and identically distributed thus facilitating tests of the null hypothesis. Assuming the usual linear model, $y = X\beta + u$, the null hypothesis of no structural change can be specified as:

$$H_0 = \beta_1 = \beta_2 = ... = \beta_n = \beta$$
$$and \quad \sigma_1^2 = \sigma_2^2 = ... = \sigma_n^2 = \sigma^2$$

(7.1)

where, β_t and σ_t^2 denote the vector of coefficients ruling in period t and the disturbance variance in that period, respectively.

The null hypothesis would be violated if the β vectors remained constant but σ^2 varies, which represents heteroscedasticity. On the other hand, the null hypothesis of no structural break would be violated if there is variation in βs. Such variance in the coefficients may be tested by using the Cusum (Cumulative Sum of Recursive Residuals) and the Cusum of Squares (Cumulative Sum of Squares of Recursive Residuals) tests.[11] Since it is known that the Cusum test is less powerful than the Cusum of Squares test, we provide both tests for evaluating the absolute export trends for India and her Asian competitors. Results of Cusum and Cusum of Squares tests are graphically shown in Figures 7.1–7.7 (presented in Appendix A.3) where, the bold curves provide the trends for respective variables along with appropriate ranges (straight lines) that mark the acceptable zone.

Generally speaking, Figures 7.1–7.7 show that the respective variable registers a 'stable' pattern if the bold curve – showing the trend – remains within the critical bounds (no intersections). Conversely, we witness an 'unstable' pattern if one or more intersections exist between the trend curve and the bounds. The Cusum of Squares test reveals instability in the export growth for most of the countries. For India, the prolonged break stretches for a decade (1994 to mid-2005) indicating substantial change in the growth structure of Indian clothing exports to the world markets as a result of the dismantling of the MFA regime. A similar trend is observed for China, which is the other beneficiary of the new regime. For China the break occurs in 1996 and lasts for almost a decade. But for both these big countries, the weaker Cusum tests show stable patterns. For Bangladesh, the Cusum test shows a break in exports growth during 2004, while the Cusum of Squares test indicates an unstable pattern between 1994 and 1997. A marginal break appeared in 1996–1997 for Pakistan, although the Cusum test does not confirm it. Indonesia is the only country with no structural break at all in its export trend as verified by both tests.

Malaysia, like Bangladesh, faces an unusual trend in exports in 2004 (Cusum test) along with a different, unstable pattern between 1994 and 2000 (Cusum of Squares test). Thailand experiences a minor structural break starting in 1994 and ending in the middle of 1996, as observed from the Cusum of Squares test. Table 7.20 summarizes the findings from the above exercises.

Table 7.21 provides the time dependence of exports via OLS estimations for all exporters in our study. Thus, total clothing exports of each country to the major regional markets taken together is considered as the dependent variable and a constant term A and Time (T, in years) are chosen as the regressors:

$$Y_{ij} = A_{ij} + \beta_{ij}T + u_{ij} \qquad (7.2)$$

where, i stands for the product type and j for the respective country. We carry out OLS regression analysis with 21 observations (from 1985–2005) for each country. The estimated values indicate that the value of exports of all these countries is positively related to the *time trend* and the coefficients are statistically significant. The coefficients along with country-wise $\bar{R}^2$s are reported in Table 7.21.

In brief, therefore, the entire exercise offers several interesting and counterintuitive results. For example, it was often claimed that since India is restrained by the quota system its withdrawal should promote production and exports for India. In reality, the export share declines (from 18 per cent to 10 per cent) between the pre-ATC to the post-ATC period over 1984–1985 and 2005 (Table 7.19).[12] Second, it is apparent from Table 7.20 that the structural break for most countries occurs in 1994 (except for China and Pakistan for which the break starts in 1996). Third, China and Bangladesh are the two real beneficiaries of the entire dismantling process whose export shares went up from 42 per cent to 61 per cent and from 4 per cent to 9 per cent respectively, while Pakistan, Indonesia, Malaysia and Thailand face sectoral contractions. Thailand is the worst affected country among all, with its export share falling from 13 per cent in 1985 to a mere 4 per cent in 2005. The downward change for Thailand started around 1996 (Cusum of Squares test). Malaysia had also seen similar change of fortune for its textile and clothing sector and these issues may be taken up for further research in future on the individual country level.

7.4 Concluding remarks

The implementation of the Agreement on Textile and Clothing by the WTO led to the complete withdrawal of the Multi-Fibre Arrangement in the year 2005. This chapter analysed the effects of this withdrawal on a number of Asian exporters of textile and clothing items to major destinations worldwide. It is common knowledge that trade-related quotas and non-tariff barriers are non-competitive in nature and removal of such restrictions create competitive field for all countries that do not necessarily enjoy the most favoured nation status with importers. At the same time, in a recent study it was pointed out that inclusion of China in the WTO and the concomitant withdrawal of MFA might turn out to be unfavourable for many smaller countries in Asia. With the help of commodity trade statistics in select items within the textile and clothing industries for seven major Asian exporters we establish that such an apprehension carries substantial credibility. In particular, during the ten-year transition of MFA phase-out we observe that countries such as China, Bangladesh, and India that were traditionally the more efficient exporters of textile merchandise have been the greatest beneficiaries. Some Asian countries that enjoyed the protection of bilateral import quotas, but were not necessarily the efficient producers, have suffered in the aftermath of MFA withdrawal.

We chose three main items within the clothing and textile industry according to their importance in overall export shares and analysed the implications for each country over a period of ten years between 1995 and 2005. In addition, we offer expected movements in the country-wise export growth path for these commodities over the next decade and illustrate stability of growth path for each. A phenomenal upsurge in the production and export from Bangladesh for all product categories in our study, along with complete diminution of the textile fibres industry in India contribute to our set of interesting results. It is observed that the competitiveness effect – one of the three components in the constant market share analysis that we deploy as a methodology – is the most dominant factor in the observed transitions. In other words, the effect of MFA phase out on countries that gained and lost can be largely explained by the competitiveness effect. Once again, much in contradiction to the earlier belief that a removal of quota shall lead to market expansion for all exporters seems unsubstantiated. This holds true for the quinquennial and the annual results for most of the countries. That countries like Thailand, Malaysia and Indonesia would suffer most in the face of competition from China and India turns out to be a natural outcome of the drive towards freeing world trade from non-competitive impediments.

A host of other issues, including the impact of textile industry on general growth and welfare levels should in the future help to understand the broader reach of the trade policy dealt with in this chapter. Similarly, it would be interesting to investigate the implications of the MFA withdrawal on the labour market in each country and discuss relevant policy aspects for the internal economies. Finally, over the last decade many Asian economies have seen unprecedented growth with avenues for trade creation among these countries opening up at a much faster rate. With more recent data, estimates of intra-Asia trade can add new dimensions to the analysis of post-MFA textile and clothing industries offered here.

Appendix

A.1 Methodology

This section presents the methodology used in Section 7.2. We use the method of CMS analysis developed by Hickman *et al.* (1979). The CMS analysis uses aggregate export data to measure the difference between constant share norms and actual export performance. The following symbols are used in the CMS model.

X_{ijt} = exports from country i to region j in year t.

$X_{it} = \sum_{j=1}^{n} X_{ijt}$ = total exports of the country i to all the n regions in year t.

$M_{jt} = \sum_{i=1}^{m} X_{ijt}$ = total imports of the jth region from all the m exporters in year t.

$W_t = \sum_{i=1}^{m} X_{it} = \sum_{j=1}^{n} M_{jt}$ = total exports to all the n regional markets by all the m

exporters or total imports by all the n regional markets from all the m exporters in year t.

$\alpha_{ijt} = \dfrac{X_{ijt}}{M_{jt}}$ = the market share of the exporting country i in region j in year t.

$\beta_{jt} = \dfrac{M_{jt}}{W_t}$ = the import share of region j of the total imports by all regions in year t.

$\gamma_{it} = \dfrac{X_{it}}{W_t}$ = the market share of the country i in terms of total exports to all regions in year t.

$j = 1 \dots n$, where, n is the number of regional markets.

$i = 1 \dots m$, where, m is the number of exporting countries to those regional markets.

0 – the subscript used to denote the base year.

Applying these definitions and summing over all the regional markets, we can derive expression (A.1.a) that decomposes total export by country i in year t, to all the regional markets taken together, into four components

$$X_{it} = \sum_{j=1}^{n} X_{ijt} = \left[\sum_{j=1}^{n} \alpha_{ij0}\beta_{j0}\right]W_t + \left[\sum_{j=1}^{n}\beta_{j0}\Delta\alpha_{ijt}\right]W_t +$$

$$\left[\sum_{j=1}^{n}\alpha_{ij0}\Delta\beta_{jt}\right]W_t + \left[\sum_{j=1}^{n}\Delta\alpha_{ijt}\Delta\beta_{jt}\right]W_t$$

(A.1.a)

Constant market share

The first term in the expression (A.1.a) gives the constant market share or the value of exports for country i in year t assuming that the ith country's share of the regional world markets taken together has remained unchanged since the base period. To show this, we note that in the base period,

$$\Delta\beta_{jt} = \Delta\alpha_{ijt} = 0$$

Therefore, expression (A.1.a) reduces to

$$X_{i0} = \left[\sum_{j=1}^{n}\alpha_{ij0}\beta_{j0}\right]W_0$$

(A.1.b)

where,

$$\gamma_{i0} = \left[\sum_{j=1}^{n}\alpha_{ij0}\beta_{j0}\right]$$

is the base period market share of total exports for country *i* such that,

$$\gamma_{i0} = \frac{X_{i0}}{W_0} \tag{A.1.c}$$

The competitiveness effect

The second term of the expression (A.1.a) summarizes the effects of changes in the *i*th country's market shares ($\Delta\alpha_{ijt}$) for all regions since the base period, holding constant the relative size (β_{j0}) of the different importing regions. This term isolates the influence of changes in the competitiveness of country *i* in specific regional markets.

The market size effect

The third term measures the net effect of shifts in the size of the various regional markets (β_{jt}) holding constant the *i*th country's share in each market (α_{ijt}). On account of this market size effect, total exports of country *i* may increase or decrease without any change in its export competitiveness (α_{ijt}). This term therefore isolates the influence of changes in the sizes of different regional markets.

The interaction effect

Finally, the last term measures the interaction between changes in market shares and market sizes. The interaction effect serves largely as a residual term and takes into account changes that cannot be attributed exclusively to either the competitiveness effect or the market size effect.

The export share for country *i* in total exports of each item to the regional world markets taken together may be obtained by dividing the expression (A.1.a) by W_t,

$$\gamma_{it} = \frac{X_{it}}{W_t} = \left[\sum_{j=1}^{n}\alpha_{ij0}\beta_{j0}\right] + \left[\sum_{j=1}^{n}\beta_{j0}\Delta\alpha_{ijt}\right] + \left[\sum_{j=1}^{n}\alpha_{ij0}\Delta\beta_{jt}\right] + \left[\sum_{j=1}^{n}\Delta\alpha_{ijt}\Delta\beta_{jt}\right] \tag{A.1.d}$$

Since the first term on the right hand side of the expression (A.1.d) is the market share of country *i* for the base period, this expression may also be written as:

$$\Delta\gamma_{it} = \gamma_{it} - \gamma_{i0} = \left[\sum_{j=1}^{n}\beta_{j0}\Delta\alpha_{ijt}\right] + \left[\sum_{j=1}^{n}\alpha_{ij0}\Delta\beta_{jt}\right] + \left[\sum_{j=1}^{n}\Delta\alpha_{ijt}\Delta\beta_{jt}\right] \tag{A.1.e}$$

Finally, the change in export share in each period can be, more conveniently, expressed in the form of a ratio to the export share of the base period, by dividing expression (A.1.e) by γ_{i0}:

$$\dot{\gamma} = \frac{\Delta\gamma_{it}}{\gamma_{i0}} = \frac{\left[\sum_{j=1}^{n}\beta_{j0}\Delta\alpha_{ijt}\right]}{\gamma_{i0}} + \frac{\left[\sum_{j=1}^{n}\alpha_{ij0}\Delta\beta_{jt}\right]}{\gamma_{i0}} + \frac{\left[\sum_{j=1}^{n}\Delta\alpha_{ijt}\Delta\beta_{jt}\right]}{\gamma_{i0}} \tag{A.1.f}$$

Therefore, expression (A.1.f) reveals that the percentage change in export share of a country in any item ($\dot{\gamma}$) can be decomposed into three constituent parts, namely,

i   percentage change in export share explained by the competitiveness effect,
ii percentage change in export share explained by the market size effect and
iii percentage change in export share explained by the interaction effect.

A.2 Tables

Table 7.1 Country-wise total export of textile fibres (*SITC-26*) to five important regional markets 1985–1994 [value in million US$]

Year	India	Pakistan	Sri Lanka	Bangladesh	Indonesia	Malaysia	Thailand	China
1985	23.42	195.91	12.57	17.51	1.35	1.30	5.64	544.57
1986	68.24	220.84	12.19	19.19	0.68	1.54	3.01	597.11
1987	51.16	273.39	11.13	17.91	0.75	2.12	4.67	805.34
1988	40.09	275.36	11.26	15.94	2.51	44.10	6.80	950.90
1989	69.76	198.15	14.55	16.86	19.51	43.40	15.86	915.30
1990	122.08	196.88	13.13	10.48	13.80	46.30	18.69	629.72
1991	49.73	144.68	16.60	20.04	14.88	38.87	30.06	622.93
1992	34.93	143.61	13.74	15.12	11.16	30.14	38.36	498.48
1993	47.79	66.21	12.20	9.66	8.12	28.76	47.57	418.98
1994	40.30	55.74	16.85	23.29	9.50	40.79	58.03	628.67

Data Source: Commodity Trade Statistics; UN Statistical Papers: Series D.

Table 7.2 Country-wise total export of textile fibres (*SITC-65*) to Five important regional markets 1985–1994 [value in million US$]

Year	India	Pakistan	Sri Lanka	Bangladesh	Indonesia	Malaysia	Thailand	China
1985	575.14	730.62	11.42	211.34	155.60	90.12	248.37	1246.26
1986	710.09	927.86	20.12	170.46	155.56	102.72	289.14	1354.70
1987	1198.74	1320.65	28.11	191.12	293.30	136.01	417.48	1965.66
1988	1134.84	1342.47	27.24	165.87	404.58	109.92	484.29	2273.28
1989	1319.15	1391.07	18.15	160.13	453.59	128.97	512.06	2358.45
1990	1630.75	1770.87	20.27	179.31	648.66	148.03	612.06	2225.72
1991	1810.79	2025.84	39.55	175.46	813.72	178.23	684.42	2458.65
1992	2191.41	2288.20	63.51	226.36	1187.49	213.94	728.95	2631.78
1993	2160.81	2324.72	81.64	229.47	1180.32	231.98	781.76	3010.98
1994	2646.16	2500.21	104.70	211.55	1256.70	282.34	846.33	3680.60

Data Source: Commodity Trade Statistics; UN Statistical Papers: Series D.

Table 7.3 Country-wise total export of textile fabrics and yarn (SITC-84) to five important regional markets 1985–1994 [value in million US$]

Year	India	Pakistan	Sri Lanka	Bangladesh	Indonesia	Malaysia	Thailand	China
1985	704.54	219.22	272.64	162.47	310.12	307.79	511.27	1659.03
1986	914.31	406.25	316.51	232.24	382.28	389.96	712.11	1919.07
1987	1284.16	517.82	411.34	406.44	563.12	578.57	1209.06	2560.04
1988	1324.38	557.31	424.26	401.36	718.90	788.37	1497.29	3034.02
1989	1928.45	664.55	479.67	428.82	1050.68	987.26	1907.12	3273.74
1990	2185.35	950.53	631.54	576.49	1500.15	1186.15	2147.05	3086.78
1991	2234.59	1131.94	1054.68	784.01	1941.36	1347.92	2593.32	5077.85
1992	2806.33	1384.35	1177.45	1037.66	2613.30	1664.49	2565.60	6795.91
1993	2673.11	1475.70	1323.52	1227.83	2877.21	1760.88	2854.32	10526.58
1994	3339.31	1509.45	1435.37	1151.10	2680.64	1844.07	2984.85	12830.48

Data Source: Commodity Trade Statistics; UN Statistical Papers: Series D.

Table 7.4 Annual percentage change In India's export performance of clothing and accessories (SITC-26) to all regional markets for 1985–1994

Year	Percentage change in export share	Percentage change in export share explained by competitiveness effect	Percentage change in export share explained by market - size effect	Percentage change in export share explained by interaction effect
1985–1986	110.924	86.655	2.721	21.548
1986–1987	–49.747	–44.001	16.645	–22.391
1987–1988	–31.841	–34.411	–4.182	6.752
1988–1989	80.194	75.570	3.687	0.937
1989–1990	115.438	127.441	–7.972	–4.031
1990–1991	–54.277	–53.658	0.415	–1.034
1991–1992	–10.956	–14.928	8.517	–4.545
1992–1993	68.307	68.195	2.148	–2.036
1993–1994	–37.939	–34.195	–4.201	0.457

Data Source: Commodity Trade Statistics; UN Statistical Papers: Series D.

Table 7.5 Annual percentage change in India's export performance of textile fabrics and yarns (*SITC-65*) to all regional markets for 1985–1994

Year	Percentage change in export share	Percentage change in export share explained by competitiveness effect	Percentage change in export share explained by market size effect	Percentage change in export share explained by interaction effect
1985–1986	8.764	3.646	4.361	0.757
1986–1987	12.128	14.310	–2.020	–0.162
1987–1988	–12.553	–9.100	–4.116	0.663
1988–1989	9.361	7.492	1.695	0.174
1989–1990	10.075	2.531	7.106	0.438
1990–1991	3.897	5.201	–1.860	0.556
1991–1992	4.481	3.142	0.990	0.349
1992–1993	–5.861	–4.096	–1.639	–0.126
1993–1994	3.016	6.277	–2.217	–1.044

Data Source: Commodity Trade Statistics; UN Statistical Papers: Series D.

Table 7.6 Annual percentage change in India's export performance of clothing (SITC-84) to all regional markets for 1985–1994

Year	Percentage change in export share	Percentage change in export share explained by competitiveness effect	Percentage change in export share explained by market size effect	Percentage change in export share explained by interaction effect
1985–1986	2.149	−2.073	4.606	−0.384
1986–1987	−1.907	−4.071	2.947	−0.783
1987–1988	−11.201	−8.597	−2.572	−0.032
1988–1989	19.340	20.313	−0.974	0.001
1989–1990	−7.439	−10.237	3.222	−0.424
1990–1991	−16.305	−15.512	−0.231	−0.562
1991–1992	1.385	5.522	−3.160	−0.977
1992–1993	−22.733	−19.551	−3.151	−0.031
1993–1994	9.317	14.506	−2.304	−2.885

Data Source: Commodity Trade Statistics; UN Statistical Papers: Series D.

Table 7.7 Quinquennial percentage changes in export shares of eight exporting countries for textile fibres (SITC-26) for 1985–1994

	India	Pakistan	Sri Lanka	Bangladesh	Indonesia	Malaysia	Thailand	China
1985–88								
Percentage changes in export share	0.918	-16.270	-59.907	-45.455	5.700	3148.400	-24.829	3.914
Percentage changes in export share explained by competitiveness effect	0.197	-21.553	-46.481	-52.541	0.550	3187.800	-9.543	5.936
Percentage changes in export share explained by market-size effect	6.231	-6.978	-6.538	39.577	35.450	-34.500	10.214	0.565
Percentage changes in export share explained by interaction effect	-5.510	12.261	-6.888	-32.773	-30.300	-4.900	-25.500	-2.587
1988–1991								
Percentage changes in export share	78.113	-24.569	110.375	81.175	701.250	25.973	535.980	-5.847
Percentage changes in export share explained by competitiveness effect	79.163	-25.314	147.263	80.275	501.500	6.570	540.060	-4.635
Percentage changes in export share explained by market-size effect	-7.130	-2.732	-5.425	14.025	-1.650	-16.139	1.080	1.667
Percentage changes in export share explained by interaction effect	6.080	3.477	-31.463	-13.125	201.400	35.542	-5.160	-2.879
1991–1994								
Percentage changes in export share	-13.665	-58.500	10.156	26.566	-31.575	12.798	107.228	8.327
Percentage changes in export share explained by competitiveness effect	-9.974	-59.803	3.256	30.095	-14.919	27.467	119.616	6.484
Percentage changes in export share explained by market-size effect	5.366	-2.682	15.661	4.257	-23.756	-22.821	-6.422	1.960
Percentage changes in export share explained by interaction effect	-9.057	3.985	-8.761	-7.786	7.100	8.152	-5.966	-0.117

Data Source: Commodity Trade Statistics; UN Statistical Papers: Series D.

Table 7.8 Quinquennial percentage changes in export shares of eight exporting countries for textile fabrics and yarns (SITC – 65) for 1985–1994

	India	Pakistan	Sri Lanka	Bangladesh	Indonesia	Malaysia	Thailand	China
1985–1988								
Percentage changes in export share	8.538	1.151	41.933	-47.994	42.213	-32.688	7.405	0.338
Percentage changes in export share explained by competitiveness effect	7.588	-0.207	50.933	-52.771	43.444	-32.848	11.854	-0.292
Percentage changes in export share explained by market-size effect	-0.474	0.179	-8.367	0.748	-6.058	-0.381	1.505	2.012
Percentage changes in export share explained by interaction effect	1.424	1.179	-0.633	4.029	4.827	0.541	-5.954	-1.382
1988–1991								
Percentage changes in export share	15.859	9.521	2.520	-22.572	46.125	19.300	2.378	-20.499
Percentage changes in export share explained by competitiveness effect	10.929	9.595	1.500	-26.961	36.735	23.511	-1.758	-16.416
Percentage changes in export share explained by market-size effect	3.906	-0.463	1.280	10.746	2.968	1.256	7.211	-4.588
Percentage changes in export share explained by interaction effect	1.024	0.389	-0.260	-6.357	6.422	-5.467	-3.075	-0.505
1991–1994								
Percentage changes in export share	0.631	-14.876	80.300	126.415	10.738	10.199	-15.098	1.551
Percentage changes in export share explained by competitiveness effect	4.527	-13.782	83.820	121.448	7.878	10.086	-14.071	-1.240
Percentage changes in export share explained by market-size effect	-2.975	-0.930	0.160	-1.457	2.239	1.927	-0.701	2.346
Percentage changes in export share explained by interaction effect	-0.921	-0.164	-3.680	6.424	0.621	-1.814	-0.326	0.445

Data Source: Commodity Trade Statistics; UN Statistical Papers: Series D.

Table 7.9 Quinquennial percentage changes in export shares of eight exporting countries for clothing (SITC-84) for 1985–1994

	India	Pakistan	Sri Lanka	Bangladesh	Indonesia	Malaysia	Thailand	China
1985–1988								
Percentage changes in export share	-10.993	20.624	-19.032	17.293	10.584	21.102	39.200	-13.391
Percentage changes in export share explained by competitiveness effect	-11.494	19.334	-8.941	32.672	23.204	36.880	26.855	-17.940
Percentage changes in export share explained by market-size effect	6.064	8.343	-13.570	-20.382	-7.960	-10.143	2.142	3.254
Percentage changes in export share explained by interaction effect	-5.563	-7.053	3.479	5.003	-4.660	-5.635	10.203	1.295
1988–1991								
Percentage changes in export share	-8.658	9.652	25.083	4.839	45.881	-6.955	-6.178	-9.504
Percentage changes in export share explained by competitiveness effect	-8.456	8.156	37.898	10.615	44.676	-2.246	-7.526	-12.163
Percentage changes in export share explained by market-size effect	0.666	1.158	-7.137	-6.872	-6.041	-6.750	3.339	3.035
Percentage changes in export share explained by interaction effect	-0.868	0.338	-5.678	1.096	7.246	2.041	-1.991	-0.376
1991–1994								
Percentage changes in export share	-19.672	-24.016	-22.659	17.201	-20.537	-22.128	-30.691	44.850
Percentage changes in export share explained by competitiveness effect	-3.415	-11.277	-16.735	20.096	-11.835	-16.728	-28.966	28.140
Percentage changes in export share explained by market-size effect	-13.107	-13.700	-3.272	-7.273	-8.242	-6.375	-4.217	15.301
Percentage changes in export share explained by interaction effect	-3.150	0.961	-2.652	4.378	-0.460	0.975	2.492	1.409

Data Source: Commodity Trade Statistics; UN Statistical Papers: Series D.

Table 7.10 Country-wise total export of clothing to three important regional markets 1995–2005 [value in million US$]

Year	India	China	Bangladesh	Pakistan	Indonesia	Malaysia	Thailand
1995	3522.23	13963.29	1005.68	1454.9	2583.77	1992.44	2923.33
1996	3554.42	14597.68	2193.34	1690.16	2748.7	2055.14	6491.23
1997	3535.24	15361.44	2655.48	1628.46	2176.22	2014.07	2995.92
1998	3726.06	15433.09	3748.45	1679.22	2167.19	2063.08	3006.09
1999	3813.8	17169.39	3493.5	1712.73	3004.95	1975.71	3003.95
2000	4596.26	21640.57	3972.02	1954.21	3815.81	2016.63	3293.15
2001	4063.99	22471.94	4218.1	1882.75	3592.82	1849.94	3124.66
2002	4651.62	23504.55	4929.06	1894.77	3101.66	1774.77	2722.03
2003	2974.64	26254.11	4951.63	2485.2	3333.65	1771.53	3114.42
2004	5028.41	30275.72	6160.36	2621.47	3697.51	1970.9	3411.04
2005	7624.68	43208.61	6364.61	3058.38	4314.98	2033.89	3489.19

Data Source: UN Database COMTRADE: Database of Commodity Trade Statistics, UN Statistical Papers; Series D.

Table 7.11 Annual percentage changes in export share of clothing for India: 1995–2005

Year	Percentage change in export share explained by competitiveness effect	Percentage change in export share explained by market size effect	Percentage change in export share explained by interaction effect	Percentage change in export share
1995–1996	–14.871	–1.518	–0.515	–16.904
1996–1997	5.101	4.444	–0.378	9.168
1997–1998	–2.350	3.003	–0.079	0.574
1998–1999	–2.018	–2.580	–0.089	–4.686
1999–2000	2.498	–2.809	0.061	–0.250
2000–2001	–10.387	–1.048	0.035	–11.399
2001–2002	5.140	5.508	0.117	10.765
2002–2003	–39.505	–2.217	2.384	–39.338
2003–2004	40.873	–1.577	3.419	42.715
2004–2005	7.614	7.080	0.316	15.010

Data Source: UN Database COMTRADE.

Table 7.12 Annual percentage changes in export share of clothing for China: 1995–2005

Year	Percentage change in export share explained by competitiveness effect	Percentage change in export share explained by market size effect	Percentage change in export share explained by interaction effect	Percentage change in export share
1995–1996	-12.875	-0.522	-0.518	-13.915
1996–1997	18.025	-2.353	-0.169	15.503
1997–1998	-0.743	-3.158	-0.230	-4.131
1998–1999	0.571	3.041	-0.014	3.598
1999–2000	2.140	2.198	-0.015	4.323
2000–2001	3.229	0.852	-0.026	4.055
2001–2002	4.526	-3.335	0.029	1.219
2002–2003	4.155	2.232	-0.430	5.958
2003–2004	-1.316	-1.190	-0.136	-2.642
2004–05	12.602	-5.352	0.998	8.249

Data Source: UN Database COMTRADE.

Table 7.13 Annual percentage changes in export share of clothing for Bangladesh: 1995–2005

Year	Percentage change in export share explained by competitiveness effect	Percentage change in export share explained by market size effect	Percentage change in export share explained by interaction effect	Percentage change in export share
1995–1996	83.429	−5.617	1.775	79.587
1996–1997	28.112	4.552	0.223	32.887
1997–1998	30.166	3.452	1.080	34.699
1998–1999	−10.840	−2.948	0.576	−13.212
1999–2000	−2.543	−3.291	−0.061	−5.894
2000–2001	7.661	−1.250	0.002	6.413
2001–2002	6.549	5.453	1.081	13.083
2002–2003	−2.745	−2.034	0.074	−4.705
2003–2004	4.266	1.134	−0.366	5.034
2004–2005	−26.894	7.095	−1.838	−21.637

Data Source: UN Database COMTRADE.

Table 7.14 Annual percentage changes in export share of clothing for Pakistan: 1995–2005

Year	Percentage change in export share explained by competitiveness effect	Percentage change in export share explained by market size effect	Percentage change in export share explained by interaction effect	Percentage change in export share
1995–1996	–2.957	0.312	–1.696	–4.342
1996–1997	2.425	4.148	–0.819	5.754
1997–1998	–5.113	3.644	–0.133	–1.602
1998–1999	–1.824	–3.095	–0.102	–5.021
1999–2000	–3.306	–2.485	0.229	–5.562
2000–2001	–2.450	–1.006	–0.003	–3.460
2001–2002	–6.552	4.385	–0.442	–2.609
2002–2003	28.245	–3.051	–0.773	24.420
2003–2004	–12.758	2.362	–0.549	–10.945
2004–2005	–18.010	7.809	–1.310	–11.510

Data Source: UN Database COMTRADE.

Table 7.15 Annual percentage changes in export share of clothing for Indonesia: 1995–2005

Year	Percentage change in export share explained by competitiveness effect	Percentage change in export share explained by market size effect	Percentage change in export share explained by interaction effect	Percentage change in export share
1995–1996	–12.021	1.269	–1.648	–12.400
1996–1997	–14.413	2.438	–1.125	–13.100
1997–1998	–8.153	2.940	0.241	–4.972
1998–1999	32.818	–2.845	–0.854	29.118
1999–2000	7.259	–1.955	–0.201	5.103
2000–2001	–4.844	–0.867	0.060	–5.651
2001–2002	–18.679	3.370	–1.148	–16.457
2002–2003	5.438	–3.145	–0.337	1.956
2003–2004	–9.050	2.924	–0.233	–6.360
2004–2005	–17.614	7.519	–1.390	–11.485

Data Source: UN Database COMTRADE.

Table 7.16 Annual percentage changes in export share of clothing for Malaysia: 1995–2005

Year	Percentage change in export share explained by competitiveness effect	Percentage change in export share explained by market size effect	Percentage change in export share explained by interaction effect	Percentage change in export share
1995–1996	-17.503	4.555	-2.117	-15.065
1996–1997	6.721	1.277	-0.430	7.567
1997–1998	-6.074	3.925	-0.105	-2.254
1998–1999	-7.849	-3.274	0.300	-10.823
1999–2000	-14.383	-1.332	0.198	-15.517
2000–2001	-7.427	-0.701	0.051	-8.078
2001–2002	-8.945	2.228	-0.443	-7.160
2002–2003	-2.136	-3.198	0.022	-5.312
2003–2004	-8.618	2.988	-0.443	-6.073
2004–2005	-26.129	6.604	-2.203	-21.728

Data Source: UN Database COMTRADE.

Table 7.17 Annual percentage changes in export share of clothing for Thailand: 1995–2005

Year	Percentage change in export share explained by competitiveness effect	Percentage change in export share explained by market size effect	Percentage change in export share explained by interaction effect	Percentage change in export share
1995–1996	74.741	1.874	6.228	82.843
1996–1997	−49.482	−1.197	1.337	−49.342
1997–1998	−7.372	2.836	0.284	−4.252
1998–1999	−4.167	−2.709	−0.069	−6.945
1999–2000	−8.362	−0.920	0.019	−9.263
2000–2001	−4.347	−0.595	0.020	−4.922
2001–2002	−17.352	1.625	0.029	−15.697
2002–2003	12.136	−4.012	0.411	8.535
2003–2004	−9.961	3.020	−0.593	−7.534
2004–2005	−26.480	6.285	−2.219	−22.414

Data Source: UN Database COMTRADE.

Table 7.18 Country-wise share in three important regional markets for clothing (1995–2005)

Year	India	China	Bangladesh	Pakistan	Indonesia	Malaysia	Thailand
1995	0.128	0.509	0.037	0.053	0.094	0.073	0.107
1996	0.107	0.438	0.066	0.051	0.082	0.062	0.195
1997	0.116	0.506	0.087	0.054	0.072	0.066	0.099
1998	0.117	0.485	0.118	0.053	0.068	0.065	0.094
1999	0.112	0.502	0.102	0.050	0.088	0.058	0.088
2000	0.111	0.524	0.096	0.047	0.092	0.049	0.080
2001	0.099	0.545	0.102	0.046	0.087	0.045	0.076
2002	0.109	0.552	0.116	0.045	0.073	0.042	0.064
2003	0.066	0.585	0.110	0.055	0.074	0.039	0.069
2004	0.095	0.569	0.116	0.049	0.070	0.037	0.064
2005	0.109	0.616	0.091	0.044	0.062	0.029	0.050

Data Source: UN Database COMTRADE: Database of Commodity Trade Statistics, UN Statistical Papers; Series.

Table 7.19 Country-wise share in important regional markets for clothing (1985–2005)

Year	India	China	Bangladesh	Pakistan	Indonesia	Malaysia	Thailand
1985	0.182	0.428	0.042	0.057	0.080	0.079	0.132
1986	0.184	0.387	0.047	0.082	0.077	0.079	0.144
1987	0.180	0.360	0.057	0.073	0.079	0.081	0.170
1988	0.159	0.365	0.048	0.067	0.086	0.095	0.180
1989	0.188	0.320	0.042	0.065	0.103	0.096	0.186
1990	0.188	0.265	0.050	0.082	0.129	0.102	0.185
1991	0.148	0.336	0.052	0.075	0.128	0.089	0.172
1992	0.149	0.360	0.055	0.073	0.139	0.088	0.136
1993	0.114	0.450	0.052	0.063	0.123	0.075	0.122
1994	0.127	0.487	0.044	0.057	0.102	0.070	0.113
1995	0.128	0.509	0.037	0.053	0.094	0.073	0.107
1996	0.107	0.438	0.066	0.051	0.082	0.062	0.195
1997	0.116	0.506	0.087	0.054	0.072	0.066	0.099
1998	0.117	0.485	0.118	0.053	0.068	0.065	0.094
1999	0.112	0.502	0.102	0.050	0.088	0.058	0.088
2000	0.111	0.524	0.096	0.047	0.092	0.049	0.080
2001	0.099	0.545	0.102	0.046	0.087	0.045	0.076
2002	0.109	0.552	0.116	0.045	0.073	0.042	0.064
2003	0.066	0.585	0.110	0.055	0.074	0.039	0.069
2004	0.095	0.569	0.116	0.049	0.070	0.037	0.064
2005	0.109	0.616	0.091	0.044	0.062	0.029	0.050

Table 7.20 Country-wise stability patterns of clothing exports

Country	Time trend		Break year	
	Cusum	Cusum squares	Cusum	Cusum squares
India	Stable	Unstable	NA	1994 to mid-2005
China	Stable	Unstable	NA	1996 to mid-2005
Bangladesh	Unstable	Unstable	2004	1994–1997
Pakistan	Stable	Unstable	NA	1996–1997
Indonesia	Stable	Stable	NA	NA
Malaysia	Unstable	Unstable	2004	1994–2000
Thailand	Stable	Unstable	NA	1994 to mid-1996

Table 7.21 Results of ordinary least square estimation for all the countries

Countries/coefficients	India	China	Bangladesh	Pakistan	Indonesia	Malaysia	Thailand
Time	232.37	1684.7	319.49	116.17	178.11	80.12	126.85
(t-ratios)	(8.96)	(12.99)	(14.31)	(16.47)	(10.63)	(6.79)	(3.65)
Constant term (A)	609.90	−4501.1	−1128.7	192.56	382.48	660.30	1297.8
(t-ratios)	(1.87)	(−2.76)	(−4.03)	(2.17)	(1.82)	(4.46)	(2.97)
Value of $\bar{R}^2$	0.7985	0.8935	0.9106	0.9311	0.8486	0.6933	0.3819

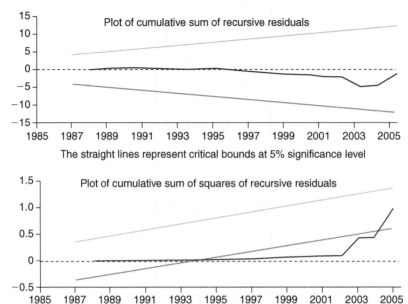

Figure 7.1 Results of Cusum and Cusum of Squares test: India.

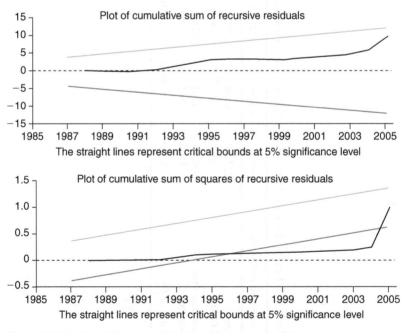

Figure 7.2 Results of Cusum and Cusum of Squares test: China.

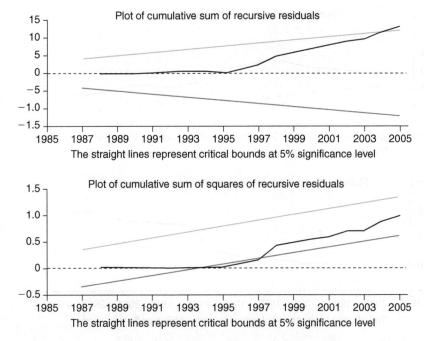

Figure 7.3 Results of Cusum and Cusum of Squares test: Bangladesh.

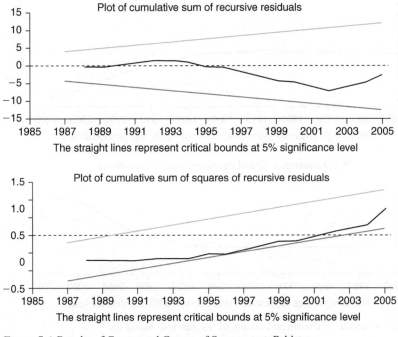

Figure 7.4 Results of Cusum and Cusum of Squares test: Pakistan.

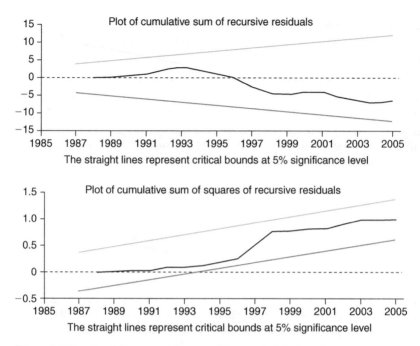

Figure 7.5 Results of Cusum and Cusum of Squares test: Indonesia.

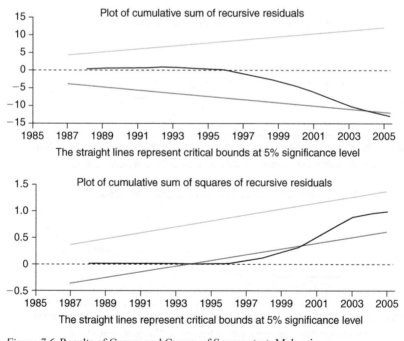

Figure 7.6 Results of Cusum and Cusum of Squares test: Malaysia.

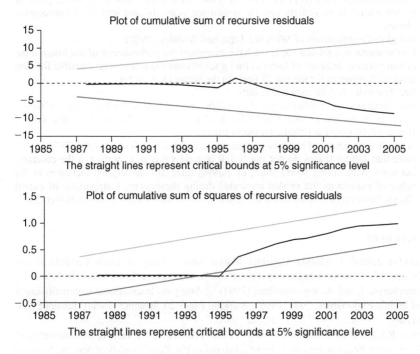

Figure 7.7 Results of Cusum and Cusum of Squares test: Thailand.

Notes

1 Mausumi Kar is indebted to Soumyen Sikdar for several important suggestions. Saibal Kar thanks S. Mansoob Murshed for very insightful suggestions on an earlier draft and Pedro Goulart for relevant discussions. Saibal Kar is also indebted to ICSSR-NWO for partial financial support towards this research. The usual disclaimer applies.

2 Dr Mausumi Kar is Assistant Professor of Economics, Women's Christian College, Kolkata, India. She has been awarded PhD in Economics from Calcutta University and has worked extensively on international trade in textile and apparel, among other things. She has published in peer-reviewed journals on topics in Public Economics and teaches undergraduate and graduate international economics. Faculty: Department of Economics, Women's Christian College, Kolkata, India.

3 Dr Saibal Kar is a Fellow in Economics (Associate Professor) at the Centre for Studies in Social Sciences, Calcutta, India and Visiting Scholar at Amsterdam School of Economics, University of Amsterdam. He has published in several reputed international journals and edited volumes on Labour Economics and International Trade. Faculty: Centre for Studies in Social Sciences, Calcutta, India and, Amsterdam School of Economics, UvA, The Netherlands.

4 Address for correspondence: Centre for Studies in Social Sciences, Calcutta R-1, B. P. Township, Kolkata 700 094, India.

5 The Uruguay Round of GATT launched at Punta Del Este led to the Agreement on

Textiles and Clothing (ATC) in 1995. It is the institutional shape given to the promise to end quotas in an orderly process within ten years divided into three consecutive phases.

6 For global implications of MFA see Trela and Whalley (1990).
7 Furthermore, in a related paper we have examined the performance of the firms in the cotton garment industry of India to find a set of important factors responsible for firm level performances for the top 25 firms in the sector (Kar 2009).
8 See Appendix A.2 for data and results.
9 For limitations and further scope of the CMS analysis, see Ahmadi-Esfahami (2006).
10 Also see Hamilton (1990); EXIM Bank of India (1995); Kathuria (1995); Gherzi Report (2003); Sarkar (2004); Hashim (2005).
11 A detailed treatment of recursive residuals is available in Johnston (1984: 207).
12 Note that falling shares do not imply fall in total value of exports. On the contrary, countries with falling world share of exports have also undergone increases in the value of exports as the market expanded during these years. Comparison of export shares, however, provides ample evidence in favour of the state of competitiveness.

References

Ahmadi-Esfahani, F. (2006) 'Constant Market Shares Analysis: Uses, Limitations and Prospects', *Australian Journal of Agricultural and Resource Economics*, 50: 510–26.
Bhattacharya, J. and A. Raychaudhuri (1994) 'A Study on International Competitiveness of India's Exportables, 1971–1990', Working Paper 20, Jabalpur (India): Jabalpur University.
Brown, R.L., J. Durbin and J.M. Evans (1975) 'Techniques for Testing the Constancy of Regression Relationships over Time', *Journal of the Royal Statistical Society, Series B (Methodological)* 37: 149–92.
Danninger, S. and F. Joutz (2007) 'What Explains Germany's Rebounding Export Market Share?' IMF Working Paper 07/24, Washington, DC: International Monetary Fund.
Davis, D.R. (1995) 'Intra-industry Trade: A Heckscher–Ohlin–Ricardo Approach', *Journal of International Economics*, 39: 201–26.
Debroy, B. (1996) *Beyond the Uruguay Round: The Indian Perspective on GATT*. New Delhi: Response Books.
EXIM Bank of India (1995) 'Indian Garment Exports: Implications of the MFA Phase-Out', Occasional Paper 34, Export–Import Bank of India.
Gherzi Report (2003) 'Benchmarking of Costs of Production of Textile Products in India vis-à-vis China, Pakistan, Indonesia, Bangladesh and Sri Lanka', Switzerland: Gherzi AG (Swiss Textile Organization).
Hamilton, C.B. (1990) *Textiles Trade and the Developing Countries: Eliminating the Multi-Fibre Arrangement in the 1990s*. Washington DC: World Bank.
Hashim, D.A. (2005) 'Post-MFA: Making the Textile and Garment Industry Competitive', *Economic and Political Weekly*, 40: 117–27.
Hickman, B.G., Y. Kuroda and L.J. Lau (1979) 'The Pacific Basin in World Trade: An Analysis of Changing Trade Patterns, 1955–1975', *Empirical Economics*, 4: 63–85.
Ichikawa, H. (1996) 'Constant-Market Share Analysis and Open Regionalism: A Study Suggestion', online, available at: www.ide.go.jp/English/Publish/Download/Apec/pdf/1996_03.pdf (accessed 15 August 2000).
James, W.E. and O. Movshuk (2004) 'Shifting International Competitiveness: An Analysis of Market Share in Manufacturing Industries in Japan, Korea, Taiwan and the USA', *Asian Economic Journal*, 18: 121–48.

Johnston, J. (1984) *Econometric Methods*. New York: McGraw-Hill Book Company.

Kar, M. (2009) 'Textile and Apparel Trade of India in the Changing Global Context', Department of Economics, Calcutta: Calcutta University.

Kathuria, S. (1995) 'Competitiveness of Indian Industry', in D. Mookherjee (ed.) *Indian Industry: Policies and Performances*, New York: Oxford University Press.

Koopmann, G. and C. Langer (1988) 'Trends in International Competitiveness of Industrial Countries', *Intereconomics* 23: 8–14.

Krugman, P. (1980) 'Scale Economies, Product Differentiation, and the Pattern of Trade', *American Economic Review*, 70: 950–9.

Krugman, P. (1981) 'Intraindustry Specialization and the Gains from Trade', *Journal of Political Economy*, 89: 959–73.

Leamer, E. and R. Stern (2006) *Quantitative International Economics*. New Brunswick, NJ: Transaction Publisher.

Lohrmann, A.-M. (2000) 'On Turkey's Export Performance: A Decomposed Constant Market Share Analysis', *Russian and East European Finance and Trade*, 36: 80–90.

Marjit, S. and A. Raychaudhuri (1997) *India's Exports: An Analytical Study*. New Delhi: Oxford University Press.

Marjit, S., T. Kabiraj and A. Mukherjee (2009) 'Quota as a Competitive Device', in T. Kamigashi and L. Zhao (eds) *International Trade and Economic Dynamics: Essays in Memory of Koji Shimomura*, Heidelberg: Springer-Verlag.

Misra, S. (1993) *India's Textile Sector: A Policy Analysis*. New Delhi: Sage Publications.

Piezas-Jerbi, N. and C. Nee (2009) 'Market Shares in the Post-Uruguay Round Era: A Closer Look using Shift-Share Analysis', Working Paper ERSD 14, Geneva: WTO.

Richardson, D.J. (1971) 'Constant Market Share Analysis of Export Growth.' *Journal of International Economics*, 1: 227–39.

Sarkar, P. (2004) 'Export Diversification, Market Shares and Issues of North–South Terms of Trade', in A. Bhattacharjea and S. Marjit (eds) *Globalization and the Developing Economies: Theory and Evidence*, New Delhi: Manohar Publishers.

Simonis, D. (2000a) 'Belgium's Export Performance. A Constant Market Shares Analysis', Brussels: Federal Planning Bureau.

Simonis, D. (2000b) 'Export performance in Eastern Europe', online, available at: www.sre.wu-wien.ac.at/ersa/ersaconfs/ersa00/pdf-ersa/pdf/176.pdf (accessed 17 May 2000).

Trela, I. and J. Whalley (1990) 'Global Effects of Developed Country Trade Restrictions on Textiles and Apparel', *Economic Journal*, 100: 1190–205.

8 The geography of trade and the network effects of economic diplomacy in the South[1]

Marie-Lise E.H. van Veenstra,[2] Mina Yakop[3] and Peter A.G van Bergeijk[4]

8.1 Introduction

Over the last decades, export promotion agencies have emerged in many countries as a popular tool to increase exports, both in developed and in developing countries (Figure 8.1). Around 1990 export promotion agencies became controversial especially in developing countries due to a lack of effectiveness, funds and business (i.e., client) orientation, while the macroeconomic policies at the time did not offer a solid basis for the social acceptance of exports, so that export promotion agencies mostly did not gain support from the business community (Keesing and Singer 1991; De Wulf 2001). In spite of heavy criticisms, most

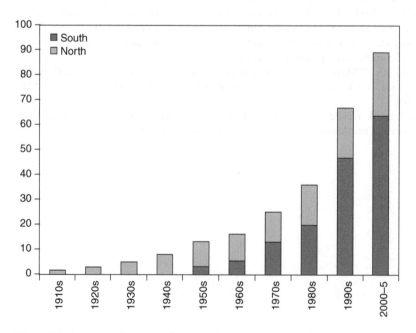

Figure 8.1 Recent studies on the impact of commercial diplomacy.

export promotion agencies were kept in business and worked hard to increase their effectiveness. The policy environment changed and the strong anti-exports bias disappeared.

The change in the policy environment was also reflected in the activities of the Foreign Service through their network of embassies and consulates with much more attention for the 'low politics' of trade and investment (Kostecki and Naray 2007). Recently, an academic discussion on the effectiveness of such bodies has emerged, triggered by Rose (2007), who found that the Foreign Service has a positive effect of about 6 to 10 percent on bilateral exports. Several authors have confirmed these findings (Table 8.1) for wide ranges of activities and wide ranges of instruments.

One drawback of the literature is that these instruments are studied in isolation. It is quite possible, however, that the instruments are interlinked in practice. For instance, public export promotion agencies often make use of the network of embassies and consulates abroad for hands-on information about a particular market. Therefore, the two types of bodies may benefit from considerable synergies. It is, however, also possible that the activities of the instruments crowd out. The only way to find this out is to evaluate the effectiveness of two instruments with respect to their influence on (bilateral) exports as we plan to do. We organize our discussion as follows. Section 8.2 discusses the economic rationale for government intervention in dealing with trade barriers and market failures. It also looks at the question of how governments can offer solutions and points at the risk of government failure. Section 8.3 presents the overall empirical analysis. We introduce the gravity model, discuss the dataset and present the overall results for a sample that consists of the 1242 bilateral trade flows of 36 countries. Section 8.4 presents and discusses the general benchmark results of

Table 8.1 Recent studies on the impact of commercial diplomacy

Study		Elasticity
Lederman *et al.* (2006)	Export impact of export promotion agencies	0.07–0.11
Rose (2007)	Export impact of embassies and consulates	0.08–0.11
Gil-Pareja *et al.* (2007)	Tourism impact of embassies and consulates	0.15–0.30
Head and Ries (2006)	Export impact of state visits (Canada)	insignificant
Nistch (2007)	Export impact of state visits (USA, France and Germany)	0.08–0.13
Yakop and Bergeijk (2009)	Export impact of embassies and consulates	0.06–0.13
Afman and Maurel (2010)	Impact of embassies and consulates on East–West trade (and vice versa)	0.07–0.17

this study. Section 8.5 delves deeper into the data as we distinguish between, on the one hand, low- and middle-income countries (the 'South') and, on the other hand, high-income countries (the 'North') in order to analyze differences related to levels of development. In particular, we take a look at differences between and within these country groupings and in this process derive some lessons for South–South and South–North trade. Section 8.6 compares our findings to earlier studies, draws conclusions and suggests some issues for further research.

8.2 Border effects, market distortions and what to do about them

Economists have always been very critical about economic and commercial diplomacy. Their theoretical argument against government intervention is straightforward. A transfer of resources to an export industry is in itself already an implicit subsidy that distorts the efficient outcome because it has to be financed by distorting taxes, but it also generates an additional terms of trade loss, because shippers will export the good up to the point where the domestic price exceeds the foreign price by the amount of the subsidy. This is the case for explicit subsidies but it is equally true for implicit subsidies, that is when the government provides certain diplomatic services for free or below market value to the private sector. Thus economists only see a role for public intervention if markets fail, that is if the efficient outcome cannot be reached for some reason. So a preliminary question is: why do exports need to be promoted, or in other words, why do productive firms not utilize their full export capacity without export promotion? We will first take a look at the barriers to trade that hinder the decision to export, then consider which market failures could motivate govern-ment action and finish with some critical remarks on government failure.

8.2.1 Barriers

Firms that want to start exporting must overcome many barriers. The existence of substantial and significant border effects suggests that although many formal (conventional) trade barriers have decreased or been removed over the last decades, there are many other – often intangible – hurdles that need to be passed in international trade. For instance, multilateral negotiations in the WTO have led to a gradual removal of many tariffs. Also, transport costs have been falling steadily. In spite of such trends, the effect of distance is increasing (van Bergeijk 2009). Cultural and institutional distance seems to take an ever more important role in international (trade) relations. Ramaswami and Yang (1990) describe several (perceived) barriers to trade for firms that want to start exporting or expand their current exports. They distinguish four categories of barriers: export knowledge (informational barriers), internal resource constraints (financial or human resources), procedural barriers (language, cultural differences, red tape) and exogenous barriers (fluctuations in the exchange rate, taxation, corruption, etc.). Most of these barriers apply in particular to developing countries (Brunetti *et al.* 1997). Keesing and Singer (1991) point out that in developing countries, exporters had more difficulty in obtaining permissions and dealing with restrictions and controls. Delivery is often slower and less reliable in developing countries, quality and service levels are often lower. Developing countries thus could gain more from (public) export promotion. For exporters in developing countries, quality standards abroad (in developed countries) are often higher than domestic standards (De Wulf 2001), making it more difficult for exporters to compete in foreign markets. (Potential) exporters in industrialized countries are hampered less by such barriers to export and especially so for exports between the most developed countries. Exports to and from developing countries are therefore most difficult in terms of crossing such barriers to trade.

8.2.2 Market failures

Theoretical trade models use neoclassical assumptions, such as perfectly competitive markets with full information and rational behavior of all concerned agents. Self-interest of actors determines the utility- and profit-maximizing behavior of consumers and producers, respectively, which should result in an optimal and efficient allocation of (scarce) resources. Supply of goods and services is then determined by market forces. In theory, this leads to a Pareto-efficient optimum, a situation where no one could do better without making anyone else worse off.

Reality, however, often diverges from such highly stylized settings. Many market failures have been recognized to exist, also in developed, free market-oriented economies, although market failures are considered to be much more severe in developing countries (Stiglitz 1989; Krueger 1990). Examples of market failures with a high incidence are the existence of informational imperfections (asymmetric, incomplete or costly information), transaction costs or agency problems (adverse selection or moral hazard) and imperfect competition (market power). Furthermore, various types of externalities can cause market failures, as well as the characteristics of certain goods (e.g., public goods), inertia (inflexible labor and product markets that are unresponsive to price signals) or uncertainty. Market failures are especially relevant in international markets and for developing countries. Entry into foreign markets requires good knowledge about foreign legislation, cultural differences and local preferences and the search for and evaluation of potential international business partners is costly and time consuming (Volpe Martincus and Carballo 2008). Exporting thus requires an investment in information that cannot be recovered if the export project fails and if the project succeeds demonstration effects will cause copy cat behavior by competitors.[5] A firm will only make an investment if it knows that this will provide a competitive edge, but is less inclined to do so if other firms are able to observe the (changed) behavior of the firm, so that they will also benefit from the information, but without making any investment (the free-rider problem) (e.g., see Hausmann and Rodrik 2003). The market therefore tends to under-provide 'trade knowledge capital' which to a large extent is a public good.

Due to these market failures private firms invest too little in trade-relevant knowledge and this may justify public intervention.

The existence of market failures offers the theoretical economic justification for active government involvement in international activities.[6] According to Krueger (1990), the compensation of market failures is even one of the most important roles of the government, next to providing 'social overhead' and 'infrastructure.' The government can improve efficiency in markets by alleviating the effects of existing market failures and provide incentives for firms to adjust themselves to become an exporter and/or to increase their export capacity.

8.2.3 Government failure

The existence of a market failure is, however, a *necessary* but never a *sufficient* condition. For one thing, one should be careful not replace a market failure by a government failure. Harris and Li (2005: 76) describe government failure as 'a hindrance to firms and markets that arises when the government has a comparative advantage in supplying a good or service (often knowledge), but fails to do this.' Government institutions with self-interested agents might commit government failures in a way that is similar to market failure, for instance delinking of costs and revenues and externalities. According to Krueger (1990), government failure in many developing countries, resulting from omission (the neglect of public transport or communication facilities) or commission (government involvement in non-public activities) and corruption, is more costly than market failure. Therefore such activities should be scrutinized as Hoekman and Javoricik (2004: 3) propose:

> Pro-active support policies of whatever stripe should be subject to cost-benefit analysis and be informed by answers to the following types of questions: where is the market failure? What is the objective of a policy? How is the performance and cost effectiveness going to be monitored? It should also be recognized that such interventions are frequently associated with the risk of misdiagnosing the problem and the possibility of capture by rent seekers.

These are relevant questions indeed and our research will attempt to provide an element of such a cost–benefit analysis in the sense that we investigate if the export promotion activities deliver on their stated goals. Clearly this is again only a necessary condition for public intervention, but it is an important question. With these caveats in mind we can now turn to the instruments of export promotion.

8.2.4 How to promote exports?

In order to promote exports, firms could be encouraged to start exporting or increase their exports by providing the right incentives (so, by providing 'carrots'). Also, exports can be promoted by removing existing barriers to export (by removing 'sticks'), but public export promotion that focuses on aspiring exporters is not sufficient and needs to be accompanied by policies that improve certain firm characteristics (such as productivity) to help exporters to become permanent exporters (Alvarez 2007). Government policies with regard to export promotion may only be worthwhile when some sort of pre-selection is done, so that only the most productive firms are assisted in their internationalization process, as only these firms will be fit enough to survive international markets (van Bergeijk 2009). In practice, these approaches and insights have already been incorporated in the many export promotion instruments that have been used in commercial diplomacy. We will not be concerned with all these commercial export promotion activities but instead focus on the network of commercial diplomacy, that is on permanent representations of countries abroad (embassies and consulates) and on export promotion agencies.[7]

Traditionally, embassies and consulates were not only representing the home country abroad, but were also the eyes and ears in the host country (an informational role). Rose (2007) argues that since communication costs have fallen, information from and about other countries is more easily accessible, reducing the importance of the informational role of the Foreign Service. Nowadays, embassies and consulates are increasingly occupied with promotion of economic and commercial interests of the home country in the host country. Many Foreign Services now state that export promotion is one of their main tasks. Embassies are thus important actors in commercial diplomacy, and more specifically in the promotion of exports.

Whereas embassies are located in or near export markets, export promotion agencies (or trade promotion organizations) are often located inside the exporting country. The objectives of most export promotion organizations include supporting the business sector in their internationalization process and improving the performance of exporting businesses, creating a positive image of the home country abroad and generally increasing the home country's competitiveness so that the scope of the agencies has broadened over the years. Lederman *et al.* (2006) divide their services into four categories: country image building, export support services, marketing, and market research and publications. Volpe Martincus and Carballo (2008) point out that export promotion agencies can alleviate information problems, distinguishing between firms that try to enter new foreign markets or sell new products abroad (extensive margin) and information problems for firms that are already exporting and attempting to increase the volume of their exports (intensive margin). Volpe Martincus and Carballo (ibid.) find evidence that export promotion agencies in Peru are most effective in promoting exports in the extensive margin, where information problems are most severe. Their findings support the idea that export promotion is effective in alleviating information problems.

8.3 Empirical analysis

For the empirical analysis in this chapter, we use an extended form of the so-called 'gravity model'; nowadays one of the most widely used models for empirical trade analyses. A gravity model quantifies factors that explain the volume of international trade flows in commodities. The form of this model is similar to the Newtonian gravity equation used in physics. Newton's Law describes the gravitational force between two bodies that depends on a gravitational constant, the two masses and the distance between the two bodies. For economic analysis – analogously – the trade between a pair of countries depends on the economic masses of these countries (i.e., national income) and the physical distance between them. The essence of the gravity model is that bilateral exports increase with economic size (GDP, population) but decrease with economic distance in all its multidimensional characteristics (physical, cultural, institutional, political). Typically, a basic gravity model used for empirical analysis consists of a log-linear equation in which bilateral trade flows between a pair of countries are related to the national incomes or gross domestic products of both countries and inversely related to the geographical distance between the two countries. We aim at estimating the impact of (bilateral) economic diplomatic efforts of embassies and export promotion agencies on bilateral exports, which makes the gravity model the obvious choice of model. Our choice for the gravity model is motivated by an excellent track record in empirical trade flow analysis as well as acknowledged theoretical foundations (van Bergeijk and Brakman 2010). It is one of the few models that measures impact of different variables on bilateral trade flows and thus the logical tool for our topic. Indeed many authors have used the model to quantify the impact of commercial and/or economic diplomacy on international exchange.[8]

We combine and extend the studies of Rose (2007) and Lederman *et al.* (2006) as we combine an extended gravity model and dataset *à la* Rose (2007) with the data on export promotion agencies collected by Lederman *et al.* (2006). Moreover, whereas the impact of different instruments of economic diplomacy so far has been measured separately, we include both embassies and export promotion agencies simultaneously in our model. We report estimates of different specifications of the following equation:

$$\ln(X_{ij}) = \beta_0 + \beta_1 \ln(D_{ij}) + \beta_2 \ln(Y_i) + \beta_3 \ln(Y_j) + \beta_4 \ln(Pop_i) + \beta_5 \ln(Pop_j)$$
$$+ \beta_6 Lang_{ij} + \beta_7 Landl_{ij} + \beta_8 Island_{ij} + \beta_9 \ln(Area_i Area_j) + \gamma EmbCon_{ij} \quad (8.1)$$
$$+ \delta StaffEPA_i + \eta(EmbCon_{ij} * StaffEPA_i) + \varepsilon_{ij}$$

where *i* denotes the exporter, *j* denotes the importer and the variables are defined as follows:

X_{ij} denotes the exports from country *i* to country *j*. Since we have a logarithmic transformation $\ln(0)$ is not defined so that we exclude 18 zero observations and thus $X_{ij} > 0$.

D_{ij} is the distance between i and j. We expect $\beta_1 < 0$ because transportation costs, transportation time and the 'economic horizon' of the exporter (all assumed to correspond roughly with the geographic distance between the exporting and importing country) have a negative impact on trade.

Y_i, Y_j represent the gross domestic product per capita of i and j, respectively. We expect $\beta_2 > 0$ and $\beta_3 > 0$ because countries with larger GDP have larger production capacity in i and larger markets j for export products.

Pop_i Pop_j refer to the population of i and j, respectively. We expect $\beta_4 > 0$ and $\beta_5 > 0$ because a larger population would also mean that the countries have larger labor supply (i) and more consumers (j).

$Lang_{ij}$ is a binary (1,0) dummy variable that is unity if the countries in the pair share the same official language. We expect $\beta_6 > 0$ because countries that share the same official language trade more easily since trading costs (repackaging, translation and marketing) are lower and because countries with similar languages often share cultural patterns and preferences.

$Landl_{ij}$ is a dummy variable (0,1,2) that denotes the total number of countries in a country pair that are landlocked. It assumes the value 2 if both countries are landlocked, 1 if only one country is landlocked and 0 if neither country is landlocked). We expect $\beta_7 < 0$ because land-locked countries trade less as their connectivity to the world market is lower and their average trading costs higher because the goods that flow in and out of these countries have to pass more borders.

$Island_{ij}$ is a dummy variable (0,1,2) that denotes the total number of countries in a country pair that are islands (value is 2 if both countries are islands, 1 if only one country is an island and 0 if neither country is an island). We expect $\beta_8 < 0$ because island economies typically have a larger distance to markets.

$Area_i Area_j$ is the product of the land areas of i and j. We expect $\beta_9 < 0$ because countries that are larger tend to trade less basically, because many products are already within their border so that internal trade may substitute for international trade.

Next we have the two variables of special interest in this research (and their interaction term):

$EmbCon_{ij}$ is the number of embassies and consulates of country i in country j.
$StaffEPA_i$ is the staff of a nation's export promotion agency (in hundreds of persons).[9]

Finally we have:

ε_{ij} which represents the residual influence on bilateral exports; assumed to be a well-behaved log-normally distributed error term.

Basically this is the specification of Rose (2007) from which insignificant variables have been dropped and to which we added the number of staff of the export promotion agency of country *i StaffEPA$_i$* and an interaction term *EmbCon$_{ij}$*StaffEPA$_i$* in order to investigate whether export promotion agencies have a complementing or substituting influence on bilateral exports.

The sample of our analysis consists of 36 countries. Like Rose and Lederman *et al.*, our analysis examines the influence of embassies and export promotion agencies across countries. The 20 exporting countries of Rose (2007) serve as a starting point, supplemented with counties for which Yakop and van Bergeijk (2011) have collected Foreign Service data and for which data was available from the survey of Lederman *et al.* (2006).[10] The resulting sample consists of 36 countries and provides 36*35 = 1,260 potential observations for bilateral trade and covers nearly half of total world exports, more than 60 percent of total world GDP and nearly a quarter of the total world population. The sample covers both high-income and low-income countries, includes OECD countries and developing countries in Africa, Asia, Latin America and the Middle East and includes small as well as large countries, both in terms of population and in terms of land area. A weak spot is that country selection has been based on the inclusion in Yakop and van Bergeijk (2011) and Lederman *et al.* (2006) so that the representativeness is not clear beforehand. The main issue is that the dataset only includes countries that have a (partly) public export promotion agency. The Appendix discusses the data sources in some detail and provides an overview table that lists and classifies the countries and gives some basic information about their embassies, consulates and export promotion agencies.

8.4 General findings

The benchmark results from estimating the core model are reported in Table 8.2. The first column provides OLS estimates for the most restricted model that does not take the influence of commercial diplomacy into account ($\gamma = \delta = \eta = 0$). The second and third column separately include the indicators for the influence of embassies and consulates ($\delta = \eta = 0$) and for export promotion agencies ($\gamma = \eta = 0$), respectively. The fourth column reports the regression results for the unrestricted model, including the Foreign Service, export promotion agencies and the interaction term.

Before discussing the coefficients of special interest (of the Foreign Service and export promotion agencies), we note that the restricted gravity model (column 1) works rather well; all coefficients are highly statistically significant, the sign and size of the different variables correspond to *ex ante* expectations and more than three-quarters of the variation in bilateral export flows is explained by the model.[11]

The coefficients of special interest are those of the variables *EmbCon$_{ij}$* and *StaffEPA$_i$* and their interaction term; they are shown in the second and third column of Table 8.2, respectively. The number of embassies and consulates that a country employs in a host country increases exports to that host country by about 0.05. This positive effect is statistically significant but economically smaller than most other standard variables in the model. The effect is similar to

Table 8.2 Benchmark estimation results for export equations (N = 1,242)

Dependent variable: Ln exports	(1)	(2)	(3)	(4)
$EmbCon_{ij}$		0.05** (0.02)		0.09*** (0.03)
$StaffEPA_i$				0.01 (0.01)
$EmbCon_{ij}*StaffEPA_i$				-0.01*** (0.00)
Ln (D_{ij})	-0.76 *** (0.05)	-0.75*** (0.05)	-0.76*** (0.05)	-0.74*** (0.05)
Ln (Y_i) (p/c)	1.24*** (0.03)	1.23*** (0.03)	1.26*** (0.04)	1.24*** (0.04)
Ln (Y_j) (p/c)	1.11*** (0.03)	1.09*** (0.03)	1.11*** (0.03)	1.09*** (0.03)
Ln (Pop_i)	1.05*** (0.04)	1.04*** (0.04)	1.08*** (0.05)	1.07*** (0.05)
Ln (Pop_j)	1.10*** (0.04)	1.06*** (0.05)	1.10*** (0.04)	1.07*** (0.05)
$Lang_{ij}$	0.87*** (0.13)	0.84*** (0.13)	0.87*** (0.13)	0.84*** (0.13)
$Landl_{ij}$	-0.45*** (0.09)	-0.44*** (0.09)	-0.44*** (0.09)	-0.44*** (0.09)
$Island_{ij}$	-0.50*** (0.10)	-0.48*** (0.10)	-0.46*** (0.10)	-0.44*** (0.10)
Ln $(Area_i Area_j)$	-0.12*** (0.03)	-0.13*** (0.03)	-0.12*** (0.03)	-0.13*** (0.03)
Adj. R^2	0.77	0.77	0.77	0.77

Note
***, **, * imply significance at 99%, 95% and 90% levels respectively.

but slightly smaller than the coefficient reported in other studies (compare Table 8.1). The influence of export promotion agencies on bilateral exports, on the other hand, is negative but not statistically significant. The combination of these two variables in column 4 results in a statistically significant coefficient of 0.09 for the Foreign Service and a coefficient for export promotion agencies that is still not statistically significant. The interaction effect is statistically significant and negative (–0.01) implying that two instruments have a rivalry character and tend to crowd each other out. Formal F-tests that test the restricted model ($\gamma = \delta = \eta = 0$) against the extended gravity equations refute the addition of $StaffE\text{-}PA_i$, while supporting the other extensions.[12]

Thus the results in Table 8.2 indicate that the bilateral diplomatic efforts of the Foreign Service promote bilateral exports, but in contrast to the results of Lederman *et al.* (2006) export promotion agencies do not promote bilateral exports. Indeed, the positive results of Lederman *et al.* need to be put into the perspective of a bilateral context by taking into account other factors that influence trade, such as distance and income levels.

8.5 Low- and middle-income (South) versus high-income countries (North)

Instructive as these general results may be, we see a need to investigate whether the development level of the trading partners influences the established relationships. The new emerging empirical literature on new and intangible barriers to trade such as a lack of trust, cultural differences and ineffective governance (a lack of an enforceable legal framework, accountability and stability) may be more relevant for developing countries as we saw in our discussion in Section 8.2 of trade barriers and market failures that hamper international exchange. If so, the instruments of commercial diplomacy could be more relevant for the developing countries. In order to investigate the proposition that export promotion is more effective in low-income countries than in high-income countries, we re-estimate the restricted and unrestricted models along the lines of Table 8.2 for different (cumulative) sub-groups of countries according to exporter's GDP per capita. We follow two procedures. First, we start with a small sample of low-income countries and investigate how the coefficients develop when we add increasingly richer countries to that sample. This procedure does not only offer an indication of how commercial diplomacy interacts with development but also provides information about the stability and robustness of the established equations. Second, we split the sample into two groups (low and middle income versus high income) and re-estimate the equations for the sub-samples and additionally for the trade flows within and between these groups.

8.5.1 Sample expansion

We start by estimating the models on the basis of data for a group of exporters that has a GDP per capita of less than $10,000. Then we enlarge this sub-sample by stepwise increasing the threshold of GDP per capita so that we have a range of sub-samples for groups of countries with ascending (cumulative) incomes.

Focusing on the fully unrestricted model specification (Table 8.2 column 4), Figure 8.2 plots the development of the coefficients of all 'standard' variables as the sample expands to include countries with higher levels of GDP per capita. The coefficients for the core variables in the gravity model remain fairly stable. Their sign and size are comparable to the results reported in Table 8.2 and in line with expectations.[13]

Now that we have established that the gravity model remains fairly stable throughout the modifications of the sample size, we can take a closer look at the influence of the Foreign Service and export promotion agencies on bilateral exports (Figure 8.3). The number of embassies and consulates that a country employs in a host country has a consistently positive effect on bilateral exports to that host country, but the influence of embassies and consulates varies and is not statistically significant for countries with an income per capita below $20,000. The Foreign Service thus helps to promote bilateral exports, but not for developing countries, most strongly for the middle-income countries and to a lesser extent for the high-income countries. The coefficient for the export promotion agency's staff consistently decreases as we include countries with higher incomes per capita. For low- or middle-income countries, the influence of export

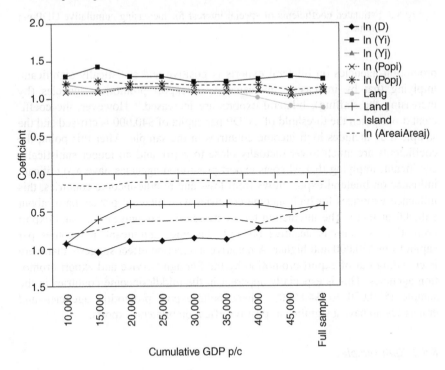

Figure 8.2 Estimated coefficients for core variables for increasing cumulative GDP per capita.

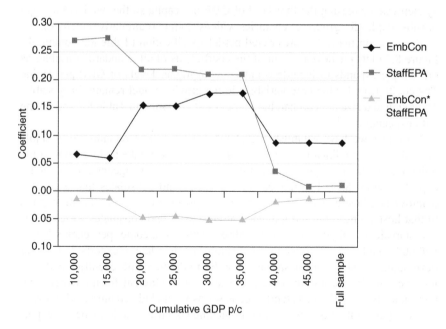

Figure 8.3 Estimated coefficients of special interest for increasing cumulative GDP per capita.

promotion agencies on bilateral exports is positive and statistically significant, implying that by increasing the capacity of export promotion agencies (by increasing the staffing), bilateral exports are increased.[14] However, the coefficient drops when the threshold of a GDP per capita of $40,000 is crossed and the sample thus includes high-income countries in the sample. After this point, the coefficients are much lower (actually close to zero), and no longer statistically significant, implying that whereas export promotion agencies have a significant influence on bilateral export flows from low- and middle-income countries, this influence vaporizes for high-income countries with incomes per capita of about $40,000 or more. The interaction term between the Foreign Service and export promotion agencies is negative but only becomes significant at incomes per capita from $20,000 and higher. A negative interaction effect suggests that there is crowding out of export promotion by the Foreign Service and export promotion agencies. This is especially apparent in the middle-income countries in the sample ($20,000 to $40,000), where both export promotion agencies and embassies do have a significant, positive effect on bilateral exports.

8.5.2 Split samples

We divide the sample in two different groups: low- and middle-income countries (18 countries with a GDP per capita of less than $11,455; 612 observations and

Table 8.3 Estimation results for export equation at different levels of per capita income

Dependent variable: Ln exports	Low and middle income (South)	High income (North)
N	612	630
$EmbCon_{ij}$	0.06 *(0.08)*	0.07* *(0.04)*
$StaffEPA_i$	0.28*** *(0.05)*	−0.02* *(0.01)*
$EmbCon_{ij}*StaffEPA_i$	−0.01 *(0.03)*	−0.00 *(0.00)*
Adj. R^2	0.70	0.84

Note
***, **, * imply significance at 99%, 95% and 90% levels respectively.

18 zero trade flows) and high-income countries (18 countries with a GDP per capita of more than \$11,455; 630 observations).[15] We repeat the OLS estimations (using the specification of Table 8.2, column 4) for the two separate groups and report the results in Table 8.3. Clearly, there are differences for the effects of export promotion through the Foreign Service or export promotion agencies between the group of low- and middle-income countries and the group of high-income countries. We first re-estimate the most extended gravity model on these sub-samples (Table 8.3). Table 8.3 studies the trade flows that originate in the low- and middle-income countries and the high-income countries, respectively, without making a distinction according to the destination of that trade.

The influence of embassies and consulates is only statistically significant for exporting countries in high-income countries. The presence of a high-income country's Foreign Service abroad has a positive effect on bilateral exports to those countries (the coefficient is 0.07 but only marginally significant at the 10 percent level). The coefficient of export promotion agencies is – as was the case with the cumulative income samples – much higher in low- and middle-income countries. The estimated coefficient for low- and middle-income countries is 0.28 and significant at the 1 percent level. In contrast we find for the high-income countries a coefficient of −0.02 that is statistically significant at the 10 per cent level. Third, although the sign of the interaction effect remains negative for both samples, the effect is not statistically significant.

8.5.3 Trade flows within and between the two groups of countries

Next we take a closer look at the trade flows within and between these country groupings and re-estimate gravity models on these sub-samples. 'Within'-trade relates to North–North trade (where we only consider the trade flows with origin and destination in the high-income countries) and South–South trade (where we only consider the trade flows with origin and destination in the low- and middle-income countries). 'Between'-trade consists of, on the one hand, North–South trade that relates to goods exported by high-income countries and imported by low- and middle-income countries and, on the other hand, South–North trade that relates to trade flows in the opposite direction.

Table 8.4 Estimation results for export equation; 'within' and 'between' effects

Dependent variable: Ln exports		*To* *Low and middle income(South)*	*To* *High income (North)*
EmbCon_{ij}	From	*Low and middle income (South)*	0.19 (0.23)	0.06 (0.07)
		High income (North)	0.25*** (0.09)	0.02 (0.03)
StaffEPA_i	From	*Low and middle income (South)*	0.29*** (0.09)	0.28*** (0.06)
		High income (North)	−0.01 (0.02)	−0.02* (0.01)
*EmbCon_{ij}*StaffEPA_i*	From	*Low and middle income (South)*	−0.06 (0.08)	−0.01 (0.03)
		High income (North)	−0.01 (0.01)	−0.00 (0.00)

Note
***, **, * imply significance at 99%, 95% and 90% levels respectively.

Regarding the impact of the Foreign Service, the coefficients are positive but only the *between* effect for North–South trade is significant. The effects of the Foreign Service on export flows *within* the same group of countries are not significant, neither is the effect of the Foreign Service in South–North trade. The coefficient for the Foreign Service in North–South trade is 0.25 and highly significant. This positive effect means that each additional embassy or consulate of a high-income exporter increases bilateral exports to a low- or middle-income host country. These results suggest a case for export promotion by way of the Foreign Service of high-income countries that is targeted to countries that are in a later stage of development (low- or middle-income countries). For high-income countries, export promotion toward other high-income countries does not have any significant effect. Commercial ties between the high-income countries are mostly already well established and barriers to trade are likely to be less severe within the group of high-income countries.

Regarding the influence of export promotion agencies on bilateral exports, the results are comparable to the results from the cumulative income samples, and therefore the coefficients for export promotion agencies seem very robust. Increasing the capacity of export promotion agencies in low- and middle-income countries increases their bilateral exports to both groups of export destinations. The estimated coefficient for the influence of export promotion agencies of low- and middle-income countries is 0.29 *within* the group of low- and middle-income countries, and 0.28 for the influence of agencies on exports from low- and middle-income to high-income countries (*between*). Both effects are highly statistically significant. For high-income countries, on the other hand, the picture is entirely different, as was also suggested by the exercise with the cumulative samples. For both the *within* and *between* effects, the coefficients remain negative. This negative effect is statistically significant for the effect *within* high-income countries but not for the effect *between* (exports from high-income countries to low- and middle-income countries). This means that increasing the capacity of export promotion agencies in high-income countries has no significant effect on bilateral exports to low- and middle-income countries, and even a negative effect on bilateral exports to other high-income countries.

Finally, the interaction effect is not significant for all four directions. Although the interaction term is negative in all cases, there is no significant effect since in all cases one of the two export promotion variables (either the Foreign Service or export promotion agencies) is not significant.

8.6 Discussion, policy implications and further research

We can summarize our empirical findings as follows. Only the Foreign Services of high-income countries (GDP per capita more than US$11,455), with embassies and consulates positioned in low- and middle-income countries (GDP per capita less than US$11,455), are effective in increasing exports and only so in the context of North–South trade. Only export promotion agencies of low- and middle-income countries are effective in increasing bilateral exports, and both to low- and middle-income countries and to high-income countries. The export promotion agencies of high-income countries even have a negative influence on bilateral exports to other high-income countries. Throughout all specifications of the model, we have not found any positive interaction effects between export promotion agencies and the Foreign Service, but instead we find negative and/or insignificant coefficients. How do these results relate to earlier findings? And what does this imply?

Before making any comparisons with the results of other studies it is important to note that the samples differ a lot. Rose (2007) uses a sample consisting of the bilateral trade flows of 20 exporting countries and 200 import destinations in the year 2002. Lederman *et al.* (2006) deal with 83 total export flows in the year 2005–6. Yakop and van Bergeijk (2011) have a symmetric trade matrix of 63 countries for the year 2006. Afman and Maurel (2010) study the bilateral trade flows between 26 OECD countries and 30 countries of the former Eastern bloc in the years 1995–2005. With so much difference it is important to note that there is strong agreement. First, the studies agree on the overall impact of export facilitation and promotion through the public sector. Our estimate of the elasticity for the Foreign Service in Table 8.2 is at the low end of the ranges reported in Table 8.1. Second, the studies agree that the impact of the instruments of commercial diplomacy differs for countries at different levels of GDP per capita[16] (Figure 8.3 and Table 8.3). In particular, the consensus that can be distilled from these studies is that North–North trade is not significantly influenced by the network of commercial diplomacy (embassies and consulates and export promotion agencies). For export promotion agencies, we find not only such *between* effects, but also *within* effects (albeit only for trade originating in low- and middle-income countries). Our finding that export promotion agencies promote overall trade may correspond to the 'overall trade enhancing' character of export promotion agencies, in contrast to the bilateral character of many other instruments of export promotion, such as foreign missions or state visits. Another consensus relates to the observation that typically significant coefficients occur in the *between* trade flows. Our findings disagree with other studies regarding the impact of embassies and consulates in South–South trade where we have positive but insignificant coefficients (Table 8.4). This may be a result of sample bias as we selected countries that are in the Lederman *et al.* (2006) dataset and thus have an export promotion agency but more likely this is a consequence of a very limited sample: we have only 288 observations on South–South trade whereas Yakop and Van Bergeijk (2011) have 462 observations. Importantly the reduction from 63 countries in their sample to 36 in the present sample may unintentionally have left out some low- and middle-income countries for which diplomacy is an important driver of trade (the most obvious candidate is China). For this reason we do not consider our evidence on the impact of embassies and consulates in South–South trade sufficiently strong to draw firm conclusions. If anything we find the positive effect relevant even though we cannot establish its significance.

These observations also guide some thoughts on future research. In particular more work needs to be done on expanding the number of countries in the dataset in a manner that generates a more balanced dataset. It is thus not the number of observations per se that needs to increase, but rather data for countries that do not involve in export promotion need to be collected.

At a general level the results offer supportive evidence for the role of governments in solving and mitigating problems related to market failures and non-traditional barriers that hinder international trade. Given that the effectiveness of government activities is larger in trade relations from and with the South and zero, if not negative, in North trade one might conjure that market failures are more severe in the developing world. Typically the analysis of low volumes of South–South trade has been concerned with infrastructure and trade facilities. Our analysis adds a new element as this chapter offers a new empirical perspective on the impact of export promotion agencies in developing countries and their potentially stimulating role in South–South trade. It should be noted, however, that it is not simply the activity of export promotion agencies that matters. The existence and size of such agencies may be a symptom of a pro-trade-oriented policy environment in developing countries. Merely establishing an export agency will not suffice as effective management, sufficient budget and supportive general trade-oriented microeconomic and macroeconomic policies should be considered necessary conditions. But with that caveat in mind we find substantial potential for increase of the trade flows between developing countries so that a case for targeted export promotion would seem to exist.

Appendix

We follow the classification used in IMF statistics and therefore define North as the major advanced economies (G7), the Euro area and other advanced economies, and newly industrialized Asian economies;

Bilateral merchandise exports (over the year 2006), in US dollars are from the IMF's Direction of Trade data (September 2007) and supplemented with data from the Comtrade Database (UN).

Data on gross domestic product, in current US dollars for 2006, and data for the total population of all countries are from the World Development Indicators Database (World Bank).

Distances are geodesic great-circle distances; this indicator uses latitudes and longitudes of the most important cities or agglomerations in terms of population, which are taken from the distances dataset of the CEPII, that also provided data for the land areas (in km^2) and the dummies (contingency, language, island, landlocked and colony).

Data for the free trade agreements and currency unions are from the World Trade Organization website and reported by Yakop and van Bergeijk (2011), who also provide the number of embassies and (career) consulates country i has in country j.

Budgets and staff of export promotion agencies are for the most recent year that the concerning export promotion agency could provide (mostly for 2005–6) and have been provided by Lederman *et al.* (2006). Since this dataset is confidential, we cannot provide results for specific countries, but must limit the reporting to results for the complete sample or groups of countries. The dataset has been supplemented with data for Belgium, the Netherlands and the USA.

Appendix 8.a.1 Data sources

We follow the classification used in IMF Statistics and therefore define North as the major advanced economies (G7), the Euro area and Other Advanced Economies, and Newly industrialized Asian economies;

Overview table

Country i	Total number of embassies and consulates of country i in other 35 countries	Total number of embassies and consulates of other 35 countries in country i	Year of establishment export promotion agency (ranking)	
North				
Australia	35	64	1985	*(17)*
Austria	48	36	1946	*(6)*
Belgium	45	52	2004	*(34)*
Czech Republic	41	31	1997	*(23)*
Denmark	52	29	2000	*(29)*
Finland	37	37	1919	*(1)*
France	88	123	2004	*(35)*
Germany	66	116	1951	*(8)*
Hungary	43	32	1990	*(18)*
Ireland	30	27	1998	*(27)*
Netherlands	62	49	1936	*(4)*
Norway	45	26	2004	*(36)*
Portugal	77	40	1949	*(7)*
Spain	93	97	1982	*(16)*
Sweden	38	45	1971	*(12)*
Switzerland	58	56	1927	*(3)*
United Kingdom	78	56	1999	*(28)*
United States	76	227	1921	*(2)*
South				
Algeria	37	32	1997	*(22)*
Bangladesh	23	15	1972	*(13)*
Brazil	54	92	2003	*(32)*
Chile	61	32	1975	*(14)*
Dominican Republic	39	18	2003	*(33)*
Ecuador	33	22	1997	*(24)*
Egypt	49	42	1997	*(25)*
Israel	41	40	1958	*(10)*
Malaysia	31	35	1993	*(19)*
Mexico	81	47	1937	*(5)*
Morocco	67	47	1981	*(15)*
South Africa	36	54	2001	*(31)*
Thailand	34	31	1952	*(9)*
Tunisia	37	24	2000	*(30)*
Turkey	65	57	1960	*(11)*
Uganda	9	13	1996	*(20)*
Uruguay	42	21	1996	*(21)*
Venezuela	49	35	1997	*(26)*

Notes

1 This chapter reports on research undertaken by student assistants in the Globalization Strategy unit of the Ministry of Economic Affairs which resulted in two MA theses supervised by Charles van Marrewijk (van Veenstra 2009) and Franc Klaassen (Yakop and van Bergeijk 2011) at Erasmus University Rotterdam and the University of Amsterdam, respectively. Comments by Charles, Franc and participants of the conference 'The Gravity Equation or Why the World is Not Flat,' Groningen 2007, are gratefully acknowledged.

2 Leiden University.

3 University of Amsterdam.

4 ISS, The Hague and CERES, Utrecht.

5 Likewise, sunk costs occur for the adaptation of export products to foreign technical and/or administrative standards or to comply with foreign regulations (Blanes-Cristóbal *et al.* 2008).

6 Kostecki and Naray (2007) list a number of non-economic reasons including visibility in the mass media, access to decision makers (both in the public and private sector), credibility and reputation.

7 Other instruments may include export credit insurance (Moser *et al.* 2006), export subsidies (Panagariya 2000), business-sector activities (Alvarez 2004), export intermediaries (Peng and York 2001) and state visits (Nitsch 2007).

8 All studies mentioned in Table 8.1 with the exception of Lederman *et al.* (2006) deploy a gravity methodology. Lederman *et al.* (2006) measure the impact of the export promotion budget per capita on the national (total) exports per capita per country using full information maximum likelihood and ordinary least squares (OLS) estimators in a model that includes amongst the regressors GDP per capita, trade restrictiveness, market access, exchange rate volatility, compliance costs and a geography-determined trade to GDP ratio.

9 In contrast with Lederman *et al.* (2006) we do not use the total budget of the agency because budget is much more difficult to measure than staff and thus less comparable across countries. Financial figures are often confidential and agencies may even find some benefit in under- or overstating the budget. Moreover, the specification of 'total budget' (which agencies had to supply in the survey of Lederman *et al.*) is problematic, as it has not been clarified what to include or exclude in the budget.

10 Countries that belong to the group of 20 exporters of Rose (2007) but do not occur in the dataset of Lederman *et al.* (2006) are Belgium, Canada, India, Indonesia, Italy, Japan, the Netherlands, Poland, Russia, South Korea and the United States. China did answer the survey but no data on either budget or staff of the export promotion agency was made available. We obtained data for the export promotion agencies of Belgium, the Netherlands and the United States.

11 Extensive econometric testing of the model and its specifications is reported in van Veenstra (2009) and Yakop and van Bergeijk (2011) including fixed effect estimates and treatments of heteroskedasticity and zero trade flows.

12 The F-statistics are 3.88, 1.38 and 4.37, respectively. The null hypothesis that the restricted model suffices is rejected for the second model ($\delta=\eta=0$) at the 5 percent significance level (the critical F-value(5%, 1, 1231) is 3.84) and largest model (final column) at the 1 percent level (the critical F-value(1%, 3, 1229) is 3.78, but for the third model ($\gamma=\eta=0$). the null hypothesis could not even be rejected at the 10 percent level (critical F-value 2.71).

13 The size of most coefficients decreases slightly for samples that include countries with higher GDP per capita, technically because the variance increases but also because 'standard' determinants of bilateral trade (such as distance) have less impact for countries with higher incomes per capita. This may suggest that exports in lower-income

countries are more susceptible to border effects and other trade determinants than are exports in high-income countries.

14 The coefficients for the samples including countries with an income per capita below $40,000 fall in a range of 0.21 to 0.28.

15 This value of $11,455 divides the sample into two sub-samples of 18 countries and is based on the country classification of the World Bank between low- and middle-income countries and high-income countries.

16 Afman and Maurel (2010) do not investigate this issue. Rose (2007) implicitly does investigate it in a sensitivity analysis. Yakop and van Bergeijk (2011) explicitly deals with this issue.

References

Afman, E. and M. Maurel (2010) 'Diplomatic relations and trade reorientation in transition countries,' in P.A.G. van Bergeijk and S. Brakman (eds.) *The Gravity Model in International Trade: Advances and Applications*, New York: Cambridge University Press.

Alvarez, R. (2004) 'Sources of export success in small and medium-sized enterprises: The impact of public programs,' *International Business Review*, 13: 383–400.

Alvarez, R. (2007) 'Explaining export success: Firm characteristics and spillover effects,' *World Development*, 35: 377–93.

Bergeijk, P.A.G., van (2009) *Economic Diplomacy and the Geography of International Trade*, Cheltenham: Edward Elgar.

Bergeijk, P.A.G., van and S. Brakman (eds.) (2010) *The Gravity Model in International Trade: Advances and Applications*, Cambridge: Cambridge University Press.

Blanes-Cristóbal, J.V., M. Dovis, J. Milgram-Baleix and A.I. Moro-Egido (2008) 'Do sunk exporting costs differ among markets? Evidence from Spanish manufacturing firms,' *Economics Letters* 101: 110–12.

Brunetti, A., G. Kisunko and B. Weder (1997) 'Institutional obstacles to doing business: Region-by-region results from a worldwide survey of the private sector,' World Bank Policy Research 1759, Washington, DC: World Bank.

Harris, R. and Q.C. Li (2005) 'Review of the literature: The role of international trade and investment in business growth and development,' Report to UKTI, Washington, DC.

Hausmann, R. and D. Rodrik (2003) 'Economic development as self discovery,' *Journal of Development Economics*, 72: 603–33.

Head, K. and J. Ries (2006) 'Do trade missions increase trade?' Working Paper Series, Sauder School of Business. Online, available at: http://ssrn.com/abstract=1015413 (accessed April 14, 2009).

Hoekman, B. and B.S. Javoricik (2004) 'Policies facilitating firm adjustment to globalization,' Policy Research Working Paper 3441, Washington, DC: World Bank.

Keesing, D.B. and A. Singer (1991) 'Development assistance gone wrong: Failures in services to promote and support manufactured exports,' in P. Hogan, D.B. Keesing and A. Singer (eds.) *The Role of Support Services in Expanding Manufactured Exports in Developing Countries*, Washington, DC: Economic Development Institute, World Bank.

Kostecki, M. and O. Naray (2007) 'Commercial diplomacy and international business,' Discussion Papers in Diplomacy, 107, The Hague: Clingendael Institute.

Krueger, A.O. (1990) 'Government failures in development,' *Journal of Economic Perspectives*, 4: 9–23.

Lederman, D., M. Olarreaga and L. Payton (2006) 'Export promotion agencies: What works and what doesn't,' World Bank Policy Research 4044, Washington, DC: World Bank.

Moser, C., T. Nestmann and M. Wedow (2006) 'Political risk and export promotion: Evidence from Germany,' Economic Studies 36, Deutsche Bundesbank.

Nitsch, V. (2007) 'State visits and international trade,' *World Economy*, 30: 1797–816.

Panagariya, A. (2000) 'Evaluating the case for export subsidies,' Policy Research Working Paper 2276, Washington, DC: World Bank.

Peng, M.W. and A.S. York (2001) 'Behind intermediary performance in export trade: Transactions, agents, and resources,' *Journal of International Business Studies*, 32: 327–46.

Ramaswami, S.N. and Y. Yang (1990) 'Perceived barriers to exporting and export assistance requirements,' in S.T. Cavusgil and M.R. Czinkota (eds.) *International Perspectives on Trade Promotion and Assistance*, New York: Quorum Books.

Rose, A.K. (2007) 'The foreign service and foreign trade: Embassies as export promotion,' *World Economy*, 30: 22–38.

Stiglitz, J.E. (1989) 'Markets, market failures and development,' *American Economic Review*, 79: 197–203.

Veenstra, M.E.H., van (2009) 'The effectiveness of export promotion by the foreign service or by export promotion agencies: A quantitative analysis,' Rotterdam: Erasmus University Rotterdam.

Volpe Martincus, C. and J. Carballo (2008) 'Is export promotion effective in developing countries? Firm-level evidence on the intensive and the extensive margins of exports,' *Journal of International Economics*, 76: 89–106.

Wulf, L., De (2001) 'Why have trade promotion organizations failed, and how they can be revitalized?' PREM notes 57, Washington, DC: World Bank.

Yakop, M. and P.A.G. van Bergeijk (2011) 'Economic diplomacy, trade and developing countries,' *Cambridge Journal of Regions, Economy and Society* (special issue Development and Geography), in print.

9 Value chain responsibility in the global South

Peter Knorringa

9.1 Introduction

Global value chain analyses have been instrumental in showing that many markets are far from being the anonymous meeting places of numerous sellers and buyers. Instead, access to global markets is often controlled by a limited number of gate keepers, namely global buyers that act as the spiders-in-the-web of global value chains. Supplying these global buyers has created new opportunities for exports from developing countries, leading to employment generation, foreign exchange earnings and sometimes upgrading of local producers. At the same time, global buyers' sourcing strategies are based on procuring the highest value for the lowest possible price of a variety of components and products, and global buyers tend to wield effectively their negotiation power.

This chapter explores where and when responsibility issues in global value chains are more likely to gain a foothold in developing countries. Most of the literature on responsibility, often under the increasingly unsatisfactory label of Corporate Social Responsibility (CSR), takes OECD based brand-name companies and OECD middle-class consumers as its point of departure. Instead, this chapter brings together theories and analytical devices to start constructing an analytical framework on where and when value chain responsibility is more likely to emerge in the global South.

Global value chain leaders and coordinators from China, India, Brazil and South Africa increasingly contract suppliers from poorer countries in Asia, Africa and Latin America, for a variety of agro-based and/or labour-intensive components and products. Through a focus on how both producers *and* consumers in the global South increasingly shape newly emerging issues like responsibility, this chapter contributes to a better understanding of new forms of South–South globalisation. One innovative aspect of this framework is the ambition to investigate opportunities for more social responsibility on both the supply and demand side. While some studies look at how production processes in the global South could become more responsible, no existing studies have included also the extent to which mainstreaming of responsible production will be determined at least partly by purchasing preferences of new middle-class consumers from the global South.

Diverging views exist on whether a more responsible and/or a more Southern-led form of globalisation are likely to emerge (Zadek 2006; Gu *et al.* 2008). What is clear is that we now find ourselves in a transition phase. The current era has been characterised by a capitalist growth logic, unsustainable use of resources and enormous prosperity in some places paired with continued poverty in others. The coming era calls for more integrated attention to sustainability, equity and solidarity. A key question is whether socially responsible and environmentally sustainable forms of capitalism are possible, and to what extent these might be built upon a strengthened morality in the private sector itself (Macdonald and Marshall 2010). But is this merely wishful thinking, or are such processes really taking shape? In this chapter I focus on social responsibility issues (see ILO (2002) for an overview of 'decent work' indicators, and Barrientos and Smith (2006), for the most comprehensive social responsibility assessment to date).

This chapter takes a first step in contributing to a more empirical debate on where and when private sector actors are more likely to prioritise responsibility issues. Section 9.2 develops an initial typology of where and when firms are more likely to make responsibility issues a part of their core business strategy, visualised through a pyramid with four layers. Section 8.3 focuses on the agency of private sector firms, and investigates factors that influence the choices made by firms on their level of engagement with social responsibility as a part of their core business strategy (their position in the pyramid). Section 8.4 brings together state, civil society and longer-term change perspectives to frame the structure in which firm agency is embedded (the shape of the pyramid and the relative size of the four layers). Section 8.5 offers preliminary conclusions on this framework and tentatively identifies possible pathways on how attention for responsibility might be mainstreamed in various institutional settings.

9.2 Responsibility and CSR: definition and initial typology

The responsibility debate so far has been dominated by the conceptualisation of CSR as a voluntary approach by firms to decide their responsibility profile, independently from public and civic actors. In this chapter I will take my cue from a conceptually more diverse and politically more integrated approach, as also advocated in recent publications like Marques and Utting (2010), and Macdonald and Marshall (2010). But before adding public and civic perspectives in Section 8.4, here I start from the CSR literature for a basic typology of firm strategies towards responsibility. Many CSR definitions by management scholars do not only include that firms need to go beyond what is required by law, but also to go beyond the interest of the firm (McWilliams *et al.* 2006). I find this counter-intuitive and counter-productive, as the more sustainable achievements in responsible production most feasibly are to be found in situations where firms can actually increase long-term profitability and responsibility by engaging in CSR as a way to differentiate themselves and their products. In a very critical, forcefully argued survey *The Economist* (2005), even goes one step further and argues that only the type of CSR where both profits and social benefits increase makes sense. Given its dislike of the CSR terminology, it prefers to label the situation where higher profits and increased social benefits go together as 'good management', so as to differentiate it from three other types of CSR which it feels are flawed. This type of 'good management' is what in much of the business-school CSR literature is referred to as the 'business case for CSR'. This implies a win–win situation, often without much emphasis on the inherent conflicts of interests among the different stakeholders in such initiatives. Two other recent special issues on CSR by development researchers, in the *International Affairs* (2005) and *Third World Quarterly* (2007) journals, shed a very different light on the debate (cf. Blowfield 2005; Jenkins 2005; Blowfield 2007; Newell and Frynas 2007). They argue that the development relevance of CSR will remain inherently limited in reach as long as only internationally operating brand-sensitive firms in consumer markets are pushed to behave responsibly, and depth remains limited as long as private sector actors can get away with defining, implementing and evaluating what is to be seen as socially responsible.

Even though philanthropy is often the first association with the idea of CSR, especially in the USA and in many developing countries, in this chapter I focus on the more strategic dimensions of CSR in terms of incorporating responsibility attributes in the day-to-day operation of the firm. In other words, while philanthropy is basically about ways to use profits to 'give back to the community', I focus on CSR as part of a business strategy or when CSR 'becomes the way in which the company does business' (Chapple and Moon 2005: 425).

The more strategic CSR literature often uses the following typology of three different but in reality often partly overlapping strategies:

- abiding by the letter and the spirit of the law (with existing regulations, laws, conventions and non-voluntary standards),
- brand protection (safeguard brand-name goodwill and company reputation by moving beyond mere compliance to public regulation, and to invest in for example voluntary codes of conduct to minimise the risk of being seen as an irresponsible actor) and
- value creation (using CSR activities as a way to compete and essentially differentiate oneself from other companies that offer similar products) (Nelson 2000: 7–28).

Next to these strategies it is important to recognise that a substantial number of firms, by far most of them operating in the informal sector of the economy, do not follow any of these strategies. The American business school led thinking about CSR focuses its attention almost exclusively on formal sector firms, and neglects the informal sector. However, with our focus on South–South interactions and on the value chain relationships through which substantial parts of production processes are subcontracted to informal sector firms, we need to explicitly give attention to the large army of invisible informal sector firms. Moreover, a large majority of informal sector firms does not produce as subcontractors for larger and internationally operating firms. They produce for local and domestic markets, and while they might engage in local philanthropy, such informal sector entrepreneurs have no incentives to incorporate responsibility attributes in their core business strategy.

These four CSR related strategies can be visualised as a pyramid. The base of the pyramid consists of the many smaller informal sector firms that do not (need to) follow a systematic responsibility strategy. On top of this base is an also very large group of formal sector firms focusing on abiding-by-the-law, which means they make sure they cannot be formally blamed or sued for any of their activities. A smaller but still substantial group of (especially brand invested) companies that aim for brand protection, and see investments in one or more voluntary initiatives as a sensible strategy to boost their marketing reputation and reinforce their supply base. Finally, the top of the pyramid is formed by a small but significant set of firms for whom achieving and maintaining responsibility is a key part of their core strategy.

The following sections will elaborate on the dynamic processes related to this virtual pyramid, starting from two basic conceptualisations. First, structure–agency thinking that helps to maintain a balance in giving attention to both the role of firms in making their own responsibility choices, and to the role of societal structures and dynamics in influencing these choices. This means economic actors make an attempt at purposive action, and any economic action is always embedded in the prevailing institutional setting (Granovetter 1985: 487). Second, with three main sets of actors in society – states, civil society and the private sector – how can one think creatively about new divisions of tasks between them? While we observe shifts in this division of labour, our conceptual approaches too often continue to employ simplistic images, such as the rule-maker, the do-gooder and the exploiter or the hero. These, however, have always been caricatures at best. In the debate about incorporating responsibility issues in global value chains, a key question is how private sector actors respond or co-develop newly emerging governance modalities to embed social responsibility concerns in soft and hard law in their value chains at global, regional, national and local levels.

These two starting points are operationalised in structuring this chapter. I first look at agency of private actors. The next section investigates how firms make choices on where they think they 'fit' in this pyramid. Moreover, firms may change their strategy and may 'move' from one segment in the pyramid to another, depending on how they interpret internal and external dynamics and a resulting preferred responsibility profile, weighing costs and benefits of achieving such a profile in line with a targeted customer profile. Next, the focus shifts to elements of structure and its dynamics. I will bring together theories and analytical devices that shed light on the shape of the pyramid (leaner and taller or broader and plumper) and on the relative sizes of the four segments.

9.3 Firms and entrepreneurs choosing positions in the pyramid

This section pulls together strands in the literature that focus on the agency of entrepreneurs. Individual entrepreneurs can and do make responsibility choices.

For example, they can choose to be among the more proactive or reactive members in a particular initiative. Nevertheless, a key point for this framework is that the question of whether they join such an initiative in the first place is determined more by structural characteristics, like the type of product they produce, its market segment and the relative importance of reputation risks. Entrepreneurs can also be incentivised to act more responsibly as a result of group pressures, like in a cluster or association. Obviously, this can also work the other way around; so one indicator would be the responsibility profile of sectoral or territorial entrepreneur organisations.

Sectoral indicators like levels of required technology, market structure, and origin, scarcity and quality sensitivity of key raw materials also play an important role in determining the scope for value chain responsibility. For example, the present breakthroughs in the cacao sector seem to crucially depend on the awareness among lead firms that the regular supply of good quality cacao beans was threatened by an exodus of producers in the few key supplier countries.

Next to the input indicators, a more important driver for value chain responsibility is market segmentation. Consumer-oriented A-brands, in particular for identity goods like clothing and certain food items, need to be much more sensitive to (potential) consumer responsibility expectations and to NGO advocacy. In contrast, sectors and firms in B2B markets have so far remained outside this limelight. Moreover, lead firms can decide among a variety of strategies to deal with these perceived challenges (Van Tulder *et al.* 2009). Another dimension is value chain governance, which has become a key dimension of value chain and global production network studies (Gereffi *et al.* 2005; Hughes *et al.* 2008). Specific configurations of how lead firms manage 'their' supply chain also provide insights in under what conditions such lead firms are more likely to be interested in value chain responsibility initiatives. For example, lead firms without a brand to protect and oriented to cut-throat price competition are much less likely to perceive incentives for joining a value chain responsibility initiative. Moreover, a fragmented value chain with many levels of subcontractors to minimise on labour costs makes it also more difficult and more costly to implement and monitor responsibility initiatives.

The individual choices by entrepreneurs, or other actors, are important acts of agency that influence newly emerging structures. Break-through advancements in value chain responsibility can be traced back often to charismatic individuals. Examples are visionary entrepreneurs, NGO leaders with an eye for business realities, or a politician or policy maker that moulds previously unimaginable new alliances. We recognise the key role of such individuals in many of the most visible value chain responsibility success stories. However, a policy-oriented framework to identify under what conditions value chain responsibility is more likely to occur cannot be predicated on such 'agents of change'. Instead, such a policy-oriented framework can more usefully investigate how it can contribute to creating enabling conditions, which enhances the likelihood that (incipient) change agents can become catalysts of value chain responsibility. Therefore, the components outlined below emphasise dimensions of structure, with an eye on making that structure more enabling for potential catalysts.

9.4 Shape and segmentation in pyramid

In terms of content, we emphasise the need for integration and dovetailing of public, private and civic governance. As the mix of public and private regulation, possibly combined with civil society pressures, will depend among others on the institutional setting, we need to explore these differences to be able to better predict the possibilities and limitations of responsible consumption in the global South (Graham and Woods 2006). Nevertheless, we present the components actor by actor, because most of the existing literature starts from one particular actor, and then looks at how they interact with other actors. But before moving into the literature on state and civil society perspectives, I briefly touch upon the importance of differences in levels of macroeconomic development.

9.4.1 Macro indicators

One crucial set of elements structuring the opportunities for more responsibility attributes are levels of economic, human and social development in a country. Without underestimating the importance of these factors, in this chapter I do not engage in elaborating on those dimensions, as indicators for these variables are well developed and easily available. The literature converges on two rules of thumb on the relationship between levels of income and likelihood of people being willing to pay a premium for products with (more) responsibility attributes. First, people can afford to start considering responsibility attributes in their purchases only once they have reached a certain level of economic security. Second, at some level of income increased sensitivity for responsibility attributes tapers off with additional increases in income.

9.4.2 State perspectives: (inter) national policy environment

Ruggie (2008) constructed a policy framework on minimally acceptable normative behaviour with a division of tasks among major societal actors. His framework and its recent attempts at further operationalisation are hotly debated in OECD policy circles. The basics of his framework are that states are obliged to protect the agreed upon minimum norms, subsequently firms are obliged to respect them, and an independent judiciary is obliged to offer remedy in case of violations. Ruggie is criticised in the literature for underplaying the extent to which firms would have more proactive legal responsibilities to actively protect human rights, instead of 'only' being obliged not to do any harm. Human rights activists in a variety of countries emphasise that the law should not be taken as a given, but as being co-shaped in the medium term by civic action and changes in societal expectations about minimal norms. In this sense, litigation can assist in developing customary international law that would raise the minimum level of expected responsibility behaviour. This also means that countries with more of a tradition in litigation, like South Africa and to some extent India, might be seen as less attractive to less responsible investors. Even though the Ruggie framework enjoys a high visibility in the OECD policy discourse, its impact on the day-to-day operations of less 'visible' firms in developing countries seems remote at best.

The Business System approach (Whitley 1999; Jacobsen and Torp 2001) aims to analyse how, in a particular country,[1] due to its political system, its culture and its history, key societal actors interact and how this influences business outcomes. This approach became very popular because it was better able than other existing approaches to explain the success of countries like Taiwan and more recently Vietnam. From our perspective, this approach is important as it provides key indicators on how the public, private and civic spheres interact or negotiate their respective roles in a specific society. For example, many observers might be inclined to suggest that Brazil, given its institutional history and present political leadership, would be more inclined to support value chain responsibility initiatives as compared to China. Moreover, civil society organisations in China are seen as less independent from state influence as those in for example India, while both countries are wary of the influence of 'international' NGOs.

Closely linked to the Business System approach is the idea of embedded autonomy (Evans 1995, 1996) that has been used to explain parts of the East Asian success stories. Embedded autonomy refers to the role of public servants in the industrialisation strategy of for example South Korea. On the one hand they need to be embedded, which means closely related to main private sector entrepreneurs and managers, in order to be able to respond effectively to real needs. At the same time, they need to be autonomous (i.e. not corrupt and not unduly influenced) in taking their ultimate decisions based on longer-term societal priorities, and not on what a particular lobby group of entrepreneurs may desire in terms of for example subsidies. Moreover, Evans emphasised the importance of social capital as a lubricant in the relationships between key policy makers, industrialists and civil society leaders. While such alliances tend to be temporary and based on a few selective common interests, if and when such a conducive environment exists, also for example value chain responsibility initiatives might fall on a more fertile ground.

Another important set of indicators emerges from the new industrial policy literature, which has taken its cue from the embedded autonomy discussion (Rodrik 2004). Industrial policy is increasingly diverse, and co-shapes the boundary conditions for value chain responsibility initiatives. New industrial policy is much less prescriptive and blueprint oriented, but is more experimental and demand driven. Emerging markets differ strongly in the extent to which they adhere to 'new' or 'old' industrial policy approaches. 'New' industrial policy offers much more scope to experiment with value chain responsibility initiatives in particular sectors, for specific market niches, targeting responsibility-sensitive consumers.

9.4.3 Civil society perspectives: how to more effectively engage the private sector?

Although most of civil society lobbying is oriented towards influencing state behaviour, civil society organisations increasingly engage also the private sector.

A basic distinction in civil society–market relations is often made between those who focus on promoting more responsible behaviour in existing markets and those who aim to develop and promote alternative development models (Howell and Pearce 2001). This distinction increasingly hides more than it reveals as previously alternative initiatives like Fair Trade now focus on mainstreaming, and mainstream businesses are developing 'alternative' niches that would be unthinkable 15 years ago. However, we can still discern a distinction between NGOs with a more confrontational versus a more collaborative stance. In its more confrontational stance, civic actors may start litigation against specific companies (usually MNCs) to create new legal springboards for further lobbying with legislators, like in the case of the oil industry (Frynas 2005), and to also raise minimal standards of acceptable behaviour as in for example Ruggie's framework. In its more collaborative stance NGOs nowadays play important roles in a variety of multi-stakeholder initiatives, like for example the Roundtable on Responsible Soy and the Roundtable on Sustainable Palm Oil. But the main point is that the real potential strength of civil society pressure seems to lie in the dynamic interactions between various initiatives on the continuum between confrontational and collaborative (Spar and La Mure 2003). Civil society can contribute most to enhancing value chain responsibility in situations where they recognise a shared responsibility towards strengthening each other's efforts and optimising overall progress. This does not mean a de-politicisation of the role of civil society organisations in engaging the private sector. Instead, it entails an engagement that is both critical and constructive and moves beyond the enemy perception of the private sector (Knorringa and Helmsing 2008). Finally, the room for manoeuvre for civil society organisations differs by institutional and political setting, as indicated above under the Business System approach.

9.4.4 New middle-class consumers in the global South: do they care?

Demand issues have not yet received systematic attention in the literature. In this sub-section we pull together the limited empirical information on the extent to which new middle-class consumers are likely to demand social responsible behaviour from lead firms in value chains. In the debate on how to improve social and environmental conditions in supply chains led by major branders and retailers, the scant attention given to the (potential) role of consumers has been limited to ethical consumers in OECD countries. So far, the possibly different role of new middle-class consumers from the global South has been ignored.

This is problematic because consumers from the global South will soon numerically dominate overall global middle-class consumption, and it is unclear to what extent these consumers from the global South will respond differently to responsibility issues. The global middle classes are growing rapidly, 'twice as fast as the overall world population' (World Bank 2007). This group of consumers, with yearly household earnings between $17,000 and $72,000, will increase from 400 million in 2005 to one billion in 2030. By 2030, 92 per cent of the global middle classes will live in developing countries (also because many

OECD upper-middle-class consumers are labelled as 'rich' because they earn more than $72,000 a year per household). Therefore, the World Bank estimates that by 2030: 'more than a billion people in developing countries will buy cars, engage in international travel, demand world-class products, and require international standards for higher education' (World Bank 2007: 69).

The question then becomes, how likely is it that the world-class products they demand will include responsible attributes? The sad truth is that we know very little about this likelihood. On the positive side, this means we cannot rule out the possibility that the new middle classes might be triggered by responsible attributes. What we do know about consumer behaviour from consumers in OECD countries does not sound very hopeful. Research indicates that relatively few (around 5 per cent) of consumers actually use their 'consumption as voting' (Shaw *et al.* 2005), while it needs to be stressed that this type of research is still in its early stages. Moreover, there seems to be a major discrepancy between what people say in surveys (around 20 per cent claim to act as ethical consumer) and their actual ethical behaviour in the store.

An interesting exploratory study by Devinney *et al.* (2005) claims that the gap between consumer commitment to responsibility in principle and in practice is explained by different factors for different institutional settings. Consumers in countries like India and China 'tended to have quite different justifications for their beliefs and behaviour' (ibid.: 15) as compared to those from the USA or from European countries. Therefore, it may well be that for example civil society organisations that aim to promote standards with higher levels of responsibility would need to follow a different strategy as compared to how they promoted awareness and commitment in Europe or the USA. This does not mean that the experience of how, for example, Fair Trade has played a catalytic role in the coffee sector on raising responsibility demands in more mainstream markets (Starbucks and others) is useless in other settings, but it does mean that history will most likely not repeat itself in the same way.

Another complicating factor is 'Bottom of the Pyramid' thinking (Prahalad 2005). The Bottom of the Pyramid debate focuses on bringing another four billion relatively poor consumers into the global market realm by 'simplifying' existing consumer products, to produce them at cost levels within reach of relatively poorer consumers. From the perspective of this study one might argue that such a simplification of product attributes would probably leave no space for 'luxury' responsibility attributes. In other words, also branded products will increasingly need to find a way to produce a broader variety of simpler products at lower price ranges with fewer if any responsibility attributes. However, this may not fully or not at all apply to the new middle classes, as they might wish to clearly distinguish themselves from a 'Bottom of the Pyramid' market segment, and may wish to be seen as consuming products at least on par with Western brand images, which would include responsibility attributes.

Moreover, given the different configuration and roles of civil society organisations, governments and large corporations in countries like China and India as compared to the USA and Europe, the ways in which consumers in for example

China and India are informed or manipulated is likely to differ. Therefore, exploring consumer behaviour – and actors that influence this behaviour – should be a key element in any attempt to understand the opportunities for promoting value chain responsibility. This important and so far ignored issue is probably most usefully approached by:

- looking across product sectors, and exploring data sources on middle-class consumption behaviour in major new consumption countries like India, China, Brazil and South Africa;
- looking at the role of consumer activism and civil society campaigning for responsible consumption behaviour in these countries, and at the ways in which firms respond to pressures or proactively raise their responsibility profile.

9.4.5 Longer-term structural changes

Sociotechnical pathways (Geels and Schot 2007) and norm life cycles (Finnemore and Sikkink 1998; Segerlund 2005) provide taxonomies that identify different stages that possess distinct potential for enhancing value chain responsibility. The basic point here is that the role, motivations and incentives inherently differ for public, private and civic actors in these various stages. Therefore, such taxonomies provide a step towards a more analytical understanding of where and when different combinations of regulatory and voluntary governance can be applied more effectively.

By way of illustration I will elaborate on how applying the norm life cycle theory helps to identify more structural changes over time in the shape of the pyramid introduced in Section 9.2. This analysis is based on experiences by OECD based branders and retailers selling predominantly to consumers in the global North. Our assumption is that this model can serve as an initial frame of reference also for production directed at middle-class consumers in the global South. The Norm Life Cycle model is a useful tool to analyse the process of how new norms can become mainstreamed (Finnemore and Sikkink 1998: 898). They distinguish three stages: norm emergence, norm cascading and norm internalisation, with a key role assigned to the 'norm tipping' that takes place between the first and second stage (Segerlund 2005: 5). In the first stage of norm emergence, altruism, empathy, idealism and commitment are seen as the main motives for 'norm entrepreneurs' to push for example for better labour standards. This refers to the frontrunners in responsible production, in particular various types of Fair Trade initiatives. Moreover, it also includes those firms that really use their responsibility image to create value (a well-known example is the Body Shop).

Once a certain critical mass of key companies has adopted such a norm, 'norm tipping' brings us to the second stage of norm cascading. In this stage legitimacy, reputation and esteem become the main motives of companies to join what is now seen as 'the right thing to do'. This is also where brand protection comes in. A-brand companies start seeing they need to invest in boosting their responsibility image, in order not to 'fall behind' those firms who used to be seen as frontrunners, but are now increasingly setting the new level of expected responsible behaviour.

In the third stage of norm internalisation the new norm has become a generally accepted minimal standard that all participants need to conform to, and at this stage for example new laws on minimum labour standards can further institutionalise the now generally accepted new norm. At this stage also those firms who focus on abiding-by-the-law need to respond to the changed situation. Adding this dynamic dimension therefore shows that firms need to actively respond to changes in norms, even when they continue to follow the same CSR strategy. Moreover, through this dynamic process of new norms becoming mainstreamed and subsequently internalised over time, the 'floor of basic compliance can be raised', and overall compliance requirements can increase over time.

The danger with these types of models is that one might be tempted to think only in terms of inevitable or 'teleological' improvements leading up to a steady state of utopia. Obviously, over time companies may move up and down through this model, and it is important not to be naive about ever reaching a state in which a majority of companies would use their responsibility profile to differentiate themselves from competitors. Nevertheless, I feel this model helps to more systematically assess trends in the occurrence of responsible production. The basic point here is that the role, motivations and incentives inherently differ for state, private and civic actors in these various stages of the Norm Life Cycle model. Moreover, this adjusted taxonomy also provides a step towards a more analytical understanding of where and when different combinations of regulatory and voluntary governance can be applied more effectively, one of the new and fashionable themes for those working on CSR and development. An emerging research theme is to investigate how to dovetail state driven legal regulation and voluntary self-regulation by corporations, with civil organisations as both watchdogs and catalysts in these processes (Braithwaite 2006; O'Rourke 2006). Perhaps because most research on CSR remains caught at the level of doing case studies, what has so far been neglected is that the relative roles, motivations and incentives for state, private and civil society actors are not simply diverging because of case-by-case contextual peculiarities.

Finally, a critical dimension of sustained success in value chain responsibility initiatives is the development of integrative institutions that promote learning and dissemination of initial results to broader groups of stakeholders. Classic and more recent literature on the social technology of institutional development will be relevant to identify trajectories that are more or less likely to foster institutional support for specific value chain responsibility initiatives (Nelson and Winter 1982; Hodgson 2007). This will include a focus on what made specific responsibility partnerships more effective and to draw some more generic indicators from these case-based experiences.

9.5 Conclusion: taking the debate forwards

This chapter has explored where and when responsibility issues are more likely to be incorporated in global value chains, with a focus on the global South as centre of production and consumption. A basic typology identifies a pyramid consisting of four layers with overlapping border zones. The base of this pyramid consists of informal sector firms that do not comply with existing minimum legal requirements in terms of responsible behaviour of firms. The next level consists of formal sector firms that do abide by the letter and the spirit of the law. A smaller but still sizeable number of firms follow a brand protection strategy, in which they invest in voluntary responsibility initiatives that go beyond legal requirements. Finally, the top layer consists of firms for whom their responsibility profile is a key part of their core value creation strategy.

The emerging framework identifies a number of key explanatory variables that influence the likelihood of value chain responsibility in the global South. It aims to tie together and investigate interaction patterns between public, private and civic actors in enhancing value chain responsibility. The chapter was structured along two major dimensions.

First, I identified factors that explain how firms position themselves in this pyramid ('agency'). Choices by lead firms in determining their responsibility profile depend among others on the type of product they produce, the type of consumers they target, and the personality traits of entrepreneurs and key managers. Second, I explored factors that explain both the shape of the pyramid in various institutional settings and the relative size of its four layers ('structure'). Such structural factors include the specific business system in a country, its actor interaction patterns, and longer-term changes in consumer behaviour and societal norms and standards of minimally expected levels of responsible behaviour.

It seems that at least three different trajectories can be identified that might result in more value chain responsibility in the global South, be it through very different routes. The first pathway requires a more open society with an active civil society and a relatively responsive or rather absent or corrupt government, in which firms are pressured through both litigation and soft power of civil society to give more systematic attention to responsibility issues. In such a societal constellation individual firms are rather free to choose their own responsibility profile, but especially in the more exacting market segments targeting final consumers, firms are likely to be pushed to at least a brand protection profile. At the same time, this relative freedom of choice also means that a large majority of firms, operating outside these types of responsibility-sensitive segments and product markets, are more likely to minimise their involvement in responsibility. In short, the pyramid is more likely to be taller and leaner, but possibly with a broad base when many firms can remain in the informal sector. South Africa and India, even though their institutional settings obviously differ in many respects, might be used in a next stage of empirical work as countries that portray important dimensions of this pathway.

The second pathway fits with a more centrally guided society. In situations where public authorities decide they wish to strengthen systematic attention for responsibility, they can and will use their implementation capacity to enforce this decision upon private and public sector enterprises. In this pathway the implementation of increased attention for responsibility takes place predominantly through regulation, and not through the soft power of civil society organisations, like in the first pathway. In this more centrally enforced pathway, making headway with responsibility is first of all a matter of public and political decision making, and if and when it is implemented, is more likely to be more generically enforced. In short, the pyramid will be plumper and broader, and fewer actors need to develop negotiated partnerships to make headway. China might serve as the example to test this pathway.

The third pathway lies in between the first two, and resembles Peter Evans' ideas on the concept of an embedded autonomy. Here the state plays an important role, but does not fully dominate the economy. Senior bureaucrats maintain close contacts with key players from the business community, but also uphold a critical level of independence with a longer-term vision on a national development strategy. Moreover, civil society organisations exist in many varieties, ranging from politically independent and critical to those strongly influenced by business interests. In such a societal constellation it is crucial to find workable combinations of private and public governance to reinforce responsibility. While in the first pathway private actors are the central players, and in the second pathway the state occupies a key role, in this third pathway progress can only be made through synergetic initiatives that incorporate at least two of the three main societal actors. Brazil, and for example South Korea, are examples of countries that might offer an appropriate institutional setting to empirically investigate this third pathway.

These pathways emerge from bringing together various strands in the literature, but are not yet empirically tested. One open question is which pathway is more likely to provide more development relevant responsibility impacts. One way in which our approach differs from mainstream CSR literature is that I do not automatically assume that the first pathway – a societal constellation resembling the USA – necessarily will achieve more development relevant responsibility impacts. Through different channels, with different lead actors, each of the three pathways may provide important lessons on how social responsibility issues can be more successfully embedded in global value chains in the global South.

Note

1 More recently, this approach has also been used to explain very diverging success or failure cases of attracting FDI in particular states or provinces in large countries like China or India. For example Andhra Pradesh is often mentioned as a case in point. While it uses the same legal framework as other states in India, it has been very successful in attracting FDI because it implements these rules in a much more flexible and 'business-friendly' manner and it had a Chief Minister who raised confidence among business men.

References

Barrientos, S. and S. Smith (2006) *Evaluation of the Ethical Trading Initiative*, Brighton: IDS.

Blowfield, M. (2005) 'Corporate Social Responsibility: Reinventing the Meaning of Development?' *International Affairs*, 81: 515–24.

Blowfield, M. (2007) 'Reasons To Be Cheerful? What We Know about CSR's Impact', *Third World Quarterly*, 28: 683–95.

Braithwaite, J. (2006) 'Responsive Regulation and Developing Countries', *World Development*, 34: 884–98.

Chapple, W. and J. Moon (2005) 'Corporate Social Responsibility (CSR) in Asia: A Seven-Country Study of CSR Web Site Reporting', *Business and Society*, 44: 415–41.

Devinney, T., G. Eckhardt and R. Belk (2005) 'Why Don't Consumers Behave Ethically? The Social Construction of Consumption (mimeo)', online, available at: www2.agsm.edu.au/agsm/web.nsf/AttachmentsByTitle/TD_Paper_SocialConstruction/$FILE/Social+Construction.pdf (accessed 10 May 2010).

Economist, The (2005) 'The Good Company: Survey on Corporate Social Responsibility', online, available at: www.economist.com/surveys (accessed 20 January 2006).

Evans, P. (1995) *Embedded Autonomy: States and Industrial Transformation*, Princeton, NJ: Princeton University Press.

Evans, P. (1996) 'Government Action, Social Capital and Development: Reviewing the Evidence on Synergy', *World Development*, 24: 1119–32.

Finnemore, M. and K. Sikkink (1998) 'International Norm Dynamics and Political Change', *International Organization*, 52: 887–917.

Frynas, J.G. (2005) 'The False Developmental Promise of Corporate Social Responsibility: Evidence from Multinational Oil Companies', *International Affairs*, 81: 581–98.

Geels, J. and J. Schot (2007) 'Typology of Sociotechnical Transition Pathways', *Research Policy*, 36: 399–417.

Gereffi. G., J. Humphrey and T. Sturgeon (2005) 'The Governance of Global Value Chains', *Review of International Political Economy*, 12: 78–104.

Graham, D. and N. Woods (2006) 'Making Corporate Self-regulation Effective in Developing Countries', *World Development*, 34: 868–83.

Granovetter, M. (1985) 'Economic Action and Social Structure: The Problem of Embeddedness', *American Journal of Sociology*, 91: 481–510.

Gu, J., J. Humphrey and D. Messner (2008) 'Global Governance and Developing Countries: The Implications of the Rise of China', *World Development*, 36: 274–92.

Hodgson, G. (2007) 'Institutions and Individuals: Interaction and Evolution', *Organization Studies*, 28: 95–111.

Howell, J. and J. Pearce (2001) *Civil Society and Development: A Critical Exploration*, London: Lynne Riemer.

Hughes, A., N. Wrigley and M. Buttle (2008) 'Global Production Networks, Ethical Campaigning, and the Embeddedness of Responsible Governance', *Journal of Economic Geography*, 8: 345–67.

ILO (2002) 'Decent Work and the Informal Economy', Geneva: ILO.

Jacobsen, G. and J.E. Torp (eds) (2001) *Understanding Business Systems in Developing Countries*, London: Sage Publications.

Jenkins, R. (2005) 'Globalization, Corporate Social Responsibility and Poverty', *International Affairs*, 81: 525–40.

Knorringa, P. and A.H.J.B. Helmsing (2008) 'Beyond an Enemy Perception: Unpacking and Engaging the Private Sector', *Development and Change*, 39: 1053–62.

Macdonald, K. and S. Marshall (2010) *Fair Trade, Corporate Accountability and Beyond: Experiments in Globalizing Justice*, Farnham (UK): Ashgate.

McWilliams, A., D.S. Siegel and P.M. Wright (2006) 'Guest Editors' Introduction: Corporate Social Responsibility, Strategic Implications', *Journal of Management Studies*, 43: 1–18.

Marques, J.C. and P. Utting (2010) *Corporate Social Responsibility and Regulatory Governance: Towards Inclusive Development?* Basingstoke: Palgrave.

Nelson, J. (2000) 'The Business of Peace: The Private Sector as a Partner in Conflict Prevention and Resolution', International Alert, The Prince of Wales Business Leaders Forum, London: Council on Economic Priorities (Forms can be downloaded from: www.international-alert.org/corporate).

Nelson, R. and S. Winter (1982) *An Evolutionary Theory of Economic Change*, Cambridge, MA: Harvard University Press.

Newell, P. and J.G. Frynas (2007) 'Beyond CSR? Business, Poverty and Social Justice: An Introduction', *Third World Quarterly*, 28: 669–81.

O'Rourke, D. (2006) 'Multi-stakeholder Regulation: Privatizing or Socializing Global Labor Standards?' *World Development*, 34: 899–918.

Prahalad, C.K. (2005) *The Fortune at the Bottom of the Pyramid: Eradicating Poverty Through Profits*, Upper Saddle River, NJ: Wharton School Publishing.

Rodrik, D. (2004) 'Industrial Policy for the Twenty-First Century', CEPR Discussion Paper 4767, Centre for Economic Policy Research.

Ruggie, J. (2008) 'Promotion and Protection of all Human Rights, Civil, Political, Economic, Social and Cultural Rights, including the Right to Development', Human Rights Council.

Segerlund, L. (2005) 'Corporate Social Responsibility and the Role of NGOs in the Advocacy of New Norms for Transnational Corporations (Licentiate's Thesis)', Department of Economic History, Stockholm: University of Stockholm.

Shaw, D., T. Newholm and R. Dickenson (2005) 'Consumption as Voting: An Exploration of Consumer Empowerment', Mimeographed, Glasgow Caledonian University.

Spar, D.L. and L.T. La Mure (2003) 'The Power of Activism: Assessing the Impact of NGOs on Global Business', *California Management Review*, 45: 78–101.

Van Tulder, R., J. Van Wijk and A. Kolk (2009) 'From Chain Liability to Chain Responsibility', *Journal of Business Ethics*, 85: 399–412.

Whitley, R.D. (1999) *Divergent Capitalisms: The Social Structuring and Change of Business Systems*, Oxford: Oxford University Press.

World Bank (2007) 'Global Economic Prospects. Managing the Next Wave of Globalisation', Washington, DC: World Bank.

Zadek, S. (2006) 'Responsible Competitiveness: Reshaping Global Markets through Responsible Business Practices', *Corporate Governance*, 6: 334–48.

10 The diverse dynamics of deindustrialization internationally

Fiona Tregenna[1,2]

10.1 Introduction

An increasingly prevalent form of structural change internationally is deindustrialization, which is most commonly defined as a decline in the share of manufacturing in total employment. Deindustrialization has been observed in many countries of the North over the past few decades. One of the contributing factors to this was the partial 'relocation' of manufacturing to countries of the South, especially to the successively emerging groups of 'Asian Tigers'. More recently, there has been deindustrialization in a number of countries of the South as well, especially in middle-income countries. This is likely to be associated, at least in part, to shifting locations of manufacturing amongst developing countries. Deindustrialization is also associated with changing dynamics of manufacturing within countries, which lead to greater reductions in the share of manufacturing in countries' total employment than in their total value-added.

This chapter analyzes experiences of deindustrialization internationally in order to unpack the very different dynamics at work in terms of not only declines in manufacturing employment but also countries' varying experiences in terms of manufacturing output level and share, the labor intensity of manufacturing, GDP growth, and labor productivity. Defining deindustrialization solely in terms of manufacturing share of employment is conceptually limiting and can also have misleading policy implications. In most of the deindustrialization cases analyzed here, the decline in manufacturing employment is associated primarily with falling labor intensity of manufacturing rather than an overall decline in the size or share of the manufacturing sector. Deindustrialization associated with falling labor intensity in manufacturing is very different from deindustrialization associated with a poor performance in manufacturing value-added, and the methods developed and applied here allow for an analysis of the different dynamics at work in individual countries as well as a typology of country experiences of deindustrialization.

Section 10.2 begins by reviewing why a sectoral structure matters for growth, and specifically in what ways manufacturing is considered to have special growth-pulling properties and hence why deindustrialization could be problematic for growth. Section 10.3 empirically investigates deindustrialization processes in 48 countries. Section 10.4 discusses the implications of the results, particularly in terms of distinguishing between different types of deindustrialization, and suggests a new definition of deindustrialization.

10.2 Sectoral specificity and deindustrialization

10.2.1 The 'special role' of manufacturing in the growth process

There has traditionally been a strong argument in branches of the heterodox economics literature that there is a sector-specificity in the economic growth process. This implies that a unit of value-added is not necessarily equivalent across sectors, notably in terms of its growth-inducing or growth-enhancing effects. Such an approach differs from the sector-neutrality implicit in neoclassical growth theory.

The Kaldorian tradition in the heterodox literature has regarded the manufacturing sector as having special growth-enhancing characteristics that are not shared by the other sectors (or at least not to the same extent).[3] The growth-supporting externalities of these characteristics may not be fully reflected in relative prices, and hence a market-based 'equilibrium' sectoral structure can be sub-optimal for growth. This implies that an intersectoral shift of employment (or similarly of other resources) may potentially increase aggregate productivity. A view of the manufacturing sector having special properties leads to it being accorded a special place in understanding the growth process, as well as suggesting that from a policy perspective there needs to be a particular focus on the manufacturing sector.[4]

Manufacturing is regarded in this literature as having the capacity or potential to 'pull along' overall economic growth in ways that growth in other sectors of the economy cannot. One dimension of this is backward and forward linkages between manufacturing and other sectors of the domestic economy. If these are indeed stronger than for other sectors of the economy, then manufacturing growth can exert a particularly powerful pulling effect on the economy.[5] Another channel through which manufacturing can act as an engine of growth relates to dynamic economies of scale, which imply that the growth of productivity in manufacturing is higher the higher the growth in manufacturing output. This is related to the notion that 'learning-by-doing' is more important in industry than it is in agriculture or in the service sector. Learning-by-doing, innovation, and intersectoral linkages are thus thought to render overall productivity growth endogenous to growth in dynamic manufacturing sectors. It is also argued that most technological change occurs in the manufacturing sector. Furthermore, most of the technological changes that occur in the rest of the economy are regarded as being diffused out from the manufacturing sector, in part through the use of higher productivity manufacturing inputs in the 'production' processes of the rest of the economy. Finally, manufacturing is considered critical to alleviating the balance of payments constraints that can impose a 'stop-go' pattern on developing countries' growth, due to issues of import income elasticities and relative tradability of manufactures.

In the Kaldorian and structuralist literature, these properties are regarded as being strongly associated with the manufacturing sector. This would imply that deindustrialization – especially premature deindustrialization – could have negative implications for the rates and sustainability of growth.

10.2.2 Deindustrialization: the current literature

Deindustrialization is typically understood in the current literature[6] as a decline in the share of manufacturing[7] in a country's total employment. Rowthorn and Coutts (2004) review five explanations of deindustrialization that have been advanced in the literature. The first of these is specialization, referring to the domestic outsourcing of activities previously performed in-house in manufacturing to specialized service providers, resulting in an apparent decline in manufacturing employment that is a 'statistical artifact' rather than real.[8] Second, a fall in the relative prices of manufactures means that they account for a smaller share of consumer expenditure. Third, the higher rate of productivity growth in manufacturing relative to services is associated with slower employment growth in manufacturing than in services, even if output increases at the same rate. Fourth, international trade might negatively affect manufacturing employment in advanced economies by increasing productivity through higher competitive pressures, eliminating low value-added activities or inefficient firms, and by replacing relatively labor-intensive activities subject to import pressures with less labor-intensive activities producing sophisticated exports. Finally, decreases in the rate of investment will tend to reduce the share of manufacturing (in both employment and GDP), since a disproportionately large share of investment expenditure is accounted for by manufactures. To these explanations Palma (2005) adds the Dutch Disease concept, understood here as a country shifting from a 'manufacturing' path to a 'primary commodity' path.

The declines in the share of manufacturing employment in developed economies in the 1980s were much more pronounced than were the declines in manufacturing share of GDP. This stands to reason, as the sources of deindustrialization reviewed above would tend to affect employment more strongly than output. The causes of deindustrialization discussed earlier would affect manufacturing output and employment in differing ways. To the extent that deindustrialization is a statistical illusion arising from outsourcing to specialized service providers, the fact that these activities are generally more labor intensive than manufacturing overall means that manufacturing employment would be reduced proportionately more than would manufacturing output. Deindustrialization associated with productivity growth in manufacturing exceeding that in services would of course only have a negative effect on manufacturing employment, not output. International trade as a source of deindustrialization would reduce employment more than output, both because the activities affected will tend to be more labor intensive than manufacturing as a whole and also because of trade-induced pressures to increase labor productivity. On the other hand, the 'consumption' source of deindustrialization – that falling relative prices of manufactures reduce total expenditure on manufacturing – would affect manufacturing output rather than employment (in fact it may even increase employment to the extent that falling prices increase actual consumption in 'volume' terms). Deindustrialization associated with a fall in the rate of investment would affect manufacturing output more than employment.

The fact that the declines in manufacturing employment share have generally exceeded those in manufacturing output might partly explain the emphasis on the fall in the share of manufacturing employment in the deindustrialization literature. The clearer trends in manufacturing employment share may have been considered more conducive for quantitative analysis than the declines in manufacturing output shares, which were not only less pronounced but were found in fewer countries. Further, apparent changes in manufacturing output share are complicated by concurrent changes in relative prices, and this could also be part of the reason for the focus in the literature on changes in manufacturing employment share.

In addition, the decline in manufacturing employment was arguably more acutely felt in a broader sense in advanced capitalist economies in the 1980s than was the decline in manufacturing output. The shedding of manufacturing jobs made this an important political and social issue. The relative visibility and 'political' nature of manufacturing job losses may have contributed to the focus on this dimension of deindustrialization.

10.2.3 What matters for growth: manufacturing output or employment?

Defining deindustrialization exclusively in terms of employment gives no explicit place to changes in the share of manufacturing in GDP. If changes in manufacturing output and employment were monotonically related as well as being of similar magnitudes, the above discussion as to the relative importance of each for the growth-pulling properties of manufacturing would not be of much practical import. But empirically, changes in the levels or share of manufacturing output and employment can be not only of very different magnitudes but even in different directions, as will be seen in the empirical analysis that follows.[9]

A falling share of manufacturing employment may be of concern for various economic, social, and political reasons, as discussed elsewhere in this chapter, but in terms of growth specifically, does it matter what happens to the share of manufacturing in GDP, or is it only the share of manufacturing in employment that has growth implications?

First, the growth-pulling effects of manufacturing through backward and forward linkages with the rest of the domestic economy are related more to the share of manufacturing in GDP and the growth of manufacturing *output*, than to its share of employment or growth in manufacturing employment. Even if manufacturing's share of employment is shrinking, if the sector as a whole is growing then this will *ceteris paribus* give rise to higher demand for inputs from backward-linked sectors as well as providing stimulus and potentially lower input costs to forward-linked sectors. Second, manufacturing might also pull growth through Keynesian-type demand multiplier effects, through wages paid. In this respect it would clearly be manufacturing *employment*, rather than output per se, that would be relevant.

Third, dynamic economies of scale would operate through both *output* and *employment*. Output and employment are both relevant to learning-by-doing. In terms of employment, on-the-job learning by workers means that the scale of employment in manufacturing affects the strength of the contribution of manufacturing to productivity and growth through this channel. However, manufacturing output is also relevant, as learning-by-doing applies not only at the level of individual workers, but also in terms of management and the planning of production and technology. Further, it is the 'replicability' of manufacturing production processes that is one of the distinguishing features of manufacturing from agriculture or most services. These (static) increasing returns to scale are effective through the output of manufacturing. Both output and employment are germane to the broader endogeneity of manufacturing productivity growth to manufacturing output growth. Nevertheless, the conceptualization of productivity growth as a function of *output* growth (as in the specification of Verdoorn's Law) suggests that it is primarily the growth in manufacturing *output* (as opposed to employment) that is most important for this dimension of dynamic economies of scale.

Another of the 'special properties' of manufacturing for growth discussed above is in terms of technological change and innovation, and it is the growth of manufacturing *output* that is more relevant to this than the growth of manufacturing employment. A final quality of manufacturing regarded as being important for overall growth is in terms of alleviating balance of payments constraints and freeing economies (developing economies in particular) from a 'stop–go' pattern of growth. It is the *output* of manufacturing that is most relevant to its net balance of payments position. Even a decline in the share (or level) of manufacturing employment would not be directly relevant to this.[10]

This assessment of the relevance of manufacturing output and employment to the channels through which manufacturing can raise overall growth suggests that both output and employment are important. The relative importance of each for an individual country is ultimately an empirical issue, contingent on the binding constraints faced by a particular economy at a particular time. However, it does seem that in general the growth of manufacturing output is at least as important as manufacturing employment. This suggests that it is inadequate to focus exclusively on changes in manufacturing's share of employment.

Defining deindustrialization as a fall in the share of manufacturing in employment is narrow as it neglects trends in the level or share of manufacturing output. This could give rise to misleading policy interpretations. For instance, a case where the share of manufacturing employment falls despite healthy growth in manufacturing output and a rising share of manufacturing in GDP, would not necessarily give rise to the negative consequences for growth typically associated with 'deindustrialization'. Such a trend may well be of concern for other reasons – especially in terms of manufacturing employment in its own right – but would not necessarily undermine the growth-pulling capacity of manufacturing or depress long-term growth.

It is these separate processes that the analysis in this chapter seeks to distinguish. That is, to understand the extent to which a fall in the share of manufacturing in total employment can be accounted for by a shrinking of the manufacturing sector as a whole on the one hand and, on the other hand, by changes in the labor intensity of manufacturing. This is important for understanding the precise character of 'deindustrialization' processes in specific countries over specific periods, the implications of these changes for the rates and sustainability of growth, as well as what 'deindustrialization' should really refer to. The next section thus develops a method for decomposing these changes, and applies it to the analysis of 'deindustrialization' experiences in various countries.

10.3 Empirical analysis of deindustrialization

10.3.1 Data and summary statistics

This study covers all 48 countries (as well as the territories of Hong Kong and Macao) for which suitable data are available and which show evidence of deindustrialization. Table 10.1 lists the countries, the time periods analyzed for each country, and the changes in the number of manufacturing jobs and in the share of manufacturing in total employment for that period.

The time periods are generally taken from the high point of manufacturing employment share prior to a sustained decline (although data is not available for the pre-1980 period). In isolated cases (such as Pakistan) a declining share of manufacturing employment over a significant period of time has since been followed by a rising share; nevertheless, the period in which the share declined is still included in this study.

Value-added and GDP data are taken from the UN national accounting data. The dollar-denominated measures of manufacturing value-added and GDP in 1990 constant prices are used. The employment data is from the International Labor Organisation (ILO) Key Indicators of the Labor Market (KILM) database.

In constructing the employment dataset each country was examined individually, in order to assess whether it met the criteria for inclusion in the sample (a sustained decline in the share of manufacturing employment), to determine the appropriate period for inclusion in the sample, and to check the continuity of the data series. Some series in the KILM database include breaks, arising from a change in methodology, scope of coverage, type of source, or repository. Data series used in this analysis generally do not traverse breaks in the series, unless scrutiny of the data suggests no significant shift in level or trend. In some cases no break is noted in the database, yet examination of the data suggests that there was in fact an unrecorded change in methodology (for example an unexplained large jump in the series), and such cases were treated as a break and excluded from this analysis. The tendency has thus been to err on the side of caution. Even so, employment data generally has wide confidence intervals, particularly at the sectoral level, and the results derived using this data could thus be treated as indicative rather than precise.

Availability of data, as well as the stringent criteria (in terms of data continuity and reliability) for inclusion in the sample, means that a number of countries that in all probability did undergo deindustrialization have been excluded from the sample. For example, Brazil is widely regarded as having deindustrialized, yet it is excluded from the sample on the basis of insufficient data continuity. The problem of having to exclude countries on grounds of data availability or quality is particularly acute for developing countries. This would have led to some 'bias' in the sample, in the sense that developing countries are underrepresented in the sample. Deindustrialization is undoubtedly less advanced in developing than in developed countries. Nonetheless, deindustrialization is somewhat more pronounced among developing countries than the sample analyzed here might suggest.

10.3.2 Summary of manufacturing output and employment trends

Table 10.2 summarizes the manufacturing performance of the sample countries, in terms of changes in the levels and shares of manufacturing employment during the relevant periods (as listed in Table 10.1). Since only countries whose share of manufacturing employment declined are included in the study, the dimension of manufacturing employment share is extraneous to the table.

Of the 48 countries, the level of manufacturing employment rose in six despite the share falling. Of the other 42 countries, in which both the share and level of manufacturing employment fell (the rightmost column of the table), in most (31 countries) the manufacturing sector grew in real terms, and in 11 of these also increased as a share of GDP. Eleven countries had an all-round decline of their manufacturing sectors: manufacturing shrank in real terms and as a share of GDP, and manufacturing employment also fell as well as declining as a share of total employment. The latter group are essentially developing and 'transition' economies. These countries clearly experienced deindustrialization (in most cases, 'premature' deindustrialization).

These dynamics are investigated further in the analysis set out below, in which we use decomposition techniques to separate out the various components of the changes in manufacturing employment. The first two decompositions analyze changes in the *level* of manufacturing employment, while the third one looks at changes in the *share* of manufacturing in total employment.[11]

10.3.3 Decomposing changes in the level of manufacturing employment into value-added and labor intensity

First, we undertake a two-way decomposition on changes in the level of manufacturing employment. This separates out changes in the value-added of the

Table 10.1 Country sample and summary data

Country	Period	Change in manufact. employment share ($\Delta\Phi_{ij}$)	Change in manufact. employment (%)	Change in manufact. employment ('000) (ΔL_{ij})
Advanced economies – G7				
Canada	1980–1993	−5.14	−13.45	−289.8
France	1980–1989	−4.37	−16.51	−907
Germany	1991–2003	−7.42	−26.77	−3029
Italy	1980–1992	−4.77	−13.96	−759
Japan	1985–2003	−6.37	−18.93	−2750
United Kingdom	1980–2003	−12.82	−39.27	−2755.52
United States	1980–2002	−8.80	−17.30	−3795
Advanced economies – newly industrialized Asian economies				
Hong Kong	1980–2003	−33.69	−71.12	−670.7
Korea	1989–2003	−8.81	−13.87	−677
Singapore	1991–2003	−10.25	−15.09	−64.83
Advanced economies – other				
Australia	1980–2003	−8.29	−13.25	−164.3
Austria	1982–2003	−10.25	−22.62	−214
Belgium	1980–1999	−7.84	−27.36	−251.99
Cyprus	1982–1995	−5.65	3.53	1.5
Czech Republic	1981–1998	−7.72	−21.16	−385.13
Denmark	1996–2003	−3.14	−13.53	−69
Finland	1981–2001	−7.14	−25.82	−164.2
Greece	1993–2002	−1.89	−6.55	−37.94
Iceland	1980–2002	−10.41	−14.98	−3.88
Ireland	1980–1997	−3.60	−0.12	−0.3
Israel	1986–1992	−2.30	8.65	27.4
Luxembourg	1980–2003	−15.28	−21.77	−9.1
Netherlands	1980–2002	−7.81	2.06	22
New Zealand	1980–2003	−10.65	−12.36	−39.3
Norway	1980–2000	−7.48	−24.02	−92
Poland	1981–2002	−8.82	−49.40	−2514.3

Portugal	1980–1997	–4.73	–7.26	–74.7
San Marino	1980–1993	–6.29	24.15	0.92
Slovenia	1993–2003	–6.99	–14.29	–44.
Spain	1980–2003	–7.68	0.49	14.3
Sweden	1980–2003	–7.97	–32.85	–337
Switzerland	1986–2003	–9.06	–21.90	–189.85
Developing economies – Central and Eastern Europe and Commonwealth of Independent States				
Estonia	1990–2003	–2.58	–35.47	–73.7
Latvia	1990–2003	–9.23	–53.46	–199.4
Mongolia	1995–2003	–2.91	–19.03	–12.9
Romania	1990–2003	–11.65	–44.67	–1613.65
Russia	1990–1996	–5.93	–32.03	–6394.9
Developing economies – Western Hemisphere				
Argentina	1992–2002	–11.17	–3.51	–38.41
Barbados	1982–2003	–8.08	–42.75	–5.9
Chile	1992–2003	–2.99	–1.97	–16.02
Colombia	1991–1999	–5.58	–10.86	–126.72
Jamaica	1992–2003	–4.15	–33.27	–33.9
Saint Lucia	1993–2000	–2.39	–2.82	–0.18
Uruguay	1987–2000	–7.71	–35.61	–87.5
Venezuela	1988–2003	–5.97	9.34	99.16
Developing economies – Asia				
Macao	1989–2003	–18.41	–37.64	–22.39
Pakistan	1981–1994	–4.49	–13.87	–505
Suriname	1990–1997	–3.01	–27.82	–2.37
Mean	15.15 yrs	–7.70	–19.21	–609.51
Weighted mean[1]		–7.52	–22.17	
Median	13.50 yrs	–7.45	–16.90	–81.10

Notes
1 Weighted by a country's manufacturing employment (mean of the beginning and end values).
Country classification based on IMF classification.

Table 10.2 Typology of changes in manufacturing

	Increase in manufacturing employment	Decrease in manufacturing employment
Manufacturing growth, share increase	0 countries	11 countries: Austria, Belgium, Estonia, Finland, Ireland, Korea, Pakistan, Poland, Slovenia, Sweden, Switzerland
Manufacturing growth, share decrease	4 countries: Cyprus, Israel, Netherlands, Spain	20 countries: Australia, Canada, Chile, Colombia, Czech Republic, Denmark, France, Germany, Greece, Iceland, Italy, Japan, Luxembourg, Mongolia, New Zealand, Norway, Portugal, Singapore, United Kingdom, United States
Manufacturing decline, share increase	0 countries	0 countries
Manufacturing decline, share decrease	2 countries: San Marino, Venezuela	11 countries: Argentina, Barbados, Hong Kong, Jamaica, Latvia, Macao, Romania, Russian Federation, Saint Lucia, Suriname, Uruguay

sector from changes in the labor intensity[12] of that sector. The object is to understand how much of each country's decline in manufacturing employment is associated with changes in the overall size of manufacturing, and how much with changes in the labor intensity of that production.

The separation of these two vectors is useful in distinguishing different types of 'deindustrialization'. For instance, a given fall in manufacturing employment could be associated with either a falling labor intensity of production, or with a shrinkage of manufacturing as a whole (or of course with a combination of these factors). These two processes would be very different, even if associated with the same change in manufacturing employment.

Let L_{ijt} be the employment in sector[13] i in country j at time t, i.e.,

$$L_{jt} = \sum_{i=1}^{n} L_{ijt}.$$

Then as an identity, $L_{ijt} \equiv \varphi_{ijt} Q_{ijt}$, where Q_{ijt} is the value-added in the sector, and φ_{ijt} is the labor intensity of sector i, measured as

$$\frac{L_{ijt}}{Q_{ijt}}.$$

Then the change in employment in a given sector over a given period h is given as follows:

$$\Delta L_{ij} = \varphi_{ijt} Q_{ijt} - \varphi_{ijt-h} Q_{ijt-h}$$

$$= \underbrace{(\varphi_{ijt} - \varphi_{ijt-h}) \left(\frac{Q_{ijt-h} + Q_{ijt}}{2} \right)}_{\text{labor intensity effect}} + \underbrace{(Q_{ijt} - Q_{ijt-h}) \left(\frac{\varphi_{ijt-h} + \varphi_{ijt}}{2} \right)}_{\text{sector growth effect}}.$$

The 'labor intensity effect' is the change in the number of jobs in sector i associated with the changing labor intensity of the sector (where labor intensity refers to the number of people employed per value-added unit of production). The 'sector growth effect' is the change in the number of people employed in the sector that is associated with a change in the size of the sector (value-added). Where sector i is manufacturing and where $\Delta L_{ij} < 0$, the labor intensity and the sector growth effects can be thought of as the two components of 'absolute deindustrialization' (referring to a fall in the *level* of manufacturing employment). These two effects could be differentially important in the loss of manufacturing jobs of different countries or in a country at different times.

Deindustrialization associated predominantly with one or other of the two effects could have different causes and implications. A loss of manufacturing jobs associated primarily with the sector growth effect might suggest – in a simplistic way of course – that the issue is primarily one of the manufacturing sector as a whole and its lack of dynamism. On the other hand, a loss of manufacturing jobs associated primarily with the labor intensity effect might suggest that the manufacturing sector as a whole is not necessarily in decline, but that the 'problem' pertains more to its labor absorbing capacity.

The cross-country results from this first decomposition are summarized graphically in Figure 10.1. Each point in the scatter plot denotes the combination of the labor intensity effect (x-coordinate) and sector growth effect (y-coordinate) for a particular country (over the time periods listed in Table 10.1). The values are normalized in terms of the country's manufacturing employment at the beginning of the period, meaning that the coordinates of each point represent the contribution of that effect to the percentage change in manufacturing employment for that country.

That is, the labor intensity effect is shown as

$$(\varphi_{ijt} - \varphi_{ijt-h}) \left(\frac{Q_{ijt-h} + Q_{ijt}}{2} \right) \left(\frac{100}{L_{ijt-h}} \right)$$

and the sector growth effect as

$$(Q_{ijt} - Q_{ijt-h}) \left(\frac{\varphi_{ijt-h} + \varphi_{ijt}}{2} \right) \left(\frac{100}{L_{ijt-h}} \right)$$

summing to the percentage change in sectoral employment

$$\frac{100 \Delta L_{ij}}{L_{ijt-h}}.$$

For example, the coordinates of the USA (−75.8, 58.5) indicate that the fall in manufacturing labor intensity accounted (hypothetically) for a 75.8 percent fall

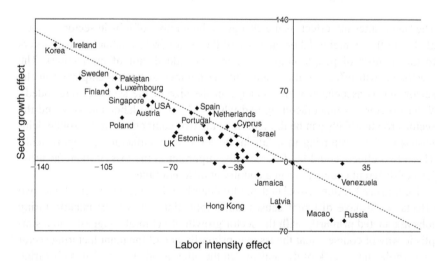

Figure 10.1 Results from first decomposition analysis.

in the level of its manufacturing employment, while the growth of manufacturing value-added accounted (hypothetically) for a 58.5 percent increase in manufacturing employment. The sum of these two effects, at −17.3 percent, is the actual percentage change in manufacturing employment in the USA, as shown in Table 10.1.

The position of a point in the north-east quadrant indicates that both the labor intensity and sector growth effects were positive, such that the change in the labor intensity of manufacturing and the growth in manufacturing value-added each accounted for manufacturing employment creation, with unambiguously positive manufacturing employment growth. Conversely, the location of a point in the south-west quadrant indicates that both effects were negative for the relevant period; in other words, the change in labor intensity and the change in manufacturing sector size each accounted for negative manufacturing employment growth, with an unambiguously negative change in manufacturing employment. A location in the north-west quadrant indicates a negative labor intensity effect and a positive sector growth effect, that is, the drop in labor intensity accounted for a negative change in manufacturing employment, while the sector growth contributed to a positive change in manufacturing employment. A point in this quadrant lying above the dashed diagonal line (along which the labor intensity effect and the sector growth effect are of equal magnitude but opposite sign) indicates that the positive sector growth effect outweighed the negative labor intensity effect, hence net manufacturing job creation; and below the line the reverse, and thus net manufacturing job loss. Finally, a point in the south-east quadrant indicates a positive labor intensity effect and a negative sector growth effect, denoting a case where the rise in labor intensity accounted for a positive change in manufacturing employment while the change in sector size accounted for a negative change in manufacturing employment. A point in the quadrant above the dashed diagonal line would have had net manufacturing employment creation, with the positive labor intensity outweighing the negative sector growth effect, with a point below the dashed line having had net manufacturing employment loss. Overall, any point falling below/to the left of the dashed diagonal line shows manufacturing employment loss for that country, while any point above/to the right of the dashed line shows manufacturing employment growth.

Several insights can be noted from these results. First, manufacturing employment increased in just six countries (Cyprus, Israel, the Netherlands, San Marino, Spain, and Venezuela), despite a fall in the share of manufacturing in total employment. These countries are located to the right of the dashed diagonal line. However, these increases are relatively small, as can be seen from their proximity to the line.

Second, there is a clustering of countries in the north-west quadrant, that is, with a negative labor intensity effect and a positive sector growth effect. For these countries, the manufacturing sector grew, yet became less labor intensive. Third, almost all of the latter group of countries fall below the diagonal line. The potential increase in manufacturing employment associated with the positive sector growth effect was outweighed by the negative labor intensity effect. Countries in this quadrant thus generally experienced a fall in the level of manufacturing employment. In those few countries in the quadrant whose manufacturing employment increased – Cyprus, Israel, the Netherlands, and Spain – the increases are of a small magnitude (as can be seen by their proximity to the diagonal line).

Fourth, no countries experienced both growth in the size of their manufacturing sector and an increase in its labor intensity (note the absence of any points in the north-east quadrant).[14] In the handful of countries in which manufacturing became more labor intensive (such as Russia and Venezuela), manufacturing value-added shrank more than did manufacturing employment.

Fifth, in 13 countries the manufacturing sector actually shrank in real terms: Argentina, Barbados, Hong Kong, Jamaica, Latvia, Macao, Romania, Russia, Saint Lucia, San Marino, Suriname, Uruguay, and Venezuela. These countries are located below the x-axis. This group of countries includes most of the developing countries in the sample, as well as the 'transition' countries of Eastern Europe/ex-USSR. These are the countries whose manufacturing sector declined in absolute terms. (Conversely, the 35 other countries of the sample experienced real growth in manufacturing output.)

10.3.4 Decomposing changes in the level of manufacturing employment into share of GDP, labor intensity, and economic growth

The first decomposition analysis separated out changes in the level of manufacturing employment into changes in manufacturing value-added and in the labor intensity of that value-added. In a second decomposition analysis, we continue to analyze changes in the *level* of manufacturing employment, but are now interested in changes in the *share* of manufacturing in GDP, as well as in changes in labor intensity. A fast-growing country could show growth in the number of manufacturing jobs even while the share of manufacturing in GDP declines *and* manufacturing becomes less labor intensive, if the economy grows fast enough.

These two additional dimensions (manufacturing share of GDP and total GDP) are thus incorporated in the following identity:

$$L_{ijt} \equiv \varphi_{ijt}\delta_{ijt}Q_{jt}$$

where φ_{ijt} is the labor intensity of sector i, defined as previously, δ_{ijt} is sector j's share of the economy (in terms of value-added) of country j at time t, measured as

$$\frac{Q_{ijt}}{Q_{jt}},$$

and Q_{jt} is the GDP of country j at time t. Then the change in employment in a given sector over a given period h is given as follows: $\Delta L_{ij}=\varphi_{ijt}\delta_{ijt}Q_{jt}-\varphi_{ijt-h}\delta_{ijt-h}Q_{jt-h}.$

This can be decomposed into the following three components:[15]

labor intensity effect

$$= \frac{1}{6}(\varphi_{ijt} - \varphi_{ijt-h})\left\{\left(\delta_{ijt-h}Q_{jt-h} + \delta_{ijt}Q_{jt}\right) + (Q_{jt-h} + Q_{jt})(\delta_{ijt-h} + \delta_{ijt})\right\};$$

sector share effect

$$= \frac{1}{6}(\delta_{ijt} - \delta_{ijt-h})\left\{\left(\varphi_{ijt-h}Q_{jt-h} + \varphi_{ijt}Q_{jt}\right) + (Q_{jt-h} + Q_{jt})(\varphi_{ijt-h} + \varphi_{ijt})\right\};$$

economic growth effect

$$= \frac{1}{6}(Q_{jt} - Q_{jt-h})\left\{\left(\varphi_{ijt-h}\delta_{jt-h} + \varphi_{ijt}\delta_{jt}\right) + (\delta_{jt-h} + \delta_{jt})(\varphi_{ijt-h} + \varphi_{ijt})\right\}.$$

The sum of these three effects is the change in employment in a sector over that period. Normalizing these by a country's manufacturing employment at the beginning of the period, the three components can be calculated as follows:

labor intensity effect

$$= \frac{1}{6}(\varphi_{ijt} - \varphi_{ijt-h})\left\{\left(\delta_{ijt-h}Q_{jt-h} + \delta_{ijt}Q_{jt}\right) + (Q_{jt-h} + Q_{jt})(\delta_{ijt-h} + \delta_{ijt})\right\}\left(\frac{100}{L_{ijt-h}}\right);$$

sector share effect

$$= \frac{1}{6}(\delta_{ijt} - \delta_{ijt-h})\left\{\left(\varphi_{ijt-h}Q_{jt-h} + \varphi_{ijt}Q_{jt}\right) + (Q_{jt-h} + Q_{jt})(\varphi_{ijt-h} + \varphi_{ijt})\right\}\left(\frac{100}{L_{ijt-h}}\right);$$

economic growth effect

$$= \frac{1}{6}(Q_{jt} - Q_{jt-h})\left\{\left(\varphi_{ijt-h}\delta_{jt-h} + \varphi_{ijt}\delta_{jt}\right) + (\delta_{jt-h} + \delta_{jt})(\varphi_{ijt-h} + \varphi_{ijt})\right\}\left(\frac{100}{L_{ijt-h}}\right).$$

These sum to the percentage change in sectoral employment:

$$\frac{100\Delta L_{ij}}{L_{ijt-h}}.$$

The 'labor intensity effect'[16] is the change in the level of employment in a sector associated with the changing labor intensity of that sector. For example, there could be a decline in manufacturing employment associated with a falling labor intensity of manufacturing production. The 'sector share effect' measures the change in employment associated with a change in the sector's share in GDP. For example, there could be a decline in manufacturing employment associated with a decline in the share of manufacturing in the overall economy. Third, the 'economic growth effect' is the change in employment in a sector associated (in a simple mechanical way) with the overall growth of the economy. So long as there is any economic growth, this effect would be positive for all sectors.

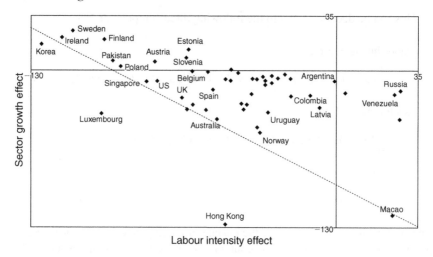

Figure 10.2 Results from second decomposition analysis.

A 'diagnosis' of absolute deindustrialization according to this decomposition would yield insights into the nature of that process in different countries or over different periods. Figure 10.2 presents the results (normalized by initial employment), focusing at this stage on the labor intensity and sector share effects. The intercepts of each point thus show for that country the percentage change in the level of manufacturing employment associated with changes in the labor intensity of manufacturing (x-axis) and with the share of manufacturing in GDP (y-axis).

The coordinates of the UK (−65.7, −23.4), by way of example, indicate that the fall in manufacturing labor intensity in that country accounted for a

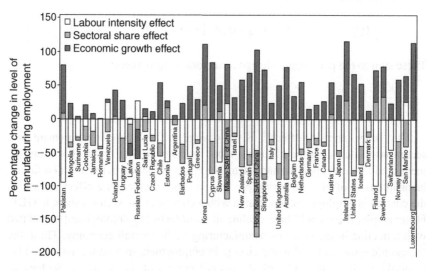

Figure 10.3 Full results of second decomposition.

(hypothetical) decrease of 65.7 percent in manufacturing employment, while the decline in the share of manufacturing in GDP accounted for a (hypothetical) decrease of 23.4 percent in manufacturing employment. Note that the overall change in countries' manufacturing employment share cannot be directly read off this chart (in the way that the net change in manufacturing employment could be seen in Figure 10.2 from the first decomposition), as the third component of this decomposition (the economic growth effect) is not included in this chart. In the case of the UK, economic growth accounted for a (hypothetical) increase of 49.8 percent. The net change in manufacturing employment in the UK was –39.3 percent (which corresponds with the figure shown in the summary of country trends in Table 10.1).

Most countries fall in the south-west quadrant: declining labor intensity of manufacturing as well as a decrease in manufacturing share of GDP, both associated with falls in the level of manufacturing employment. For countries in this quadrant, which, nevertheless, experienced manufacturing employment growth, this can be accounted for entirely by overall economic growth (i.e. manufacturing was a declining share of a growing economy).

Manufacturing in countries located in the north-west quadrant also became less labor intensive but grew as a share of GDP. Interestingly, these countries generally tend to be somewhat better performers in the sample in terms of overall GDP growth.

Figure 10.3 shows the results of this second decomposition in more detail, by also including the economic growth effect as well as giving a sense of the relative contributions of the labor intensity and sector share effects. The vertical axis shows the percentage change in the level of manufacturing employment in each country. For each country, each of the three bars thus shows the percentage change in manufacturing employment that can be accounted for by the labor intensity effect, the sector share effect, and the economic growth effect. The sum of the three bars gives the net percentage change in the level of manufacturing employment in each country (corresponding to the middle column of figures in Table 10.1). For example, in Pakistan the normalized labor intensity effect, sector share effect, and economic growth effect are –94.9 percent, 8.3 percent, and 72.7 percent, respectively, summing to –13.9 percent, which is the net decline in manufacturing employment in that country. In this case the fall in the level of manufacturing employment is entirely accounted for by the fact that manufacturing became less labor intensive.

The labor intensity effect is negative for almost all countries (the exceptions being Venezuela, Russia, Saint Lucia, Macao, and San Marino; only the first two of these are of real empirical significance). The sector share effect is somewhat more mixed, but is negative in 37 of the 48 countries. The labor intensity effect exceeds (in absolute terms) the sector share effects for most countries. In other words, for most countries the falling labor intensity of manufacturing can primarily account for falls in manufacturing employment or, in cases where manufacturing employment increased, for these increases not being higher than they actually were. The economic growth effect is positive for all but three countries (Russia, Latvia, and Romania). Of course, even where the economic growth effect is positive, had growth been higher than it was this might have led to better performance in manufacturing employment.

10.3.5 Decomposing changes in the share of manufacturing employment into share of GDP, labor intensity, and labor productivity

The two decomposition exercises undertaken above analyze changes in the level of manufacturing employment. The first decomposition disaggregated these changes into those associated with changes in manufacturing value-added and manufacturing labor intensity, respectively; the second was a three-way decomposition into changes associated with manufacturing labor intensity, manufacturing GDP share, and overall economic growth, respectively. Now, in the third and final decomposition we analyze changes in the *share* of manufacturing in total employment. This is particularly relevant as deindustrialization is conventionally defined in terms of a decline in the share of manufacturing employment.

In order to decompose changes in the share of manufacturing in total employment we define σ_{ijt} as the sectoral share of employment and set up the following identity:

$$\sigma_{ijt} \equiv \frac{L_{ijt}}{L_{jt}} \equiv \varphi_{ijt}\delta_{ijt}\theta_{jt}$$

with all terms as previously defined and the introduction of

$$\theta_{jt} = \frac{Q_{jt}}{L_{jt}},$$

the economy-wide labor productivity.[17]

This allows for a separation of changes in the sectoral share of employment into components associated with changes in sectoral labor intensity, sectoral share of GDP, and economy-wide labor productivity respectively, as follows:

labor intensity effect

$$= \frac{1}{6}(\varphi_{ijt} - \varphi_{ijt-h})\left\{\left(\delta_{ijt-h}\theta_{jt-h} + \delta_{ijt}\theta_{jt}\right) + (\theta_{jt-h} + \theta_{jt})(\delta_{ijt-h} + \delta_{ijt})\right\}$$

sector share effect

$$= \frac{1}{6}(\delta_{ijt} - \delta_{ijt-h})\left\{\left(\varphi_{ijt-h}\theta_{jt-h} + \varphi_{ijt}\theta_{jt}\right) + (\theta_{jt-h} + \theta_{jt})(\varphi_{ijt-h} + \varphi_{ijt})\right\}$$

labor productivity effect

$$= \frac{1}{6}(\theta_{jt} - \theta_{jt-h})\left\{\left(\varphi_{ijt-h}\delta_{jt-h} + \varphi_{ijt}\delta_{jt}\right) + (\delta_{jt-h} + \delta_{jt})(\varphi_{ijt-h} + \varphi_{ijt})\right\}.$$

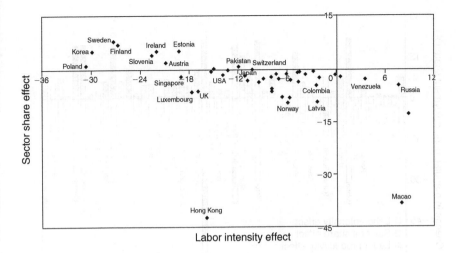

Figure 10.4 Results from third decomposition analysis.

Figure 10.4 shows the labor intensity and sector share effects of the sample countries. We focus initially on the labor intensity and sector share effects, which are of principal interest to this study.

The only quadrant in which no countries fall is the north-east quadrant: none had both positive labor intensity and sector share effects. In other words, in none of the 48 sample countries did manufacturing increase as a share of GDP *and* become more labor intensive.[18] There are five countries in which manufacturing became more labor intensive but declined as a share of GDP; 11 countries in which manufacturing became less labor intensive but increased as a share of GDP; and in the remaining 32 countries both effects were negative: manufacturing fell as a share of GDP while also becoming less labor intensive. The most extreme of the latter cases is that of Hong Kong. Indeed, Hong Kong experienced the largest absolute fall in manufacturing share of employment as well as the largest proportional decline in the number of manufacturing jobs of all countries studied.

Figure 10.5 shows the full results from the third decomposition, displaying all three components of the change in manufacturing employment share (that is, the changes in manufacturing employment share associated with changes in manufacturing labor intensity, manufacturing GDP share, and economy-wide labor productivity, respectively). The sum of these is, of course, the net change in manufacturing employment share for each country. To take the case of South Korea, for example, the (hypothetical) fall in the manufacturing employment share associated with declining labor intensity outweighed the positive sector share effect and the (economy-wide) labor productivity effect; the share of manufacturing in GDP fell by 8.8 points overall.

The labor intensity effect was negative in all but five cases, and these were all countries experiencing serious economic problems. The sector share effect was

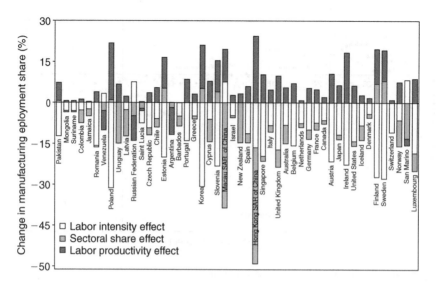

Figure 10.5 Full results of third decomposition.

positive in 11 countries – generally relatively better performing countries (such as South Korea and Ireland). The economy-wide labor productivity effect accounted for a positive component of the change in manufacturing employment share in 42 of the 48 countries.

10.3.6 Summary of results and a typology of 'deindustrializations'

Table 10.3 consolidates the basic results of all three decompositions, abstracting from the relative magnitudes of the various components and focusing on the signs of each component by country. The labor intensity effect, shown in the first column, was calculated in all three decompositions, and although the magnitude of this component varies across the decompositions the sign of the effect is consistent for each country. The sector growth effect was calculated in the first decomposition. The sector share effect was derived from the second and third decompositions (with the sign of this component being consistent, for each country, across both decompositions). The economic growth effect was calculated in the second decomposition, and the labor productivity effect in the third decomposition; both of these are economy-wide variables. We classify countries into four broad categories as discussed below, based on the results from all three decompositions. Within each category, countries are shown ordered in terms of their income grouping.

In the first set of countries, from South Korea to Pakistan, the sector growth effect, sector share effects, economic growth effect, and labor productivity effect are all positive. These are, in fact, the only countries for which the sector share effects are positive (i.e., in which manufacturing grew as a share of GDP). The declining shares of manufacturing in the total employment of these 11 countries are primarily accounted for by the fact that their manufacturing became less labor intensive (that is, labor productivity rose in manufacturing), as evidenced by the negative labor intensity effects. These are primarily advanced countries, and they are also countries which experienced relatively good economic performance.

The second set of countries, from Canada to Colombia, differs from the first set in that the sector share effect is negative. The decrease in the share of manufacturing in total employment in these countries is accounted for both by the negative labor intensity effect and by the negative sector share effect. Half of the countries in the sample fall within this category. It includes all the G7 countries as well as the largest group of other advanced countries in the sample.

In the third set of countries, from Hong Kong to Suriname, not only is the sector share effect negative (as in the second category), but the sector growth effect is also negative (i.e. manufacturing value-added shrank in real terms). The economic growth and labor productivity effects are positive for most, but not all, of these countries, unlike the first and second sets of countries for which these two effects are uniformly positive. The countries in this category are essentially middle-income countries.

Finally, the fourth set of countries are the only ones with positive labor intensity effects. The fact that manufacturing share of employment fell in these countries nonetheless is accounted for by the negative sector share effect as well as by a negative economic growth effect or negative labor productivity effect in certain of the cases. It is worth noting that the two cases in this sample with significant economic size – Russia and Venezuela – were particularly poor performers during the periods analyzed here.

There is, of course, considerable heterogeneity amongst each of these sets of countries, as this typology is based only on the signs of the components of the decompositions. In the earlier discussions we considered the relative magnitude and importance of each component in accounting for changes in the level and share of manufacturing employment in each country. The implications of this broad typology are considered in the next section.

10.4 Discussion and conclusion

A fall in manufacturing employment associated primarily with changes in the labor intensity of production is very different from a fall in manufacturing employment associated primarily with declining manufacturing output. These two types of falling manufacturing employment are quite different phenomena, likely to have different causes, different implications for growth, and to require different policy interventions should they be deemed undesirable. These distinctions render the analysis of this chapter important, both conceptually and from a policy perspective.

If a decrease in manufacturing employment share is primarily accounted for by falling labor intensity of manufacturing (as in the cases of, for example, Finland,

Table 10.3 Summary of signs of components from decompositions 1–3

Country	Country grouping	Labor intensity effect	Sector growth effect	Sector share effect	Economic growth effect	Labor productivity effect
Korea	Advanced – NIAE	−	+	+	+	+
Austria	Advanced – other	−	+	+	+	+
Belgium	Advanced – other	−	+	+	+	+
Finland	Advanced – other	−	+	+	+	+
Ireland	Advanced – other	−	+	+	+	+
Sweden	Advanced – other	−	+	+	+	+
Switzerland	Advanced – other	−	+	+	+	+
Slovenia	Advanced – other	−	+	+	+	+
Poland	Developing – CEE/CIS	−	+	+	+	+
Estonia	Developing – CEE/CIS	−	+	+	+	+
Pakistan	Developing – Asia	−	+	+	+	+
Canada	Advanced – G7	−	+	−	+	+
France	Advanced – G7	−	+	−	+	+
Germany	Advanced – G7	−	+	−	+	+
Italy	Advanced – G7	−	+	−	+	+
Japan	Advanced – G7	−	+	−	+	+
United Kingdom	Advanced – G7	−	+	−	+	+
United States	Advanced – G7	−	+	−	+	+
Singapore	Advanced – NIAE	−	+	−	+	+
Australia	Advanced – other	−	+	−	+	+
Czech Republic	Advanced – other	−	+	−	+	+
Denmark	Advanced – other	−	+	−	+	+
Greece	Advanced – other	−	+	−	+	+

Iceland	Advanced – other	+	+	−	+
Luxembourg	Advanced – other	+	+	−	+
Netherlands	Advanced – other	+	+	−	+
New Zealand	Advanced – other	+	+	−	+
Norway	Advanced – other	+	+	−	+
Portugal	Advanced – other	+	+	−	+
Spain	Advanced – other	+	+	−	+
Cyprus	Advanced – other	+	+	−	+
Israel	Advanced – other	+	+	−	+
Mongolia	Developing – CEE/CIS	+	+	−	+
Chile	Developing – WH	+	+	−	+
Colombia	Developing – WH	+	+	−	−
Hong Kong	Advanced – NIAE	+	+	−	−
Latvia	Developing – CEE/CIS	+	−	−	−
Romania	Developing – CEE/CIS	−	−	−	−
Argentina	Developing – WH	−	+	−	−
Barbados	Developing – WH	+	+	−	−
Uruguay	Developing – WH	+	+	−	−
Jamaica	Developing – WH	−	+	−	−
Suriname	Developing – Asia	−	+	−	−
San Marino	Advanced – other	+	−	−	+
Russia	Developing – CEE/CIS	+	+	−	+
Saint Lucia	Developing – WH	−	+	−	+
Venezuela	Developing – WH	−	+	−	+
Macao	Developing – Asia	+	+	−	−

Note
Country groupings based on IMF classification. Advanced economies are divided into three categories: G7; Newly Industrialised Asian Economies (NIAE); and other advanced economies excluding the aforementioned two groups. Developing and emerging countries in the sample are divided into three groups: Central and Eastern Europe and Commonwealth of Independent States (CEE/CIS); Western Hemisphere (WH); and Developing Asia.

Sweden, Switzerland, Ireland, or South Korea), this calls into question the extent to which 'deindustrialization' is an appropriate characterization. This is especially relevant in cases (the countries mentioned above and all those in the first set of Table 10.3) where the manufacturing sector is growing in real terms as well as increasing its share of GDP. There could be various underlying economic causes behind falling labor intensity in manufacturing, which might relate to the sub-sectoral composition of manufacturing and/or to processes within sub-sectors (including as a defensive response to cheap manufacturing imports from lower-wage countries). In an 'optimistic' scenario, falling labor intensity could essentially amount to exogenous increases in labor productivity, driven by factors such as improved skills or technology. On the other hand, falling labor intensity could be caused by labor-displacing capital intensification. The actual causes of falling labor intensity would vary across countries and time periods, and are not the focus of this study. The point is that a fall in the share of manufacturing employment that is mostly accounted for by falling labor intensity of manufacturing (i.e. increasing labor productivity of manufacturing) would not *necessarily* have a negative impact on growth. The impact on growth would be contingent on various conjunctural factors, including what the causes of the fall in labor intensity might be.

This is very different from the case (such as in Norway, Colombia, Latvia, or Hong Kong) where the fall in the share of manufacturing employment is associated primarily with a decline of the manufacturing sector as a share of GDP (and especially in cases such as the latter two where manufacturing shrank in real terms as well). In such a scenario, an economy would be particularly at risk of losing out on the growth-pulling effects of manufacturing. This could be associated with a diminution of long-term growth prospects (although of course this would be contingent on the country's stage of development, on the nature of the manufacturing sectors in decline, of the sectors whose share of GDP is growing,[19] and so on). This strongly suggests the need to go deeper into the black box of falling share of manufacturing employment – as this chapter has attempted to do – before the effects on growth can be assumed.

One insight that emerges from this analysis is the significant heterogeneity of experiences that would be characterized as 'deindustrialization' when considered exclusively in terms of the share of manufacturing in total employment (as per the conventional denotation of deindustrialization). The common denominator of the 48 countries of the sample, over their respective time periods included in this study, is that they experienced a reduction in the share of manufacturing in total employment. Yet amongst these countries the share of manufacturing in GDP grew in some and fell in others; manufacturing value-added increased in some and fell in others; and countries underwent diverse experiences in terms of the labor intensity of manufacturing, economic growth, and overall labor productivity.

This heterogeneity points to the difficulty in formulating a generic definition of deindustrialization. We would argue that a case in which the sector growth effect, sector share effect, economic growth effect, and labor productivity effects are all positive and the decline in manufacturing employment level and/or share is accounted for entirely by a negative labor intensity effect should not be characterized as deindustrialization in any real sense. If labor productivity rises more rapidly in manufacturing than in the rest of the economy – as might be expected if manufacturing does indeed have the Kaldorian properties attributed to it – and if manufacturing does not increase its share of GDP commensurately, then the share of manufacturing in total employment would of course fall.

Yet it does not seem meaningful to characterize such a process as deindustrialization, particularly when associating deindustrialization with negative implications for growth. Rather than defining deindustrialization in terms of the single dimension of falling share of manufacturing in total employment, as in the current literature, we propose that deindustrialization should be regarded as occurring when there is a *sustained decline in both the share of manufacturing in total employment and the share of manufacturing in GDP.*

This would mean that the 11 countries grouped in the top category in Table 10.3, in which manufacturing actually grew as a share of GDP, would not be regarded as having deindustrialized (at least over the periods analyzed in this chapter). These countries are: Austria, Belgium, Finland, Ireland, South Korea, Sweden, Switzerland, Estonia, Slovenia, Poland, and Pakistan. Note that in these countries manufacturing value-added also grew (in real terms), as well as economy-wide labor productivity increasing and overall economic growth being positive.

In the other 37 countries of the sample, manufacturing fell as a share of GDP (as well as decreasing in its share of total employment). These countries would meet the criteria of deindustrialization suggested here. The empirical analysis presented here is helpful in distinguishing between different types of deindustrialization amongst these countries. For instance, countries in which manufacturing grew in real terms despite falling as a share of GDP (the second set of countries in Table 10.3, such as Japan, Denmark, and Portugal) need to be distinguished from those in which manufacturing actually shrank in real terms (the third set of countries in Table 10.3, which are either developing countries or Eastern European countries).

The methodology developed in this chapter can also be helpful in distinguishing between 'positive' and 'negative' deindustrialization, a distinction originally introduced by Rowthorn and Wells (1987) and which has been discussed further in the subsequent literature. Positive deindustrialization is regarded as

> the normal result of sustained economic growth in a fully employed, and already highly developed, economy [which] occurs because productivity growth in the manufacturing sector is so rapid that, despite increasing output, employment in this sector is reduced, either absolutely or as a share of total employment.
>
> (ibid.: 5)

For Rowthorn and Wells, in positive deindustrialization any workers displaced from manufacturing find employment in new jobs in the services sector, such that unemployment does not increase. This is contrasted with negative deindustrialization, which is 'a product of economic failure and occurs when industry is in severe difficulties ... labor shed from the manufacturing sector – because of falling output or rising productivity – will not be reabsorbed into the service sector' and unemployment will therefore increase (ibid.: 6).[20]

The empirical results obtained through the methodology proposed in this chapter, considered in conjunction with the overall employment performance of an economy, can shed light on the 'positive' or 'negative' character of specific deindustrialization experiences. For instance, the decomposition analysis is suggestive as to the extent to which increases in labor productivity in manufacturing account for deindustrialization in each country, and the relationship between changes in manufacturing output and employment. The empirical analysis also draws attention to the heterogeneity of experiences among rich countries, and hence the difficulties in using a generic definition of 'positive deindustrialization'.

A full analysis of deindustrialization also needs to take other considerations into account, such as whether any workers who lose their jobs in manufacturing can readily find jobs elsewhere in the economy, and the nature of the activities that are 'replacing' manufacturing employment.

Of course, a fall in manufacturing share of employment can, in its own right, have a negative effect on growth, as discussed earlier. Some of the Kaldorian channels of manufacturing growth-pulling operate through employment, and hence a fall in manufacturing employment would be of concern irrespective of the performance of manufacturing output.

Falling manufacturing may also be regarded as a problem in its own right, over and above any effects on aggregate growth and its sustainability. Loss of manufacturing jobs (in terms of levels) is of obvious concern, particularly if other sectors cannot absorb these workers. A fall in the share of manufacturing employment can also be problematic, even putting aside any implications for growth. There are various reasons as to why manufacturing jobs may be regarded as more desirable than jobs in other sectors of the economy, such that a fall in the share of manufacturing in total employment would be undesirable. Blue-collar manufacturing jobs generally tend to develop higher levels of skills than equivalent jobs in the rest of the economy. Employment security in manufacturing tends to be superior to that in agriculture or services, and there is lower scope for and actual trends towards casualization and other forms of atypical employment. Manufacturing is also easier to unionize than is agriculture and many services sectors, making manufacturing an important mainstay of trade union organizations.

All of these characteristics make manufacturing employment important, arguably more important than employment in most other (private) sectors of the economy. A decline in the share of manufacturing employment is thus of concern in its own right. It may have various negative consequences, particularly in terms of distribution.

A study of the data on sectoral levels and shares obscures the human dimension of these shifts and the upheaval wrought in people's lives. Behind the glibness of economic models or policies, people whose manufacturing jobs are lost may struggle to find new jobs or may never work again and if they do, the jobs may not be at an equivalent level of remuneration or job security. The experience of acute deindustrialization suggests that a displaced auto or textile worker who does manage to gain new employment is likely to have a relatively insecure, non-unionized, low-paid services job. The long-lasting social problems in regions that have undergone severe deindustrialization are testimony to the devastation belied by the economic data.[21]

The empirical analysis of this chapter does not address these distributional and social ramifications of deindustrialization. The concerns typically associated with deindustrialization in the economics literature relate principally to the growth-pulling properties of manufacturing. A decline in the share of manufacturing employment remains relevant to these properties, especially in terms of learning-by-doing, and thus may well have deleterious effects on sustainable economic growth. However, the share of manufacturing output in GDP and the growth of manufacturing output are also highly relevant to the growth-pulling properties of manufacturing.

A proper empirical analysis of deindustrialization thus needs to take into account trends in manufacturing output as well as employment. This study has considered both, attempting to disentangle the components of falling manufacturing employment associated with changes in declines in manufacturing output and in the labor intensity of this output. In most country experiences of 'deindustrialization' analyzed here, falling manufacturing employment is accounted for primarily by decreases in the labor intensity of manufacturing, rather than by an overall decline in manufacturing GDP or manufacturing share of total GDP.

As discussed earlier, data availability and quality has limited the extent to which developing countries that have undergone deindustrialization have been included in the sample. Although it is primarily upper-income countries that have undergone deindustrialization, in recent times middle-income countries have increasingly experienced deindustrialization as well. As Palma (2005) has noted, 'premature deindustrialization' in developing countries has often been associated with policy changes, in particular trade and financial liberalization. Besides this, based on observed trends of manufacturing tending to fall (in both employment and GDP but especially the former) at higher levels of income per capita rises, it can be expected that deindustrialization will in the future become more pronounced in countries currently classified as middle income. Amongst the developing countries analyzed here, there is considerable heterogeneity in the dynamics of their manufacturing sector, with a country such as South Korea not actually considered as having deindustrialized according to the definition advanced here, whereas on the other extreme in countries such as Venezuela and Jamaica manufacturing performed dismally.

Notes

1 Department of Economics and Econometrics, University of Johannesburg, South Africa.

2 I thank Rolph van der Hoeven, Karel Jansen, Gabriel Palma, two anonymous reviewers, and the editors of this publication especially Pedro Goulart for their helpful comments and suggestions.

3 By Kaldorian I refer to the 'laws' that Kaldor advanced in explaining the differences in growth rates internationally. The first of these laws states that the faster the rate of growth in manufacturing, the faster the rate of growth of the economy as a whole (in a fundamental causal sense associated with rates of productivity). The second law, also known as Verdoorn's Law, is that the growth rate of labor productivity in manufacturing is endogenous to the growth rate of manufacturing output. According to the third law, aggregate productivity growth is positively related with the growth of manufacturing output and employment and negatively related with non-manufacturing employment.

4 This chapter does not seek to investigate the empirical validity of these arguments. There is however an existing corpus of work that has found some empirical support for the validity of Kaldor's laws, using various techniques and testing across a range of countries and time periods. Recent studies include Leon-Ledesma (2000), Wells and Thirlwall (2003), Bernat (1996), Pons-Novell and Viladecans-Marsal (1999), Harris and Liu (1999), Diaz Bautista (2003), and Libanio (2006).

5 See Tregenna (2008) for an analysis of the strength of intersectoral linkages in South Africa.

6 See for instance Palma (2008), Rowthorn and Coutts (2004), and Rowthorn and Ramaswamy (1997). A prominent exception to this has been the approach of Singh (1977, 1987), who considers deindustrialization to be problematic insofar as it is a manifestation of structural disequilibrium in the economy, in the sense that manufacturing becomes unable to not only satisfy domestic demand at least cost but also to export enough to pay for full employment level of imports (at a 'reasonable' exchange rate).

7 Note that although manufacturing is one sector within 'industry' as per national accounting classifications, 'deindustrialization' refers specifically to manufacturing and not to industry as a whole.

8 See Tregenna (2010) for an estimation of the magnitude of outsourcing from manufacturing to services for the case of South Africa.

9 Disparate trends in the shares of manufacturing in total employment and in GDP can be understood in terms of changes in the labor intensity of production. An expanding manufacturing sector could show declining levels of employment if falling labor intensity outweighs the growth in the sector. Similarly, the share of manufacturing in GDP could rise concurrently with a fall in the share of manufacturing in total employment if changes in manufacturing labor intensity exceed those in the rest of the economy by a sufficient magnitude to outweigh the increase in manufacturing's share of GDP.

10 In fact, a decline in manufacturing output in the absence of a commensurate decline in manufacturing employment could even improve a country's balance of payments position, through a channel of reduced demand for imports arising either from lower absolute levels of employment or the shifting of jobs to lower-paid employment in other sectors such as agriculture or low-wage private services.

11 Note that decomposition analysis is a mechanical technique which does not necessarily shed light on the underlying economic causes of the changes being examined, nor on the endogeneity of each of the components to the other. As will be discussed below, it simply distinguishes between different aspects of the changes in manufacturing employment, with the aspects as specified in the initial identity on which each of the decompositions is based.

12 Throughout this chapter, labor intensity refers to the ratio of employment to value-added.

13 Sector i is manufacturing in this chapter. However, the methods proposed here could also be used for the analysis of changes in other sectors.

14 This is, in part, related to sample selection, which is limited to countries and periods in which the share of manufacturing in total employment declined.

15 See Tregenna (2009) for technical details concerning the derivation of terms in this and the subsequent decomposition.

16 Note that the 'labor intensity effects' calculated in the three decompositions do not measure exactly the same thing, as they are based on different initial specifications, yet all are measures of the changes associated with changes in manufacturing labor intensity and the sign of the effect is constant for each country across the three decompositions.

17 Note that this term is simply the inverse of the economy-wide labor intensity.

18 Again, this is in part related to the sample being limited to cases where manufacturing fell as a share of employment.

19 For instance, Hong Kong developed a dynamic financial services sector.

20 Rowthorn and Wells also identify a third type of deindustrialization, in which the matter of net exports shifts away from manufactures toward other goods and services, leading to a transfer of labor and resources from manufacturing to other sectors of the economy (Rowthorn and Wells 1987: 6).

21 For example, Rowthorn and Webster (2008) document the significant impact of deindustrialization in increasing female lone parenthood in the United Kingdom.

References

Bernat, G. (1996) 'Does manufacturing matter? A spatial econometric view of Kaldor's laws', *Journal of Regional Science*, 36: 463–77.

Diaz Bautista, A. (2003) 'Mexico's industrial engine of growth: Cointegration and causality', *Momento Economico*, 126: 34–41.

Harris, R. and A. Liu (1999) 'Verdoorn's law and increasing returns to scale: Country estimates based on the cointegration approach', *Applied Economics Letters*, 6: 29–33.

Leon-Ledesma, M. (2000) 'Economic growth and Verdoorn's law in the Spanish regions, 1962–91', *International Review of Applied Economics*, 14: 55–69.

Libanio, G. (2006) 'Manufacturing industry and economic growth in Latin America: A Kaldorian approach', Second Annual Conference for Development and Change (December 2006), Campos Do Jordaõ: Brazil.

Palma, G. (2005) 'Four Sources of "De-Industrialisation" and a New Concept of the "Dutch Disease"', in J.A. Ocampo (ed.) *Beyond Reforms: Structural Dynamics and Macroeconomic Vulnerability*, New York: Stanford University Press and World Bank.

Palma, G. (2008) 'Deindustrialisation, Premature Deindustrialisation, and the Dutch Disease', in L. Blume and S. Durlauf (eds) *The New Palgrave: A Dictionary of Economics*, Basingstoke: Palgrave Macmillian.

Pons-Novell, J. and E. Viladecans-Marsal (1999) 'Kaldor's laws and spatial dependence: Evidence for the European regions', *Regional Studies*, 33: 443–51.

Rowthorn, R. and K. Coutts (2004) 'Commentary: Deindustrialisation and the balance of payments in advanced economies', *Cambridge Journal of Regions*, 28: 767–90.

Rowthorn, R. and Ramaswamy, R. (1997) 'Deindustrialisation: Causes and implications', IMF Working Paper no. 97/42, Washington: International Monetary Fund.

Rowthorn, R. and D. Webster (2008) 'Male worklessness and the rise of lone parenthood in Great Britain', *Cambridge Journal of Regions, Economy and Society*, 1: 69–88.

Rowthorn, R. and J. Wells (1987) *De-industrialization and Foreign Trade*, Cambridge: Cambridge University Press.

Singh, A. (1977) 'UK industry and the world economy: A case of de-industrialisation', *Cambridge Journal of Economics*, 1: 113–36.

Singh, A. (ed.) (1987) 'Manufacturing and De-industrialization', in J. Eatwell, M. Milgate, and P. Newman (eds) *The New Palgrave: A Dictionary of Economics*, London: Macmillan.

Tregenna, F. (2008) 'The contributions of manufacturing and services to employment creation and growth in South Africa', *South African Journal of Economics*, 76: 175–204.

Tregenna, F. (2009) 'Characterising deindustrialisation: An analysis of changes in manufacturing employment and output internationally', *Cambridge Journal of Economics*, 33: 433–66.

Tregenna, F. (2010) 'How significant is intersectoral outsourcing of employment in South Africa?' *Industrial and Corporate Change*, 19: 1–31.

Wells, H. and A. Thirlwall (2003) 'Testing Kaldor's laws across the countries of Africa', *African Development Review*, 15: 89–105.

Part III
Country case studies

11 The 'dragon' and the 'elephant' and global imbalances

Max Spoor[1]

11.1 Introduction

This chapter analyses the complex manner in which the emerging developing economies of East, South and South-East Asia (in particular China and India) have been influencing the main imbalances in the world economy before the global economic crisis and after, how the global crisis has affected them, and how in particular the 'dragon' (China) and to a lesser extend the 'elephant' (India) stimulate the world economy's recovery. It will be argued that 'developing Asia' is contributing to the rebalancing of a highly unbalanced world economy, but with its spectacular growth it was also part and parcel of growing global financial imbalances, while furthermore causing new ones to emerge.

Global imbalances are the outcome of growing unequal trade flows, caused by an insatiable US consumer demand, fed by cheap Asian consumer goods and other exports, leading to a high trade and a growing current account deficit, which is financed by the purchase of US treasury bonds and other dollar denominated securities by private investors and Asian governments. However, the world economy has known another, more fundamental imbalance as the US economy has been for long the largest economy, also dominating world trade (with the EU and Japan) in the past century, in which most trade was actually originating in and destined for industrialized high-income countries (Ocampo and Martin 2003). Furthermore, as an outcome of this traditional dominance of the US economy, the US dollar functions as a reserve currency. As countries, such as the emerging Asian economies that are greatly dependent on trade and finance, wish to shield themselves from external shocks and exchange rate fluctuations, they accumulate dollar reserves, creating the necessity for the US to run ever larger deficits.

The very high growth rates of 'developing Asia', and in particular China started to redress some of this structural imbalance. Since the 2000s China and India together were rapidly approaching the size of the Japanese economy, which for long has been the second economy in the world in size. By 2010 China is overtaking Japan in size, confirming its role as a major player at the world's stage, although still following the US economy at a sizeable distance (see Table 11.1). Therefore, the world economy is changing from one which was fully dominated by the OECD economies, towards a multi-polar one with various large economies, including China. The role of India might become important in the near future, but its growth model has been structurally different (and with growth rates that were substantially lower than the Chinese ones), as it has been largely based on growth of internal consumption rather than exports (such as is the case in China). Dollar (2009) confirms this point of view by arguing that the current century will become a 'multi-polar century' rather than an 'Asian century', which is sometimes being suggested (Mahbubani 2008), as the size and exports of the other Asian developing economies (including India) are much smaller than China as yet.

World trade is also changing substantially, as a much greater volume of merchandise and services is now exchanged in Asian markets (if compared with the early 1990s when China started to focus on external trade). Again this effect is particularly caused by emerging Chinese exports (and imports), although we should not ignore that Chinese exports are often still dominated by (Western-based) multinational companies (Fischer 2010). Asia as a whole by 2007 was already the second largest 'trade bloc' in the world (see Table 11.2), particularly stimulated by spectacular growth rates of Chinese trade volumes. While this contributes to redressing the first mentioned more structural imbalance in the world economy, at the same time it has fuelled the emerging global financial imbalances, as some Asian economies (in particular China) became the main supplier of the American consumer goods market, while the accumulated reserves (as outcome of the huge trade surpluses of China) emerged as the main funder to cover the growing US current account deficit. Hence, emerging China contributed to these global imbalances in the form of 'cure' and 'cause' of the problem.

Next to these developments, the chapter will also show that Asia's growth (fuelled by the spectacular emergence of China), and its recent appearance as a major world player is also contributing to a number of new imbalances. These are, first, the growing appetite for energy, hydrocarbons and metals, which has been driving up world market prices. China and India are both relatively energy inefficient economies, hence high growth rates translate in much higher incremental energy demand than the OECD countries. Energy inefficiency in India is mainly due to weak infrastructure, while in China it is primarily caused by the many – energy inefficient – industries. While China and India both already represented an important part of the incremental demand for hydrocarbons and mine products in the past years (see Figure 11.2), also their overall volume of demand for energy has become substantial, and has a major influence in the world market prices for hydrocarbons.

Second, until the global financial crisis a marked differentiation started to appear between a number of current account surplus countries (mostly in Asia, except for India) and current account deficit countries (the Western economies, except for Germany). This has led to a growing concentration of international reserves, with China and Japan dominating the scene, holding more than half of the global volume of international reserves. These are not used to stimulate domestic investment or consumption, but 'hoarded' in the form of US treasury

bonds, in part to defend themselves against external shocks and currency specu-
lations. As a consequence, finance flows to the richest economy, namely, the US.
Also Russia, as the main exporter of oil and natural gas in the world, accumulated large international reserve holdings, especially after the price hikes in the
oil market during 2008.

There was also a shift in foreign direct investment (FDI) flows, now that more
and more FDI is moving to these rapidly growing economies, bypassing the rest
of the developing world. Moreover, renewed bilateralism has been entering in
international relations, in particular where China wanted to guarantee its current
and future energy supplies. Some of these bilateral agreements, such as between
China and African countries have included substantial funding for investment
and development projects, in particular in infrastructure, counter-balancing the
negative influence from diminished development finance (see de Haan 2009),
but leaving aside the resource-poor economies in the developing world. While in
the past some of the surpluses in one OECD country were 'recycled' in portfolio
investment in a deficit OECD country, this venue is not possible for China,
which has not any other alternative than to use most of the reserves to buy US
treasury bonds.[2]

Overall, the chapter argues that with the emergence of China, and to a lesser
degree of India, a process of structurally rebalancing the world economy has initiated, but the differential growth processes (with a slow growing non-saving
importing US, versus a non-consuming exporting China) currently produces and
worsens global imbalances, while also causing other ones. This development has
already led to reduced access for the poorer developing countries to capital
flows, as the latter are pulled towards the US, other Western economies or recycled between financial institutions in high-income countries before reaching the
LDCs. The global crisis even seems to aggravate this picture, with the Western
economies running into even larger fiscal deficits, while the emerging Asian
economies are partly focusing more on their own recovery.

Indeed, since the Asian and Russian crises of the late 1990s, the growth rates
of nearly all Central, East, South and South-East Asian economies became sustained and very high. The Chinese economy experienced an even longer path of
such spectacular growth, which has been uninterrupted since the early 1980s.
The performance of large Asian (developing) economies, such as China and to a
lesser extent India, although in size still smaller than the US, EU and Japanese
economies, pulled the chart of growth during the past decade, particularly as
Japan has been stagnating during most of that same period.

The growing importance of the emerging Asian developing economies (next
to the traditional role of Japan) seems to redress part of a long-standing imbalance in the world economy. In fact, global economic power has been dominated
since the mid-1800s by Europe and the United States. With the strong recovery
of Japan in the second half of the twentieth century and in spite of the successful
emergence of the Asian Tigers (such as South Korea and Taiwan), the high-
income OECD countries (including Japan) still largely dominate the world
economy and world trade.

This highly skewed economic development, with wealth concentrated in fairly small areas of the world, seems now to be gradually but steadily transforming. By 2007 the Chinese and Indian economies together were close to the size (measured in gross national income (GNI) at market prices; see Table 11.1) of the Japanese economy, while already being substantially larger if measured at purchasing power parity (PPP) prices. By 2010 the Chinese economy has become larger in size than the Japanese economy, becoming the second largest economy in the world.[3] Of course, with regards to per capita incomes there are still huge inequalities, but if only taking the total size of these economies, the highly unbalanced world economy has indeed been changing. Over the past two decades this was particularly influenced by the developments in international trade until the global crisis started, in which particularly China has become an important new player. Furthermore, China has become a formidable player in international political relations on the world scene, and is an exponent of 'soft power' (de Haan 2009).

This chapter analyses the growing importance of Asia in the world economy as follows. In the second section, we will show that the rapid growth of the economies of Central, East, South and South-East Asia, leads to at least a partial redressing of the existing structural imbalance of the world economy. It also briefly looks at how the global crisis influences China and India, and how a resumption of rapid growth in these countries might 'pull' the world economy out of the recent deep recession.

In the third section, the spatial shifts in international trade are addressed, which has seen a transformation in particular since the late 1990s, from a predominance of intra-high-income country trade towards a growing role of trade originating from low- and medium-income countries. This is primarily caused by rapidly expanding merchandize trade of China (Acharya 2009; Dollar 2009). In this section also the influence of the increased appetite for hydrocarbons and metals by the rapidly growing developing economies of Asia, in particular China and India, is discussed.

In the fourth section, we will analyse global financial imbalances that have emerged, in particular the current divide between current account (CA)-deficit and CA-surplus countries, with a growing concentration of international reserves in the hands of some of the Asian economies (such as China and Japan), and look at its effects, and what influence the global economic crisis has in this respect.

In the concluding section it will be stressed that the growth of China and to a lesser extent of India is influencing existing and new global imbalances. It will be concluded that there is an important negative impact for the much slower growing (and often resource-poor) rest of the developing world, in particular with regards to the inverse flow of finance (from fast-growing China to slow-growing US), the availability of FDI, its overall significance for development finance and the rising energy prices caused by rapidly growing additional demand for carbohydrates and bio-fuels by China and India.

11.2 The 'dragon' and the 'elephant': stabilizers of the crisis?

While Japan has been the largest Asian economy for several decades, it suffered stagnation since the Asian crisis of the late 1990s. China's sustained and high growth rates have meant that by 2007, its GNI at market prices had reached the size of 64.7 per cent of the GNI of Japan (Table 11.1, based on the World Development Indicators of the World Bank). According to the IMF in 2010 the Chinese economy has overtaken the Japanese as second economy of the world, although if we compare import and export shares of China (in the world total) with the US and Europe, these data somewhat overstate the importance of China. At the same time, the US economy has been losing its global dominance, representing 26.3 per cent (at market prices) of the world economy in 2007, and 'only' 21.0 per cent at PPP prices, although still by far remaining the largest single economy of the globe (see Table 11.1).

Although in 2007 (on the eve of the global crisis) the OECD countries still represented the largest share of the world's GNI, namely 71.5 per cent (in PPP terms 54.2 per cent) the balance is indeed changing, and the traditionally unbalanced income distribution (between countries) is partly being redressed (IMF 2008). The current global economic crisis will affect this distribution even further, in particular because the size of the OECD economies has shrunk with around 4 per cent in 2009, while most of the Asian economies (such as China and India) have still substantially grown (between 5 and 8 per cent).[4] This regional shift towards a greater weight of some by the largest Asian economies in the global economy, is an outcome of sustained high growth rates in the Asian continent (except for Japan), which were and are much higher than those in the OECD countries. For example, if we take the period 1991–2001, growth in Japan was on average 1.1 per cent, in the United States 3.5 per cent and in the EU 2.4 per cent, while developing countries (including China), grew by 4.8 per cent

Table 11.1 Global GNI (OECD and developing countries), 2007

	GNI USD (billions)	GNI PPP USD (billions)	GNI/capita	GNI PPP/capita
World	52,850.42	65,752.31	7,995	9,947
OCED	37,808.28	35,642.70	39,158	36,915
High income	39,685.90	38,386.03	37,572	36,341
Middle income	12,393.46	25,666.19	2,910	6,027
Low income	744.29	1,929.70	574	1,489
Least developed countries	383.63	935.73	494	1,171
East Asia and the Pacific	4,172.76	9,503.13	2,182	4,969
South Asia	1,388.68	3,853.61	880	2,532
United States	13,886.42	13,827.20	46,040	45,840
Japan	4,828.91	4,440.21	37,790	34,750
China	3,126.01	7,150.54	2,370	5,420
India	1,071.03	3,082.54	950	2,740

(UNCTAD 2008). In the period 2001–08, during which the world economy was confronted with a trough during 2001–02 (as a consequence of 9/11), Japan grew with 1.7 per cent, the US economy with 2.6 per cent and the EU with 2.1 per cent per annum (ibid.). In contrast, the developing countries of Asia (with China) grew with 6.4 per cent, while China alone had an average annual growth of 10.3 per cent and India 7.7 per cent (ibid.).

Although the Chinese and Indian economies together started to approach the size of the Japanese (or at PPP even approach the US economy) by the midst of the decade, income inequality measured at per capita income levels remains very large.[5] As can be read from Table 11.1, average GNI per capita (2007) ratios between the US, China and India were distributed as 48: 2: 1, while at PPP prices this was 17: 2: 1.

The spectacular growth rates in the various parts of Central, East, South and South-East Asia and the Pacific are on average high, but still quite differentiated between various sub-regions, as is shown in Figure 11.1. These very high growth rates emerged in the current decade, and notably the growth rate of those Central Asian countries which emerged from the former Soviet Union were the highest in the region during the period 2004–08 (between 10 and 12 per cent),[6] while growth rates of GDP in East and South Asia were consistently around 8 per cent, still much higher than in the OECD region.

Hence, Asia led current global growth until the global economic crisis and continues – albeit at slightly lower levels during the crisis. The differential rates of growth have only become larger as in 2009 the OECD countries were in deep recession, while China and India were growing still quite fast. In particular China showed a speedy recovery to growth rates close to 10 per cent, although there are some concerns about 'overheating' (to be seen in higher inflation occurring in early 2010). China has become the new manufacturing centre of the world, to be compared with Manchester during the first industrial revolution, with growth largely being industry and export led.[7] In parallel, India transforms

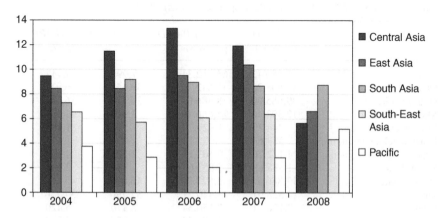

Figure 11.1 GDP growth in Asian region (source: ADB (2008)).

itself into an important service centre, in particular for IT services. China focused on manufacturing exports, for which it also demands more and more industrial inputs, primary commodities and energy sources, while India is already making a gradual transition towards high-tech exports, which generate more value added. Both countries have been influencing the global trade patterns and flows and were also, in the crisis, affected by the dramatic slowdown of the demand for their exports, especially China, which has chosen to boost domestic demand, to compensate for the losses incurred in the export sector. The export sector was also the first to recover, positively influencing the resumption of growth of the OECD economies with its renewed high growth in 2010.[8]

While the US, EU and Japanese economies – in late 2008 and the whole of 2009 – have been going through the largest economic contraction since the 1929 'crash', this crisis had a different impact on China and India. Growth slowed down in both countries, but substantially positive growth rates have been kept in the depth of the crisis, where Japan showed a 12.7 per cent contraction in the fourth quarter of 2008 and the US economy did so with 6.2 per cent. China's growth rate slowed down to 6.8 per cent in the same period, while India reported 5.3 per cent growth. Nevertheless, even this relatively slower growth rate had dramatic consequences. For example in China, an estimated 20 million workers lost their jobs in the fourth quarter of 2008 and the first quarter of 2009 (IMF 2009). Absorption of rural labour in industrial/urban centres needs a minimal growth rate of 10 per cent. Employment was also negatively affected by the dramatic drop in Chinese exports in 2009 (when they still slightly grew, but at a much slower pace than in the previous years, when export growth rates of 20–30 per cent/annum had become the standard). Hence, although it seems from the outside that China and India were hardly affected by the global recession, this was not the case. Both the OECD countries in deep recession as well as China, suffering from insufficient growth rates to keep absorbing the enormous migration from rural areas into the cities, chose for huge fiscal stimulus packages, championed by China who provides an enormous boost to its economy the period 2009–11.[9]

Economic recovery is stimulated in a Keynesian manner, with increased public investment in infrastructural projects, communications and employment generation. It seems that it indeed has stabilized the economy's slowdown, with first signs of recovery towards former high growth rates already seen by the fourth quarter of 2009. India was somewhat less affected by the global recession, although some export (service) sectors were also hit hard in terms of employment. India has also responded in a less interventionist manner to contain the crisis, but has been able to stabilize its economic growth in 2009–10, as increased domestic (and in particular rural) demand kept on boosting the economy. India did use fiscal stimulus packages which meant that its relatively low fiscal deficit as share of GDP more than doubled (to above 6 per cent) in 2009.

11.3 Asian trade and the world economy

Using data provided by Ocampo and Martin (2003) to look at the history of trade, for most of the twentieth century, exports were dominated by the industrialized world. In 1973, Europe, North America and other industrialized countries had respective shares of 50.3, 19.1 and 9.6 (total 79.0) per cent of world merchandise exports. In 1990, in spite of the implementation of structural adjustment in many developing countries[10] (and with a greater openness of the OECD countries as part of the GATT agreements), these shares remained stable, with 51.9, 17.0 and 11.0 (total 79.9) per cent. By 1998, they had slightly gone down to 47.4, 18.6 and 9.5 (total 75.5) per cent (ibid.). In the 2000s this reduction continued, with an increasing share for low- and middle-income countries. Their growth in exports was largely absorbed by other low- and middle-income countries, whose share went up from 7.1 to 14.3 per cent in the same period (very much representing the increased role of Chinese exports in world merchandise trade). The exports to high-income countries only grew from 17.0 to 20.9 per cent. The latter, however, continues to grow, and if services exports would be taken into account, the increase would be even more visible.

In Table 11.2, which shows inter-regional merchandise trade for 2007, just before the global economic crisis started to unfold, we can note that Asia's trade (including Japan) as share of total exports represents already 27.9 per cent, well beyond the share of North America, but still below that of Europe, which – by the way – is largely trading within Europe itself (73.5 per cent of all regional trade), while this share is less than half (49.7 per cent) for Asia.

11.3.1 From Mao to the WTO

The growing importance of Chinese exports is extraordinary, especially considering that China started as a very isolated economy in the period before the reforms in 1978. Growth during the 1980s was largely endogenous, based on a rapid growth of the agricultural sector and rural savings. At that era the first steps towards an export-led economic strategy were becoming visible in some of the later Asian Tiger economies, albeit mixed with import substitution industrialization. In contrast, growth of the Chinese economy was largely endogenous until the early 1990s. It was primarily investment-led growth, and in the early stages, after the introduction of the household responsibility system in agriculture, financed by rapidly improving peasant incomes and household savings. Since the early 1990s, FDI started flowing into the country, which followed sustained and rapid growth, rather than causing it (see Spoor 2007). However, FDI soon did become much more important, in particular when it became a crucial mover of more technology-intensive and innovative production sectors, hence a catalyst for further modernization. Exports became more and more the motor of its growth strategy and, during much of the 1990s, China followed a strategy of export promotion (rather than liberalization), with import protection diminishing gradually, in order to prepare for the membership of the WTO, which was realized in 2001 (Anderson *et al.* 2004).

Table 11.2 Inter-regional merchandise trade, 2007

Origin		Destination							
		NA	SCA	EUR	CIS	AF	ME	AS	World
World		2,517	451	5,956	397	355	483	3,294	13,619
North America	NA	951	131	329	12	27	50	352	1,854
South and Central America	SCA	151	122	106	6	14	9	80	499
Europe	EUR	459	80	4,244	189	148	153	434	5,772
Commonwealth of Independent States	CIS	24	6	288	103	7	16	60	510
Africa	AF	92	15	168	1	41	11	81	424
Middle East	ME	84	4	108	5	28	93	397	760
Asia	AS	756	92	715	80	91	150	1,890	3,800

Since the mid-1990s, China's exports (and in its shadow those of India as well, although at much lower levels still, see Acharya (2009)), have reached yearly growth levels which are much higher than any other country (see Table 11.3). Its growth rates have been stable at around 25 per cent per annum since 2001 until the current global economic crisis. Exports from China grew by rates of 10–30 per cent per annum and at 10–20 per cent for India during the years 2001–08 (see Table 11.3). Similarly, but overall less, imports also grew in a spectacular manner. Faster growth of imports than exports has meant that India gradually increased its trade deficit (ibid.).

Asia's (but in particular China's) fast growing exports have of course meant that the trade balance in most of the region has become very positve, except for South Asia, which has a large negative trade balance under the influence of a trade gap for India (which in 2007 was US$90.0 billion; see for regional trade balances Table 11.4). The latter might be explained by the much smaller share in terms of heavy industry (and manufacturing industry in general) in comparison to countries such as China and the Tiger economies, and hence its dependence on imports of intermediate goods.

It is also important to note that in the Central Asian region and the Caucasus, only for Kazakhstan and Azerbaijan the trade surplus is growing because of rapidly expanding oil exports and the high prices for oil. For all other countries in this region the absence of those resources or a thriving manufacturing sector

Table 11.3 Growth of export volumes, 1996–2008

	Export volume					
	1996–2000	*2001–04*	*2005*	*2006*	*2007*	*2008*
World	7	6	6	9	6	4
Developed economies	7	4	5	8	4	3
Japan	6	6	5	12	7	5
United States	7	1	7	11	7	6
Europe	7	5	6	9	3	3
Developing economies	8	9	9	11	8	5
China	12	26	27	25	22	13
India	8	13	16	10	13	7
S.E. Europe and CIS	1	9	0	5	7	19

Table 11.4 Trade balance Asian regions, 2004–08

	2004	*2005*	*2006*	*2007*	*2008*
Central Asia	7,719	14,222	23,971	30,477	62,483
East Asia	104,505	178,597	255,955	353,243	351,442
South Asia	–44,456	–68,340	–85,048	–115,438	–
South-East Asia	75,512	74,624	107,904	116,464	86,747

provides pressures for growing imports, which led to only slightly positive trade balances in the early part of the decade (before the windfall profits gained from oil and natural gas). This is contrary to what is visible for East Asia (dominated by China), where the trade surplus became nearly US$351.4 billion in 2008, in which China alone covered for US$315.4 billion (Table 11.4, and ADB (2009)).

Taken together, the success of the South and East Asian region in terms of export performance is spectacular compared to the performance of Latin America and the Caribbean (LAC), Africa and West Asia. The Asian miracle of the 1980s was already the success of the interventionist developmental states of Japan and the Tiger economies, with an appropriate mix of import substitution and export orientation.[11] The combined Asian region established much quicker a predominance of manufactured exports than any of the other developing regions. LAC is also partly undergoing this transition, but is doing so at a much slower pace (UNCTAD 2008). LAC has also been struck much more severely by the global recession, which has particularly hit manufactured exports, providing a drawback to the above described process of industrial transformation within the export portfolio.

In the developing world (or the low- and middle-income countries), comparing between continents it is clear that East and South Asia have been making the transition to higher value exports and moving away from fuels and non-fuel primary exports, while these commodities are still dominant in the exports portfolio of Africa and West Asia (see UNCTAD 2005). While Africa was still 50.6 per cent dependent on fuels in exports during the period 1999–2003, this was 72.2 per cent for West Asia (Middle East) and only 16.2 per cent in LAC. For South and East Asia together this only represented 4.9 per cent, as most countries are energy importers. In the non-fuel primary commodity exports, the shares for the other regions went down to respectively 24.0, 6.1 and 25.7 per cent. For the South and East Asia region, this dropped to 9.1 per cent. Finally, the share of manufactured exports increased for Africa, West Asia and Latin America to respectively 23.0, 21.0 and 56.6 per cent, while this was 84.8 per cent in the 1999–2003 period for South and East Asia, a development primarily pushed by China. The transition that the South and East Asian region has made in this respect has been faster than that of any other developing region. This becomes especially apparent when comparing 1980–83 with the 1989–92 averages, and slightly less so between the latter period and 1999–2003, when LAC seems to catch up in terms of the importance of manufactured goods in total exports (ibid.). In recent years LAC has had enormous windfall profits and income from price hikes in primary commodities, in part caused by the growing demand generated by the Asian economies. This has unexpectedly re-emphasized the pre-dominance (for some countries) of primary commodity exports.

Elaborating on some of the Asian economies and this qualitative transformation of exports there are some long-term trends mentioned by ADB (2006). On the one hand, to show the importance of manufactured exports, we can note the increasing share of electronics in the export value. Japan from 1965 to 2003, raised this share from 7.5 to 22.6 per cent, South Korea, during the same period, from 0.9 to 35.8 per cent, while a 'latecomer' such as China has managed to do the same, from 3.4 to 30.3 per cent, within a much shorter time span, namely from 1987 to 2003. As stated above, India is much less involved in manufacturing exports, and only lifted its share of electronics exports in the total export value from 0.8 to 1.9 per cent since 1975 (ibid.). On the other hand, China dropped from 37.7 to 9.2 per cent its share of primary commodities in its exports (during the period 1987–2003), while for India this share went down from 55.1 to 23.0 per cent over an even longer period (1975–2003). These trends have continued in the years to follow (see ADB 2009).

11.3.2 China's insatiable appetite for raw materials

As another aspect of the rapid changes in international trade, Asian developing economies, such as China and to a lesser extent India, have been strongly influencing the rising additional demand in the world markets for oil, metals and minerals, and primary agricultural commodities, such as soybeans (primarily produced in the USA and Brazil). The appetite for resources of these rapidly emerging economies has been boosting world market prices for commodities such as oil, steel, copper and tin, which provides additional income for the producing countries,[12] such as in oil when during 2008 the price of crude skyrocketed to a level of more than US$140 per barrel. During the global economic crisis of 2008–09, prices dropped again, but it can be expected that with economic recovery, an upward pressure on primary commodity prices will be felt again, which was already noticeable in early 2010, at the time of final revisions made to this chapter.

China has been signing many bilateral agreements with African and Latin American countries, to safeguard its energy and input needs for the coming decades, while the Indian economy might start to express similar needs, although not as profound as it is still less industrialized and in that field possibly with a time-lag of between five to 20 years behind China.[13] This increase in demand for energy resources and other primary commodities has slowed down during the 2008–09 crisis, although China has launched an ambitious investment programme to boost domestic demand, which seems to be working.[14]

China is also investing in energy efficiency, and environmental measures to contain increasing pollution, measures which in the future might well reduce the projected incremental demand that is projected at the moment. While in 1980 primary oil demand was still largely dominated by the OECD economies (41.8 million barrels/day versus all the developing countries together only using 11.3 million barrels/day), this picture is rapidly changing. By the year 2000 the oil demand from the side of developing countries already had risen to 23.1 million barrels/day, with China alone represented by 4.7 million barrels/day (IEA 2007). In Figure 11.2, it can be seen how some years further (in 2003) China's demand for oil accounted for 7.0 per cent of world exports, while in metals and minerals this was already 19.1 per cent.

These shares have been rapidly growing in the years to follow. This can be seen by looking at additional demand, which in 2004 came for oil for 31.2 per cent from

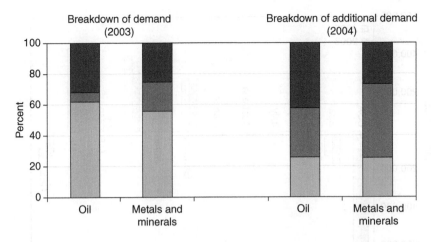

Figure 11.2 Increased developing country demand, 2003–04 (source: World Bank (2005)).

China, and for even 47.0 per cent for metals and minerals, caused by the rapidly growing Chinese industrial sector (ibid.). It has been estimated that this trend has continued and that in 2010 the demand for oil in the OECD countries is around 49.0 million barrels/day, while in the developing countries this has grown rapidly to 33.7 million barrels/day (with China standing for 9.0 and India for 3.1 barrels/day alone). The expected demand from the side of the Chinese economy in 2030 is estimated to be 16.5 barrels/day, just more than half of the US demand (ibid.).

The non-oil-exporting (and energy-poor) developing countries, which form the majority, will be negatively affected by the increased demand for carbohydrates in the next few decades, as rising prices will increase their import bills. While at the same time development finance will be less available, this might well create a financial squeeze for many of the developing countries, which is a new imbalance that is the indirect consequence of the structural rebalancing of the world economy as was analysed in Section 11.2.

11.4 Old and new global imbalances

The rapid expansion of trade, and in particular of exports, in and from the East Asian region is one of the most important reasons for the increasing surpluses on the CA of a number of these Asian economies, in particular China and Japan (IMF 2008, 2009). Looking more broadly, in Figure 11.3 an overview is depicted for 2007–08 of the CA balances of a group of OECD (and CEE) countries with large deficits, which are compared with others which have large surpluses, such as Germany, the CIS and the Middle East (because of oil revenues), and the already mentioned China and Japan (Figure 11.3).

Apart from the above-mentioned Asian economies, there are a number of European countries which also have substantial CA surpluses, such as Germany,

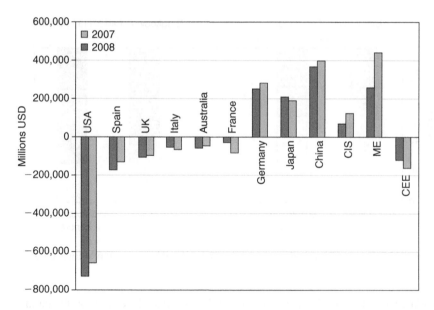

Figure 11.3 Current account balances, 2007–08 (source: ADB (2009)).

Norway and Sweden. However, at the other side of the spectrum, apart from the United States, there is a group of Western economies, formed by Spain, the United Kingdom, France, Australia and Italy having substantial CA deficits.

The accumulated deficit in 2008, held by these six countries, was estimated at US$1,094 billion, with the US accounting for an estimated and staggering US$664 billion. If the CEE countries are added (which have been hit very hard during the 2008–09 crisis), the CA deficit accumulates to US$1,258 billion. In comparison, Germany, China, Japan, the CIS (in particular Russia) and the Middle East, the mentioned CA surplus countries, held an accumulated surplus of US$1,439 billion in 2008 (ADB 2009). The CA deficits have been reducing in 2009, but this was mainly caused by the recession rather than a structural change in the imports and exports of the OECD countries.

As was shown in Section 11.1, sustained growth of the Asian economies, fuelled by a growth of exports, is actually redressing a long-standing imbalance, in which the global economy is largely dominated by a small number of high-income countries (the OECD group). However, the export growth (and the movement of FDI) has contributed to global financial imbalances which emphasize a new division into two groupings. One is 'headed' by the United States which has built up an unprecedented CA deficit, with some other OECD economies (including the CEE countries) that have much smaller deficits, while the other group, led by some Asian economies, in particular by China and Japan, shows an increasing CA surpluses, while furthermore some European countries, in particular Germany, and furthermore Russia belong to this group. The crisis and the differential impact of contraction of the global economy possibly reiterate this global imbalance.

Although in theory there is no problem, as long as current account and capital account balance, in reality things are not that simple (McKinley 2006). Before the credit crunch and financial crisis there was already an increasing pressure on the USA dollar, but the US government looked particularly at China, asserting pressure to appreciate its currency. However, it seems that the latter is only happening very gradually, not to endanger the excellent export performance of the Chinese economy has had until now, and particularly its rapid recovery late 2009 and early 2010.[15] A further realignment of the dollar–renminbi exchange rate might be desirable, but it is not going to transform the structural foundations of the imbalances, such as the 'over-consumption' in the US (Akyüz 2010).

As a consequence of the global financial imbalances there is a peculiar situation in which inverse financial streams have emerged, from low- and middle-income countries (such as China) to high-income countries, principally the USA, excluding other (weaker) developing countries from these financial flows (Izurieta and McKinley 2006; McKinley 2006). As growth has slowed down in 2008 and a full-blown contraction took place in the OECD (and other) regions, financial flows will further reduce, or partially directed to the Western economies in crisis and domestically used, with continued exclusionary effects for the weaker developing countries.

International reserves have been increasingly accumulated by China and Japan (and to a much lesser extent by the USA and Russia). These two Asian economies hold more than half of the world's international reserves, emphasizing even more the global financial imbalances. In particular the reserves accumulated by China, but also in other Asian economies are increasingly hoarded, and converted in (relatively low-performing) US treasury bonds (see Dollar 2009), rather than invested in the domestic economy, to boost consumer demand, which could – at least in the long run – redress some of the existing global financial imbalances. It has been suggested that this relatively cautious behaviour of Asian policy makers has been inspired by the devastating influence of the previous financial crisis in 1997–98, which had its origin in a collapse of banking institutions in the region itself. International financial institutions were incapable to intervene, and when they did their actions were largely contra-productive (Stiglitz 2003). Holding large international reserves has become a new form of self-defence of the emerging Asian economies (see Vos, in this volume).

McKinley (2006: 11) argues that the US dollar reserves held in Asia help to 'finance the gargantuan US Current Account deficit', while:

Many of the developing countries holding large foreign-exchange reserves, particularly those in Asia, have systematically tried to sterilize their impact on their domestic money supply. This has aborted the expansion of domestic credit, which could have stimulated private investment and closed the gap of investment with domestic savings.

This has led something rather counter-intuitive to happen, namely finance moves to the economy which least needs it (ibid.). Since the global economic crisis of late 2008 to early 2009 this is even more true, and it can therefore be understood that Mrs Hilary Clinton, the US Secretary of State of the new Obama administration, went first to China with the preoccupation that it would continue to finance the US deficit. China may be wondering whether the US is 'still good for its money', i.e. the treasury bonds, but on the other hand will continue to finance the gap on the US CA, because of obvious inter-dependency of the two economies.

11.5 Conclusion

The structural global imbalance of high-income versus low- and middle-income countries and their traditional dominance in international trade has been positively addressed by the rapid growth of the developing economies in East, South and South-East Asia. This is likely to continue in the decades to come. In 2010 China has already become the second economy of the world, taking the place of Japan. Before the global economic crisis emerged, Asia's trade volume (including that of Japan) had overtaken already that of the US, and is approaching the volume of EU trade. Furthermore, although there are still very large differences in per capita income, the fast growing economies of China and India have the potential to become larger than respectively the US or Japanese economies within several decades, leading to a multi-polar world economy with the economies of the US, EU and Asia as the most important ones. However, there are other global financial imbalances that have emerged in parallel with this development. Most pertinent amongst these is the differentiation between CA surplus and CA deficit economies, with global savings moving towards the richest economy (the USA), even more than before the global crisis emerged. As a consequence of fast growth, positive trade balances and influx of FDI, China (with Japan) has built up very positive current account balance. The emerging Asian economies have actually hoarded the international reserves they have accumulated in the past decade, sterilizing the effects on their domestic economies, and not using them to stimulate domestic consumption. However, rather than criticizing the Chinese for undervaluing the RMB (*yuan*), the CA deficit countries need to become more competitive, innovative and investment rather than consumption led and export oriented.

Finally, new imbalances are emerging, such as the expansion of demand for raw materials (energy, metals, minerals and agricultural commodities) generated by China and to a lesser extend India, until the eve of the global crisis, and in the years after the current global recovery, is also benefiting the carbohydrate exporting development countries. However, this could easily lead to 'Dutch Disease' effects for these exporting economies, withholding them from becoming competitive in manufactured commodity markets, a transition that just had started in the past decades. It can also mean that some middle-income developing countries, such as Argentina and Brazil are becoming (even more than they are already) main suppliers of agricultural raw materials for Developing Asia, be it for the growing animal husbandry sector to feed the expanding middle classes, or for the production of bio-fuels. Energy-poor developing countries will feel mostly detrimental effects from this development, as energy prices will rise again, and their import bills as well. China's demand for raw materials has temporarily slowed down in 2008. However, its domestic demand for inputs in industries has been stimulated by the large-scale stimulus package, which is focused on infrastructural investments.

The global imbalances which have been analysed in this chapter, in particular the financial imbalances which influence large 'inverse' capital flows towards the slow-growing CA-deficit and consumption-led Western economies, have to be redressed, as these are detrimental for other developing countries, in particular those who are dependent on energy and primary commodity imports. However, the recovery from the global crisis, and the public finance that has been utilized to bail out the banks or finance the stimulus packages, will make this process of restoring balances even longer, negatively affecting the poorer developing countries. China and India will likely recover rapidly their previous rates of economic and export growth, as the first signs of 2010 already seem to indicate. The high-income countries are benefiting substantially from the fast growth of China and India. Nevertheless, global financial imbalances will not be redressed if China does not direct more of its reserves towards the domestic economy in terms of increasing consumer demand, while the US (and some of the other CA-deficit OECD economies) should redirect their growth models to more savings (and investment) based, more competitive and export directed economies (Dollar 2009; Vos, in this volume).

Notes

1 This chapter benefited from detailed comments by Alex Izurieta, and the editors of this volume, Mansoob Murshed and Pedro Goulart. I also gratefully acknowledge the research support received from Koen Voorend and Marijn Nieuwenhuis.
2 This point was made by Alex Izurieta in a personal communication, indicating that FDI is much less symmetrical than in the past.
3 The data of IMF (2009), published in April, has been used here.
4 UNCTAD (2009) – is used as reference here. There are quite some conflicting data on the differential impact of the global crisis though.
5 The differences between per capita income of OECD countries and China or India are still huge, and global income inequality, taking this into account, has possibly increased (see Milanovic 2005), especially if growing domestic inequality is taken into account.
6 These high growth rates are mainly to be explained by the spectacular carbohydrate-driven growth rates in Kazakhstan and Turkmenistan.
7 Fischer (2010: 21) however, argues that it is mostly processing industry, observing that China has a 'subordinate third or even fourth-tier position' within East Asian production networks, and that more than 50 per cent of exports come from foreign dominated transnational companies in China.
8 Izurieta and Singh (2010), argue correctly that the emergence of China and India and their pattern of industrialization has actually provided positive impacts on the US

economy (contrary to the popular idea that they only pose a threat, in particular to jobs), such as providing cheap consumer goods consumed by low-income US citizens; apart from the purchase of US treasury bonds which also avoided lower growth of the US economy.

9 According to UNCTAD (2010: 2):

> China has done more than any other emerging economy to stimulate domestic demands ... According to several estimates, Chinese private consumption increased by 9% in 2009 in real terms, dwarfing all the other major countries' attempts to revive their domestic markets.

10 Structural adjustment was initially expected to boost foreign trade through a rapid liberalization of markets and the reduction of tariffs. However, it did not translate in an improvement of relative shares for most developing countries.

11 It is always good to remember what Alice Amsden argued; namely that fast growth and industrialization took place precisely because South Korea had their prices deliberately 'wrong' (see Amsden 1992).

12 However, these windfall profits and increased inflows of forex also meant for some of the exporting countries effects of 'Dutch Disease', strengthening their traditional role of primary commodity exporter.

13 Acharya (2009) argues that there is also a permanent qualitative difference in growth models between China and India. Hence, not only there is a substantial time lag in development, but he states that India will not go through a similar industrialization, and hence will influence world demand for energy resources in a different manner.

14 In the first quarter of 2010 China's growth was already close to 10 per cent.

15 Early 2010 domestic inflation was suddenly surging, which could be a sign of overheating of the Chinese economy. An effort to slow down (stimulated by increased interest rates to contain inflation) could include a further appreciation of the exchange rate.

References

Acharya, S. (2009) 'India's Growth: Past and Future', in N. Dinello and S. Wang (eds) *China, India and Beyond: Development Drivers and Limitations*, Cheltenham: Edward Elgar for the Global Development Network.

ADB (2006) 'Asian Development Outlook', Manila: Asian Development Bank.

ADB (2008) 'Asian Development Outlook, 2008', Manila: Asian Development Bank.

ADB (2009) 'Asian Development Outlook', Manila: Asian Development Bank.

Akyüz, Y. (2010) 'Global Economic Prospects: The Recession may be Over but Where Next?', Research Paper, Geneva: South Centre.

Amsden, A. (1992) *Asia's Next Giant: South Korea and Late Industrialisation*, Oxford: Oxford University Press.

Anderson, K., J. Huang and E. Ianchovichina (2004) 'Will China's WTO Accession Worsen Farm Household Incomes?' *China Economic Review*, 15: 443–56.

de Haan, A. (2009) 'Will China Change International Development As We Know It?' Working Paper, The Hague: Institute of Social Studies.

Dollar, D. (2009) 'Asian Century or Multipolar Century?' in N. Dinello and S. Wang (eds) *China, India and Beyond: Development Drivers and Limitations*, Cheltenham: Edward Elgar for the Global Development Network.

Fischer, A. (2010) 'Will China Change International Development As We Know It?' Working Paper, The Hague: Institute of Social Studies.

IEA (2007) *World Energy Outlook: China and India Insights*, Paris: International Energy Agency.

IMF (2008) 'World Economic Outlook Database, 2008', IMF.

IMF (2009) 'World Economic Outlook Database, 2009', IMF.

Izurieta, A. and T. McKinley (2006) 'Addressing Global Imbalances: A Development Oriented Policy Agenda', Working Paper, Brasilia: UNDP Poverty Centre.

Izurieta, A. and A. Singh (2010) 'Does Fast Growth in India and China Help or Harm US Workers?' *Journal of Human Development and Capabilities*, 11: 115–41.

McKinley, T. (2006) 'The Monopoly of Global Capital Flows: Who Needs Structural Adjustment Now?' Working Paper, Brasilia: UNDP Poverty Centre.

Mahbubani, K. (2008) *The New Asian Hemisphere: The Irresistible Shift of Global Power to the East*, New York: Public Affairs.

Milanovic, B. (2005) *Worlds Apart: Measuring International and Global Inequality*, Princeton, NJ: Princeton University Press.

Ocampo, J.A. and J. Martin (eds) (2003) *Globalization and Development: A Latin American and Caribbean Perspective*, Palo Alto, CA: Stanford University Press, for Eclac and the World Bank.

Spoor, M. (2007) 'Growth and Regional Inequality in Asia's "New Dragons"', in M. Spoor, N. Heerink and F. Qu (eds) *Dragons with Clay Feet? Transition, Sustainable Land Use and Rural Environment in China and Vietnam*, Lanham, MD, and Oxford: Rowman and Littlefield, and Lexington Books.

Stiglitz, J. (2003) 'The East Asian Crisis: How IMF Policies Brought the World to the Verge of a Global Meltdown', in J. Stiglitz (ed.) *Globalization and its Discontents*, New York: Norton.

UNCTAD (2005) 'Trade and Development Report', Geneva: United Nations Commission for Trade and Development.

UNCTAD (2008) 'Trade and Development Report', Geneva: United Nations Commission for Trade and Development.

UNCTAD (2009) 'Trade and Development Report', Geneva, United Nations Commission for Trade and Development.

UNCTAD (2010) 'Global Monetary Chaos: Systemic Failure need Bold Multilateral Responses', Policy Brief, Geneva: United National Conference on Trade and Development.

World Bank (2005) 'Global Development Finance, 2005', Washington, DC: The International Bank for Reconstruction and Development/The World Bank.

12 Trade integration after the great recession

The case of Argentina[1]

Leandro A. Serino[2]

12.1 Introduction

The Great Recession, as the current global economic crisis is known (see for instance Borio 2009), is not just another financial crisis. The crisis has led to the collapse of financial institutions, seriously affected the functioning of global financial markets and also has had significant real effects. Some of these are the collapse of investment, the contraction of GDP and the rise of unemployment, particularly in developed countries, and the large reduction of trade and industrial production worldwide (Eichengreen and O'Rourke 2009). More important, in contrast to previous financial crises which principally affected the developing world, is the fact that this crisis started in industrialized countries and has been the consequence of an explosive combination of lax financial regulations, the development of new (and risky) financial instruments and the rise of households' indebtedness to preserve their standards of livings in a more unequal world (Blankenburg and Palma 2009; Serino and Kiper; 2009).

At the moment of the crisis developing countries were in a strong position. Many of them learned the costly lessons from previous financial crises and implemented macroeconomic regimes that reduced their exposure to volatile capital flows and the instability of financial markets. Economists coined the term 'decoupling' and by the end of 2008 considered that developing countries were not going to be affected by the current world economic crisis. Unfortunately, they have proven not to be immune to it.

Although the crisis so far has not led to the collapse of macroeconomic regimes in developing countries, as happened during the financial crises in the 1990s, it has been affecting them through different mechanisms. Some developing countries, especially those implementing inflation targeting regimes and more integrated into the web of global financial markets (e.g., Peru and Colombia), suffered from the reversion of capital flows, as uncertainty spread out and institutional investors decided to move to 'safe' financial assets.

In an increasingly integrated world economy, the crisis has been affecting most developing countries through the trade channel. First via the collapse of world trade between the second half of 2008 and the beginning of 2009. Second, through falling external demand, as industrialized economies went into recession and, in spite of China, world output contracted in 2009.

An additional and "paradoxical" mechanism through which the recent transformations have been influencing developing countries, has been the fast recovery (and sustained expansion) observed in primary commodity prices, which, after falling strongly, have increased 20 per cent in US dollar terms since March 2009, according to the Index of Primary Commodity Prices elaborated by Argentina's Central Bank. This a priori constitutes a positive external shock for natural resource exporting countries, as many developing countries are, which is linked in part to expansionary monetary policies that rich economies have put in place to overcome the crisis.

This chapter discusses how the persistence of some of the abovementioned effects of the crisis will influence the economic performance of Argentina. This is an interesting case because the country, first, is a primary commodity exporter and second, has been implementing a stable and competitive exchange rate regime (SCER) in recent years. The strategy underpinning both these factors is to promote its non-traditional tradable sector and diminish the vulnerability of the economy to the moods of international financial markets. This analysis focuses on two connected transformations. One is the recovery of the expected 2010 world output growth on the basis of a continuous supportive policy stance and given that persistent vulnerabilities do not undermine the recovery process (United Nations 2010). The other transformation focuses on the rebound in primary commodity prices and associated improvements in the price of Argentina's traditional exports.

The analysis is performed using a structuralist computable general equilibrium (CGE) model and a stylized social accounting matrix (SAM) of the Argentine economy. The CGE model and the SAM were especially designed to capture structural features of the Argentine economy (see Serino 2009b, 2009a), like for example the presence of a natural resource exporting sector and other tradable sectors operating under different economic rationale. Most features of the model are embedded in the structuralist tradition (see for instance: Taylor 1990; Gibson and D. van Seventer 2000b; Gibson 2005). The relevant ones for the analysis in this chapter are: fix-flex closure rules in commodity markets, endogenous productivity growth in the manufacturing sector and demand-driven output. This closure rules implies that Argentina's macroeconomic performance is linked to the dynamism of the external sector and thus to the swings in world output and the international competitiveness of the Argentine economy.

The analysis presented here shows that the recovery of primary commodity prices and GDP growth in Argentina's trading partners will both be expansionary, yet they have different mesoeconomic implications. The predicted recovery in world output is expected to contribute to GDP growth in Argentina and to provide an impulse to resume the process of productive and export diversification that took place in the country in the period 2003–2008. These stimuli, however, will be weaker than before the crisis and therefore call both to encourage further economic integration among developing countries, which are the fastest growing economies today, and for expansionary fiscal policies. This chapter also shows that the growing primary commodity prices in Argentina, a wage-goods exporting country, will be expansionary, yet depending on the exchange rate regime may crowd out non-traditional exports. It is shown that a competitive exchange rate policy (implemented in combination with export taxes) is necessary to partly counteract Dutch Disease adjustments, which are commonly associated with positive primary commodity shocks, and to encourage domestic savings and investment.

12.2 Argentina during the golden years, the Great Recession and beyond

12.2.1 The golden years: Argentina in the period 2003–2008

The international crisis has brought Argentina's longest sustained economic expansion in decades to a halt. According to the Ministry of Economy and Public Finance, seasonal adjusted output expanded for 26 consecutive quarters between mid 2002 and the third quarter of 2008, when financial problems in advanced countries turned global.

Figure 12.1 shows real GDP growth and the contribution of aggregate demand components to output growth between 2003 and 2009. It also shows how these variables are expected to evolve in 2010, whereas Table 12.1 displays aggregate demand figures in addition to other key macroeconomic data. As can be observed through these data, Argentina expanded fast between 2003 and 2008. Output grew on average more than 8 percent per year during this period; an expansion that has been promoted by the sustained growth of all components of aggregate demand[3] (which was only at first linked to the recovery from 2001–2002

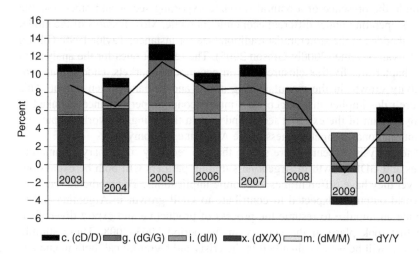

Figure 12.1 Output growth and contribution of aggregate demand components.

Table 12.1 Growth in output and aggregate demand and external and macroeconomic balances. Selected years and periods

| | (billions of Arg $ at 1993 prices) | | | | | | (% of GDP[a]) | | | |
| | GDP | Consumption | | TOT INV | EXP | IMP | TRADE BCE | CC AA | GOV PR S | GOV FC S |
		Private	Public							
1998	288.1	197.6	35.2	63.4	30.8	38.9	−1.04	−4.8	0.2	
2003	256.1	168.0	34.3	39.0	35.1	20.4	13.2	6.4	2.3	0.5
2004	279.1	183.9	35.2	44.2	38.0	28.6	8.7	2.1	3.9	2.6
2005	304.7	200.3	37.4	58.3	43.1	34.3	7.2	2.8	3.3	1.8
2006	330.6	215.9	39.4	68.6	46.2	39.6	6.5	3.6	3.5	1.9
2007	359.2	235.3	42.3	78.8	50.4	47.8	5.1	2.7	3.2	1.1
2008	383.4	250.6	45.3	90.9	51.0	54.4	3.9	2.2	3.1	1.4
2009	380.6	248.2	46.9	80.2	47.4	42.1	4.8	2.7	1.7	−0.2
2010[b]	397.8	258.2	50.1	85.5	53.3	49.3				
	Annual average growth rate						Period average			
2003–2008	8.41	8.34	5.69	18.43	7.77	21.7	3.9	2.2	3.1	1.55
2008–2009	−0.73	−0.99	3.79	−11.75	−7.08	−22.54	4.35	2.45	2.4	0.6
2009–2010	4.50	4.03	6.69	6.58	12.42	17.04				

Source: Secretary of Economic Policy, MEPF (Ministry of Economy and Public Finance).

Notes

TOT INV = total investment; EXP = exports; IMP = imports; TRADE BCE = trade balance; CC AA = current account balance; GOV PR S = government primary surplus; GOV FC S = government financial surplus.

a Positive (negative) values stand for surplus (deficit).

b projected.

economic crisis in Argentina and the deflationary years which preceded it). Table 12.1 shows that investments (although starting from low levels) and exports (until the outbreak of the international crisis in 2008), which are two key variables for the sustainability of growth processes in developing countries, expanded faster than output during Argentina's *golden years*. Investment, it is worth noting, reached a historical peak in 2008, as the investment rate grew to 24 percent and accounted for 50 percent of expansionary demand impulses (see Figure 12.1).[4] Private consumption in these years grew at a similar rate of output and government consumption grew on average slower than other variables.

Economic growth in Argentina has been in part related to international conditions. It benefited from fast economic growth and trade in the world economy, but especially from the good performances in developing countries. As shown in Table 12.2, whereas advanced economies grew around 2.5 percent between 2003 and 2007, output levels in the developing world and in South America (the largest destination of Argentina's industrial exports), grew 6.8 percent and 5.2 percent per year, respectively. In addition to a growing export demand, Argentina in these years experienced a sustained improvement in the external terms of trade. The ratio between Argentina's exported and imported goods improved 2.7 percent per year between 2002 and 2005, and at an annual rate of 7.5 percent between 2005 and 2008 (see Table 12.2).

Improvements in Argentina's external terms of trade have been in part due to skyrocketing primary commodity prices. As shown in Table 12.2, mounting demands for food and raw materials from rapidly growing China and India and speculation in financial markets increased the dollar price of primary commodities at an annual rate of 23 percent in the period 2005–2008.

Although Argentina faced favorable international conditions before the crisis, economic policies also played a critical role in shaping the country's macroeconomic performance, improving socio-economic conditions and encouraging a more diversified export structure. Argentina's competitive exchange rate policy has been of particular importance in this respect. The policy regime, which included export taxes in addition to the Central Bank's interventions in the foreign exchange market, have since 2003 encouraged industrial production, exports and employment (see Table 12.3 and Tavosnanska and Herrera 2010). Together with the renegotiation of Argentina's external debt in 2005, the policy regime contributed to achieving surpluses in current account and primary and financial government accounts (see Table 12.1). In so doing, the regime limited vulnerabilities that had historically conditioned Argentina's economic development.

Argentina's economic authorities, it is also worth mentioning, imposed capital controls in 2005 to discourage speculative capital inflows and actively prevented Dutch disease type adjustments during the recent primary commodity boom (Serino 2009b). This approach to dealing with external shocks, which differs from the one taken in other South American countries like Brazil and Chile, where capitals inflows have been encouraged and the exchange rate has been used as the adjustment variable, expresses Argentina's decision to integrate in the international economy that is based on trade – rather than financial flows.

Table 12.2 External impulses to the Argentina economy: output and trade growth in the world economy and changes in international prices. Selected years and periods

	Output growth (1)					Trade growth (1)		TOT Arg.(2)	IPCP. (US$) (3)
	GDP world	GDP a'ced	GDP dev.	GDP SAC	Arg. TP (EXP MOI)	Exp. world	Exp. dev.	1993 = 100	1995 = 100
2001	1.7	1.4	3.0	1.00	0.93	-1.1	-1.9	105.5	70.6
2003	2.7	1.8	5.30	1.80	1.02	5.6	9.8	114.8	85.5
2005	3.5	2.5	6.70	5.10	3.13	8	12.7	113.8	100.9
2007	3.9	2.6	7.60	6.50	4.01	6.6	9.1	125	144.5
2008	2.1	0.5	5.40	5.30	3.27	2.8	2.1	141.2	189.1
2009	-2.6	-3.5	1.90	-0.10	-0.79	-12.6	-8.9	135.6	146.3
2010[a]	1.6	1.3	5.30	3.70	2.67	5.5	6.5		150[b]
Annual average rate									
2003–2007	3.6	2.5	6.8	5.2	3.2	8.08	11.4	2.2	14.1
2002–2005						7.47	10.9	2.7	10.7
2005–2008						6.7	8.6	7.5	23.3

Sources: (1) UN World Economic and Social Prospects (2010); (2) Secretary of Economic Policy, MEFP; (3) BCRA: Central Bank of the Argentine Republic.

Notes
a Projected.
b Average January and February 2010.
GDP a'ced = GDP advanced economies; GDP dev. = GDP developing economies; GDP SAC = GDP South American countries; Arg. TP (EXP MOI) = Argentina's trading partners (industrial exports); Exp. world = exports world; Exp. dev. = exports developing; TOT = terms of trade; IPCP = index of primary commodity prices.

Table 12.3 Production and exports in selected sectors and main crops in Argentina. Selected years and periods

	Export quantity index (1) (1993 = 100)			Production (1) (1993 = 100)		Production of cereals and oil crops (millions tons) (1)			
	PP	MOA	MOI	Industry	Agriculture	Soybeans	Maize	Wheat	Sunflower
2001	208.9	179.9	239.5	94	124				
2003	195.8	226.3	235.5	97	131				
2005	250.5	291.7	302.8	117	145				
2007	285.0	317.8	397.8	137	162				
2008	262.1	286.3	467.7	143	158	46.2	21.3	16.3	4.6
2009	178.5	296.3	472.8	139	143	31.0	13.1	8.4	2.4
2010[a]						52.0	18.0	7.5	2.2
Annual average growth rate									
2003–2008	6.0	4.8	14.7	8.07	3.79				

Source: (1) Secretary of Economic Policy, MEFP.

Notes

a Projected.

PP = primary products; MOA = manufactures of agricultural origin; MOI = manufactures of industrial origin.

This type of integration in the world economy differs from the one Argentina implemented in the 1990s and has diminished the country's vulnerability of the economy to the moods of international financial markets. It therefore has limited the negative consequences of the recent international financial crisis. In contrast to other developing countries, especially those implementing inflation targeting strategies, Argentina has not been hit by the sudden stops and massive reversions in capital flows after the collapse of Lehman Brothers. The country has however, not been immune to the international crisis.

12.2.2 The Great Recession

The international crisis affected Argentina *first* through the contraction of world trade and Argentina's exports. As shown in Table 12.2, after growing at an annual rate of 8 percent (11 percent) between 2003 and 2007, the volume of world (developing countries') exports slowed down in 2008 and fell by 12 percent (9 percent) in 2009. Exported volumes fell due to lower primary commodity prices (an issue to which we turn next) and due to the contraction of world output, following the Great Recession affecting advanced economies and some developing ones and the slowdown in output growth taking place in fast growing East Asian countries. According to the UN's World Economic and Social Prospects (United Nations 2010), output in 2009 fell by 2.6 percent in the world economy, 3.5 percent in industrialized countries, while growing less than 2 percent in the developing world (see Table 12.2). Although a large fraction of Argentina's exports goes to developing countries, output of Argentina's trading partners contracted by 0.7 percent in 2009.

Deflation in primary commodity prices, as mentioned above, has been the second mechanism through which the international crisis hit Argentina. According to the IPCP, prices in dollar terms rapidly deflated with the advent of the international financial crisis. Commodity prices fell 22 percent on average between 2008 and 2009 (see Table 12.2), and in March 2009 were down by 40 percent from the peak observed in June 2008. Two additional facts on this issue are worth noting. One is that primary commodity prices in March 2009, however, were 50 percent higher than in 2003 and at the level of April 2007, before the run up that led to the international financial crisis (see Figure 12.2). The other fact worth mentioning is that, as the price of Argentina's imports also fell during the crisis, the country's external terms of trade fell 4 percent in 2009, which is less than the 22 percent adjustment observed in primary commodity prices (see Table 12.2).

Output in Argentina contracted in 2009, as the economic crisis unfolded and became global. As shown in Table 12.1 and Figure 12.1, the contraction of investment (down by 12 percent) and exports (down by 7 percent) have been the main negative demand impulses. Investment fell as the crisis increased uncertainty, rationed credit and limited demand. Exports, on the other hand, fell as a consequence of the crisis, but also due to internal factors. One is the political dispute between the government and agricultural producers over the distribution of the

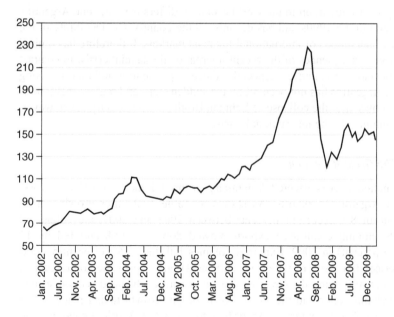

Figure 12.2 Index of primary commodity prices.

gains from growing primary commodity prices in 2008. The other is the severe drought that constrained agricultural production in 2009. Production in agriculture fell by 3 percent in 2008 and 10 percent in 2009, while exports of primary products, expressed in quantitative terms, were down by 10 percent and 30 percent each year; and agro-industry exports fell by 10 percent in 2008 but resumed growth in 2009 (see Table 12.3). Argentina's industrial exports, the fastest growing export group between 2003 and 2008, have been hardly hit by the international crisis. After growing 18 percent in 2008 (and at an annual rate of 14 percent during the *golden years*), industrial exports stagnated in 2009 (see Table 12.3).[5]

Imports and government consumption have been the two components of aggregate demand acting countercyclically in 2009 (see Figure 12.1). Imports were down by 22 percent in 2009, due to a decline in investments and private consumption, but also as a consequence of government administrative measures designed to discourage imports in 2009. In contrast to other variables (and other periods of crisis in Argentina), government consumption was up by 4 percent and different transfer mechanisms have been put in place to support employment and private consumption demand.[6] This has reduced the primary surplus by 50 percent and, for the first time in many years, turned financial government balances from surplus into deficit (see Table 12.1).

12.2.3 Future prospects

Although financial vulnerabilities have not disappeared, as can be seen from the recent crises in Dubai and Greece, and (probably sooner than later) the public sector in advanced economies may start devoting public income to repay debt rather than to encourage demand, the global economy is projected to move out of recession in 2010. According the UN WESP (United Nations 2010), which take account of persisting vulnerabilities and therefore is less optimistic than projections from other international institutions, the world economy is expected to grow by 1.6 percent in 2010. Global GDP growth is explained in part because advanced countries (though not all) have been showing signs of recovery. After falling sharply, industrial production in the US, the EU and Japan has been recovering since mid 2009 (and Japan had already achieved positive growth rates in December 2009). It is also the consequence of fast output growth in developing countries, with China and India in front, which are expected to grow more than 5 percent in 2010 (as they had done in 2008).[7]

The recovery of global output will be accompanied by an expansion in the volume of trade, which is a process that has already started in the second half of 2009, and which will be more apparent in the developing countries (Table 12.2 above shows the projected expansion in the volume of exports). These projections are good news for Argentina's exporting sectors, but especially for its manufactures. Indeed, the dynamism of Argentina's non-traditional exports, and thus the prospects for further productive and export diversification, will be linked to the economic performance of Argentina's trading partners, trends in world trade and the competitiveness of the country's economy. All these factors are expected to provide positive impulses to Argentina's external sector, though smaller than prior to the crisis. The main impulses to Argentina's external sector are listed below.

First, output in the US, Brazil, other South American countries and two 'small' European economies, such as the Netherlands and Switzerland, which are among the top ten destinations of Argentina's industrial exports and stand for nearly 80 percent of these exports, is expected to grow on average in 2010 by 2.7 percent (see Table 12.1). Second, world exports are expected to grow, although less than in the 2003–2007 period in which the overall volume of exports expanded at an average annual rate of 8 percent and 11 percent for developing countries. Third, Argentina's price competitiveness has improved in the second half of 2009, as soon as exchange rates in Argentina's trading partners stabilized after the crisis (see Figure 12.3). The expected recovery in the production of Argentina's principal crops, which fell close to 40 percent between 2008 and 2009 but is expected to expand by more than 45 percent this year, will provide an additional boost to Argentina's exports (Table 12.3).

Fast output growth in China and low interest rates in the developed world have promoted the recovery of primary commodity prices. After a large and fast adjustment between June 2008 and March 2009 (down by more than 40 percent), primary commodity prices have been growing again, and in February 2010 were close to 15 percent higher than in March 2009 (the lowest point in the aftermath of the crisis), according to the IPCP (see Figure 12.2 and Table 12.2). Although it is difficult to know how primary commodity prices are going to evolve, especially in a world of very volatile financial flows, prices have remained higher

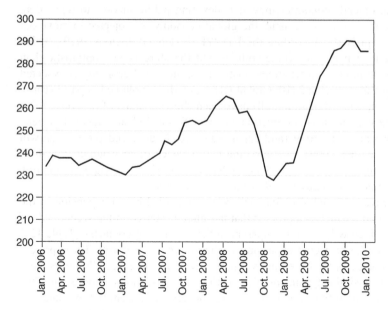

Figure 12.3 Multilateral real exchange rate.

than in previous recessions. This has occurred in part because demand for food and raw materials from fast growing economies persists (Brahmbhatt and Canuto 2010).

Argentina is, after a period of adjustment, this year (2010) therefore expected to experience positive impulses in its external sector. It bears mentioning that these impulses will be weaker than those prevailing before the international crisis. The country will experience two different positive natural resource shocks: one linked to the recovery of primary commodity prices and the other associated to the expansion of traditional crops and exports. Argentina is also expected to benefit from the recovery of the international economy and global trade. The effects of these positive changes are analyzed in the coming sections through counterfactual simulations run with the support of a structuralist CGE model.

12.3 A structuralist CGE model for Argentina

12.3.1 General remarks

I employ a structuralist CGE model and a stylized SAM of Argentina to explore how exogenous shocks after the great recessions may affect Argentina's macro- and mesoeconomic performance. Although the model is dynamic, simulations are based on a static version, due to uncertainties about the evolution of the world economy in the coming years.

They SAM and model were designed to capture some structural features of the Argentine economy. The model draws on existing applied models and is embedded in the structuralist tradition.[8] Key characteristics of the model are fix-flex closure rules in the commodity markets, mark-up prices and quantity adjustment in the industrial sector, the inclusion of wage, trade and investment equations and the Keynesian closure rule for the saving–investment balance.

Other relevant features of model (and the SAM) are the classification of commodities and economic activities. I distinguish five commodity groups and five economic sectors that produce them:[9] primary products (PP); resource intensive manufacturing products (MR); other manufacturing products (MO); producer services (PS); consumer services (OS). Their key characteristics are summarized in Table 12.4 at the end of this section, together with other relevant features of the model.

Following the tradition for multisectoral models of the Argentine economy,[10] the sectors linked to Argentina's natural resources (PP and MR) are assumed to (i) have a price competitiveness advantage, (ii) operate at full-capacity and (iii) sell to the domestic or the international market depending on the relative profitability of one or the other product destination. Excess capacity and quantity adjustments, on the other hand, are the norm in the non-natural resource manufacturing sector MO and in sector PS, hence output in these sectors is demand-determined and depends on domestic and world income and the price and non-price competitiveness (and the events affecting them) of these sectors.

The model finally distinguishes between producer-oriented services and consumer-oriented ones. The reason for this particular classification of the service sector is to distinguish the group from modern services, which as for instance software, transportation and financial services can be exported or as some public utilities, communication and specialized services are key determinant of the overall competitiveness of the economy, from other services such as commerce, leisure and informal services.[11]

12.3.2 The CGE model

The material balance equation and demand components

A synthetic description of the model is provided in this section, which highlights the features of the CGE model that are relevant for the applied analysis; the reader is referred to Serino (2009b, 2009a) for its full specification.

Together with the commodities and economic sectors (denoted with supraindex c and a), the model distinguishes ten factors of production (one capital and nine labor categories, characterized with supraindices k and l) and identifies three types of institutions: households (H), government (G) and rest of the world (W).

Equation (12.1) presents the material balance equation:

$$XC_{c,t} = AINTD_{c,t} + \sum_h CDH_{c,h,t} + IO_{c,t}^{priv} + IO_{c,t}^{gov} + CDG_{c,t} + E_{c,t} - M_{c,t} \quad (12.1)$$

In the above equation, XC_c is commodity c demand, $AINTD_c$ is domestic intermediate inputs, $CDH_{c,h}$ refers to household consumption, IO_c^{priv} and IO_c^{gov} to private and public investment, CDG_c to government current expenditure, E_c stands for exports and M_c for imports.

The external sector: exports supply and demand, and the competitiveness of the non-natural resource tradable sectors

The economic rationale for exporting natural resource products is different from that for other exports and therefore they are modeled differently. Exports of natural resource-related products (PP or MR) are supply-determined and producers decide the destination of production according to relative profitabilities. The decision between exporting or selling to the domestic market is modeled using a constant elasticity of transformation (CET) function that links exports ($E_{c,t}$) and supply to the domestic market ($QDDA_{c,t}$) to the relative price prevailing in the external and domestic market

$$\left(\frac{PE_{c,t}}{PDC_{c,t}}\right).$$

This function is defined in equation (12.2):[12]

$$\frac{E_{c,t}}{QDDA_{c,t}} = \left(\frac{PE_{c,t}}{PDC_{c,t}} \cdot \frac{\left(1-\psi_c^{cet}\right)}{\psi_c^{cet}}\right)^{1/\rho_c^{cet}-1} \tag{12.2}$$

The exponent parameter depends on the elasticity of the transformation between the domestic and export supply, which captures the ability of producers to shift from one market to another. To reproduce the capacity of Argentina's natural resource sector to export its surpluses, the model assumes high elasticity of transformation. This permits an easy reallocation of production between the domestic and external markets and increases the pass-through of international to domestic prices. It thus serves to evaluate the adjustment to positive terms of trade shocks in wage-goods exporting countries.[13]

Output in sectors MO and PS is assumed to be demand-determined. It depends, among other things, on the demand for exports and the competitiveness of production in these sectors. Equation (12.3) defines the export demand equation for MO and PS products.

$$E_{c,t} = E_{c,t-1} \cdot (RERE_{c,t})^{\xi_{EP}} \cdot (y^W)^{\xi_{Ey}} \cdot \left(\frac{ID_{a,t}^{priv}}{ID_{a,t-1}^{priv}}\right)^{\xi_{ENP1_c}} \cdot \left(\frac{QA_{APS,t}}{QA_{APS,t-1}}\right)^{\xi_{ENP2_c}} \tag{12.3}$$

The export demand equation goes beyond traditional specifications.[14] Exports are the function of conventional factors, as changes in world income (y^W) and the price competitiveness of the products concerned, as captured by the sector-specific real exchange rate (RER_c). Yet, in this CGE model, the competitiveness of exports depends on factors other than price.

Following Leon-Ledesma's (2002) Kaldorian growth model, the equation incorporates two non-price determinants of competitiveness. The first links the competitiveness of production to sector-specific private investment

$$\left(\frac{ID_{a,t}^{priv}}{ID_{a,t-1}^{priv}} \right),$$

which enters the equation to account for factors facilitating access to foreign markets, as embodied technical progress and investment in machinery and equipment. The second one associates export competitiveness with output increases in sector PS

$$\left(\frac{QA_{APS,t}}{QA_{APS,t-1}} \right).$$

This is included to capture the contribution of the producer services to the competitiveness of exports, an effect emphasized in Ros (2001) and the analytical model developed in Serino (2009b: chapter 3).

The price competitiveness of non-traditional exports is defined by the sector-specific real exchange rate and depends on the nominal exchange rate and domestic prices in sectors *MO* and *PS* as defined in equation (12.4):

$$PDA_{a,t} = (1 + TAUV_{a,t})VC_{a,t} \tag{12.4}$$

Prices in these sectors depend on the mark-up rate $TAUV_a$, which changes according to sectoral output, and variable production costs (VC_a), which are a function of intermediate input prices and unitary labor costs, as defined by nominal wages W_l and labor productivity.

The model also assumes that the price of labor is institutionally determined, depending on the growth of labor productivity (*LPRODG*), the evolution of consumer prices (*CPI*), changes in the rate of unemployment (*UN*) and an exogenous policy variable (*wpol*) which accounts for changes in government wage policy.

$$WL_{fl,t} = WL_{fl,t-1} \cdot \left[1 + \omega_1 \cdot \frac{\sum_a LPRODG_{fl,a,t}}{a} + \omega_2 \cdot \hat{CPI}_t - \omega_3 \, \hat{UN}_{fl,t} + \omega_4 wpol \right] \tag{12.5}$$

Labor productivity growth is assumed to be endogenous in the model and determined by demand and supply factors. Demand-determined productivity growth is referred to in the literature as the Kaldor–Verdoorn effect and links productivity growth to learning and specialization economies that arise with an expansion in demand. Modeling-wise, productivity is linked to changes in economy-wide capacity utilization. Supply-side determinants of productivity growth (i.e., human capital accumulation) are assumed to be exogenous in the model.

The specification of imports resembles the export demand equation, but includes real output instead of world income.

Domestic demand

The specification of domestic demand, to a large extent, follows the traditional structuralist CGE models. Demand for intermediate inputs is based on a Leontief function and consumption demand is defined according to a linear expenditure system (LES).

Output also responds to changes in investment and government expenditure, which thus are determined according to particular behavioral equations or are defined as exogenous and determined by economic policies.

Private investment is defined below:

$$ID_{a,t}^{priv} = ID_{a,t-1}^{priv} \cdot \begin{bmatrix} 1 + \gamma_{1a}\, U\hat{A}V_t + \gamma_{2a}\, I\hat{D}_t^{gov} \\ + \gamma_{3a}\, P\hat{R}FR_{a,t} - \gamma_{5a}\, R\hat{I}R_t \end{bmatrix} \cdot IADJ_t \tag{12.6}$$

The model defines an investment equation for each economic sector; each equation incorporates an accelerator parameter γ_1, linking capital accumulation to changes in economy-wide capacity utilization, and a crowding-in parameter γ_2 that relates private investment to changes in public investment. Investment is also a positive function of the profit rate $P\hat{R}FR_{a,t}$ and is negatively linked to the real interest rate $R\hat{I}R_t$, which accounts for the cost of borrowing.[15]

Government consumption and public investment are the remaining components of aggregate demand. The benchmark specification of the model assumes that *government expenditure (consumption and investment)* is exogenous and changes according to a predefined rule (*cdgrule* and *idgrule* in equations (12.7) and (12.8)), but that can be modified so as to simulate the impact of alternative government expenditure policies. The model allows for alternative specifications of government spending, for this also can be endogenous and adjust to balance government accounts (*GCADJ*) and (*GIADJ*),[16] or can be a function of government income from export taxes (*CDGTC_{c,t}*) and (*IGTI_{c,t}*).

$$CDG_{c,t} = \begin{bmatrix} CDG_{c,t-1} \cdot (1 + cdgrule) + CDGTC_{c,t} \end{bmatrix} \cdot GCADJ_t \tag{12.7}$$

$$ID_t^{gov} = ID_{t-1}^{gov} \cdot \begin{bmatrix} (1 + igrule) + IGTI_t \end{bmatrix} \cdot GIADJ_t \tag{12.8}$$

In the model, public income is invested exclusively to improve the provision of infrastructure. It occurs, therefore, in sector *PS*.

Production and labor demand

In the model, supply depends on capital accumulation and, thus, on investment, as defined in Gibson and van Seventer (2000a) and equation (12.9). Based on the assumption of price adjustment in sectors PP, MR and OS, equation (12.9) determines effective output in these sectors. In sectors MO and PS, where output is demand-determined, the equation defines potential output.

$$QA_{a,t} = \left(\kappa_a \cdot K_{a,t-1} + QA_{a,t-1} \right) \tag{12.9}$$

In (12.9) κ_a is the sector-specific incremental capital–capacity ratio, and $K_{a,t-1}$ and $QA_{a,t-1}$ respectively denote capital stock and output in the previous period. The rate of capacity utilization ($U_{a,t}$) equals:

$$U_{a,t} = \frac{XA_{a,t}}{QA_{a,t}} \tag{12.10}$$

Capacity utilization equals 1 in sectors PP, MR and CS, the sectors for which the model assumes full employment and price adjustment, and is defined as the ratio of demand-determined ($XA_{a,t}$) to potential output ($QA_{a,t}$) in the other two sectors.

Sectoral labor demand depends on the endogenous labor output coefficients and output, as shown in equation (12.11).[17]

$$LD_{fl,a,t} = LOCF_{fl,a,t} \cdot XA_{a,t} \tag{12.11}$$

Macroeconomic balances, system constraints and closure rules

The final elements of CGE models are macroeconomic balances. These concern balances in government and external accounts, which define public and external savings, and the macroequilibrium relation between savings and investment. Table 12.4 summarizes the main characteristic of the CGE model: the main features of economic sectors, the *numeraire* to express relative prices and the closure rules[18] that define how the factor and commodity markets adjust to excess demand and how the economy achieves the various macroeconomic balances.

As shown in the Table 12.4, the nominal wage for unskilled and informal labor is defined as the *numeraire*, and a fix-flex closure rule characterizes the commodity market, with mark-up sectors MO and PS showing quantity adjustments, and sectors PS, MR and OS adjusting to excess demand via price adjustments. Quantity adjustments are the regulating mechanism in the labor market – in 2009 unemployment affected 8 percent of Argentina's labor force.

In the case of macroeconomic balances, the benchmark specification of the model assumes a fixed exchange rate (an assumption consistent with the managed exchange rate regime implemented in Argentina), exogenous government expenditures and a Keynesian closure rule for the saving–investment

Table 12.4 Main features of the dynamic CGE model

Market	Adjustment mechanism	Other properties
Micro closure		
Commodity markets:		
PP (primary) and MR(resource intensive manufacture)	Price adjustment to excess demand	Price competition; full capacity utilization and CET function to determine export supply
MO (non-resource manufacture) and PS (producer services)	Quantity adjustment	Non-price competition; excess capacity and mark-up pricing
OS (consumer-oriented services)	Price adjustment to excess demand	
Labour market	Quantity adjustment	Institutionally determined wages
Macro closure		
Foreign Exchange Market	Fixed/Flex exchange rate regime	
Saving-Investment Balance	Investment driven/Saving driven	
Numeraire		
FWLNP1	Nominal wage of unskilled and informal wage labor	

balance, where output adjusts to ensure the savings required to finance the exogenously determined investment.

12.3.3 The model parameters

The model is calibrated to reproduce the initial equilibrium of the SAM using different parameter values. Average and distribution parameters are calibrated to the SAM,[19] values for exogenous variables are obtained from different official sources, as shown in Table 12.a.1 (in the Appendix to this chapter), and parameters for behavioral equations and exogenous or policy variables are calibrated using available information, borrowed estimations or as defined on the basis of guesstimates. This section makes a short description of the calibration.[20]

The model assumes a high elasticity of transformation (sigma = 5) to capture the ability of the natural resource producers to sell their surplus on the international market. Although high parameter values may overestimate the economic or sectoral response to changes in international conditions or trade policy (Vos 2007), a high elasticity of transformation is a realistic and relevant assumption to describe the behavior of sectors PP and MR in Argentina.

Demand for exports from sectors MO and PS is assumed to have unitary price elasticity, in line with figures from Catao and Falcetti (2002). The income elasticity of exports for these sectors equals 0.94, which is the short run elasticity for Argentina's exports estimated by Senhadji and Montenegro (1999). Price and income import elasticities are calibrated, taking Catao and Falcetti's (2002) estimations into account. The short term price elasticity of imports is 0.25 and the income elasticity of imports has the value 1.92. These values illustrate the strong connection between Argentina's imports and the economic cycle and their unresponsiveness to changes in relative prices, especially in the short term. Due to a lack of empirical estimations, the elasticity of imports and exports to the determinants of non-price competitiveness is assumed to have very low values (equal to 0.025).[21]

Labor productivity grows due to labor-saving technical change, which is assumed to be exogenous and increases by 2 percent per year, but also varies according to changes in aggregate demand. The Kaldor–Verdoorn parameter capturing this relationship equals 0.5, as commonly assumed (see, e.g., Ros 2001; Leon-Ledesma 2002).

Price and income elasticities of household demand are taken from Berges and Casellas (2002) and are employed to calibrate the intercept and marginal propensities of the household linear expenditure system according to the Frisch methodology.

The parameters of the wage and investment equation were defined considering estimations from a structural macroeconometric model for the period 2003–2006 (see Panigo *et al.* 2009).[22] The calibration of the wage equation considers (i) an intermediate response of wages to labor productivity growth, with the respective coefficient taking a value equal to 0.5, (ii) an indexation parameter equal to 0.8 and (iii) a moderate elasticity to the situation of the labor market, since the coefficient linking wage growth to changes in unemployment equals 0.28. Parameters for the investment equation suggest a weak response of total investment to output growth, public investment and increases in the cost of capital, and that profits are the main driving force behind investment (see Table 12.a.1).

Together with parameter values and sources, Table 12.a.1 shows the range of values for which the CGE model works. None of the model's parameters, as shown in columns 2 and 3 of Table 12.a.1 is at bound, but rather is distant from the values that make the CGE model unstable. This suggests that the functioning and stability of the model do not depend on any particular parameter value and that the CGE model works for values close to those defined in this calibration.

12.4 Life after the Great Recession: positive (and moderate) external shocks and domestic adjustment in Argentina

12.4.1 Positive primary commodity shocks and macroeconomic policies

The chapter discusses first how recent trends in primary commodity prices may affect the Argentine economy. It is assumed that commodity prices will remain high, but will not increase as before the crisis. The first simulation therefore considers that the international price of primary commodities in 2010 will grow by 2.5 percent, which is the growth rate at which prices have increased on average between 2009 and the first months of 2010. Unless stated otherwise, all simulations are run using the benchmark closure rules described in Table 12.5: quantity adjustments in mark-up sectors and the labor market, exogenous government expenditure, a managed exchange rate regime, where the nominal rate does not clear the foreign exchange market and the Keynesian closure rules for the saving–investment balance.

Simulation results for a selected group of variables are presented in Table 12.5, where figures refer to percentage changes to the base run (BR) simulation. The positive change in world prices for Argentina's exports has small expansionary effects. As shown in column (1), output expands 0.3 percent in relation to the baseline as the shock increases available income in the economy and with it consumption (up 0.5 percent from the BR), and higher domestic demand, capacity utilization and prices promote investment (up 2.5 percent from BR).[23]

The shock however reduces exports. Sales to external markets contract first as more natural resource products, particularly wage-goods, are devoted to the domestic market. Exports also decline because increases in primary commodity prices also augment domestic prices (as the assumption of an easy reallocation of primary production between the domestic and the international market implies that the pass through between international and domestic prices shows a one-to-one relationship), jeopardizing the competitiveness of non-traditional exports, which contract 2 percent in relation to the baseline (see Table 12.5 column (1), rows (7) to (12)).

Table 12.5 (Moderate) positive primary commodity shocks and domestic adjustment. Alternative exchange rate and closure rules

	(1) 2.5% inc. PW_{PP} and PW_{MR}	(2) 2.5% inc. PW_{PP} and PW_{MR}	(3) 2.5% inc. PW_{PP} and PW_{MR}	(4) 2.5% inc. PW_{PP} and PW_{MR} and 10% inc. export tax
	BM CR	Flex ER	NCL CR	BM CR
	% change to baseline			
Macroeconomic variables				
(1) Real GDP	0.31	0.23	-0.17	0.15
(2) Private investment	2.54	1.88	-1.02	1.24
(3) Total consumption	0.51	0.79	0.03	0.25
(4) Total Exports	-0.92	-1.53	0.03	-0.46
(5) Current account deficit (% GDP)	-2.1	-1.98	-2.56	-2.29
(6) Government primary. surplus (% GDP)	3.30	2.95	3.15	3.34
(7) Consumer price index	2.53	-0.46	1.54	1.15
(8) Domestic price (PP and MR)	2.42	-0.93	2.07	1.06
Variables external sectors				
(9) Real exchange rate M-up sectors (MO + PS)	-2.1	-2.60	-1.13	-0.96
(10) Output M-up sectors (MO + PS)	0.7	0.53	-0.40	0.36
(11) Exports PP and MR	-0.3	-0.98	0.70	-0.21
(12) Exports MO and PS	-2.0	-2.57	-1.23	-0.94
Socio-economic variables				
(13) Total employment	0.21	0.16	-0.07	0.10
(14) Av. real wage	0.31	0.63	-0.49	0.17
(15) Labor share	-0.23	0.05	-0.70	-0.10
(16) Income (YHQ1)/YHQ5	-0.11	-0.05	0.04	-0.05

Source: model computations.

Notes

Benchmark (BM) closure rule: quantity adjustment the labour market; fixed exchange rate regime; exogenous government expenditure and Keynesian closure rule for the saving–investment balance; Flex ER = flexible exchange rate; NCL CR = neoclassical closure rule saving–investment balance; $PWE_{PP(MR)}$ = export price primary products (resource-intensive products); inc. = increase; YHQ1(5): income quintile 1 (5).

The shock promotes employment growth and in an economy with unemployment levels lower than in previous periods and with active wage negotiations, real wages will (despite rising domestic prices) grow. This however, is not sufficient to improve income distribution, as the price shock increases incomes in the richest households more than in the poorest ones and reduces the wage share (see column (1), rows (13) to (16)).

The response to this positive external shock is not neutral to the macroeconomic regime. Instead of trying to promote a competitive exchange rate, Argentina's economic authorities could have opted to allow market forces to determine the adjustment in the external market. This has to some extent been done in other Latin American countries, for example in Chile, during the primary commodity shock prior to the international crisis.

Column (2) in Table 12.5 illustrates the effects of the positive primary commodity shock under a flexible exchange rate (Flex ER) regime. Although increases in primary commodity prices remain expansionary, the economy may experience additional changes worth discussing.

As expected, the shock promotes a stronger exchange rate and this has its positive and negative consequences. The good news is linked to the stability in domestic prices and the related improvements in real wages vis-à-vis the baseline and the adjustment to the shock in the context of a managed exchange rate regime (see Table 12.5, columns (1) and (2), rows (7) and (8)). The negative aspects of the alternative exchange rate regime comes from Dutch disease type adjustments, as the stronger exchange rate further reduces non-traditional exports.[24] Although (in spite of lower exports) production in these sectors expand, this may change in the medium term. As shown in Serino (2009a), increases in primary commodity prices over various periods of time, such as those between 2005 and 2008, can lead to an absolute decline in industrial production. This could even potentially make the positive shock contractionary, if the adjustment in external accounts is left to market forces (Berges and Casellas 2002). This may happen as a consequence of stronger exchange rates but also because productivity and non-price competitiveness tends to be procyclical in modern industrial sectors. Because, as mentioned in the previous section, attempting to foresee the evolution of exogenous variables beyond 2010 is neither advisable nor feasible, the analysis is based on static simulations and the abovementioned effects do not materialize.

Simulation results in column (2) also show that under a flexible exchange rate the primary commodity shock reduces the current account surplus. Although the exchange rate adjustment does not turn external accounts into a deficit that needs to be financed from abroad, the point is worth mentioning because, as happened in Argentina in the 1990s, strong exchange rates and positive foreign savings have not encouraged investment but rather led to unsustainable consumption booms. On the contrary, the competitive exchange rate regime in place between 2003 and 2008 – and to some extent preserved today – has promoted consumption, but also household and government savings, and these have been one of the pillars of the fast and steady expansion of investment and output in Argentina before the international crisis.

The negative association between investment and foreign savings observed in Argentina in the last 20 years goes against the propositions of neoclassical models. Whereas from a Keynesian perspective investment depends on profits, demand and financial costs, according to neoclassical approaches investment is a function of available finance. Running current account deficits to receive savings from abroad, as international financial institutions once and again advise developing countries, is therefore a key mechanism to promote investment and long term growth. By the same token, whatever improves external accounts will reduce investment. Hence, as shown in column (3), increases in primary commodity prices in simulations run using the neoclassical closure rule may reduce investment and be contractionary. As recent history has shown, reality may be rather different.

Turning back to the adjustment of Argentina's exporting sector, it is worth noting that Dutch disease adjustments may happen if the nominal exchange rate appreciates, but also if the *pass through* of international to domestic prices is large, a particular relevant issue in Argentina, a wage-goods exporting country. Export tax to natural resource exports may contribute to limit this adjustment. Column (4) in Table 12.5 shows the results from a simulation where the government raises export taxes 10 percent to cope with the primary commodity shock. The policy puts a wedge between international and domestic prices and limits domestic price increases, particularly of natural resource goods. In so doing, export taxes reduce the contraction in non-traditional exports (down by 0.9 percent instead of 2 percent in the alternative scenario without changes in export taxes) and diminish (but do not eliminate) the negative impact of the shock on income distribution.[25]

Argentina has reintroduced export taxes in 2002 and until 2007 has made discrete adjustments to adapt to changes in the international environment. However, since 2008, after the political crisis over the distribution of the gains of primary commodity shocks, there is no scope for adjustments in export taxes. This may not be problematic if prices remain high but expand slowly, as in the simulations, but may require rethinking the macroeconomic regime if for instance commodity prices expand at an annual rate of 20 percent (14 percent), as between 2005 (2003) and 2008 (see Table 12.2).

12.4.2 Positive external and internal shocks to Argentina's exporting sectors and government demand impulses

Since the end of 2009, the world economy has been showing signs of recovery and international organizations, with varying degrees of optimism, are forecasting that output will expand in most economies. Although countries from the North, with the exception of China, have done the largest effort in terms of expansionary fiscal and monetary policies, global recovery in 2010 will be guided by developing countries (see Table 12.2).

This recovery is beneficial for developing counties not only because it has contributed to the recovery of primary commodity prices, but also because is

Table 12.6 Positive exogenous and supply shocks and alternative demand impulses from the government (%)

	(1)	(2)	(3)	(4)	(5)	(6)	(7)	(8)
Macroeconomic variables								
(1) Real GDP	0.2	0.4	1.9	0.5	1.5	1.7	1.8	3.5
(2) Private investment	0.04	0.1	13.7	2.6	4.5	4.8	5.0	11.3
(3) Total consumption	0.2	0.4	3.0	0.7	1.8	2.9	2.1	3.9
(4) Total exports	0.6	1.1	-4.2	-0.4	1.6	-0.2	-0.7	-2.3
(5) Current account deficit (GDP)	-2.1	-2.1	-2.7	-2.2	-2.4	-1.8	-1.6	-0.6
(6) Government primary surplus (GDP)	2.9	3.0	5.0	3.3	3.6	2.7	2.7	4.2
(7) Consumer price index	0.3	0.6	14.7	2.8	4.8	6.6	8.1	9.0
(8) Domestic price (PP and MR)	0.1	0.2	13.7	2.5	3.0	3.7	3.8	4.5
Variables external sectors								
(9) Real exchange rate M-up sectors (MO + PS)	-0.30	-0.60	-10.80	-2.35	-3.87	-5.08	-5.89	-7.57
(10) Output M-up sectors (MO + PS)	0.45	0.89	4.52	1.18	1.62	2.11	2.22	6.04
(11) Exports PP and MR	-0.33	-0.65	-2.14	-0.66	3.12	1.05	0.81	-1.07
(12) Exports MO and PS	2.23	4.40	-7.96	0.16	-1.39	-2.61	-3.45	-4.74
Socio-economic variables								
(13) Total employment	0.09	0.18	1.22	0.30	0.75	0.89	0.97	2.01
(14) Av. real wage	0.27	0.54	1.68	0.57	1.67	1.83	1.82	5.00
(15) Labor share	0.14	0.27	-1.21	-0.10	0.17	0.17	0.06	2.19
(16) Income (YHQ1)/YHQ5	-0.05	-0.10	-0.57	-0.16	0.09	0.05	-0.01	-0.48

Source: model computations.

Simulations
(1) World output expands 2.7%, the growth projected for of Argentina's trading partners (industrial exports).
(2) World output expands 5.3%, the growth rate projected for Developing countries in 2010.
(3) External shocks prior to the international crisis: world output expands 3.2% and primary commodity prices growth at an annual average rate of 14%, figures observed in the period 2003–2007.
(4) External shocks after the international crisis: world output expands 2.7% and primary commodity prices 2.5%.
(5) Simulation (4) plus 5% increase in agriculture production in Argentina.
(6) Simulation (5) and endogenous government transfers to households.
(7) Simulation (5) and endogenous government consumption.
(8) Simulation (5) and endogenous public investment.

Note
All simulations run using the Benchmark (BM) closure rule: quantity adjustment the labour market; fixed exchange rate regime; exogenous government expenditure and Keynesian closure rule for the saving-investment balance; YHQ1(5): income quintile 1 (5).

bringing about world trade on the expansionary path. To analyze how this may affect output dynamics in Argentina, I simulate that world output expands by 2.7 percent, which is the weighted average growth rate predicted for the top ten countries importing industrial products from Argentina.[26] The shock is expansionary, mainly because it stimulates exports of non-traditional exports products. As shown in Table 12.6, industrial and service exports go up more than 2 percent vis-à-vis the baseline, but natural resource exports contract, as when the Argentine economy expands a larger fraction of wage-goods is devoted to the domestic market. The shock also increases employment, real wages and the wage share, but worsens income distribution (see column (1), rows (12) to (15)).[27]

Larger trade integration between Argentina and countries from the South,[28] other than Latin America ones,[29] as shown in Table 12.6 column (2), which simulates that global output expands 5 percent in 2010,[30] which is the growth rate predicted for developing countries, will further expand industrial exports and reinforce the process of export diversification that has been taking place in Argentina in the twenty-first century. This will certainly require active policies and efforts from the private sector, but need not be impossible as Argentina's industrial products are exported to the European and North American markets.

Although there is life after the Great Recession, impulses from the international economy will play a smaller role in determining the evolution of output than before the crisis. Columns (3) and (4) in Table 12.6 compare positive external shocks before and after the crisis. Column (3) summarizes the results from the simulations, assuming that world output increases by 3.2 percent and primary commodity prices rise by 14 percent, which are the average growth rates observed in Argentina's trading partners and primary commodity prices between 2003 and 2007. Column (4), on the other hand, illustrates the impact of the changes predicted for 2010 (world output growing by 2.7 percent, as in Argentina's trading partners, and commodity prices increasing by 2.5 percent).

As shown in Table 12.6, simulations of impulses as those observed before the international crisis promote expansions in real GDP, investment and consumption, as well as employment and real wages that are three times larger or more than impulses projected for 2010 (see Table 12.6, columns (3) and (4), rows (1), (2), (3), (13) and (14)). Certainly, there are differences between the two periods and other shocks may be necessary or expansionary fiscal policies may have to be designed to provide the missing demand.

After two years of stagnation for political and climatic reasons, traditional agricultural production will expand in Argentina in 2010 and therefore provide an additional expansionary impulse. Data in Table 12.6 column (5) show simulation results of a 5 percent increase of output in the primary sector. This positive supply shock in Argentina's natural resource sectors sponsors an expansion in all components of aggregate demand and may expand output one percentage point vis-à-vis the scenario of exogenous impulses but not from the domestic economy (see Table 12.6, columns (5), (1) and (4), rows (1) to (4)). The shock increases total exports due to larger sales of traditional products (up by 1.5 percent and 3 percent vis-à-vis the baseline correspondingly). However, industrial and other non-traditional exports contract in relation to the baseline and the 'post crisis' scenario due to the so-called Dutch disease spending effect.[31]

In addition, three alternative expansionary fiscal policies can be envisaged to provide demand impulses in the aftermath of the crisis: increases in government transfers to households, and larger government consumption or investment. To analyze how these policies can add to the previous impulses, I modify the closure rule governing public expenditure decisions. I assume in these three final simulations that the government's financial requirements are constant and that changes in government revenues are used alternatively to increase transfers, consumptions or investment.

All three policies are expansionary but financing public investment has the largest expansionary effect (see Table 12.6, columns (6) to (8), rows (1) and (2)). In the context of a crisis, however, the economy may need policies focused to vulnerable sectors rather than projects that take time to realize. The decision between implementing transfers to poor households and expanding government consumption (as for instance through an expansion of employment or increases in wages in the public sector) will be made depending on the objective of government authorities. If preferences are in favor of expanding aggregate demand with the lowest impact on domestic prices, transfers may be a better policy than government consumption.

12.5 Final thoughts

In 2008 and 2009 economists were busy comparing the adjustments in world trade and industrial productions with those in the 1930s. Due to large fiscal and monetary stimuli packages but also thanks to the consolidation of Asia as the new engine of global growth, the crisis has not turned into a depression. Although financial vulnerabilities and the risks of a downturn remain, the world economy has returned to an expansionary mode of development. Having learnt from previous crises, this time Argentina, like many other developing countries, has been less exposed to the up and downs of financial markets. The country today is therefore in a condition to benefit from the moderate recovery of global growth and trade that is projected for 2010.

This chapter has discussed how impulses from the international economies may affect the economic performance of Argentina in the aftermath of the crisis, in particular the recovery of primary commodity prices and output growth in Argentina's trading partners. The counterfactual simulations performed with the use of a structuralist GCE model have shown that these two positive external shocks will be expansionary. Impulses from the international economy, however, have also shown to be weaker than prior to the crisis. Argentina will therefore have to intensively promote trade with developing countries to preserve its process from previous years of export growth and diversification. It also would be wise to implement expansionary fiscal policies to provide the exogenous impulses that vanished with the crisis.

There is certainly life after the Great Recession. Yet, benefiting from greater integration with the world economy is very much related to the macroeconomic policies, and in particular the exchange rate regime. This concerns the Central Bank interventions and other policies like export taxes, (particularly in wage-goods exporting countries) and capital controls, a policy which today is recommended even by the IMF (Ostry *et al.* 2010). A competitive exchange rate regime is critical to prevent Dutch disease adjustments, associated with positive external shocks, and to promote an environment favorable to investment. The latter can be achieved through demand impulses, increases in the profitability of tradable production and higher domestic savings.

Appendix

Table 12.a.1 Parameter value of the CGE model: parameter values, stability ranges and sources

Behavioral parameters	PV	Range of PV a/		Source
		Max.	*Min.*	
Elasticity of transformation CET Fn. (c = PP and MR)	5.00	0.10	55	Guesstimate
Export equation (EE) price elasticity (c = MO and PS)	1.00	0.00	7.00	Guesstimate
EE income elasticity (c = MO and PS)	0.94	-5.00	5.00	Senhadji and Montenegro (1999)
Import equation (IM) price elasticity (c)	0.25	0.00	3.00	Guesstimate
IM income elasticity (c)	1.92	0.00	4.00	Catao and Falcetti (2002)
EE/IM elasticity to sector specific investment	0.025	0.00	1.00	Guesstimate
EE/IM elasticity infrastructure and productive linkages	0.025	0.00	3.00	Guesstimate
Labour saving technical change	0.025	0.00	1.50	Guesstimate
Kaldor–Verdoorn parameter 2004–2007 (2010)	0.5	0.00	1.50	Guesstimate
Intercept LES consumption Fn				Based on Berges and Casellas (2002)
Mg. propensity to consume LES Fn.				Based on Berges and Casellas (2002)
Wage equation (WE), productivity	0.50	-1.00	5.00	Based on Panigo et al. (2009)
WE, change in CPI	0.82	-0.75	2.00	Based on Panigo et al. (2009)
WE, change in unemployment	0.28	0.10	1.70	Based on Panigo et al. (2009)
WE, wage policy	1.00			

	PV		a	Source
Investment equation (IE), response to changes in capacity utilization	0.03	−2.00	2.00	Based on Panigo et al. (2009)
IE, changes in public investment	0.13	−0.50	0.85	Based on Panigo et al. (2009)
IE, changes in the sectoral profit rate	2.05	−0.70	3.25	Based on Panigo et al. (2009)
IE, changes in real interest rate	0.01	−2.00	1.25	Based on Panigo et al. (2009)
Labour supply adj. to wage differentials	0.05	0	2	Guesstimate
Mark-up elasticity to changes in total demand for MO (PS) commodities	0.1 (0.085)	0	3	Guesstimate
Exogenous variables				
Capacity output ratio (%)	74.83 (2008) 74.03 (2009)			INDEC
Base run unemployment rates (%)	8.77 (2009)			INDEC
Nominal interest rate (%)	16.44 (2009)			BCRA
Labor force growth (%)	1.92			INDEC
Depreciation rate (%)	8.8			MEFP

Notes
PV = Parameter value; MECON = Ministry of Economy and Production; adj. = adjustment.
INDEC = National Bureau of Statistics and Census; BCRA: Central Bank of the Argentine Republic.
a Range of parameters values giving a stable dynamic solution for the period 2004–2007.

Notes

1 A previous version of this chapter has been presented at the Fourth Annual Conference in Development and Change, which took place in Johannesburg, April 9–11, 2010. The chapter benefited from comments from the participants at the conference. Any possible error is however the author's responsibility.

2 Researcher, Institute of Sciences, University of General Sarmiento (UNGS), Argentina. J. M. Gutierrez 1150. Pcia de Bs. As. – Argentina. PC. 1613.

3 As a consequence of internal and internal factors exports have not contributed to output growth in 2008.

4 In spite of representing 20 percent of total output in the period 2003–2008, more than 40 percent of changes in real GDP are linked to investment growth.

5 Indeed, Argentina's industrial exports fell dramatically during the first two quarters of 2009 and only resumed growth in the fourth quarter.

6 The most important policies in this respect are the employment programme *REPRO*, through which the government subsidizes workers' training as a mechanism to prevent lay-offs, and the *Asignación Universal por Hijo* subsidy for children from households whose head is unemployed or an informal worker.

7 China is expected to grow close to 9 percent in 2010 and India 6.5 percent, according to UN WESP (2010).

8 The model has many points in common with the models developed in Gibson (2005), Gibson and van Seventer (2000b, 2000a) and Taylor (1990).

9 Primary and industrial products are classified using the CTP-DATA taxonomy proposed by Peirano and Porta (2000) and follows the taxonomy proposed by Pavitt (1984), adapted by Gurrieri (1989, 1992, quoted in Peirano and Porta 2000), and used in the SELA study (1994, quoted in Peirano and Porta 2000) to analyze the pattern of trade specialization in Latin American countries. The classification distinguishes products and sectors according to their main competitiveness factors (endowments, economies of scale, economies of specialization, technological intensity, etc.) and their reliance on price and non-price competitiveness advantages.

10 For different analytical specifications of Argentina's agricultural sector as the main exporting sector operating at full capacity, see papers by Diamand (1972), Canitrot (1975), Kostzer (1994). Nicolini-Llosa (2007b, 2007a), Porto (1975), Serino (2009a) and Visintini and Calvo (2000).

11 As discussed in Ros (2001) and Serino (2009a, chapter 3), Dutch disease adjustments to positive external shocks follow from the expansion of the consumer-oriented service sector but not necessarily from an expansion of sector PS, which can counteract such adjustments.

12 In equation (12.2) ψ_c^{cet} and ρ_c^{cet} respectively are the share and exponent parameter of the CET function.

13 The CGE model specification differs from the specification in Serino (2007). In that model sectors producing natural resource base products are indifferent as to the destination of production since they can charge the international price in the domestic market and export their surpluses. Modeling-wise this specification implies fixed price and quantity adjustments for the natural resource sectors. This specification, however, is not included in the CGE model since it would reduce its flexibility – with four out of five sectors adjusting through quantities to excess demand.

14 See, e.g., Dervis *et al.* (1982 : chapter 7).

15 Variable *IADJ* is included to allow for alternative saving–investment closure rules: it is endogenous under the neoclassical closure and exogenous with alternative closure rules.

16 Changes in government closure rule are also applicable to transfers to households and the rest of the world.

17 The labor supply grows according to an exogenous growth rate and responds to wage

differential among labor categories. Because labor categories differ in terms of the skills of the labour force, which are acquired through working experience or participation in the education system, the response to wage differentials is assumed to be slow.

18 See Robinson (1989) and Sánchez Cantillo (2004) for a comprehensive discussion of closure rules, and Taylor (1990) for an exposition of fix-flex closure rules.

19 Average and distribution parameters represent the largest group of parameters, and include household saving rates, household income and expenditure structure, input–output coefficients and tax rates, among others.

20 The reader is referred to Serino (2009b: chapter 6), for a comprehensive discussion of the calibration and validation of the CGE model used in this chapter.

21 Low parameter values are consistent with Catao and Falcetti's findings that capital accumulation influences exports in the long run but not in the short run. They also reflect Argentina's structurally high import dependency.

22 Parameter values employed to calibrate the wage and investment equations of the model do not necessarily coincide with estimations from Panigo *et al.* (2009), for these have been taken as a benchmark for the calibration.

23 This is in part because investment in Argentina in recent years has been very responsive to the profit rate (see Panigo *et al.* 2009).

24 Exports fall 25 percent more than under the alternative exchange rate regime.

25 As they take income out of the economy and limit price increases, export taxes reduce the expansionary effects of the primary shock. This additional characteristic of the adjustment has been particularly relevant in Argentina before the crisis, a period of strong demand impulses (see Serino 2009b). However, during the crisis or recovery period, export taxes may be used to underpin the recovery of aggregate demand.

26 The first top ten destinations received close to 80 percent of Argentina's industrial exports in 2008. In order of importance, the largest markets for Argentine products are: Brazil, USA, Chile, Uruguay, Mexico, Venezuela, Switzerland, Bolivia, Peru and the Netherlands.

27 This is because the shock impacts on sectors where skilled and formal employment predominates, which tend to belong to the richest household groups.

28 Murshed, Goulart and Serino (Chapter 1), this volume, review the process of integration among developing countries that have taken place in recent years.

29 Latin American countries represent approximately 70 percent of Argentina's industrial exports and these countries have been a very active source of external demand in the years before the crisis.

30 This is certainly an over-optimistic figure but is useful to show the benefits of integrating with countries from regions that will be growing faster than Argentina's main trading partners in the coming years. According to UN WESP, Africa is expected to grow 4.3 percent and East Asia (excluding China) 3.8 percent in 2010.

31 The positive shock encourages household consumption and this leads to higher prices of non-tradable goods (the CPI expands 60 percent more than prices of traditional tradable goods) which limit the price competitiveness of non-traditional exports vis-à-vis the baseline and simulations of positive external shocks but no supply shock (see Table 12.6, columns (4) and (5)).

References

Berges, M. and K. Casellas (2002) 'A Demand System Analysis of Food for Poor and Non-Poor Households. The Case of Argentina', доклад на 10 конгрессе; EAAE, Exploring Diversity in the European Agri-Food System (August 28–31, 2002), Zaragoza (Spain).

290   *L.A. Serino*

Blankenburg, S. and J.G. Palma (2009) 'Introduction: the global financial crisis', *Cambridge Journal of Economics*, 33: 531–38.

Borio, C. (2009) 'The financial crisis of 2007–?: macroeconomic origins and policy lessons', Mumbai, India: G20 Workshop on the Global Economy.

Brahmbhatt, M. and O. Canuto (2010) 'Natural Resources and Development Strategy After the Crisis'. Online, available at: www.voxeu.org/index.php?q=node/4696 (accessed March 2011).

Canitrot, A. (1975) 'La Experiencia Populista de Distribución de Ingresos', *Revista Desarrollo Económico*, 15.

Catao, L. and E. Falcetti (2002) 'Determinants of Argentina's external trade', *Journal of Applied Economics*, 5: 19–57.

Dervis, K., J. de Melo and S. Robinson (1982) *General Equilibrium Models for Development Policy*, New York: Cambridge University Press.

Diamand, M. (1972) 'La Estructura Económica Desequilibrada Argentina y el Tipo de Cambio', *Revista Desarrollo Económico*, 45.

Eichengreen, B. and K.H. O'Rourke (2009) 'A Tale of Two Depressions'. Online, available at: www.voxeu.org/index.php?q=node/3421 (accessed March 8, 2010).

Gibson, W. (2005) 'The transition to a globalized economy: poverty, human capital and the informal sector in a structuralist CGE model', *Journal of Development Economics*, 78: 60–94.

Gibson, W. and D. van Seventer (2000a) 'Real wages, employment and macroeconomic policy in a structuralist model for South Africa', *Journal of African Economies*, 9: 512–46.

Gibson, W. and D. van Seventer (2000b) 'A tale of two models: comparing structuralist and neoclassical computable general equilibrium models for South Africa', *International Review of Applied Economics*, 14: 149–71.

Kostzer, D. (1994) *A Model of the Argentine Economy*, Buenos Aires: Mimeo.

Leon-Ledesma, M. (2002) 'Accumulation, innovation and catching-up: an extended cumulative growth model', *Cambridge Journal of Economics*, 26: 201–16.

Nicolini-Llosa, J.L. (2007a) 'Essays on Argentina's Growth Cycle and the World Economy', Amsterdam: University of Amsterdam.

Nicolini-Llosa, J.L. (2007b) 'Tipo de Cambio Dual y Crecimiento Cíclico en Argentina', *Desarrollo Económico: Revista De Ciencias Sociales*, 47: 249–83.

Ostry, J.A., K.H. Ghosh, M. Chamon, M. Quereshi and D. Reinhardt (2010) 'Capital Inflows: The Role of Controls', IMF Staff Position Note SPN 10/04, IMF.

Panigo, D., F. Toledo, D. Herrero, E. López and H. Montagu (2009) *Modelo Macroeconométrico Estructural para Argentina*, Buenos Aires: S.d.P. Económica.

Pavitt, K. (1984) 'Sectoral Patterns of Technical Change: Towards a Taxonomy and Theory', *Research Policy*, 13: 343–73.

Peirano, F. and F. Porta (2000) 'El Impacto de las Preferencias Comerciales sobre el Comercio Intraregional. Análisis del Mercosur y los Acuerdos Bilaterales de Chile', REDES, 18.

Porto, A. (1975) 'Un Modelo Simple sobre el Comportamiento Macroeconómico Argentino en el Corto Plazo', *Desarrollo Económico*, 59.

Robinson, S. (1989) 'Multisectoral models', (Chapter 18) in H. Chenery and T. Srinivasan (eds) *Handbook of Development Economics Volume II*, Amsterdam: North Holland.

Ros, J. (2001) 'Política Industrial, Ventajas Comparativas y Crecimiento', Revista de la CEPAL 73, Washington, DC: CEPAL.

Sánchez Cantillo, M.V. (2004) 'Rising Inequality and Falling Poverty in Costa Rica's Agriculture during Trade Reform', PhD Thesis,The Hague: ISS.

Senhadji, A. and C. Montenegro (1999) 'Time Series Analysis of Export Demand Equations: A Cross-country Analysis', IMF Staff Papers 46, Washington, DC, IMF.

Serino, L. (2007) 'Diversificación productiva en países que producen bienes salario: el caso de Argentina', Documento de Trabajo de la Secretaría de Política Económica del Ministerio de Economía y Finanzas Públicas de la República Argentina.

Serino, L. (2009a) 'Positive Natural Resource Shocks and Domestic Adjustments in a Semi-industrialized Economy: Argentina in the 2003–2007 Period', ISS Working Paper Series 484, The Hague: ISS. Online, available at: http://biblio.iss.nl/opac/uploads/wp/wp484.pdf (accessed March 2011).

Serino, L. (2009b) 'Productive Diversification in Natural Resource Abundant Countries: Limitations, Policies and the Experience of Argentina in the 2000s', PhD Thesis, The Hague: ISS.

Serino, L. and E. Kiper (2009) 'El trasfondo macroeconómico de la crisis internacional', Paper presented at 1st Annual Conference AEDA (Asociación de economía para el desarrollo de Argentina), Argentina.

Tavosnanska, A. and G. Herrera (2010) 'La industria Argentina a comienzos del siglo XXI: Aportes para una revisión de la experiencia reciente', in A. Müller (ed.) *Industria, Desarrollo, Historia: Ensayos en homenaje a Jorge Schvarzer, CESPA*, Buenos Aires: CESPA.

Taylor, L. (1990) 'Structuralist CGE models', in L. Taylor (ed.) *Social Relevant Policy Analysis*, Cambridge: MIT Press.

United Nations (2010) 'World Economic Situation and Prospects, 2010 (WESP)', New York: United Nations, DESA.

Visintini, A. and S. Calvo (2000) 'Macroeconomía y Agricultura: una Propuesta Metodológica para su Análisis', Anales de la AAEP.

Vos, R. (2007) 'What We Do and Don't Know about Trade Liberalization and Poverty Reduction', DESA Working Paper 50; ST/ESA/2007/DWP, DESA.

13 The macroeconomics of remittances

The case of the Philippines

Veronica Bayangos and Karel Jansen[1]

13.1 Introduction

Workers' remittances are an important financial flow to developing countries and in recent years there has been an increased interest in their economic impact.[2] It is recognized that remittances are important for a number of reasons.

First of all, at the aggregate global level, workers' remittances have become a sizeable financial flow. Recorded remittances have been increasing rapidly from US$31 billion in 1990 to US$167 billion in 2005 (World Bank 2006: 88). The World Bank's *Global Development Finance 2009* reports estimates for 2008: workers' remittances at US$305 billion, against US$583 billion for FDI, US$16 billion for net portfolio investment flows, US$20 billion for net official flows and US$108 billion for net private debt flows. In terms of size, remittances are second to FDI only and more important than other financial flows to developing countries.[3] It is thus not surprising that remittances have been the subject of intensive research. Studies have focused on determinants of remittances and on their impact on economic growth and poverty alleviation. In this chapter we focus on the short-run macroeconomic effects of remittances: we are mainly interested in the cyclical dynamics of remittances and the challenges this creates for short-term macroeconomic management.

A second aspect that is emphasized is that remittances are more stable than other financial flows. The current financial crisis originated in the advanced countries but developing countries are feeling the impact strongly. Exports are falling and capital inflows are projected to drop sharply. Many developing countries are now placing their hope on workers' remittances which are presumed to be a more stable financial flow. Studies have shown that the volatility of remittances is less than that of most other financial flows to developing countries. Even so, remittances cannot escape the impact of the global financial crisis: the World Bank's Global Economic Prospects 2009 observes that while remittances accounted for 2 percent of recipient country GDP in 2007, this fell to 1.8 percent in 2008 and is projected to decline further to 1.6 percent in 2009 (World Bank 2009: 16 and 38). Even in more normal times remittances do fluctuate from year to year and, for countries where remittances are a large share of GNP, such fluctuations may well be of macroeconomic significance and a matter of concern to policy makers.

The aggregate data on global remittances flows hide large differences between countries; remittances are rather concentrated. The amount of remittances received by the top 20 remittances receiving developing countries accounts for about 60 percent of all remittances going to developing countries.[4] Expressed as percentage of GDP, for the top 20 remittances receiving developing countries, remittances account for more than 10 percent of GDP (for the total group of developing countries remittances are equal to about 2 percent of GDP).

For countries where remittances are an important financial flow the fluctuations in remittances will pose macroeconomic problems. Just like most developing countries have to adjust to reduced capital flows after the global financial crisis, remittances receiving countries will have to adjust to reduced inflows. In this chapter we are particularly interested in the impact of fluctuations in remittances flows on financial markets and on macroeconomic variables and the challenges this sets for macroeconomic policy, in particular for monetary policy.

Fluctuations in remittances have direct and indirect effects on variables that the monetary authorities target, such as aggregate demand (and thus the output gap), inflation and the exchange rate. Shocks to remittances also have an impact on the domestic interest rate, thus affecting the instrument the monetary authorities is targeting. When remittances are substantial and fluctuations in remittances significant, such impacts will affect the conduct and the effectiveness of monetary policy.

Globalization exposes developing countries to the volatility of international markets. In the literature on financial globalization there is considerable attention for the volatility of capital flows (e.g., Prasad *et al.* 2003). The surges of inflows and flight of capital have severe effects on the economy. In many developing countries remittances are a financial flow that is as important, and in some cases more important, as capital flows. It is often noted that remittances are more stable than capital flows to developing countries but even so also remittances are subject to shocks. The ups and downs of capital flows and remittances have direct effects on aggregate demand, on the liquidity of financial markets, on foreign exchange markets, etc. In other words, the volatility of financial flows creates significant challenges for monetary policy makers.

Some studies suggest that remittances are counter-cyclical; increasing during hard times at home and thus providing an automatic stabilizer that reduces the need for monetary policy action. Other studies, however, suggest a more pro-cyclical pattern. In this chapter we will make two contributions to these discussions, using the experience of the Philippines. First, we will explore statistically the cyclical dynamics of remittances to the Philippines and, second, and more importantly, we will analyze the macroeconomic impact of remittances and the monetary policy implications. Remittances are a crucial financial flow to the Philippines: in recent years annual inflows amounted to 10 percent of GDP.

We will use a correlation analysis and Granger causality tests to assess the cyclical dynamics of remittance flows to the Philippines. We find that remittances are strongly pro-cyclical with economic activity in major host countries, such as the USA. Remittances are also pro-cyclical with Philippine real GDP. In the second endeavor we analyze monetary policy behavior in a quarterly structural macroeconometric model for the Philippines (see Bayangos 2007). To a large extent, our macro model shares features with that of the New Keynesian model (see Ball 1999) that assumes inflation and output to be backward-looking. We have also assumed that there is excess capacity in the economy and the asset markets are imperfect. Central to our macro model are important nominal rigidities in describing the Philippine macroeconomy. In addition, there are lags in the transmission mechanism.

In the benchmark version of the model, remittances are exogenous and do not affect monetary policy. In a new version of the model, developed for this chapter, we have made remittances endogenous. Shocks to remittances arise from the business cycle in the main host countries (the USA) and these shocks have an impact on disposable income, personal consumption, money supply, the domestic market interest rate and the labor force. We simulate the impact of a shock to US GDP on the Philippine economy in the two versions of the model. Our results show that the impact is very different when remittances are included in the model and that the appropriate monetary policy response is significantly different.

The chapter is organized as follows. The next section goes over the relevant literature on remittances and discusses their determinants and impacts. Section 13.3 provides some basic information on remittances with regards to the Philippines. Section 13.4 estimates the cyclicality of remittances and the subsequent sections introduce the model and the model simulations. The final section concludes.

13.2 Background

In the literature on financial globalization the volatility of capital flows has been approached using the dichotomy of 'push' and 'pull' (e.g., Taylor and Sarno 1997). The pull factors are country-specific indicators that pull capital to the country. They include the expected return on assets in the country and the country risk, reflected in indicators like the growth rate, inflation, current account, external debt and international reserves. The push factors reflect conditions in the major source countries (OECD), such as interest rates and the output gap. When these are not favorable, capital will flow out of OECD in search for higher returns elsewhere.[5]

Empirical work suggests that both push and pull factors are important in explaining capital movements. Push factors may be most important in explaining the total level of capital flows to developing countries, while pull factors determine their distribution over individual countries (see, e.g., Taylor and Sarno 1997; Hernandez *et al.* 2001; Mody and Taylor 2004).

The push and pull approach raises the issue of the interaction between capital flows and business cycles. The push factors suggest a relationship between capital flows to developing countries and the business cycle in the OECD. The pull factors suggest a relationship between capital inflows and the business cycle in developing countries. Kaminsky *et al.* (2004) formulate the following stylized facts from an analysis of data of a large sample of developed and developing countries:[6] (1) net capital flows are pro-cyclical in developing countries; (2) fiscal policy tends to be pro-cyclical and monetary policy is pro-cyclical in most developing countries; and (3) in developing countries the capital flow cycle and the macroeconomic policy cycle re-enforce each other.

Where the literature on capital movements has its push and pull factors to explain the flows, the literature on remittances has its own dichotomy: remittances are driven by altruistic or investment motives (see, e.g., Buch *et al.* 2002; Bouhga-Hagbe 2004; Alleyne *et al.* 2008). The first sees remittances as a form of altruism on the part of relatives overseas, who care for the family back home. The investment motive states that the overseas worker will have a tendency to invest her/his savings in the home country. But behind this simple dichotomy there lies a more complex set of factors.

It may be pure altruism when the overseas worker has the family welfare in her/his utility function and supports the family, certainly during hard times at home. But such support may also be driven by self-interest. If the worker expects to return home at some stage she needs to maintain the home base or her transfers may ensure her share in the family wealth. Migration may also be analyzed as a household strategy to manage risk. Sending one family member abroad diversifies the income sources and reduces risk. Such an insurance motive would be stronger when credit markets are imperfect and cannot be used to compensate shocks. Remittances can also be seen as a repayment. The family has invested in the education of the migrant worker and may have financed travel cost and other costs related to her moving abroad. The remittances are in such a case considered to be the repayment on this investment.

The investment motive is similarly complex. If the migrant worker expects that her time abroad will be limited and that she eventually will return home, she will have an incentive to invest her savings in her home country. Even if she expects to stay abroad for longer she may have good information about investment opportunities at home and networks to exploit these opportunities. But there is reason to be sceptical about the investment motive, for if the investment opportunities in the home country would be so good there would be little reason to migrate.

One oft-cited advantage of remittances is that they are not so volatile. The IMF (2005a) uses data for a large group of developing countries over the period 1980–2003 to establish that the volatility of remittances (measured by the standard deviation of its ratio to GDP) is smaller than that of aid, FDI, private capital flows and exports. Buch *et al.* (2002) analyzed the volatility of remittances and found that in 107 out of 135 countries the volatility of remittances is smaller than that of private capital flows, in 70 countries lower than that of official capital flows and in 62 countries remittances are less volatile than both private and official flows. Lueth and Ruiz-Arranz (2007) observe that remittance receipts in Sri Lanka are less volatile than ODA, FDI and portfolio flows.

Still, when remittances are a significant share of GDP, even modest volatility can result in fluctuations in the inflows that are of macroeconomic significance. Economic policy makers will be concerned about such fluctuations and will need to understand the determinants of the patterns in the flows. The main motives for sending remittances suggest possible cyclical patterns. Three scenarios could be suggested.

In the first scenario conditions in the host country determine remittance flows. When the host economy is booming employment opportunities abound and wages are good so that migrant incomes rise and they can send more to the family back home. In this scenario remittances are driven by the business cycle of the host country and are not associated with the cycle of the home country (a-cyclical). It is possible that remittances are one of the channels through which the business cycle of the home country becomes correlated with the cycle of the host country. If such a co-movement occurs the remittance flows will appear pro-cyclical.

In the second scenario the migrant worker has a clear idea about how much money she wants to transfer home over the longer term, but she will adjust the installments on the basis of the conditions in her home country. When economic times at home are hard, she will send some more and then compensate for when times are better. In this scenario remittances will be clearly counter-cyclical and perform a welcome stabilization function.

In the final scenario the migrant worker acts as an investor. She has gone abroad to build up lifetime assets and is looking for the best opportunities to invest her savings. Given her knowledge of, and contacts in, her home country and her desire to eventually return there, she will be quite interested in good investment opportunities at home. This behavior may lead to a pro-cyclical pattern in remittances as investment opportunities at home are better when the economy is booming. However, in this case the investment behavior could be more complex. The portfolio of the overseas investor is likely to contain financial and non-financial assets of the home and of the host country. Portfolio theory tells us that the investor will always hold a diversified portfolio and that adjustments to the portfolio follow changes in relative returns on assets. If the boom in the home country is accompanied by a recession in the host country, the investor will shift to home assets but, if the business cycles of home and host country are synchronized, a boom will lead to no adjustment in the portfolio.

This interaction becomes even more complex through the increasing synchronization of business cycles around the world. There is some evidence that the growing intensity of trade and financial integration, which are part of the rapid globalization of the last two decades, have led to an increased co-movement of business cycles amongst OECD countries and between the OECD countries and the main emerging market economies (see Kose *et al.* 2003; Imbs 2004; Kose *et al.* 2005; Imbs 2006).

The literature on the cyclicality of remittances is inconclusive. Is there a correlation between cyclical fluctuations of GDP and remittances? Many argue that remittances are counter-cyclical, as more money is sent home during hard times but this is not the general case. Loser *et al.* (2006) see a counter-cyclical pattern in the remittances flows to seven Latin American countries that they studied and they quote a number of other studies that come to the same conclusion. Sayan (2006) studied 12 developing countries in which remittances are significant and finds that only four show a statistically significant cyclical pattern: in two countries remittances are counter-cyclical and in two they are pro-cyclical. Lueth and Ruiz-Arranz (2007) show that remittances in Sri Lanka are strongly pro-cyclical. The case of Mexico is researched by Vargas-Silva (2008) who finds that remittances are counter-cyclical with respect to the country's business cycle. This result is, however, not robust enough to the use of different measures of remittances. Giuliano and Ruiz-Arranz (2005) correlate the cyclical components of remittances and GDP for a sample of about 100 developing countries over the period 1975–2002 and find in about two-thirds of the cases a positive correlation (i.e., remittances are pro-cyclical).

Dean Yang has done a number of interesting studies on remittances in the Philippines. He starts by observing that the correlation between (the cyclical components of) GDP and remittances do not say much about causality, as there are various possible interactions. Remittances may be invested by the receiving household and lead to income growth. But remittances may also induce households to reduce their work effort and thus reduce income. And remittances may respond to income shocks that hit the household. To deal with this problem, Dean tries to identify exogenous shocks and then trace their impact on remittances. In one paper (Yang and Choi 2007) regional variations in rainfall are used to instrument for changes in household income. In households that have a migrant working abroad there is a significant negative relationship: when the household is hit by a negative income shock, remittances increase. In households without migrants no such a relationship between income shocks and remittances can be observed.

In another study (Yang 2008) on the Philippines the shock is the sudden change in exchange rates during the Asian crisis. At that time the peso depreciated strongly with respect to the currency of main migrants' host countries (such as Middle East, USA) while at the same time households in the Philippines were suffering from the negative impact of the crisis. Comparing household surveys of June 2007 and October 2008, the study observes that a 10 percent depreciation of the peso was followed by a 6 percent increase in peso remittances.[7]

Both these studies are consistent with the altruistic or insurance approach to remittances. The migrant's utility function includes the welfare of the family back home and she decides on the level of remittances in view of the shocks that occurred. These microeconomic studies would thus suggest a counter-cyclical pattern of remittances. This is in sharp contrast with the conclusions of studies that use a macroeconomic approach to analyze the cyclicality of remittance flows to the Philippines. From a panel of 113 countries for the period 1970–1999, Chami *et al.* (2003, 2006) showed that in the case of the Philippines remittances are not profit-driven, but are compensatory in nature, and, hence, have a strong negative correlation with growth. Chami *et al.* (ibid.) argue that remittances do not appear to be intended to serve as capital for the economic development, but as compensation to poor economic performance. However, a study at the central bank (Bangko Sentral ng Pilipinas, BSP) re-estimated the same equation and revealed that such relationship fades away when the appropriate correction is made for serial correlation (Dakila and Claveria 2007). Tuaño-Amador *et al.* (2007) conducted a simple correlation test between (detrended) GDP and remittances and conclude to pro-cyclicality. Dakila and Claveria (2007) come to the same conclusion using VAR analysis. On the other hand, Burgess and Haksar (2005) find that the correlation between the growth of GDP and remittances is very low and not significant and their VAR analysis does not find an impact of GDP shocks on remittances. Our own analysis, using an economy-wide macro-econometric model of the Philippines, reveals that overseas Filipino remittances are pro-cyclical not only with the Philippine output but with those of major host countries, including the US.

In an economy where remittances are important, shifts in the remittances flows will have short-term macroeconomic effects to which policy makers may need to respond. An increase in remittances will have direct effects on aggregate demand as the purchasing power of remittance receiving households rise. Most studies (see, e.g., Chami *et al.* 2003) find that the majority of remittances are consumed and that the small part that is saved is not invested very productively (e.g., in real estate).[8] Part of this will be spent on traded goods: imports will rise and exports may fall so that the trade balance deteriorates. The direct effect on the current account will however, be positive as part of the increased remittances will be spent on non-traded goods. This increased demand for non-traded goods will push up their prices. These direct demand effects will be re-enforced by the multiplier effect.

The increase in the price of non-traded goods will increase the domestic cost of production. The inflow of remittances on the foreign exchange market may also lead to an appreciation of the exchange rate, the so-called Dutch disease effect. Both these effects will hurt the competitiveness of exporters. If these effects are strong, together with the demand effects on the trade balance, the total impact may well be that the current account deteriorates. Many studies have confirmed this effect (see, e.g., Amuedo-Dorantes and Pozo 2004; Loser *et al.* 2006). Tuaño-Amador *et al.* (2007) found some evidence for the Dutch disease effect.

The higher remittances flows will increase liquidity in financial markets, which may push down the interest rate and lead to an expansion of credit. The lower interest rate may invite an increase in expenditure. Increased investment of remittances in real estate or the stock market can push up asset prices, which may exert a wealth effect.

The total demand impact of an increase in remittances is the sum of these various effects: the direct expenditure effect, the multiplier effect and the interest rate effect will have a positive impact, while the exchange rate appreciation could have a negative impact.

There could also be a supply effect. Some have argued that an increase in remittance income will induce the household to supply less labor or to reduce work effort (Chami *et al.* 2003). Yang (2008) finds that the increase in remittances to the Philippines during the Asian crisis had no significant effect on the total number of hours worked.[9] Potentially, the labor supply effects in the Philippines could be strong. The number of overseas Filipinos is above eight million and this number has increased significantly in recent years. This is equivalent to more than 20 percent of the Philippine labor force. It could be expected that the withdrawal of such a large group from the labor market would have an effect on wages and that it would have a negative impact on production (this effect is similar to the Dutch disease effect but now working through the labor market rather than through exchange rates). This may be particularly the case if, as seems to be the case in recent years, migration concentrates on skilled workers. If, on top of that, the receipt of remittances would induce households to reduce work efforts, the impact could be even more severe.

The net effect of all these effects on the output gap is an empirical matter. If the positive demand effects dominate the negative exchange rate and labor supply effects, the output gap will narrow.

The increase in remittances will also have an effect on inflation. The demand pressures generated by the higher expenditure will push up prices and the adverse labor supply effect may help raise wages, while the exchange rate appreciation will reduce the domestic prices of imported goods. If the demand pressures dominate, inflation will increase.

In the impact assessment it is also relevant to take into account any second round effects. Studies into the determinants of remittances have established that changes in the exchange rate, the interest rate, inflation, home income may influence the decision to remit funds. The empirical evidence on these relationships is often mixed. For instance, Alleyne *et al.* (2008) find a positive impact of the interest differential (domestic minus foreign interest rate), but Bouhga-Hagbe (2004) finds a negative relationship.

When we assume a monetary authority that follows a Taylor rule, we would expect monetary policy to respond to these changes. If indeed the output gap tightens and inflation rises, the policy rate should be increased. And if the whole process of adjustment would indeed lead to a deterioration of the current account balance, the need for a tighter monetary policy would further increase. It is possible that the monetary authority is also concerned about the exchange rate and would be worried that the appreciation of the exchange rate would undermine the competitiveness of the export sector. Such a concern could reduce the willingness to increase interest rates.

In deciding on the appropriate monetary policy response, the cyclicality of the remittances is crucial. If remittances are pro-cyclical, the above policy conclusions apply. The booming economy itself would already require cautious monetary policy and the increase in the remittances would have impacts on the output gap and inflation that would strengthen that need. It should be noted at the same time that the increase in remittances will make the monetary policy less effective. As noted above, the increase in remittance inflows increase liquidity on financial markets and put a downwards pressure on the interest rate and monetary policy action will have to be strong to counter these impacts. At the same time, monetary policy can easily become perverse: if the central bank tries to cool down the booming economy and the spurt in remittances through an increase in the interest rate, the growing interest rate differential may invite even more remittances or private capital flows.

If remittances are counter-cyclical the policy response will be different. When a domestic recession is compensated by an increase in remittances, the increase in expenditure is welcome as they compensate the decline in domestic demand and therefore monetary policy can be less active than would have been desirable in the absence of the remittances. Under these conditions the inflationary effects of the increase in remittances is also likely to be less strong.

We noted above that globalization has increased the co-movement of business cycles (Kose *et al.* 2003, 2005; Imbs 2006). When the business cycles of the home and source country are synchronous a recession would reduce earnings in the source country and thus make it more difficult to send money home, while at the same time hard times at home would increase the need for compensating inflows. While during a boom it could be easier to send money, the need to do so would be less, although the investment motive will be stronger.

13.3 Recent trends in migration and remittance flows in the Philippines

The remittances in this chapter cover transfers sent both by Filipino migrants and overseas workers. In the Philippines, remittances data are sourced from the balance of payments statistics. Overseas Filipino (OF) remittances surged particularly in the 1990s.

Figure 13.1 shows the rapid growth of remittances since 1981 and Table 13.1 relates remittances to some other economic variables to show their relative importance. As of end-December 2007, remittances reached US$14.5 billion, the highest level since the 1980s. The latest available data for 2008 (January to October) show the OF remittances at US$13.7 billion.

In 1996, remittances accounted for only 5.2 percent of GDP. This has risen to around 10 percent in recent years. Remittances are equivalent to 28 percent of exports of goods and services and exceed FDI inflows. They are also much larger than external debt service payments.

Tuaño-Amador *et al.* (2007) presented three major factors behind the uptrend in OF remittances since 1996. First, that there is a trend rise in the number of deployed workers, as indicated by the stock of overseas Filipino workers and migrants.

Second, there has been a change in the skill composition of Filipino workers and migrants. From 1995 to 2007, there was a significant rise in the number of deployed Filipino workers in the services and professional categories. In fact in 2007, the number of higher-paid and skilled workers, such as those working in the medical, health-care, information technology, food and hotel services continued to rise, despite the decline in the number of professional workers.

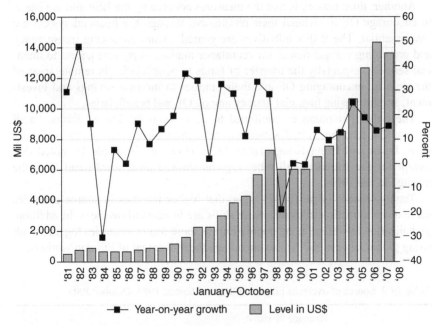

Figure 13.1 OF remittances, 1981–2008.

Table 13.1 Relative size of overseas Filipino (OF) remittances: level, growth rate and as a percentage of selected economic indicators[1]

Year	Level (US$B)	Growth rate (%)	As % of				
			GDP	XGS	FDI	GIR	DSB
1996	4.3	11.3	5.2	28.9	118.9	36.6	85.7
1997	5.7	33.3	7.0	36.9	681.1	65.3	102.6
1998	7.4	28.3	11.3	35.7	365.5	68.0	144.6
1999	6.0	−18.3	8.9	20.8	544.9	40.0	91.5
2000	6.1	0.5	8.0	17.1	270.1	40.2	96.6
2001	6.0	−0.3	7.9	20.8	3,092.8	38.4	92.4
2002	6.9	14.2	8.4	21.3	446.6	42.1	88.7
2003	7.6	10.1	8.9	22.7	1,543.4	42.4	95.4
2004	8.6	12.8	9.1	23.1	1,242.7	52.7	118.5
2005	10.7	25.0	10.0	27.5	576.5	57.8	140.2
2006	12.8	19.4	10.0	27.3	436.9	55.6	161.5
2007	14.5	15.3	9.2	28.7	493.5	30.6	204.8

Source of data: Department of Economic Statistics, Bangko Sentral ng Pilipinas.

Notes
1 Refers to cash remittances passing through the banking system.
GDP = gross domestic product.
XGS = exports of goods and services.
FDI = foreign direct investment.
GIR = gross international reserves.
DSB = debt service burden.

Another, third reason, is that the measures adopted by the BSP and the banks to encourage OF to channel their remittances through the financial system are also essential. The BSP's initiatives are geared toward enhancing transparency and promoting competition in the remittance market; improving access to financial services, especially the transfer of funds to beneficiaries in remote areas of the country; encouraging OF and their families to increase savings and investment; and increasing financial literacy among OF and beneficiaries.

The bulk of remittances continued to come from the United States, Saudi Arabia, Canada, the United Kingdom, Italy, the United Arab Emirates, Singapore, Japan and Hong Kong (Table 13.2). However, it should be noted that except for the Americas, all other regions showed an upward trend from the average in the 1990s.

Tuaño-Amador *et al.* (2007) argue that higher incomes in source countries serve as an attraction to those whose skills are in demand overseas. In addition, globalization as well as aging populations in some source countries together with rising global labor mobility also encourage the movement of Filipino workers.

Table 13.2 Source of overseas Filipino (OF) remittances, 1985–October 2008

| Region/country | Average % share | | | January–October | |
	1985–1989	1990–1999	2000–2007	2007	2008
Total*	100.0	100.0	100.0	100.0	100.0
Asia	5.4	8.6	12.9	11.1	10.9
Japan	2.7	2.9	4.7	3.3	3.0
Hong Kong	1.2	3.3	3.2	2.5	2.6
Singapore	1.1	1.6	2.3	3.1	2.7
Americas	41.8	69.1	58.0	56.1	55.1
USA	41.5	68.7	55.7	48.1	50.8
Canada	0.3	0.3	55.7	48.1	50.8
Oceania	0.8	0.3	1.7	7.5	3.8
Australia	0.8	0.9	0.4	0.8	0.6
Europe	5.2	7.7	12.9	16.5	16.9
Italy	0.1	1.1	3.9	4.3	4.4
Germany	0.9	2.2	1.1	1.9	1.6
United Kingdom	1.6	2.6	3.2	4.8	4.9
Middle East	32.5	4.2	14.1	15.4	16.1
Kuwait	1.0	0.5	0.9	0.8	1.3
Saudi Arabia	30.5	3.5	9.9	8.5	8.3
UAE	0.0	0.1	2.2	3.9	4.0
Africa	0.0	0.0	0.1	0.1	0.1
Others	14.3	9.5	1.5	0.0	0.0

Source of data: Department of Economic Statistics, Bangko Sentral ng Pilipinas.

Note
* Breakdown may not add up to totals due to rounding off.

An Asian Development Bank (ADB) (2004) study provided some information based on survey data on the potential source of remittances for capital formation and development. The study specifically addressed the issue on how remittances can be channeled to strategic areas and sectors of the economy. Among the constraints reported by the survey included the difficulty experienced by OF in accessing remittance services of the host country (or source country). However, the gap was addressed by Philippine banks, courier services and informal channels of transmission. The ADB (2004) also revealed that 80 percent of respondents regularly remit through banks and other regulated channels. However, out of this group of respondents, 90 percent were able to save some money, but only 45 percent had a savings account.

Table 13.1 has shown the growth and the relative importance of remittances in the Philippine economy. Table 13.3 uses these data to calculate the volatility of remittances relative to the volatility of other foreign exchange inflows.

The volatility, as measured by the coefficient of variation, is indeed lower for remittances than for the various types of capital flows but a bit higher than the volatility of export earnings.

The studies so far of the impact of remittances on the economy have relied either on partial equilibrium analysis based on econometric estimation, or survey approaches. The study of Goce-Dakila and Dakila (2006) utilized an economy-wide (general equilibrium) approach that allows for interactions between all major sectors in the economy. The empirical results of the study reveal that the main beneficiary (measured in peso terms) of remittance increases are the middle-income classes, across all regions. The second best beneficiaries are the low-income households, again for all regions, with the notable exception of the National Capital Region and Mindanao, where the high-income households are the second highest beneficiaries of remittances.

13.4 Estimating the cyclicality of remittances

Economies indeed undergo significant cyclical variations of distinct pattern and origin with differences in depth and length. In duration, a cycle varies from more than one year to 12 years, and comprises a boom (or expansionary phase) and a recession (or contractionary phase). In order to estimate the cyclical fluctuation of a macroeconomic series it is common to use a filter to decompose the series into a slow moving component (or trend) and a cyclical component.

Several key issues surround the use of the appropriate technique to estimate the cyclical component of a macroeconomic series. Yap (2003) expounds the several research strategies that have been employed for the potential output estimations in the Philippines. A common weakness runs across these; that is, the estimates are largely dependent on the sample period. Changing the sample therefore creates large deviations in the estimates.

Baxter and King (1995) propose the use of a band-pass filter to obtain the cyclical component of a series. The Baxter–King filter is usually preferred over high pass filters (e.g., Hodrick and Prescott 1997), because in addition to

Table 13.3 Relative magnitude and volatility of selected foreign exchange inflows, 1996–2007[1]

Year	Of remittances		Exports of goods and services		External borrowings[2]		Foreign direct investments		Portfolio investments	
	Level	% of GDP	Level	% of GDP	Level	% of GDP	Level	% of GDP	Level	% of GDP
1996	4.31	5.2	14.91	18.0	2.89	3.5	3.62	4.4	4.15	5.0
1997	5.74	7.0	15.56	18.9	3.47	4.2	0.84	1.0	3.07	3.7
1998	7.37	11.3	20.66	31.7	4.83	7.4	2.02	3.1	3.31	5.1
1999	6.80	8.9	32.62	42.8	6.24	8.2	1.25	1.6	3.92	5.1
2000	6.05	8.0	35.48	46.7	6.85	9.0	2.24	3.0	0.26	0.3
2001	6.03	7.9	29.03	38.2	7.98	10.5	0.20	0.3	1.08	1.4
2002	6.89	8.4	32.40	39.6	7.22	8.8	1.54	1.9	1.37	1.7
2003	7.58	8.9	33.38	39.1	7.21	8.4	0.49	0.6	1.38	1.6
2004	8.55	9.1	37.02	39.5	5.47	5.8	0.69	0.7	−0.80	−0.9
2005	10.69	10.0	38.92	36.4	4.07	3.8	1.85	1.7	3.62	3.4
2006	12.76	10.0	46.66	36.6	1.05	0.8	2.92	2.3	4.61	3.6
2007	14.45	9.2	50.40	32.1	0.79	0.5	2.93	1.9	3.57	2.3
Average	8.10	8.7	32.25	35.0	4.84	5.9	1.72	1.9	2.46	2.7
SD	3.04		11.04		2.42		1.08		1.73	
CV	37.48		34.22		50.07		62.92		70.36	

Source of data: Department of Economic Statistics, Bangko Sentral ng Pilipinas.

Notes
1 Consistent data on OF remittances and other indicators started in 1996.
2 Include short, and medium-to-long-term loans of the BSP.
SD = Standard deviation.
CV = Coefficient of variation, computed as standard deviation/average *100.

removing low frequency components it also removes high frequency components (irregular or fast moving components). However, limitations of the Baxter–King filter ensue when the time series is short.

Some studies suggest that fitting a trend on output, while using the Hodrick–Prescott (HP) filter, yields more benefits in terms of trend–cycle component of output but other studies seem to be weary of using the HP filter (Cogley and Nason 1995; Ravn and Uhlig 2001). There are of course limitations on using HP filter, as it depends on what adjustment factor has been used in smoothing the time series. There are rules that are widely used in practical work, but these are rules of thumb and arbitrary.

This section uses the HP filter procedure. After Burns' and Mitchell's influential work on pre-World War II US business cycle regularities, the length of the business cycles were widely accepted to vary between one-and-a-half and eight years (Burns and Mitchell 1946). Consequently, filters were specified to cut off components at higher or lower frequencies in order to capture better the cyclical component. Rand and Tarp (2001) observe that business cycles in developing countries, as opposed to cycles in industrialized countries, are significantly shorter in duration.

Leitner (2005) provides an overall picture of the Philippine business cycles covering the period 1981 to 2003, by characterizing them in terms of volatility, co-movement and persistence. As a trend–cycle decomposition technique, the most frequently used HP filter was applied. The period under investigation brought about three cycles: 1983–1989, 1989–1997 and 1997–2000 with initially very erratic, but over time smoother fluctuations.

Remittances of overseas Filipinos refer to transfers sent both by Filipino migrants and overseas workers. In the Philippines, remittances data are sourced from the balance of payments statistics. Output is measured as seasonally adjusted real GDP for all the host countries' output – Hong Kong, Japan, Italy, the United Kingdom and Canada. The Philippine output is obtained from the website of the National Statistical and Coordination Board, while the output of major host countries' are obtained from the IMF International Financial Statistics website.

As shown in Table 13.2 in the previous section, the sources of remittance flows are geographically diverse, reflecting the pattern of migration flows. In 1985 to 1989, the Middle East and the USA accounted for around three-quarters of total remittances. Later the share of the Middle East declined, but in the period 2000–2007 these two regions still accounted for about two-thirds of total flows. Other significant source countries include Canada, the United Kingdom, Italy, Singapore, Japan and Hong Kong.

We estimated the cyclical component of major host countries' business activity. We used the GDP of the United States, Hong Kong, Japan, Italy, the United Kingdom and Canada. Initially, we included Saudi Arabia, the United Arab Emirates and Singapore. While those of Saudi Arabia and the United Arab Emirates are not available, that of Singapore yielded insufficient data. We estimate the cyclical component of Philippine real GDP from 1994 to 2007 using two methods. In the first method we relied on the HP filter, described earlier, and for the second method we used the updated Deveza-Bascos (2006) methodology. In Deveza-Bascos (2006), the identification of business cycles goes in steps. The first step is the selection of the appropriate measure of economic activity. The second step is the identification of the turning points (peaks and troughs) of the underlying business cycles. The third step involves the validation of results.

After the cyclical components have been estimated, the next step consists of estimating the correlation between the cyclical components of remittances and those of the Philippine's real GDP and the country's major host countries' output. Using a pairwise correlation matrix, Table 13.4 shows the contemporaneous and lagged (up to three-quarters) cross-correlation of Philippine real GDP and its major host countries' business activity. Remittances in the Philippines (in US dollars, deflated by US CPI) seem to be strikingly pro-cyclical with economic activity in the main host countries, such as the United States, Hong Kong and Japan. These three countries account for about two-thirds of total remittance inflows. However, remittances and business activities of Italy, the UK and Canada appeared to be counter-cyclical.

In particular, remittances and Philippine GDP, when detrended by the HP filter (with no lags), show a correlation of almost 41 percent over the period from 1994 to 2007. Using Deveza-Bascos methods, remittances appeared to be similarly pro-cyclical with Philippine real GDP. Meanwhile, Philippine GDP seems to move along with the business activities of the United States, Hong Kong (albeit not significant) and Japan.

The Granger causality is a technique for determining whether a time series is useful in explaining another. Using a lag of two-quarters, we run the Granger causality test to determine whether the null hypothesis holds: the coefficients on the lagged indicators are statistically significant in explaining the behavior of other indicators. We run Granger causality tests on the following indicators at 5 percent and 10 percent levels of significance: component of US (USGDP) and Philippine real GDP (GDPHP), inflation (2000 base), OF workers' remittances (REMIT), real personal consumption expenditure (PCE), real disposable personal income (DISY), real money supply (MS), real bank deposit liabilities (DEPLIAB), nominal peso–dollar rate exchange rate (FXR), current account balance (CA), overnight RRP (RRP), 91-day Treasury bill (TBILL), labor force (LF) and compensation index for non-agriculture workers (1985 base). Except for RRP and TBILL, all variables are in logarithm.

At 10 percent level of significance, the (Granger) causation appears to run from remittances (REMIT) to inflation (INFL), remittances to 91-day Treasury bill rate (TBR91), real money supply (MS) to remittances, real deposit liabilities (DEPLIAB) to remittances, remittances to nominal peso–dollar rate (FXR), real disposable personal income (DISY) to remittances, non-agriculture real compensation index, a proxy for wages, (QSE1P) to remittances, remittances to current account balance (CA) (see Table 13.5).

Table 13.5 also shows that there is bi-directional causality between remittances and real personal consumption (PCE), real disposable personal income,

Table 13.4 Cross correlation matrix, remittances, Philippines and its major host countries' output, 1994–2007

	No lag		Lag of one-quarter		Lag of two-quarters		Lag of three-quarters	
	Remit	Philippines	Remit	Philippines	Remit	Philippines	Remit	Philippines
Remit	1.000		1.000		1.000		1.000	
Philippines	0.410*	1.000	0.400*	1.000	0.394*	1.000	0.373*	1.000
US	0.133*	0.442*	0.126*	0.412*	0.079*	0.334*	0.029*	0.233
Hong Kong	0.002	-0.361*	0.233	0.254	0.469*	0.115	0.666*	0.029
Japan	0.293**	0.522*	0.262	0.426*	0.292**	0.212	0.343*	0.021
Italy	-0.084	0.284**	-0.086	0.131*	-0.082	0.082	-0.104	-0.024*
UK	-0.141	0.594*	-0.175	0.501*	-0.222	0.328**	-0.292**	-0.023
Canada	-0.257	0.421*	-0.260	0.283**	-0.259	0.085	-0.311**	-0.087

Notes
* Significant at 5% level of confidence; ** Significant at 10% level of confidence; the remaining coefficients are not significant.

Table 13.5 Pairwise Granger causality tests

Null hypothesis	Obs	F-statistic	Prob.	Significance
LOG(PCE) does not Granger Cause LOG(REMIT)	40	6.680	0.014	5%
LOG(REMIT) does not Granger Cause LOG(PCE)	40	5.908	0.020	5%
INFL does not Granger Cause LOG(REMIT)	40	2.966	0.093	10%
LOG(REMIT) does not Granger Cause INFL	40	2.896	0.073	10%
TBR91 does not Granger Cause LOG(REMIT)	40	2.384	0.131	Not significant
LOG(REMIT) does not Granger Cause TBR91	40	3.159	0.084	10%
LOG(MS) does not Granger Cause LOG(REMIT)	40	5.493	0.025	5%
LOG(REMIT) does not Granger Cause LOG(MS)	40	0.057	0.813	Not significant
LOG(DEPLIAB) does not Granger Cause LOG(REMIT)	40	5.550	0.024	5%
LOG(REMIT) does not Granger Cause LOG(DEPLIAB)	40	4.284	0.071	10%
FXR does not Granger Cause LOG(REMIT)	40	2.890	0.118	Not significant
LOG(REMIT) does not Granger Cause FXR	40	3.061	0.097	10%
LOG(GDPHP) does not Granger Cause LOG(REMIT)	40	4.487	0.041	5%
LOG(REMIT) does not Granger Cause LOG(GDPHP)	40	7.853	0.008	5%
LOG(DISY) does not Granger Cause LOG(REMIT)	40	3.465	0.0711	10%
LOG(REMIT) does not Granger Cause LOG(DISY)	40	2.089	0.082	10%
LOG(XINFL) does not Granger Cause LOG(REMIT)	40	2.542	0.120	Not significant
LOG(REMIT) does not Granger Cause LOG(XINFL)	40	0.344	0.561	Not significant
RRP does not Granger Cause LOG(REMIT)	40	1.215	0.277	Not significant
LOG(REMIT) does not Granger Cause RRP	40	0.652	0.425	Not significant
LOG(LF) does not Granger Cause LOG(REMIT)	40	2.865	0.099	10%
LOG(REMIT) does not Granger Cause LOG(LF)	40	3.638	0.064	10%
LOG(QSE1P) does not Granger Cause LOG(REMIT)	40	4.086	0.048	5%
LOG(REMIT) does not Granger Cause LOG(QSE1P)	40	3.018	0.065	10%
CA does not Granger Cause LOG(REMIT)	40	0.367	0.548	Not significant
LOG(REMIT) does not Granger Cause CA	4.753	0.036	5%	
LOG(USGDPHP) does not Granger Cause LOG(REMIT)	40	4.566	0.039	5%
LOG(REMIT) does not Granger Cause LOG(USGDPHP)	40	18.636	0.000	5%

Notes
Sample: 1994Q1; 2007Q4.
Lags: 2.

real deposit liabilities, inflation, Philippine real GDP, labor force, non-agriculture compensation and the US real GDP. This analysis shows that remittances are an important force in the Philippines with impacts on many aspects of its economy. Of course the Granger tests conducted here deal only with bi-variable relationships while in fact the relationships are more complex involving simultaneous interaction amongst many variables. To deal with these a full-fledged macroeconomic model is needed in which the main facts around remittances are integrated.

The initial analysis we have so far reveals that it is justified to dig deeper into the macroeconomics of remittances and challenges to Philippine monetary policy. However, there are limitations of our analyses, the most important of which is the issue of endogeneity. This is seen as remittances are part of GDP, as they immediately are reflected in expenditure which leads to a positive correlation that does not mean very much. Chami *et al.* (2003), for instance, use the two-stage least squares (instrument variable) approach. This problem is aggravated in a panel data framework, due to potential dynamic heterogeneity over the cross-sections. In the study of Alleyne *et al.* (2008), they show how the fully modified ordinary least squares can be adjusted to make inferences in cointegrated panels with heterogeneous dynamics, while overcoming the problems in OLS, including that of endogeneity. In our model, we used the Chami *et al.* (2003) method of two-stage least squares to address the issue of endogeneity.

13.5 The macroeconomics of remittances

The purpose of this section is to determine the impact of remittances on the Philippine macroeconomy. Indeed, the literature on the relationship between remittances and growth is controversial. Moreover, the empirical relationship between remittances and growth is complicated by problems of endogeneity, associated difficulties in finding adequate instruments to explain the behavior of remittances and measurement issues.

In the first part of the chapter we argued that the total demand impact of an increase in remittances is the sum of various effects – the direct expenditure effect, the multiplier effect and the interest rate effect have a positive impact on aggregate demand, while the exchange rate appreciation and the labor supply effect have a negative impact. The rise in aggregate demand, the increase of prices of non-traded goods and the increase in wages will push up prices, although the appreciation of the exchange rate may dampen the inflationary effects. In the previous section, we established the correlation and causality relationship between remittances and a number of economic variables. These two approaches strongly suggest that remittances are part of a complex set of economic interactions. In an economy where remittances are significantly large, as in the Philippines, these interactions need to be taken into account when analyzing economic shocks and economic policies. In this section we include these effects in a quarterly macroeconometric model. We address the endogeneity and measurement issues by using two-stage least squares on some important indicators.

13.5.1 *Structure of the model*[10]

Our study builds on Bayangos' (2007) dynamic, structural and quarterly macro-econometric model for the Philippines. Our dataset covers the period from March 1989 to December 2007.

To a large extent, our macroeconometric model shares features with the New Keynesian model of Ball (1999). The Ball model assumes that inflation and output are backward-looking, thus it deliberately abstains from any optimizing foundation. Central to this model are important nominal rigidities in describing the macroeconomy. In addition, there are lag effects in the transmission mechanism.

We assume there is excess supply in the economy; hence, aggregate output is demand-determined in the short to medium run. However, the goods markets are monopolistically competitive (Blanchard and Kiyotaki 1987), leading to profits for firms that charge non-competitive sticky prices (Calvo 1983), which clear all of domestic production to satisfy demand (net of imports) for consumption, investment, government spending and exports. Firms make a mark-up when setting prices which are responsive to demand and monetary conditions. Meanwhile, households and firms negotiate a non-competitive real wage, engaging in sticky nominal contracts (ibid.).

Nevertheless, asset markets are imperfect. The nominal exchange rate is allowed to transitorily deviate from purchasing power parity (PPP) so that movements occur in the real exchange rate. In addition, the nominal short-term interest rates play the leading role as the instrument of monetary policy, with the money supply having a limited role in describing the monetary stance.

The main features of the model are the following: (1) the policy interest rate of the BSP responds to inflationary, output gap and exchange rate pressures; (2) changes in the BSP policy rate affect changes in the nominal exchange rate based on the uncovered interest parity (UIP) condition; and (3) the nominal peso–dollar rate is an effective transmission mechanism, as both direct and indirect pass-through effects to inflation are relatively above average.

The original model (Bayangos 2007) did not give much attention to remittances. The remittances were an exogenous inflow on the current account. Shocks to remittances would lead to changes in the current account balance and this would have a small effect on the exchange rate, which would subsequently affect imports and exports. The innovation of this chapter is that we have explicitly introduced remittances into the model as an endogenous variable with a number of impacts on the macroeconomy.

13.5.2 *Channels of remittances toward growth and inflation*

Figure 13.2 provides a schematic and simplified overview of overseas Filipino remittances and the Philippine monetary transmission. The 67 equations are grouped into seven major blocks: monetary sector (bottom left), public sector (bottom right), prices (middle left), expenditures including balance of payments (middle right), production (upper right) and employment (upper left). In particular,

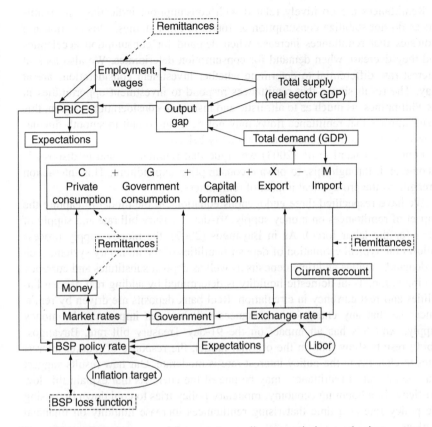

Figure 13.2 OF remittances and the monetary policy transmission mechanism.

remittances are seen to affect the supply of money, current account, total demand and labor supply.

Our chapter traces the impact of changes in remittances to the Philippine monetary policy transmission mechanism, by adding and respecifying the model in line with the suggestions from the empirical literature in Section 13.2 and the analysis in Section 13.4 of this chapter.[11]

We base the revised model on our empirical finding that remittances are pro-cyclical with the Philippine aggregate demand, but they also cause demand to change. This bi-directional causality implies that remittances are determined by real personal consumption demand but also by US real output. Remittances are therefore pro-cyclical both with the Philippine and the US business cycle (which confirms our finding that the US and Philippine cycle are correlated). Remittances are further driven by the interest rate differential as indicated by the difference between the 91-day Treasury bill rate and the 90-day Libor: a higher level of US GDP, personal consumption as well as higher interest rate differentials lead to higher remittances.

Remittances are positively related with consumption, indicating that remittances do not stabilize consumption as found in most studies. This relationship indicates that remittances increase when demand for consumption accelerates and they decrease when demand for consumption deteriorates. We also look at interest rate differential to determine whether investment considerations are at play. The result shows that remittances respond to investment opportunities in the Philippines, as much as to altruistic and insurance considerations. Again, this result implies that remittance flows may not be as important to smooth fluctuations or shocks in the economy as commonly believed.

Following Chami *et al.* (2003) we argue that remittances add to disposable income and, through this, to private consumption expenditure. This interaction strengthens the pro-cyclical impact of remittances.

We have respecified three endogenous equations in the model to capture the impact of remittances on money supply, 91-day Treasury bill rate and supply of labor (or the labor force). As in Bayangos (2007), the money supply process follows the typical estimation of deposit liabilities of the monetary system, such as demand, savings and time deposits as well as deposit substitutes and currency in circulation. Total domestic liquidity is determined by adding real deposit liabilities and real currency in circulation. Real bank deposits are driven by remittances so that any change in remittances will have an impact on the money supply. And this has an impact on the 91-day Treasury bill rate. Bayangos' (ibid.) results show that, in the original model, the response of market interest rates to changes in the policy interest rate is moderate. Our new results suggest that the impact of remittances may be one of the channels that explain this low elasticity. In a booming economy, monetary policy tries to cool down by raising the policy rate at a time that rising remittances increase liquidity on financial markets.

Following Chami *et al.* (2003) and Yang (2008) we see that an increase in remittances will have a negative effect on the labor force supply. Members of households receiving remittances reduce their work effort. Thus the labor supply falls at a time when the demand impulse from the increased remittances increases the demand for labor. This reduces the unemployment rate and increases wages.

13.6 Challenges to monetary policy

We use the open and dynamic macro model presented in the previous section to identify the channels of Philippine monetary policy transmission. In this chapter we are particularly interested in how shocks to remittances affect the economy and monetary policy effectiveness. For instance, in standard macro models, as in the original (Bayangos 2007) version of our model, a recession in the US will affect the Philippines mainly through the trade balance with a US recession reducing demand for Philippine exports. In the revised model, the US recession would also result in a decline in remittances from the US and a fall in disposable income so that, on top of the decline in export demand, also private consumption demand declines. Moreover, the shock to remittances will also have impacts on the money supply, domestic interest rates and labor supply. The adjustment process will thus be more complex and the task of monetary policy more challenging.

The strategy we follow to assess the impact of remittances on the macroeconomy in general and on monetary policy in particular is straightforward. We simulated a sustained one percentage point reduction in the US GDP growth rate on the estimated macro model from first quarter 1994 to fourth quarter 2003 through two versions of the Philippine quarterly model. In the first version of the model (the Bayangos 2007 version) remittances are exogenous. A US recession is thus only felt through the trade account and remittances remain constant. The second version of the model has made remittances endogenous. In this version the US recession leads to a decline in remittances, which in turn has effects on consumption demand, money supply and interest rates and labor supply. We compare the outcomes of the two models, with and without the remittance channel.

Annualized quarterly growth as well as volatility using the coefficient of variation (CV) are computed. Volatility is a measure on the basis of how wild or quiet an indicator is relative its history. The CV is a comparative measure defined as the ratio of the standard deviation to the mean.

The impact of a sustained one percentage point reduction in the US real GDP growth on BSP credibility is based on the estimated BSP objective function (or the welfare loss of a policy rule or the 'policy loss function'). The idea is to map the impact of simulations to the BSP's objective function over time, not to derive the optimizing policy loss function. A welfare or credibility loss (gain) to the BSP is measured by a higher (lower) value of the policy loss function. The impact on interest rates, the exchange rate, the money supply, components of GDP and finally inflation and inflation expectations are also assessed.

The objective function of the BSP is assumed to exhibit the standard quadratic form, with some modifications:

$$L = \frac{1}{2}\left[\varpi(\pi_t^f - \pi_t^*)^2 + \rho(q_t - q_t^*)^2 + \gamma(E_t e_{t+1}^n - e_t^n)^2 \right] \qquad (13.1)$$

where π_t^f is the inflation forecast, π_t^* is quarterly inflation target announced by the government, q_t is actual quarterly real GDP growth, q_t^* is potential real GDP, E_t denotes expectations conditional upon the information set available at time t and e_t^n is the average quarterly nominal peso–dollar exchange rate. Meanwhile, ϖ, ρ and γ, represent, respectively, the BSP's aversion to inflationary pressure, real GDP growth fluctuations around the potential (the output gap) and nominal peso–dollar exchange rate fluctuations around the expected rate.

In the subsequent analysis we will focus on the impact of a one percentage point reduction in the US GDP growth rate during the inflation targeting (IT) period 2001–2003 (for reference: Table 13.6 also shows the results for the pre-IT and pre-Asian crisis period 1994–1996.). In the original model, the US GDP shock was felt through trade. As the US economy declines, exports of the

Table 13.6 Impact scenario: a sustained one percentage point reduction in the US GDP growth

Economic indicators	Percent changes from baseline model							
	Without remittance channel				With remittance channel			
	1994–1996		2001–2003		1994–1996		2001–2003	
	Average	CV	Average	CV	Average	CV	Average	CV
GDP components								
Personal consumption (growth)	−0.05	−0.09	−0.18	−0.05	−0.82	−0.11	−1.07	−0.01
of which: disposable income (growth)	–	–	–	–	−1.41	−0.02	−1.48	0.00
Gross capital formation (growth)	−0.15	−0.08	−1.42	−0.14	−0.28	−0.19	−0.37	−0.09
Current account (growth)	−1.01	−0.07	−1.47	−0.33	−1.52	−0.39	−2.34	−0.82
of which: remittances (growth)	–	–	–	–	−4.00	−0.03	−4.17	0.00
Labor force (growth)	0.02	0.03	0.08	0.64	0.35	0.10	0.45	0.01
Non-agriculture compensation index (growth)	−0.08	−0.12	−0.13	−0.15–0.23	−0.05	−0.32	−0.09	
Financial indicators (%)								
Money supply (year-on-year growth)	−0.08	−0.03	−0.15	−0.04	−1.45	−0.26	−2.93	−1.25
RRP (%)	−0.12	−0.02	−0.08	−0.61	−0.10	−0.11	−0.16	−0.09
91-day Treasury bill rate (%)	−0.09	−0.02	−0.07	−0.09	−0.08	−0.02	−0.12	−0.08
Nominal peso–dollar rate (growth)	0.39	0.24	1.08	0.21	1.06	0.08	1.18	0.79
Macroeconomic indicators (%)								
Real GDP (growth)	−0.07	−0.10	−0.12	−0.08	−0.38	−0.14	−0.89	−0.08
Output gap (growth)	−0.03	−1.57	−0.33	−1.91	−0.18	−3.89	−1.73	−1.38
CPI-inflation	−0.10	−0.20	−0.13	−0.87	−0.14	−0.10	−0.18	−0.10
CPI-inflation forecast (two years ahead)	−0.12	−0.15	−0.15	−0.18	−0.15	−0.13	−0.17	−0.06
CPI-inflation expectations (long run)	−0.02	−0.02	−0.03	−0.08	−0.03	−0.10	−0.15	−0.10
BSP objective function								
With exchange rate	0.11	0.09	0.08	0.03	0.05	0.08	0.50	0.12
Without exchange rate	0.13	0.08	0.33	0.05	0.01	0.08	0.27	0.11

Philippines fall, which leads to a fall in aggregate demand and output, a deterioration of the current account and a depreciation of the exchange rate.

When we introduce remittances into the model the adjustment becomes richer. The remittances become another transmission channel, next to the trade linkage, of the US shock. The direct effect on the current account now includes the fall in export demand, as well as the decline in remittance transfers; the current account deteriorates to a greater extent: Table 13.6 shows that while in the original model the current account declines by 1.47 percent, in the model with remittances the decline is 2.34 percent. This is despite some mitigating effects: the US GDP shock leads to a fall in remittances with an immediate impact on disposable income and private consumption demand; this reduces imports. The sharper deterioration of the current account also implies a stronger depreciation of the exchange rate with impacts on exports and imports. Moreover, the fall in remittances increases the labor supply which leads to a decline in wages and prices and thus an improvement of the real exchange rate. All the countervailing effects are not so strong as to turn the current account around. The decline in the current account is stronger in the model with endogenous remittances.

The decline in remittances has a direct effect on personal consumption expenditure. In the original version of the model the decline in consumption spending is relatively small (−0.18), the result of the decline in GDP growth due to falling export demand. But once remittances are endogenous the impact is stronger: the decline in remittances, next to the other negative impacts of the US recession, causes private consumption to fall by 1.07 percent. This deepens the aggregate demand impact of the US recession on the Philippine economy.

In the original model, the monetary effects are small. The fall in the GDP growth reduces the money supply and the decline in the output gap lowers inflation. The decline in the output gap and in inflation invites a downward adjustment of the policy rate (RRP) and the market interest rate TBR91 falls as the policy rate and inflation decline. Again, when remittances are endogenous, the effects are stronger. The output gap and the money supply fall by more and inflation declines as the output gap and the money supply fall and wages decline as labor supply increases. The decline in the money supply, induced by the fall in remittances, would lead us to expect an increase in the market interest rate, but in fact the TBR91 falls. The impact of falling inflation and reductions in the BSP policy rate dominates. But to achieve this effect on market interest rates, the BSP has to take stronger policy action: the policy rate (RRP) is reduced by 0.16 (compared to 0.08 in the original version of the model).

The fall in the market interest rate helps private investment although the negative impacts of the depreciating currency and the fall in GDP dominate. Still the decline in capital formation is smaller in the model with remittances.

The larger current account deficit and the stronger fall of the market interest rate have their effect on the nominal exchange rate. While the peso–dollar rate depreciates with 1.08 percent in the original version of the model, it falls by 1.18 in the new version.

A final impact of declining remittances is felt on the labor market. According to the model, the labor supply increases when remittances decline: households seek alternative income to compensate the cut in transfers.[12] Table 13.6 shows a stronger labor force growth in the model with endogenous remittances and, as a result, a stronger decline in non-agricultural wages. This helps to curb inflation.

Comparing the two versions of the model, there is thus a stronger direct effect on aggregate demand, reflected in a much stronger decline in real GDP growth and a decline in the output gap, inflation falls by more and the exchange rate shows a stronger depreciation. These variables are in the BSP objective function and we can thus expect a different policy response. As shown in Table 13.6, the policy rate (RPP) declines by 0.08 percent in the original version of the model but by 0.16 percent in the model with endogenous remittances.

It should be noted that monetary policy becomes rather complex when remittances are endogenous. The worsening of the output gap invites a stronger monetary policy response and, as the decline in remittances helps to reduce inflation, a stronger policy response seems also feasible. On the other hand, the direct effect of the fall of remittances on the money market creates an upward pressure on the market interest rate; to counteract that pressure, the monetary policy response needs to be stronger. Moreover, the fall in remittances imply a stronger depreciation of the exchange rate, compromising the BSP objective of stabilizing fluctuations around the exchange rate. To stabilize the exchange rate the central bank should actually increase the policy rate. It may be reluctant to do so as the depreciation gives some much-needed support to exporters. There is thus a trade-off between stabilizing output and stabilizing the exchange rate. Such trade-offs will increase the loss function.

The volatility measure in Table 13.6 indicates that the BSP's reaction toward inflationary pressure, output gap and exchange rate fluctuations generated, from the baseline, lower volatility of inflation, the two-year-ahead inflation forecast, long-run inflation expectations but higher in the nominal peso–dollar exchange rate. As real GDP growth slowed and the output gap widened, lower volatility compared to the baseline was seen. With these results, the BSP's preference to react toward inflationary pressure, output gap and exchange rate fluctuations resulted in the decline of its credibility, as the policy loss estimate rose during the IT period and the forecast IT period.

Finally, we look at the BSP loss function. Table 13.6 shows that losses increase in all cases. This is not surprising, after all a negative shock to the economy affects the output gap negatively and leads to adjustments in the exchange rate. These negative impacts on the central bank's objective functions are somewhat mitigated by the decline in inflation but an overall welfare loss remains. When the BSP objective function includes exchange rate stabilization the loss increases more strongly in the model with endogenous remittances. This is the impact of the policy trade-off that we identified above. Without the exchange rate in the objective function there is not much difference in the credibility loss between the two versions of the model.

13.7 Conclusion

At the time of writing this chapter (in late 2009) the global economy and the Philippines are hesitantly emerging from the global recession. In the current commentary it is noted that weak demand in the US, Europe and Japan will reduce the demand for exports from developing countries and that the turmoil on global financial markets will reduce capital flows (FDI, portfolio investment, loans) to the developing world. This will require a painful adjustment and an aggressive policy to mitigate the impact of the recession. This chapter has argued that, in the assessment of the impact of the global recession, we should also start to consider remittances as a transmission channel, certainly for countries such as the Philippines, where remittances are substantial. Remittances are a crucial element of the Philippine economy and we have established that remittances are driven by the economic cycle of the main host countries and that the ongoing recession will thus lead to a significant slowdown in transfers (see, e.g., World Bank 2008). We have also established that the fluctuations in remittance flows over the years are of a magnitude that is significant enough for policy makers to take notice.

Through our model we have been able to trace the impact of changes in remittances on important economic variables, like that of aggregate demand, money supply and interest rates, exchange rate and labour supply and wages. The model simulations have shown that the impact of the US recession on the Philippine economy is more severe once we take account of the endogeneity and procyclicality of remittances. Our simulations clearly show that it is desirable that central banks take this endogeneity into account when formulating monetary policy.

Notes

1 Veronica B. Bayangos works at the Bangko Sentral Sentral ng Pilipinas (BSP). Karel Jansen at the Institute of Social Studies at The Hague. We are grateful to BSP Deputy Governor for Monetary Stability Sector Diwa C. Guinigundo and BSP Director from the Center for Monetary and Financial Policy, Francisco G. Dakila and an anonymous referee for their comments. The usual institutional disclaimer applies.
2 See, e.g., the World Bank's 'Global Development Finance' (2003) which has a chapter on workers' remittances, the IMF's World Economic Outlook (2005b) with a chapter on remittances and development, the World Bank's 'Global Economic Prospects' (2006) that was devoted to the economic implications of remittances and migration and the UNDP's Human Development Report (2009) on Human Mobility and Development.
3 It is believed that these official data on remittances may seriously underestimate actual flows since remittance flows through formal channels may be underestimated and since there are substantial unrecorded flows that go through informal channels.
4 The top 20 recipient countries of workers' remittances in 2006 include Mexico, the Philippines, Spain, Lebanon, China, Morocco, Pakistan, Bangladesh, Egypt, Colombia, Portugal, Guatemala, El Salvador, Brazil, Poland, Nigeria, Dominican Republic, Jordan, Indonesia and Ecuador (World Bank, Migration and Remittances Factbook).
5 Mody and Taylor (2004) follow a slightly different approach; they set up a demand–supply model to explain capital flows with the possibility of credit rationing due to

asymmetric information. Demand for capital in developing countries is mainly driven by country-specific factors (like the pull factors) while supply is dependent on country-specific factors but also on global push factors.

6 The study uses data for 104 countries over the period 1960–2003 (see Kaminsky *et al.* 2004).

7 This implies that the dollar amount remitted was reduced but that the peso amount that the household received was increased. This is what you would expect if the utility function of the migrant includes both her own and her family's consumption.

8 Yang (2008) finds no significant effect of the increase in remittances on consumption in answer to the exchange rate shocks of the Asian crisis. That may be because he is looking at the short-term impact of a shock that was sudden and may have been perceived as temporary. In line with the Permanent Income Hypothesis such shocks will not lead to immediate adjustment of consumption patterns.

9 But he did find a significant effect on children. The increase in remittances meant that more children were kept in school and children spent less time working (Yang 2008). But it should be noted that this study only looks at the very short-term impact of the increase in remittances.

10 The complete specification is found in Bayangos (2007, chapter 5), Model Specification and Estimation Results.

11 See Appendix A of Bayangos and Jansen (2009) for details on the adjustments to the model that were made to capture the full impact of remittances.

12 Alternatively, it could be argued that as employment opportunities abroad decline due to the US recession, workers stay in the Philippines or return to the Philippines to seek employment.

References

Alleyne, D., C. Kirton and M. Figueroa (2008) 'Macroeconomic Determinants of Migrant Remittances to Caribbean Countries: Panel Unit Roots and Cointegration', *Journal of Developing Areas*, 41: 137–53.

Amuedo-Dorantes, C. and S. Pozo (2004) 'Workers' Remittances and the Real Exchange Rate: A Paradox of Gifts', *World Development*, 32: 1407–17.

Asian Development Bank (2004) 'Enhancing the Efficiency of Overseas Workers Remittances', Technical Assistance Final Report, July, ADB.

Ball, L.M. (1999) 'Policy Rules for Open Economies', in J.B. Taylor (ed.) *Monetary Policy Rules*, Chicago, IL: University of Chicago Press.

Baxter, M. and R.G. King (1995) 'Measuring Business Cycles: Approximate Band-pass Filters for Economic Time Series', NBER Working Paper 5022.

Bayangos, V. (2007) *Inflation Targeting and Exchange Rate Uncertainty*, Maastricht (The Netherlands): Shaker Publishing.

Bayangos, V. and K. Jansen (2009) 'The Macroeconomics of Remittances in the Philippines', Working Paper 470, The Hague: Institute of Social Studies.

Blanchard, O.J. and N. Kiyotaki (1987) 'Monopolistic Competition and the Effects of Aggregate Demand', *American Economic Review*, 77: 647–66.

Bouhga-Hagbe, J. (2004) 'A Theory of Workers' Remittances with an Application to Morocco', IMF Working Paper 04/194, Washington, DC: IMF.

Buch, C., A. Kuckulenz and M.L. Manchec (2002) 'Worker Remittances and Capital Flows', Kiel Working Paper 1130, Kiel (Germany): Kiel Institute for World Economics.

Burgess, R. and V. Haksar (2005) 'Migration and Foreign Remittances in the Philippines', IMF Working Paper 05/111, Washington, DC: IMF.

Burns, A.F. and W.C. Mitchell (1946) *Measuring Business Cycles*, New York: National Bureau of Economic Research.

Calvo, G. (1983) 'Staggered Prices in a Utility Maximizing Framework', *Journal of Monetary Economics*, 12: 383–98.

Chami, R., C. Fullenkamp and S. Jahjah (2003) 'Are Immigrant Remittances Flow a Source of Capital for Development?' IMF Working Paper 03/189, Washington, DC: IMF.

Chami, R., T.F. Cosimano and M.T. Gapen (2006) 'Beware of Emigrants Bearing Gifts: Optimal Fiscal and Monetary Policy in the Presence of Remittances', IMF Working Paper 06/61, Washington, DC: IMF.

Cogley, T. and J. Nason (1995) 'Effects of the Hodrick–Prescott Filter on Trend and Difference Stationary Time Series: Implications for Business Cycle Research', *Journal of Economic Dynamics and Control*, 19: 253–78.

Dakila, F. and R. Claveria (2007) 'Identifying the Determinants of Overseas Filipino's Remittances: Which Exchange Rate Measure is more Relevant?' BSP Working Paper 2007–02, November.

Deveza-Bascos, T. (2006) 'Early Warning System on the Macroeconomy Identification of Business Cycles in the Philippines', *Bangko Sentral Review*, January.

Giuliano, P. and M. Ruiz-Arranz (2005) 'Remittances, Financial Development, and Growth', IMF Working Paper 05/234, Washington, DC: IMF.

Goce-Dakila, C. and F. Dakila Jr (2006) 'Modeling the Impact of Overseas Filipino Workers Remittances on the Philippine Economy: An Inter-Regional and Economy-Wide Approach', BSP Working Paper 2006–02, Manila (Philippines): Bangko Sentral ng Pilipinas.

Hernandez, L., P. Mellado and R. Valdes (2001) 'Determinants of Private Capital Flows in the 1970s and 1990s: Is there Evidence of Contagion?' IMF Working Paper 01/64, Washington, DC: IMF.

Hodrick, R.J. and E.C. Prescott (1997) 'Postwar U.S. Business Cycles: An Empirical Investigation', *Journal of Money, Credit, and Banking*, 29: 1–16.

Imbs, J. (2004) 'Trade, Finance, Specialization and Synchronization', *Review of Economics and Statistics*, 86: 723–34.

Imbs, J. (2006) 'The Real Effects of Financial Integration', *Journal of International Economics*, 68: 296–324.

IMF (2005a) 'Two Current Issues facing Developing Countries (Chapter 2)', April 2005, Washington, DC: IMF.

IMF (2005b) *World Economic Outlook; Globalization and External Imbalances*, Washington DC: IMF, April.

Kaminsky, G., C.M. Reinhart and C.Végh (2004) 'When it Rains, it Pours: Procyclical Capital Flows and Macroeconomic Policies', NBER Working Paper 10780.

Kose, M.A., E.S. Prasad and M.E. Terrones (2003) 'How does Globalization Affect the Synchronization of Business Cycles?' *American Economic Review*, Papers and Proceedings of the One Hundred Fifteenth Annual Meeting of the American Economic Association, Washington, DC, January 3–5, 2003, 93: 57–62.

Kose, M.A., C. Otrok and C.H. Whiteman (2005) 'Understanding the Evolution of World Business Cycles', IMF Working Paper 05/211, Washington, DC: IMF.

Leitner, S. (2005) 'The Business Cycle in the Philippines', PIDS Discussion Paper, 2005–10, June, PIDS.

Loser, C., C. Lockwood, A. Minson and L. Balcazar (2006) The macroeconomic impact of remittances in Latin-America: Dutch disease or Latin cure? *Inter-American Dialogue*.

Lueth, E. and M. Ruiz-Arranz (2007) 'Are Workers' Remittances a Hedge against Macro-economic Shocks? The Case of Sri Lanka', IMF Working Paper 07/22, Washington, DC: IMF.

Mody, A. and M. Taylor (2004) 'International Capital Crunches: The Time-Varying Role of Informational Asymmetries', Royal Economic Society Annual Conference 2004 113, Royal Economic Society.

Prasad, E., K. Rogoff, S. Wei and M.A. Kose (2003) 'Effects of Financial Globalization on Developing Countries: Some Empirical Evidence', Washington, DC: IMF.

Rand, J. and F. Tarp (2001) 'Business Cycles in Developing Countries: Are they Different?' CREDIT Research Paper 01/21.

Ravn, M. and H. Uhlig (2001) 'On Adjusting the HP-Filter for the Frequency of Observations', CESifo Working Paper 479, Munich (Germany), Center of Economic Studies and Ifo Institute for Economic Research.

Sayan, S. (2006) 'Business Cycles and Workers' Remittances: How do Migrant Workers Respond to Cyclical Movements of GDP at Home?' IMF Working Paper, 06/52, Washington, DC: IMF.

Taylor, M.P. and L. Sarno (1997) 'Capital Flows to Developing Countries: Long- and Short-Term Determinants', *World Bank Economics Review*, 11: 451–71.

Tuaño-Amador, C., R. Claveria, F. Co and V. Delloro (2007) 'Philippine Overseas Workers and Migrants' Remittances: The Dutch Disease Question and the Cyclicality Issue', *Bangko Sentral Review* 9: 1–23.

UNDP (2009) 'Overcoming Barriers: Human Mobility and Development', Human Development Report, 2009, New York: UNDP.

Vargas-Silva, C. (2008) 'Are Remittances Manna from Heaven? A Look at the Business Cycle Properties of Remittances', *North American Journal of Economics and Finance*, 19: 290–303.

World Bank (2003) 'Global Development Finance 2003 (Chapter 7)', Washington, DC: World Bank.

World Bank (2006) 'Global Economic Prospects 2006', Washington, DC: World Bank.

World Bank (2008) 'RP Unemployment Poverty higher in 2009-WB', *Business Mirror* (News Article), Washington, DC: World Bank, December 11, 2008.

World Bank (2009) 'Global Development Finance 2009', Washington, DC: World Bank.

Yang, D. (2008) 'International Migration, Remittances and Household Investment: Evidence from Philippine Migrants' Exchange Rate Shocks', *Economic Journal*, 118: 591–630.

Yang, D. and H. Choi (2007) 'Are Remittances Insurance? Evidence from Rainfall Shocks in the Philippines', *World Bank Economic Review*, 21: 219–48.

Yap, J. (2003) 'The Output Gap and its Role in Inflation Targeting in the Philippines', *Bangko Sentral Review (Bangko Sentral ng Pilipinas)* V(2).

14 Regional integration and South–South trade expansion

The case of Senegal in WAEMU

Diadié Diaw and Thi Anh-Dao Tran[1,2]

14.1 Introduction

While the international debt crisis and the poor economic performance of most developing countries revealed the failure of import substitution industrialization, the rapidly growing newly industrializing countries (NICs) of East Asia confirmed the early evidence pointed out by Little *et al.* (1970) about international trade as an engine of growth.[3] This difference in performance played an important role in reshaping development strategies. From the 1980s onwards, international organizations began to recommend export-oriented policies based on market-oriented reforms, reduction of trade barriers and the opening of domestic markets to foreign competition. These requirements embarked most countries in a generalized trade liberalization and strengthened integration into the world economy. As a result, the overall growth in developing countries since 1998 has been driven by export earnings. From 29 percent in 1996, their share in world trade increased to 37 percent in 2006 (UNCTAD 2007).

Equally, there has been increasing interest in a variety of trade agreements. Since the early 1990s, preferential trade arrangements (PTAs) have spread as an alternative to unilateral or multilateral trade liberalization in the scope of the Doha Agenda for Development (DAD). From 20 in 1990, the number of trade agreements notified to the World Trade Organization (WTO) rose to 86 in 2000 and 159 in 2007 (UNCTAD 2007). This renewal of interest for trade agreements, as another way to integrate markets, became a fundamental topic in the public policy debate during the last decade (Baldwin and Venables 1995). How do PTAs influence the industrialization process in developing countries? Do such agreements encourage convergence or divergence of real income?

Traditional analysis answers these questions using the ideas of trade creation and trade diversion (Viner 1950). According to this approach, early experiments of South–South RTAs in Africa and Latin America demonstrated a welfare reduction for the poorest members, trade diversion prevailing over trade creation in most cases (Foroutan 1993; Cadot *et al.* 2000). More globally, South–South integration (or 'horizontal regionalism') tends to lead to divergence among member countries (Venables 2003). This result is explained by the initial income level of member countries and the small size of integrated markets, hardly conducive to efficient industries. The low potential for trade creation also results from the fact that pro-competitive effects, as well as dynamic gains associated with economies of scale could not be exploited between Southern firms (Mayda and Steinberg 2006). Should South–South integration increase trade between member countries, it would be done at the expense of non-members.

In contrast, if RTAs include relatively high-income countries, it is the poorest ones that experience welfare gains from trade creation. North–South integration ('vertical regionalism') would cause convergence, thus bringing an incentive for developing countries to establish trade partnerships with developed countries (Schiff and Winters 2003). Although characterized increasingly by bilateral agreements between developing and developed countries,[4] the dynamics of regional integration has been prominently conducted by North–South PTAs.

Relying on an analysis in terms of trade creation versus trade diversion, North–South arrangements are better than South–South arrangements from the point of view of the participating Southern countries. However, the renewal of economic geography, along the lines of Krugman (1991) and Krugman and Venables (1995), has provided new theoretical insights on these phenomena and explain industrial agglomeration as a cumulative causation of centripetal forces. According to Puga and Venables (1998) for instance, economic development can be thought of as the spread of concentration of firms from country to country, and different trading arrangements may have a major impact on this agglomeration process. These authors argue notably that North–South PTAs are likely to offer better prospects for Southern countries.

However, many developing countries have, instead, undertaken growing experiments of South–South RTAs: the Common Market of the South (MERCOSUR) or the Andean Common Market in Latin America; the West African Economic and the Monetary Union (WAEMU) or the Economic and Monetary Community of Central Africa (CEMAC) in Africa; the ASEAN Free Trade Area in South-East Asia. Relying on these stylized facts, Rieber and Tran (2004) also developed a model of economic geography to investigate the intra-zone disturbances induced by different scenarios of South–South regional arrangements. Most importantly, their results highlighted the costs of non-cooperation among the Southern countries.

In line with this argument, South–South trade integration has gained growing interest since the beginning of the new millennium, due notably to a globalization era driven by China and India. For instance, an ASEAN–China Free Trade Agreement was signed in 2002 and is expected to become effective by 2012. By the same token, relaxed tensions between India and Pakistan led to the formation of the South Asia Preferential Trade Agreement in January 2004. Yet, despite the implementation of numerous PTAs, intra-regional trade in Africa, and their external trade in broad terms, still remains very small. On the contrary, trade has drastically increased in the South-East Asian area, boosted by the rapid emergence of the two Asian giants and the deepening of regional integration through favorable trade policies. This parallel evolution makes us wonder if such intra-regional trade development in South-East Asia has not been undertaken at the expense of non-Asian countries.

Accordingly, our chapter examines the potential for South–South trade by focusing our analysis on the case of Senegal in the WAEMU. More specifically, we seek whether Senegal's participation in the WAEMU might improve its external trade and eventually allow expansion of South–South trade in the sub-region. To do this, we start by examining the country's recent trade flows and participation in RTAs. We then compare international specialization of the WAEMU members by calculating three trade indicators: the Balassa's Revealed Comparative Advantage (RCA) index, a Contribution to the Trade Balance (CTB) index, and a relative trade balance index describing the position (POS) of individual countries on world markets. Finally, the magnitude of competition among WAEMU members is assessed with the help of a calculation of export similarity indices.

The rest of the chapter is organized as follows: Section 14.2 presents an overall description of Senegal's trade sector in comparison to other countries in the sub-region. Section 14.3 analyzes its international specialization quantitatively by using trade indicators. Section 14.4 concludes and summarizes our main results.

14.2 Senegal's foreign trade: an overview

14.2.1 Trade regime

Since 2001, Senegal is a West African developing country that belongs to the least developed countries (LDCs) listed by the United Nations. Among factors explaining this classification are bad socio-economic indicators (mainly low education enrollment and high child mortality rate), macroeconomic instability and low income. Furthermore, Senegal presents overall the characteristics of a pre-industrialized society, as its economy is mainly driven by small activities in the agricultural and service sector. In 2005, the primary and tertiary sectors accounted for 17 percent and 59 percent of GDP respectively, while the former employed more than 70 percent of the total labor force.[5]

After achieving independence, Senegal pursued an import substitution policy, common at that time in most developing countries. This policy orientation had very negative effects on the country's export and growth performance (Annabi *et al.* 2005). In the early 1980s, with the implementation of the World Bank's structural adjustment program, the country adopted a set of export-oriented policies based on market-oriented reforms, a reduction of trade barriers and the opening of domestic markets to foreign competition. Over the past few years, Senegal has undertaken a set of policies aimed primarily at reducing poverty. Its trade policy stands mainly in the continuity with measures undertaken within the framework of institutional reforms, as well as its participation in RTAs.

In 1975, Senegal embarked on a regional arrangement with 14 other West African countries known as the Economic Community of West African States (ECOWAS). The agreement was designed to strengthen regional integration in West Africa in order to promote intra-regional trade, seen as favorable to growth

Table 14.1 Senegal's participation in RTAs

Agreements	Type	Date	Countries
West African Economic and Monetary Union (WAEMU), formerly Economic Community of West Africa (CEAO)	Customs union	Created in 1973 Notified to the WTO on 27 October 1999 and into force since 1 January 2000	Senegal, Benin, Burkina Faso, Guinea Bissau, Ivory Coast, Mali, Niger, Togo
Economic Community of West African States (ECOWAS)	Free trade agreement	Created on 1975 Revived in 24 July 1993 Notified to the WTO on 9 July 2005	WAEMU countries, Mano River Union (Guinea, Liberia, Sierra Leone), Nigeria, Ghana, Gambia Cape Verde
CFA Franc Zone	Common currency		WAEMU countries, CEMAC countries (Cameroon, Central African Republic, Chad, Congo, Equatorial Guinea, Gabon)

Source: Schiff and Winters (2003).

and economic development. The treaty of this agreement was later modified in 1993 to allow for deeper progress toward an economic and monetary union. The new treaty included the objectives of creating a central bank, a court of justice, a parliament, an executive secretariat and an economic and cultural council.

In January 1994, following the devaluation of the CFA franc,[6] seven of the fifteen countries of ECOWAS, which share the CFA franc as a common currency, initiated a sub-regional market called the West African Economic and Monetary Union (WAEMU). These countries were later joined by Guinea-Bissau in 1997 (Table 14.1). In addition to these two sub-regional agreements, Senegal has signed various bilateral trade agreements with other countries or groups of countries. There are three agreements that Senegal signed independently from other countries of the WAEMU, namely Vietnam, the Czech Republic and Uganda.

RTAs are common in Sub-Saharan Africa and reflect an aspiration to overcome the limitations of small states. In connection with this, progress has been made in the continent over the past decade: average applied most favoured nation (MFN) tariffs were cut by half between 1990 and 2003. In 2007, half of the countries in the region made at least one positive reform to facilitate business, putting Sub-Saharan Africa in fourth place in business reforms. FDI increased 13-fold between 1990 and 2005, from US$1.2 billion to US$16.5 billion (UNCTAD 2007).

Although African countries belong to numerous RTAs, this has not always been accompanied by significant intra-regional trade. Despite severe reduction of applied MFN tariffs, non-border barriers still restrict internal trade: in particular, most countries in the region face high transport costs and have weak institutions which would facilitate trade. Among the regional integration schemes at work, the CEMAC displays the lowest intra-regional trade share with less than 2 percent of total trade during the period 2003–2006 (UNCTAD 2007). In contrast, trade links within the WAEMU and between the WAEMU and other sub-regions in Africa are much more developed. In 2006, 26 percent of WAEMU's exports went to ECOWAS and 32 percent to Africa as a whole. Moreover, trade integration in the WAEMU has advanced more rapidly and is more successful than the ECOWAS in terms of policy-making and an institutional framework. Among the reasons for better progress is the presence of a common currency (the CFA franc) in the WAEMU. Also, the WAEMU has become a total customs union since 2000 with the adoption of a common external tariff (CET) and the dismantling of trade barriers within the union.[7] In short, it is commonly argued that the recent RTAs in Africa have had more impact on outward-looking trade liberalization, and thus on trade outside the region, than on intra-regional trade.

14.2.2 Trade structure

Senegal is relatively open to trade in comparison with its WAEMU partners: in 2005, its merchandise trade as a percentage of GDP climbed to 55 percent, slightly above the WAEMU average. However, the country has registered a persistent trade deficit since the early 1990s, as imports grow on average faster than exports (respectively at a rate of 7.1 percent and 4.9 percent per year during the period 1990–2005). This trade balance is consistent with Senegal's early stage of development and in line with most other West African countries: as domestic demand is mainly supplied by foreign producers, imports of goods and services accounted for 43 percent of GDP in 2005, against 27 percent for exports.

Table 14.2 illustrates Senegal's trade structure by commodity; data used here are from the United Nations' division of statistics and the Commodity Trade Statistics Database (COMTRADE). Although Senegal is a rice producer, this type of cereal is among its most imported products; the same is true for dairy products. The bulk of the country's imports still remains manufactured goods, which is due to production shortages. Finally, Senegal also imports a great quantity of oil products to serve the local or sub-regional market after processing.

In face of such heavy import constraints, Senegal has a very low export capacity on the world markets. Indeed, its exports are mainly concentrated in a very limited number of commodities: namely, petroleum products, aquatic and chemical products. In the period under consideration, more than 40 percent of exports consisted of zero to two SITC aggregates, in which more than 60 percent were fishery products. Fuel and oil products also contributed to more than 40 percent of total exports, of which refined petroleum products and inorganic chemicals accounted for around 30 percent and 25 percent respectively. Finally, in spite of impressive improvements, manufactured products still remain low and are mainly attributable to a few monopolistic firms in heavy industries.

Regarding trading partners, we find that the principal exporter to Senegal is France, which is the result of the country's colonial legacy, although it is no longer the first destination of Senegal's own exports. On the sub-regional level, Senegal imports mainly from Nigeria, because Nigeria is the largest oil producer in the area. The second country is the Ivory Coast, which provides Senegal mainly with manufactured and agro-industrial goods. The amount of imports from the ECOWAS remains, however, low when compared on a global level. Less than 15 percent per year of Senegal's imports comes from the ECOWAS, while the bulk of suppliers are European (France and United Kingdom being the most significant).

Senegal's imports from Asia are rising steadily. While the Asian countries are mainly suppliers of cereal products (particularly rice), the emergence of China and India has boosted Senegal's imports from the region. These countries export manufactured products to Senegal, such as electronic and electric products in the case of China, or vehicles and other machines from India. Trade with Asian countries, in contrast to that with European countries, is on an upward sloping trend with India representing the largest share of Senegalese exports to Asia.

Senegal exports more to, than it imports from, the West African area, particularly and does particularily well in its trade with the countries of WAEMU. Since the agreement came into force in 2000, exports to the WAEMU have been steadily rising. They jumped from 13.12 percent in 2000 to 31.65 percent in

Table 14.2 Senegal's trade structure by commodity

Imports	1990	1994	2000	2001	2005
0 to 2	30.34	24.96	23.08	27.20	28.69
of which: 042 rice	18.79	18.73	30.52	30.30	36.73
022 milk and cream	7.75	16.15	7.81	6.94	7.82
3 to 5	27.74	36.26	35.89	30.57	34.76
of which: 333 crude petroleum and oils obtained from bituminous minerals	29.03	11.27	52.51	31.88	31.39
334 petroleum products, refined	25.29	37.56	7.42	14.72	27.19
6 to 8	41.92	38.63	41.02	42.22	36.49
of which: 781 passenger motor vehicles (excluding buses)	6.83	5.32	7.53	8.69	7.37
673 iron and steel bars, rods, shapes and sections	3.11	5.98	2.49	2.99	5.51
9	0.00	0.15	0.01	0.01	0.05

Exports	1990	1994	2000	2001	2005
0 to 2	48.51	28.65	48.91	43.77	31.60
of which: 034 fish, fresh, chilled or frozen	22.90	16.88	28.34	36.72	27.60
036 crustaceans and molluscs, fresh, chilled, frozen, salted, etc.	10.11	4.12	48.68	26.98	15.24
3 to 5	43.90	57.72	41.22	44.65	44.51
of which: 334 petroleum products, refined	28.06	28.24	27.78	34.70	35.06
522 Inorganic chemical elements, oxides and halogen salts	21.36	27.80	23.43	21.49	28.54
6 to 8	7.58	13.58	9.76	11.33	22.09
of which: 661 lime, cement and fabricated construction materials	3.22	2.48	9.35	10.99	16.38
784 motor vehicle parts and accessories	0.71	0.50	0.13	0.80	11.99
9	0.00	0.05	0.11	0.25	1.80

Source: Authors' calculations from COMTRADE.

Notes
Group "0 to 2" are all goods of the SITC Revision 2, which are raw animals and vegetal products. Group "3 to 5" are chemicals, fuel and oil. Group "6 to 8" are manufactured goods. Group "9" are all unclassified products.

Table 14.3 Senegal's trade structure by country

Imports	1990	1994	2000	2001	2005
WAEMU	4.70	3.95	2.73	3.12	3.59
Ivory Coast	95.36	99.16	96.60	91.72	97.15
Togo	0.03	0.01	0.12	1.27	0.57
ECOWAS (out of WAEMU)	7.75	4.60	19.26	10.35	10.89
Nigeria	97.73	98.31	98.48	95.05	95.44
Ghana	0.00	0.33	1.03	3.01	3.87
NPI2 + 3	6.48	7.46	12.28	13.42	15.03
Thailand	45.65	50.54	43.54	57.29	33.09
China	35.68	33.73	21.84	18.27	23.80
ROW	81.07	83.98	65.74	73.12	70.49
France	40.88	41.24	41.82	38.13	29.79

Exports	1990	1994	2000	2001	2005
WAEMU	13.30	16.00	13.12	14.06	31.65
Mali	58.79	66.41	49.56	56.14	68.52
Guinea Bissau	4.74	5.65	13.64	0.00	11.60
ECOWAS (out of WAEMU)	3.93	6.44	9.91	10.37	11.12
Gambia	24.64	28.40	50.93	37.65	50.80
Guinea	54.48	28.40	16.90	43.26	30.62
NPI2 + 3	13.77	20.16	15.02	15.55	16.13
India	85.02	86.85	86.12	90.99	90.77
China	0.40	0.05	12.92	7.58	6.91
ROW	69.00	57.39	61.95	60.02	41.10
France	55.52	36.43	31.40	31.79	25.09

Source: Authors' calculations.

Note
NPI2 denotes Indonesia, Malaysia, Philippines and Thailand. NPI3 are China, India and Vietnam.

2005, with Mali as the first export market. Outside the sub-region, India is the second largest client of Senegal, mainly for chemicals. This is the result of the Indian partnership in the Chemical Industries of Senegal (ICS)[8] (most notably in the industry's recapitalization). Finally, in the list of its key clients, we find European countries such as France, Italy or Spain to which Senegal exports mainly fishery products.

The evolution of the import structure remains significantly different from that of the country's exports. Generally we find that even if the share of the West African sub-region remains very low, Senegal is increasingly exporting to these countries. We also notice that trade with countries of the two sub-regional blocs (WAEMU and ECOWAS) is not uniform, and this becomes particularly apparent on the import side, where only two countries account for almost all imports (Ivory Coast and Nigeria).

Before the devaluation of the CFA franc, Senegal's manufacturing sector experienced serious problems of competitiveness on global markets. This was caused by a failure in total factor productivity, partly attributable to the import substitution policy conducted in the early decades and to other structural problems (Latreille and Varoudakis 1996). This weakness of productivity gains and the over-valuation of the real exchange rate justified a devaluation of the CFA franc. Annabi *et al.* (2005) point out that despite Senegal's participation in a large number of PTAs and its LDC status since 2001, with all the benefits it might have induced in terms of treatment, this has not stimulated its exports significantly. The authors argue that the low competitiveness of domestic products is due to non-conformity with international quality standards, high production costs and the multiplicity of grants and subsidies that favor foreign competitors in export markets.

14.3 Regional integration and South–South trade

14.3.1 A short review of the empirical literature

There exists considerable literature which addresses regional integration and its impact on economic welfare. South–South RTAs remain a puzzling issue as the empirical evidence is mixed, suggesting a case-by-case assessment (UNCTAD 2007).

A first set of studies relies on trade data to assess whether international specialization according to comparative advantage may alter economic welfare by creating and diverting trade flows. Regional integration may then improve economic welfare, if there is simultaneously an increase in trade among member countries and an overall improvement in their comparative advantage. For instance, Yeats (1998) or Cadot *et al.* (2000) in the specific case of PTAs in Africa, as well as Schiff (1997) for South–South regional trade agreements in general, showed that developing countries are unlikely to create trade flows among themselves. Should their trade flows expand, this would happen at the expense of more efficient non-members. In the same vein, the World Bank

(2000) concluded that trade diversion is more likely to happen when the initial level of CET jointly defined by member countries in the case of customs unions is high. More globally, empirical studies relying on comparative advantage suggest that the overall effect on welfare would depend on the characteristics of member countries, the existing degree of trade dependence, initial cost differences and the degree of complementarity in their productive structures.

A second set of studies uses Computable General Equilibrium (CGE) models in order to measure the actual changes in trade flows and welfare resulting from specific regional arrangements. For example, Evans (1998) and Lewis *et al.* (1999) showed that in some Sub-Saharan RTAs, trade creation prevailed. Flores (1997) came to the same results in the case of the MERCOSUR. Overall, the majority of empirical studies using CGE models report small effects on both members and non-members, with net trade creation the more likely outcome and positive overall welfare gains (UNCTAD 2007).

Finally, recent studies use gravity models to focus on the influence of historical and geographical forces on trade. Indeed, assuming that most countries trade relatively more with their neighbors than with more distant trading partners, there is an unavoidable spatial dimension to regional integration (the so-called 'neighborhood bias'). Using gravity techniques, Mayda and Steinberg (2006) showed that Uganda's participation in the Common Market of East and South Africa (COMESA) has not created trade flows with other countries. The main explanation is that these countries are not 'natural' trading partners arising from geographical proximity, thereby any policy measures aimed at stimulating trade among themselves would be inefficient. However, this 'neighborhood bias' argument is not convincing from the perspective of Southern countries, as transaction costs are not a direct function of distance but may depend on supply bottlenecks, infrastructure, macroeconomic conditions, etc. As mentioned in an UNCTAD report (2007), transaction costs for certain countries in Africa are lower when trading with countries in other regions than with neighboring countries. The growing number of PTAs, linking African and Asian countries, provides strong evidence for this argument.

In order to assess the potential for South–South trade in the WAEMU, our investigation adopts the first (comparative advantage) approach. Assuming that such potential depends mainly upon static gains at the first stage of regional integration, our study stresses the existing degree of trade dependence and complementarity of productive structures among member countries. On the basis of foreign trade data available for Senegal and its trading partners, we calculate the indicators of comparative advantage. The results will be complemented by an analysis of export structure similarity.

14.3.2 Indicators of comparative advantage and export similarity

Traditionally, the index of RCA proposed by Balassa (1965) measures comparative advantage by calculating a country's world share of exports for a particular product:

All displayed tables in this chapter should have thin spaces around mathematical symbols

$$RCA_{ij} = \frac{X_{ij}}{\sum_i X_{ij}} \bigg/ \frac{\sum_j X_{ij}}{\sum_i \sum_j X_{ij}} \tag{14.1}$$

where: X_{ij} is country j's exports of commodity i,

$$\sum_i X_{ij}$$

is country j's total exports,

$$\sum_j X_{ij}$$

is world exports of commodity i and

$$\sum_i \sum_j X_{ij}$$

is total world exports.

RCA_{ij} reveals a comparative advantage if country j's share of exports of a certain commodity i in its total exports is greater than the corresponding world share; that is when RCA is greater than one. The index allows comparisons between countries at any time (here, the WAEMU members) and similarly permits changes in the structure of comparative advantage to be tracked over time. Thus, RCA indices and their evolution provide broad information about a country's specialization pattern relative to the structure of world trade.

The RCA indices are, however, derived from export data only. The conclusions could thus be misleading, since the product-based RCA might reveal a country's comparative advantage in one product, when in fact it imports components and conducts the labor-intensive activities of assembling. In such a case, arguing that the country has a comparative advantage in the corresponding good, while ignoring its high level of imports, could be considered to be unconvincing. Furthermore, the RCA indices might be biased by the size of the country's market and the influence of changes, which are not specific to the country but instead result from fluctuations of each commodity in world markets.

In order to eliminate such distortions, the CEPII[9] has developed an analytical indicator of comparative advantage based on the trade balance instead of relative export structures. For product i and country j, the balance is first expressed in thousandths of purchasing power parity (PPP) GDP in current dollars of country j (GDP$_j$).

$$y_{ij} = 1000 * \frac{X_{ij} - M_{ij}}{GDP_j}$$

where M_{ij} denotes imports by country j of product i.

The contribution of product i to total trade balance (CTB), in relation to GDP, is defined by:

$$CTB_{ij} = y_{ij} - \left(\frac{W_i}{W}\right) * y_j$$

where world trade of product i is

$$W_i = \sum_j (X_{ij} + M_{ij}),$$

world trade of all products is

$$W = \sum_i \sum_j (X_{ij} + M_{ij})$$

and total trade balance of country j in relation to GDP is

$$y_j = 1000 * \frac{X_j - M_j}{GDP_j}.$$

The indicator depends on the spread between the trade balance of product i (relative to GDP) and the global trade balance, weighted by the share of product i in world trade. Defined in this way, the indicator reveals a comparative advantage pattern, as any deviation of the specific product to the overall balance corresponds to an advantage (disadvantage), given that the contribution to the overall balance is positive (negative). Indeed, this leads to the following index:

$$CTB_{ij} = 1000 * \frac{W_i}{GDP_j} * \left[\frac{(X_{ij} - M_{ij})}{W_i} - \frac{X_j - M_j}{W}\right] \qquad (14.2)$$

Thus, the contribution of product i to the total trade balance of country j corresponds to the spread between the country's position on the international market for product i (hereafter POS_{ij}) and its global position. In interpreting the results, two points should be borne in mind:

First, the market position of each country j on product i (POS_{ij}) measures its international competitiveness. It is defined by its relative trade balance, defined as follows:

$$POS_{ij} = 100 * \frac{(X_{ij} - M_{ij})}{W_i} \qquad (14.3)$$

Second, country j enjoys comparative advantage in product i, if the latter contributes positively to the overall balance (CTB>0). The relative trade balance on i then exceeds the overall balance, either when they are both positive or, conversely, when they are both negative. In the latter case, country j may have a comparative advantage on product i (CTB>0) even though it is not competitive on its world market (POS<0).

Finally, in order to assess the degree of export similarity or trade competition among the WAEMU members, we use here the *Cosinus* index[10] (COS_{ij}) that, by definition, determines the angular distance between two export vectors. Country i and j will have the same export structure on world markets, if their two export vectors have a cosine equal to one: hence, they will be in competition on the same products. Conversely, their exports will be completely different, if their two export vectors are perfectly orthogonal (cosine equal to zero). In this case, the two countries will have a complementary export supply. By denoting products by the subscript k, the COS index is defined as follows:

$$COS_{ij} = \frac{\sum_k X_{ik} * X_{jk}}{\sqrt{\sum_k X_{ik}^2 * \sum_k X_{jk}^2}}$$
(14.4)

All these trade indicators are computed for the WAEMU members using COM-TRADE at a three-digit SITC level. The data on PPP GDP are from the World Development Indicators of the World Bank. Due to data availability, we have excluded Guinea-Bissau from our calculations.

14.3.3 Interpretation of results

Table 14.4 depicts first the number of comparative advantages by country compared to the WAEMU average. It shows a striking picture for Senegal, with a number always higher than that of the WAEMU average. However, Senegal has a relative trade surplus for only 24 SITC categories on average during the period 1996–2003. It is ranked fourth in the sub-region: behind the Ivory Coast with 58 products, Togo with 35 products and Niger with 27 products. Taken as a whole, the results of calculation for all 239 three-digit SITC indicate that the WAEMU countries register relative trade surplus (i.e., international competitiveness) for around 10 percent of the products. Their weak position in global markets contrasts with the other developing areas.

The POS index contributes to highlighting the relative good performance of Senegal in terms of comparative advantage. Indeed, a country may register a positive CTB index in one product, provided that its relative trade deficit is lower than the overall trade deficit. As mentioned before, Senegal's trade balance has continuously worsened during the last ten years, despite government policies aimed to improve it. Among the WAEMU countries, only the Ivory Coast has registered a trade surplus over the period under consideration, while Senegal recorded the highest trade deficit. However, this is mainly attributable to trade dependency on a very small number of imported products (rice, closely followed by crude oil). That is why any assessment of a country's comparative advantage would be biased without looking deeper into its trade structure.

Table 14.4 Number of products with comparative advantage by indicator

Indicators	Countries	1996	2000	2003
RCA > 1	Benin	15	15	14
	Burkina Faso	17	27	17
	Ivory Coast	32	34	32
	Mali	13	12	na
	Niger	18	28	17
	Senegal	*30*	*32*	*37*
	Togo	33	33	42
	WAEMU average	*23*	*26*	*27*
CTB > 0	Benin	66	76	82
	Burkina Faso	94	113	112
	Ivory Coast	32	34	32
	Mali	75	71	na
	Niger	24	84	76
	Senegal	*112*	*103*	*109*
	Togo	103	83	68
	WAEMU average	*72*	*81*	*80*
POS > 0	Benin	18	17	17
	Burkina Faso	18	18	15
	Ivory Coast	57	58	58
	Mali	15	17	na
	Niger	32	34	12
	Senegal	*18*	*27*	*27*
	Togo	36	31	42
	WAEMU average	*28*	*29*	*29*

Source: Authors' calculations.

Table 14.5 reports the strengths and weaknesses of Senegal's trade specialization, according to the RCA and CTB indices of comparative advantage. We have also compiled the same indicators for all other WAEMU members. Unsurprisingly, their comparative advantage lies mainly in unprocessed products, either from the sea or sub-soil extraction. However, Senegal often enjoys a comparative advantage in products, in which its trading partners in the sub-region face a comparative disadvantage. Conversely, it has a comparative disadvantage in products which are not necessarily exported by the other WAEMU members.

Even though some products began with a disadvantage in 1994, they have seen their uncompetitiveness reduced and in some cases even turned it into a comparative advantage. The indicator, for instance, shows that Senegal has now a much more pronounced comparative advantage in fishery products, chemical products and petroleum products. It also has an advantage, but of a lesser magnitude, in some agricultural products (e.g., rice, cotton and other cereals) and in cement among other construction materials.

The CTB indices show that Senegal's comparative advantage has deteriorated drastically in some animal and vegetables products, petroleum products and basic industrial products. Among the 30 products with the greatest comparative disadvantage in 2005, there were three which had a comparative advantage in the early 1990s (SITC-423, 011 and 333).[11] There are also 13 products, which had an advantage in 1990, but lost it in 2005. For products at the bottom of the range, a few have won in 'competitiveness' in 2005: they are mainly in the SITC-7 category (SITC-773, 749 and 713)[12] and experienced a significant reversal from a negative to a positive position. As a final note it bears mentioning that during the investigated period, rice (SITC-042) has proven to be the weakest point of the Senegalese economy, suffering a worsening comparative disadvantage.

The COS index allows us to assess whether countries tend to compete on export markets or rather complement one another. In general, exports of West African countries are rather different. In the case of Senegal, the values of the COS index are all below 20 percent, with the exception of Togo which, in the early years, exceeded 40 percent, but has steadily declined (Table 14.6). The small similarities in terms of exports between the WAEMU countries is in contradiction with what the conventional theory predicts. Indeed, one of the main explicative arguments for the low intensity of economic exchanges between Southern countries is the similarity of their productive output. That supply similarity is such that output imported by a Southern country could not be produced efficiently by the other one belonging to the same PTA, thereby any requirement should be imported from more efficient non-members.

Following our calculation of the COS indices for the WAEMU area, it should be noted that only Burkina Faso has tended to have very high indices of export similarity with its WAEMU partners (Table 14.7). We note a very strong export similarity among three other countries in the sub-region: Benin (with an index around up to 1 and very stable over the period), Mali (with an index starting from 0.9, but constantly declining) and Togo (about 0.6). Early calculations of RCA and CTB indices support this high export similarity between the four WAEMU members. Burkina Faso and its three trading partners have tended to gain a comparative advantage on the same products. These empirical results suggest, therefore, a potential export rivalry among the member of this sub-group, this in contrast to Senegal's experience with its WAEMU partners.

14.4 Conclusion

Since the beginning of the new millennium, South–South trade integration has gained a growing interest, due notably to the rapid emergence of some Asian developing economies and the deepening of regional integration. The growing number of South–South regional blocs, as well as the composition of intra-regional trade, suggests an important potential for trade expansion among developing countries in support of export diversification and industrial development. Accordingly, our chapter has examined the potential for South–South trade in Africa by focusing our analysis on the case of Senegal in the WAEMU. More specifically, we have raised the question of whether Senegal's participation in the WAEMU improved the country's external trade and whether or not it

Table 14.5 Senegal's comparative advantage

RCA indices (%)

Commodity	1996	Commodity	2005
Top ranking			
271 Fertilizers, crude	400,45	522 Inorganic chemical elements, oxides and halogen salts	44,45
522 Inorganic chemical elements, oxides and halogen salts	76,43	036 Crustaceans and molluscs, fresh, chilled, frozen, salted, etc.	42,38
263 Cotton	32,66	042 Rice	39,02
562 Fertilizers, manufactured	31	034 Fish, fresh, chilled or frozen	29,34
278 Other crude minerals	15,47	951 Armored fighting vehicles, war firearms, ammunition	26,90
334 Petroleum products, refined	10,78	661 Lime, cement and fabricated construction materials	20,69
692 Metal containers for storage and transport	9,44	263 Cotton	18,90
211 Hides and skins, excluding furs, raw	7,6	278 Other crude minerals	12,25
423 Fixed vegetable oils, soft, crude refined or purified	5,74	037 Fish, crustaceans and molluscs, prepared or preserved	11,60
282 Waste and scrap metal of iron or steel	5,08	423 Fixed vegetable oils, soft, crude refined or purified	11,16
Bottom ranking			
656 Tulle, lace, embroidery, ribbons, trimmings		724 Textile and leather machinery, and parts thereof	
897 Gold, silverware, jewellery, articles of precious materials		711 Steam boilers and auxiliary plant; and parts thereof	
881 Photographic apparatus and equipment		871 Optical instruments and apparatus	
277 Natural abrasives		689 Miscellaneous non-ferrous base metals	
842 Mens and boys outerwear, textile fabrics		268 Wool and other animal hair (excluding tops)	
515 Organo-inorganic and heterocyclic compounds		233 Synthetic rubber, latex; waste, scrap of unhardened rubber	
761 Television receivers		676 Rails and railway track construction materials	
664 Glass		072 Cocoa	
662 Clay and refractory construction materials		671 Pig and sponge iron, spiegeleisen, etc., and ferro-alloys	
843 Womens, girls', infants outerwear, textile		091 Margarine and shortening	

CTB indices (%)

Top ranking

Commodity	1996	Commodity	2005
522 Inorganic chemical elements, oxides and halogen salts	6,66	522 Inorganic chemical elements, oxides and halogen salts	8,42
752 Automatic data processing machines and units thereof	3,98	034 Fish, fresh, chilled or frozen	6,40
562 Fertilizers, manufactured	3,58	036 Crustaceans and molluscs, fresh, chilled, frozen, salted, etc.	4,92
271 Fertilizers, crude	3,12	784 Motor vehicle parts and accessories, NES	3,25
781 Passenger motor vehicles (excluding buses)	2,69	776 Thermionic, microcircuits, transistors, valves, etc.	3,01
784 Motor vehicle parts and accessories	2,44	931 Special transactions, commodity not classified	2,91
764 Telecommunication equipment, NES	2,33	759 Parts, and accessories for machines of 751 or 752	1,78
792 Aircraft and associated equipment, and parts thereof	2,19	752 Automatic data processing machines and units thereof	1,60
263 Cotton	2,13	553 Perfumery, cosmetics, toilet preparations, etc.	1,39
778 Electrical machinery and apparatus	1,42	037 Fish, crustaceans and molluscs, prepared or preserved	1,25

Bottom ranking

Commodity	1996	Commodity	2005
782 Lorries and special purposes motor vehicles		248 Wood, simply worked, and railway sleepers of wood	
673 Iron and steel bars, rods, shapes and sections		783 Road motor vehicles, NES	
098 Edible products and preparations, NES		341 Gas, natural and manufactured	
692 Metal containers for storage and transport		334 Petroleum products, refined	
022 Milk and cream		541 Medicinal and pharmaceutical products	
061 Sugar and honey		424 Other fixed vegetable oils, fluid or solid, crude, refined	
423 Fixed vegetable oils, soft, crude refined or purified		673 Iron and steel bars, rods, shapes and sections	
333 Crude petroleum and oils		022 Milk and cream	
042 Rice		333 Crude petroleum and oils obtained from bituminous minerals	
334 Petroleum products, refined		042 Rice	

Source: Authors' calculation.

Note
NES: Not elsewhere specified.

Table 14.6 Indicator of export similarity for Senegal

COS index[a]		1995	1996	1997	1998	1999	2000	2001	2002	2003	2004
WAEMU	Mali	–	0.15	0.16	0.12	0.05	0.02	0.01	–	–	–
	Togo	0.48	0.43	0.34	0.26	0.25	0.11	0.13	0.12	0.12	0.17
	Benin	0.14	0.13	0.13	0.12	0.06	0.04	0.05	0.07	0.12	0.09
	Ivory Coast	0.15	0.20	0.21	0.15	0.19	0.21	0.00	0.14	0.16	–
	Burkina Faso	0.20	0.16	0.17	0.15	0.06	0.06	0.05	0.07	0.13	0.11
	Niger	0.01	0.01	0.02	0.02	0.03	0.02	0.01	0.03	0.03	–
ECOWAS	Nigeria	–	0.01	0.01	0.00	0.01	0.08	0.07	0.09	0.14	–
	Ghana	–	0.04	0.03	0.03	0.07	0.05	0.10	–	0.02	0.05
	Gambia	0.03	0.08	0.06	0.03	0.05	0.26	0.26	0.07	0.27	0.08
	Guinea	0.19	0.13	0.09	0.13	0.18	0.07	0.10	0.22	–	–

Source: Authors' calculation.

Note

a Some ECOWAS countries are excluded from calculation due to unavailable data.

Table 14.7 Indicator of export similarity for the other WAEMU members

COS Index		1995	1996	1997	1998	1999	2000	2001	2002	2003
Niger	Ivory Coast	0.01	0.01	0.01	0.01	0.01	0.03	0.00	0.01	0.01
	Togo	0.02	0.03	0.03	0.02	0.03	0.03	0.00	0.01	0.00
	Benin	0.02	0.04	0.06	0.51	0.02	0.02	0.00	0.01	0.01
	Burkina Faso	0.03	0.05	0.04	0.03	0.05	0.08	0.06	0.04	0.01
	Mali		0.06	0.01	0.00	0.01	0.01	0.00		
Mali	Togo		0.69	0.68	0.56	0.61	0.30	0.01		
	Benin		0.79	0.75	0.65	0.69	0.54	0.13		
	Ivory Coast		0.07	0.08	0.09	0.08	0.09			
	Burkina Faso		0.98	0.98	0.78	0.69	0.53	0.06		
Benin	Togo	0.46	0.57	0.51	0.52	0.73	0.59	0.27	0.40	0.42
	Ivory Coast	0.08	0.06	0.07	0.09	0.10	0.14		0.07	0.09
	Burkina Faso	0.67	0.82	0.74	0.83	0.98	0.98	0.98	0.86	0.99
Togo	Ivory Coast	0.28	0.25	0.24	0.15	0.20	0.18		0.12	0.13
	Burkina Faso	0.67	0.68	0.67	0.62	0.72	0.58	0.27	0.45	0.41
Ivory Coast	Burkina Faso	0.10	0.08	0.09	0.10	0.10	0.14	0.06	0.06	0.08

Source: Authors' calculation.

allowed for an expansion of South–South trade in the sub-region. In our pursuit of finding an answer to these questions, we have calculated and compared indicators of comparative advantage for the WAEMU members: Balassa's revealed comparative advantage (RCA) index, a contribution to the trade balance (CTB) index and a relative trade balance index describing the international market position (POS) of individual countries by product. Finally, in order to assess the magnitude of competition among WAEMU members in foreign markets, we have looked at the export similarity indices.

Overall, Senegal has been one of the fastest growing economies in Africa during the last ten years; it has achieved greater success than its WAEMU partners in terms of GDP per capita growth. Despite a comprehensive extension of trade arrangements with its neighbors, however, Senegal's imports from WAEMU still remain negligible. Senegal has increasingly diverted its import flows from developed countries (and especially its historical partner France) in favor of imports from successful South and South-East Asian economies. Senegal's exports to the WAEMU have contributed to more than 75 percent of the overall growth of its exports. This trade reorientation toward regional partners has occurred at the expense of its traditional partners (notably France). This positive trend leads us to consider if the integrating area is going to experience trade creation or diversion. Calculations of trade indicators show that Senegal is one of the countries registering the highest number of comparative advantages in the WAEMU. Additionally, its export supply structure is different from that of its trading partners, suggesting lower risks of competition between them. Moreover, the apparent increase of comparative advantage in manufactured products, albeit still weak, suggests an overall improvement in export diversification.

Therefore, contrary to conventional predictions, Senegal's actual experience of regional integration has little to do with trade diversion. Instead, in the newly Asian-led era of globalization, it seems that trade between developing countries has expanded mainly at the expense of the former industrialized country partners. In summary, we conclude that Senegal has taken advantage of a favorable international trade pattern in which there is significant scope for improving trade among developing countries.

Notes

1 Corresponding author: University of Rouen, Faculty of Law, Economics and Management: 3, Avenue Pasteur F-76186 Rouen Cedex 1 (France). Also Associate Researcher at the Centre for Economics of Paris-North (CEPN, University of Paris 13).

2 The authors are research affiliates at the Centre for Analysis and Research in Economics: *Globalization and Regulations Research Group* (CARE, University of Rouen).

3 See Edwards (1993), Bhagwati and Srinivasan (1999) for a broad survey of literature on the relationship between trade orientation and economic performance in the developing countries.

4 This phenomenon is also called 'New regionalism', because it embraces broader areas than trade of goods and organizes a deep integration that goes beyond what the multilateral framework would allow.

5 *World Development Indicators*, World Bank.
6 The franc of the African Financial Community (*Communauté Financière Africaine* in French) is the standard monetary and currency unit, of the following countries: Benin, Burkina-Faso, Cameroon, the Central African Republic, Chad, Congo, Ivory Coast, Equatorial Guinea, Gabon, Mali, Niger, Senegal and Togo.
7 Since its creation, it was expected that ECOWAS should move toward a monetary and customs union. However, the project has not moved forward because of some difficulties in the negotiations. The community decided in January 2006 to begin the implementation of the CET, which converges to the same structure as the WAEMU. The transitional period for its implementation spanned the period from January 1, 2006 to December 31, 2007. But at the end of this period, there remained unsolved problems, including the establishment of the list of products that will not be subject to the final CET in the case of Nigeria.
8 In Senegal, the Indian Farmers Fertiliser Co-operative has set up a joint venture with the local government to save the country's ailing phosphates producer, the ICS. The creation of the joint venture has secured the Indian fertilizer company with raw material supplies as most of the output is exported to India.
9 The Centre for Prospective Studies and International Information is a French public institution. For further details, see online, available at: www.cepii.fr/anglaisgraph/bdd/chelem.htm.
10 Similarly, some studies used the Finger–Kreinin index to measure the degree of export similarity (see Finger and Kreinin 1979). It compares the sectoral distribution of two countries' export supply in a reference market. If these two countries have totally identical export structures, the share of each product in one country's total exports should be the same than for the other country. The indicator varies between 100 (if there is total similarity) and zero (otherwise).
11 That is: 011 (meat and edible meat offal, fresh, chilled or frozen); 333 (crude petroleum and oils obtained from bituminous minerals); 423 (fixed vegetable oils, soft, crude, refined or purified).
12 That is: 713 (internal combustion piston engines, and parts thereof); 749 (non-electric parts and accessories of machinery); 773 (equipment for distribution of electricity).

References

Annabi, N., F. Cissé, J. Cockburn and B. Decaluwé (2005) 'Trade Liberalisation, Growth and Poverty in Senegal: a Dynamic Microsimulation CGE Model Analysis', CIRPEE Working Paper 05–12, CIRPEE, University of Laval, Canada.

Balassa, B. (1965) 'Trade Liberalization and Revealed Comparative Advantage', *Manschester School*, 33: 99–133.

Baldwin, R.E. and A.J. Venables (1995) 'Regional economic integration', in G. Grossman and K. Rogoff (eds) *Handbook of international economics* (Volume III), Amsterdam: North-Holland.

Bhagwati, J. and T.N. Srinivasan (1999) 'Outward Orientation and Development: Are Revisionists right?' Center Discussion Paper 806, Economic Growth Center, Yale University.

Cadot, O., J. De Melo and M. Olarreaga (2000) 'L'intégration régionale en Afrique: où en sommes-nous?' *Revue d'Economie du Dévelopement*, 1: 247–61.

Edwards, E. (1993) 'Openness, Trade Liberalization and Growth in Developing Countries', *Journal of Economic Literature*, 31: 1358–93.

Evans, D. (1998) 'Options for Regional Integration in Southern Africa', IDS Working Paper 94, Institute of Development Studies, Sussex.

Finger, J.M. and M.E. Kreinin (1979) 'A Measure of "Export Similarity" and its Possible Use', *Economic Journal*, 89: 905–12.

Flores, R.J. (1997) 'The Gains from MERCOSUR: A General Equilibrium, Imperfect Competition Evaluation', *Journal of Policy Modelling*, 19: 1–18.

Foroutan, F. (1993) 'Regional Integration in Sub-Saharan Africa: Past Experience and Future Prospects', in J. De Melo and A. Panagariya (eds) *New dimensions in regional integration*, Cambridge: Cambridge University Press.

Krugman, P. (1991) *Geography and trade*, Cambridge, MA: MIT Press.

Krugman, P. and A.J. Venables (1995) 'Globalization and the Inequality of Nations', *Quarterly Journal of Economics*, 110: 857–80.

Latreille, T. and A. Varoudakis (1996) 'Croissance et compétitivité de l'industrie manu-facturière au Sénégal', Document technique OCDE 118, OCDE, Paris.

Lewis, J.D., S. Robinson and K. Thierfelder (1999) 'After the Negotiations: Assessing the Impact of Free Trade Agreements in Southern Africa', TMD Discussion Paper, International Food Policy Research Institute, Washington, DC.

Little, I., T. Scitovsky and M. Scott (1970) *Industry and trade in some developing countries*, London and New York: Oxford University Press.

Mayda, A.M. and C. Steinberg (2006) 'Do South–South Trade Agreements Increase Trade? Commodity-Level Evidence from COMESA', UNU-CRIS Occasional papers 19, United Nations University, Comparative Regional Integration Studies, Brugge.

Puga, D. and A.J. Venables (1998) 'Trading Arrangements and Industrial Development', *World Bank Economic Review*, 12: 221–49.

Rieber, A. and T.A.D. Tran (2004) 'Intégration régionale Sud-Sud et répartition intra-zone des activités', *Revue Economique*, 55: 41–64.

Schiff, M. (1997) 'Small is Beautiful: Preferential Trade Agreements and the Impact of Country Size, Market Share, and Smuggling', *Journal of Economic Integration*, 12: 359–87.

Schiff, M. and L. Winters (2003) 'Regional Integration and Development', Washington, DC: World Bank.

UNCTAD (2007) 'Trade and Development Report 2007', New York and Geneva: United Nations.

Venables, A.J. (2003) 'Winners and Losers from Regional Integration Agreements', *Economic Journal*, 113: 747–61.

Viner, J. (1950) 'The Customs Union Issue', Carnegie endowment for international peace, New York.

World Bank (2000) *Trade Blocs*, New York: Oxford University Press.

Yeats, A. (1998) 'What can be expected from African Regional Trade Arrangements? Some Empirical Evidence (Mimeo)', Washington, DC: World Bank.

Index

Page numbers in *italics* denote tables, those in **bold** denote figures.

344 *Index*